Professional Java Security

Jess Garms
Daniel Somerfield

Wrox Press Ltd. ®

Professional Java Security

First Printed May, 2001

Published by Wrox Press Ltd,
Arden House, 1102 Warwick Road, Acocks Green,
Birmingham, B27 6BH, UK
Printed in the United States
ISBN 1861004257

Trademark Acknowledgements

Credits

Authors
Jess Garms
Daniel Somerfield

Managing Editor
Paul Cooper

Technical Architects
Craig Berry
Ian Blackham

Development Editor
Greg Pearson

Technical Editors
Allan Jones
David Mercer

Author Agent
Emma Batch

Project Manager
Chandima Nethisinghe

Index
Adrian Axinte
Andrew Criddle

Technical Reviewers
Yogesh Bhandarkar
Jason Bock
Carl Burnham
Chris Crane
Jeremy Crosbie
Alexander Konstantinou
Hang Lau
Jim MacIntosh
Jacob Mathew
Vinay Menon
David Schultz
Rohini Sulatycki
Andrew Watt

Production Manager
Simon Hardware

Production Project Coordinator
Mark Burdett

Figures
Shabnam Hussain

Cover
Chris Morris

Proof Reader
Christopher Smith

About the Authors

Jess Garms

Jess Garms is co-founder and Chief Technical Officer of ISNetworks, a company providing Java-based security software. He is responsible for coordinating development and investigating new technologies.

Jess would like to thank the following people:

Dave Rueter and Joe Mobley for their help in organizing the book and helping me to understand what readers would want in this book.

Josh Eckels, for developing much of the code in Chapter 11, and for his tireless work on editing .policy files.

And finally, Lisa, for putting up with me this past year while writing this book.

Daniel Somerfield

Daniel Somerfield is CEO and co-founder of ISNetworks. He is responsible for strategic planning and software architecture for the company and its clients. Daniel manages projects for diverse companies, both national and international in scope.

Daniel would like to thank:

Josh Eckels, Dave Rueter, and Joe Mobley for their help in developing the code for the book and for being the best development team I've ever worked with.

Table of Contents

Table of Contents

Table of Contents

Table of Contents

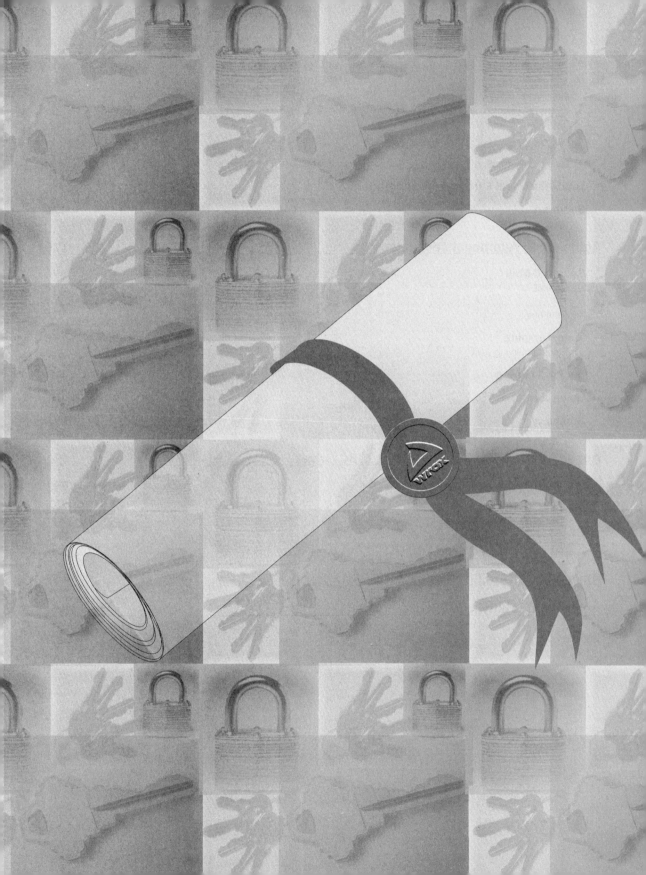

Introduction

Security is always a concern for developers – at any IT conference the seminars on this topic will always be packed out. The huge growth in use of the Internet for e-commerce has heightened the public awareness of the need for secure applications and the problems that are caused by failure in this area. For an e-commerce company, breaches in computer security aren't matters for internal embarrassment, but are items that will reduce public confidence in not only that company, but the fledgling world of consumer e-commerce as well. Similarly for B2B companies such breaches will damage working relationships and partnerships.

Computer security covers a multitude of topics – a secure application should be able to withstand certain types of disruptive attack (such as denial of service or viruses), and be resistant to eavesdropping, unauthorized access, or having data tampered with. Thus, in this book, we'll consider such areas as data encryption, authentication, and non-repudiation.

This book could be realistically sub-titled *Protecting your applications with cryptography and the Java security model*, since our main focus in this book is to look at application development. Computer security is a vast area, and while we quickly look at the context of application security in Chapter 1, we are not going to spend much time thinking about network and OS-level issues. Suffice to say that, when thinking about security, you should consider the application from end-to-end, and look for vulnerabilities at all points in the architecture. Systems need to be layered – applications should be secure and so should the underlying architecture. Of course security must be integral to the development process and not an afterthought.

At the start of the book we'll build a comprehensive understanding of the application of cryptography to programming, specifically in the context of the Java language and the Java platform. To support this we'll look at core Java security features. Armed with the knowledge we gain we'll be in a position, by the end of the book, to design and build an application that is secure from browser or client application, through the middle tier, to the data store.

Who is this Book For?

This book presents everything a Java programmer needs to know about designing and programming secure applications. Although we begin with simple examples and descriptions, towards the end of the book these ideas are collected together to provide a comprehensive set of solutions for building an application that is secured from end-to-end.

This book is aimed at intermediate to advanced Java programmers, familiar with the concepts underpinning distributed application development such as Java sockets, RMI, JDBC, and J2EE technologies such as servlets and JSPs. As such the book will concentrate on teaching approaches to security, and carefully explaining how the key Java cryptography components can be employed. For readers interested in enhancing their background knowledge in the core Java technologies mentioned we recommend *Professional Java Programming* (*ISBN 1-861003-82-X*) and *Professional Java Server Programming – J2EE Edition* (*ISBN 1-861004-65-6*) both published by Wrox Press.

What's Covered in this Book

To begin the book, in **Chapter 1**, we'll provide a brief overview of the different areas that need to be considered, when thinking about developing secure computer systems, and from there quickly discuss the various technologies used in such systems before homing in on the core theme of the book – developing secure Java based applications. Since the word security in this context covers such a diversity of subjects **Chapter 2** looks at general approaches for writing secure code that won't introduce unwelcome 'features' into your applications.

Chapter 3 introduces the topic of cryptography and, via illustrations based on a well-known Shakespeare play, gives an accessible, yet comprehensive insight, into the use of cryptography to facilitate encryption of data and authentication of entities. Furthermore the support Java gives for cryptography is introduced with a description of the **Java Cryptography Architecture** (**JCA**) and the **Java Cryptography Extension** (**JCE**). The themes of encryption are developed in **Chapters 4** and **5** where symmetric and asymmetric encryption are discussed and practical examples of each presented, while in **Chapter 6** authentication is covered when we provide examples of using message digests, digital signatures, and digital certificates.

In **Chapter 7** we look at the Java 2 security model and applet security. While this is an area of Java security many have a certain degree of familiarity with, our previous coverage of cryptography will give allow us to build a good appreciation of the implementation of the model. **Chapter 8** moves further into the arena of enterprise application development when we look at additional security aspects of the Java platform associated with servlets, Enterprise JavaBeans (EJBs), and the **Java Authentication and Authorization Service** (**JAAS**). To build secure applications that run over HTTP, **SSL** (**Secure Sockets Layer**) was developed. Built upon the cryptographic principles covered earlier, this technology facilitates much of the e-commerce running over the Web, and, in **Chapter 9** we show how programmers can apply SSL to their applications.

Our next two chapters pull together all the concepts presented previously. In **Chapter 10** we discuss approaches to securing databases, both by making the connections to the database less vulnerable and encrypting the data *within* the database. Then in **Chapter 11** we show how the concepts of encryption and authentication can be used inside a full-blown enterprise-type application.

Finally in **Chapter 12**, we'll provide information on how to program your own cryptographic provider.

To support our main text we have a number of appendices that detail additional information that lies outside the main flow of the book, such as additional techniques for enhancing application security including secure e-mail and timestamping, and also installation details for some of the software used within the book.

What You Need to Use this Book

Clear details of the software needed for a particular sample application are included in each chapter, but we'll mention them here. The code examples in this book require the use of the following software installed on your machine:

- ❑ The Java 2 Platform, Standard Edition SDK (JDK 1.3)
- ❑ The Java 2 Platform, Enterprise Edition SDK 1.2.1 Reference Implementation

The following extensions to the platforms are also used in this book:

- ❑ Java Authentication and Authorization Service (JAAS)
- ❑ Java Secure Sockets Extension (JSSE)
- ❑ A Java Cryptography Extension (JCE)

All of these are available from http://java.sun.com, and we used JAAS v1.0 and JSSE v1.0.2. While JCE v.1.2.1 is also available, for the reasons discussed in Chapter 3 this book makes extensive use of the Bouncy Castle Cryptography API v1.04 (available from http://www.bouncycastle.org). This is a freely available provider, and one of the more complete implementations available.

We are aware that future versions of Java will probably incorporate changes in this area, however, because we only want to provide solid technical information, we've concentrated on the situation as of the time of writing. Where appropriate, we'll draw your attention to issues that are most likely to change.

We'll also be using the following software at various points in our discussion of security:

- ❑ JavaSoft's HTML Converter – This software is freely available for download from Sun's web site at http://java.sun.com/products/plugin/1.2/features.html. It converts a call to a Java applet in a web page into a format that can be run in multiple browsers.
- ❑ Internet Explorer – Available from http://www.microsoft.com/downloads/.
- ❑ Netscape and Netscape's Capabilities API – The browser is available at http://home.netscape.com/download/index.html?cp=djuc1. Netscape's Java security model is a bit different from the standard 1.1 or 1.2 model and Netscape calls this the Capabilities API. In order to run applets under Netscape, we'll need the Capabilities API. These capability classes can be downloaded from http://developer.netscape.com/docs/manuals/signedobj/capsapi.html.
- ❑ Microsoft's SDK for Java – In order to create and sign .cab files to be able to run applets under Internet Explorer, you'll need Microsoft's SDK for Java. You can download it from http://www.microsoft.com/java/. At the time of this writing, the most recent version was 4.0.

❑   A database and appropriate JDBC driver – We've chosen to use MySQL (from http://www.mysql.com), and the code discussed in this book is designed to be used with this database. Other SQL92-compliant databases such as Oracle, SQL Server, or PostgreSQL could equally well be used but code modifications will be needed. JDBC drivers for MySQL can be obtained from a number of places such as http://mmmysql.sourceforge.net. Appendix B discusses database installation and JDBC driver issues.

❑   An XML Parser – We've chosen to use the Xerces XML parser to run the examples in this book. Xerces can be downloaded from http://xml.apache.org/xerces-j/index.html. We used v1.3.1 when testing this code.

❑   A Web Server – For the secure application that we'll build in Chapter 11, we're going to use Tomcat 3.2.1, which supports SSL directly (available from http://jakarta.apache.org/tomcat/index.html). Other servlet engines could be used, such as iPlanet from Sun and Netscape, or WebSphere from IBM, but as with the database, we're only providing set-up information for Tomcat.

Source Code

The complete source code from the book is available for download from: http://www.wrox.com.

Due to the nature and likely areas of application of security type code your attention is drawn to the disclaimer in the preliminary pages of this publication, specifically:

The author and publisher have made every effort in the preparation of this book to ensure the accuracy of the information. However, the information contained in this book is sold without warranty, either express or implied. Neither the authors, Wrox Press nor its dealers or distributors will be held liable for any damages caused or alleged to be caused either directly or indirectly by this book.

The code in the book will work on a single machine, provided it is networked (that is, it can see http://localhost through the local browser). The only exception to this is the SSL-tunneling (Tunnel Server) example in Chapter 10, which will require the use of two separate computers.

The application in Chapter 11 has been designed to be applicable to multiple computer systems, however for simplicity the download code is configured for a single machine.

Conventions

To help you get the most from the text and keep track of what's happening, we've used a number of conventions throughout the book.

For instance:

> **These boxes hold important, not-to-be forgotten information that is directly relevant to the surrounding text.**

The background style is used for asides to the current discussion.

As for styles in the text:

❑   When we introduce them, we **highlight** important words.

❑   We show keyboard strokes like this: *Ctrl-A*.

❑   We show filenames and code within the text like so: doGet()

❑   Text on user interfaces and URLs are shown as: Menu.

We present code in several different ways. Command line and terminal output is shown as:

```
C:\> java showStyle
When the command line is shown, it's shown in the above style, while terminal
output
is in this style.
Output needing a: response
is shown like this
```

Definitions of methods and properties are shown as follows:

```
protected void doGet(HttpServletRequest req, HttpServletResponse resp)
                throws ServletException, IOException
```

Example code is shown:

```
In our code examples, the code foreground style shows new, important,
    pertinent code
while code background shows code that's less important in the present context,
    or has been seen before.
```

Customer Support

We want to know what you think about this book: what you liked, what you didn't like, and what you think we can do better next time. You can send your comments, either by returning the reply card in the back of the book, or by e-mail (to feedback@wrox.com). Please be sure to mention the book title in your message.

Errata

We've made every effort to make sure that there are no errors in the text or the code. However, to err is human, and as such we recognize the need to keep you informed of any mistakes as they're spotted and corrected. Errata sheets are available for all our books at http://www.wrox.com. If you find an error that hasn't already been reported, please let us know.

E-mail Support

If you wish to directly query a problem in the book page with an expert who knows the book in detail then e-mail support@wrox.com, with the title of the book and the last four numbers of the ISBN in the subject field of the e-mail. A typical e-mail should include the following things:

❑   The **name of the book**, **last four digits of the ISBN**, and **page number** of the problem in the Subject field.

❑   Your **name**, **contact info**, and the **problem** in the body of the message.

We *won't* send you junk mail. We need the details to save your time and ours. When you send an e-mail it will go through the following chain of support:

❑   Customer Support – Your message is delivered to one of our customer support staff who are the first people to read it. They have files on most frequently asked questions and will answer anything general immediately. They answer general questions about the book and the web site.

❑   Editorial – Deeper queries are forwarded to the technical editor responsible for that book. They have experience with the programming language or particular product and are able to answer detailed technical questions on the subject. Once an issue has been resolved, the editor can post the errata to the web site.

❑   The Authors – Finally, in the unlikely event that the editor can't answer your problem, they will forward the request to the author. We try to protect the author from any distractions from writing. However, we are quite happy to forward specific requests to them. All Wrox authors help with the support on their books. They'll mail the customer and the editor with their response, and again all readers should benefit.

P2P.WROX.COM

For author and peer support join the Java mailing lists. Our unique system provides **programmer-to-programmer™ support** on mailing lists, forums and newsgroups, all *in addition* to our one-to-one e-mail system. Be confident that your query is not just being examined by a support professional, but by the many Wrox authors and other industry experts present on our mailing lists. At p2p.wrox.com you'll find a number of different lists aimed at Java programmers, and developers interested in security, that will support you, not only while you read this book, but also as you develop your own applications. Particularly appropriate to this book are some of the Security lists, but there are many other relevant ones within the Java category.

To enroll for support just follow this four-step system:

1. Go to p2p.wrox.com.

2. Click on the Java or Security button.

3. Click on the mailing list you wish to join.

4. Fill in your e-mail address and password (of at least 4 alphnumeric characters) and e-mail it to us.

Why this System Offers the Best Support

You can choose to join the mailing lists or you can receive them as a weekly digest. If you don't have the time, or facility, to receive the mailing list, then you can search our online archives. Junk and spam mails are deleted, and your own e-mail address is protected by the unique Lyris system. Any queries about joining or leaving lists, or any other queries about the list, should be sent to listsupport@p2p.wrox.com.

Considering Security

Computer security is difficult to define succinctly. It encompasses a number of areas, but security is mostly concerned with controlling access to resources. Security comes into play when you are writing an application and you find yourself asking questions such as:

❑ How do I transmit sensitive information, like credit card numbers?

❑ How do I store sensitive data?

❑ How can I be sure that this code is from a trusted source?

❑ How do I ensure that only authorized users can access the system?

There are many other questions, but they all revolve around how to protect information and resources.

The first thing you should learn about computer security is that there is no such thing as a secure system. All systems can be hacked, and there are no exceptions to this rule. At the very least, your network could be compromised by a simple physical attack, such as unplugging the network cable from the server. What you as a computer *programmer* can do is make it harder for an attacker to break into your systems, and easier for you to restore them if they have been compromised. In this book we'll discuss many ways to improve your applications, keeping these goals in mind.

The main focus of this book is to show you how to protect your Java applications with cryptography and the Java security model, but before we get into code and encryption details we should provide some context for your work. So in this chapter we'll look at:

❑ The high-level considerations needed when designing secure applications

❑ Some practical considerations regarding building secure systems

❑ Some basic security aspects of the Java language and platform

❑ An illustration from Hamlet that will aid our discussions on security

Let's begin by discussing the goals of security applications.

Philosophy of Security

There are three security goals that we should concentrate on when writing applications:

1. **Protect sensitive data** – The first goal is fairly obvious. This is what most people think of when they consider computer security. The canonical example of sensitive data is customers' credit card numbers, but there are many more, such as passwords, financial data, and medical histories. A good application should store this data safely. Usually this is done by using encryption. One of the oft-quoted rules in computer security is that it should cost more to break into a system than the contents of the system are worth.

2. **Control access to resources** – When storing sensitive data, occasionally it will need to be used, but it's important that access to that data be strictly controlled. This is done using some form of authentication. In most applications this is username and password, but in this book we're going to examine more secure methods, such as digital certificates. One use of access control is in stopping **denial of service (DoS)** attacks. A denial of service attack is an attempt to clog resources with fake requests, preventing legitimate users from accessing the system. By controlling access to resources, you can keep these attacks to a minimum.

3. **Log activity** – This goal is straightforward; there should be a record somewhere of who is performing what activity. If a compromise occurs, a log can help pinpoint the source of the compromise, and in certain cases can even help to reassemble the data that was lost. In some systems, however, the logs themselves should be considered sensitive data and need to be protected. We're not going to focus very strongly on logging in this book, as it's a fairly simple task and doesn't require any special Java APIs. Just bear in mind that it's important to log access in any production system.

To aid you in your considerations on how to reach these goals it's useful to have a **security policy**.

Security Policy

A security policy is an explicit statement of what actions are and are not allowed within an organization. It will help define the limits of what your application needs to protect against. It will also help you to identify what your important resources are, so you can start planning how to secure them. A security policy defines such things as acceptable use of corporate resources, remote access policy, and user privileges. It should be written in plain English and be available to anyone in your organization who might need it. A company's security policy is quite different from Java's security policy files, which we will be discussing in later chapters.

> *The first step in securing an application is to read your organization's security policy. If you are part of a small organization, one may not exist. In that case, you should write one.*

In this book, we'll be securing applications, not an entire organization. But that security still exists within a larger framework, so it is important to understand how your application's security needs will fit into the whole. We will be touching on many issues that will be affected by overall business needs.

Security Requirements

After studying your security policy or writing one, you can begin examining the security requirements of your application. We can break this topic down into the areas of **risk assessment** and **data exposure**. Of course any system will need to be grounded in practicality, which of course will lead to compromises being made.

Risk Assessment

A risk assessment is an attempt to quantify the security risks of your application. This will help you determine what resources need to be explicitly protected, and how valuable they are. Some questions to ask yourself are:

❑ How much would it cost if my data were destroyed?

❑ How much would my data be worth to someone else?

❑ How much would the destruction of my data be worth to someone else?

❑ How valuable is the use of the application?

❑ How much would it cost if unauthorized clients were using our application?

❑ How likely are people to know of our application?

Once you have determined the rough value of your resources, you have to ask yourself what your weakest links are. Who would be most likely to attempt to break in to your system? Who would try to steal your data, log in to your application, or destroy your system? Who would have the most to gain by any of these actions? If you can't come up with anyone, you still need to deal with potential vandals, crackers who will try to break into your machines just for the sheer joy of it. In some cases, it is the last group of people who are most likely to attack your systems.

Data Exposure

The next factor you must examine is the idea of **data exposure**. When will your data be easiest to access – in the corporate database, on users' computers, on backup tapes? Examine these areas to determine the most likely places that your data could be stolen or deliberately corrupted.

After this, you'll need to examine those areas closely to determine which are most in need of strengthening. To do this you will need to perform a thorough and frank assessment of the weakest points in your organization. The two areas on which to focus most closely are people and access points where the system is most vulnerable to attack.

People

Unfortunately, the people inside your organization are the greatest liability because they know more about how the system works than anyone else. People also have the annoying tendency to paste their password to their monitor, or share their passwords with co-workers. They have the most ability to do damage because they require greater access to the data than any snoop or hacker outside on the web.

> **For this reason, it is extremely important to divide your systems into sub-systems and grant permission to access data only as necessary.**

Again, the degree to which you spend time and money to subdivide and secure your data is dependent on how valuable the data is and how likely it is to be violated. A helpful strategy can be to design your security around *roles* instead of people. In other words, instead of planning to grant Jeannine access to resource X and Joe access to resource Y, you can grant DBAs access to resource X and Sales Associates access to resource Y. That will help you clarify the roles people serve in your organization in terms of your systems and data.

Additionally, assigning roles can help when people join, leave, and move around within your organization. This way of thinking will also help you move from the more theoretical design of your secure system to implementation. The concept of user roles translates nicely into a public key infrastructure and cryptographic strategies such as **certificate chaining**, which we will discuss later in the book.

Vulnerability Points

Once you have your internal roles defined, the second most crucial issue becomes securing potential points of vulnerability in your systems. These points will vary greatly from one system to another. Some will be obvious and other less so. Obvious and common examples are:

- ❑ Any point at which internal systems are connected, directly or indirectly to the Internet
- ❑ Machines that are physically located in a public or semi-public location
- ❑ Machines that provide remote services
- ❑ In-production storage mechanisms for sensitive or valuable data, such as databases

Some less obvious examples are:

- ❑ Backup storage such as tapes or CDs
- ❑ Inconspicuous physical access to a machine

Although some of these may sound obvious, it is incredible how many people will take these for granted and forget that a completely network secure un-hackable machine isn't worth much if any unauthorized person can walk up to it, boot off a floppy disk and format the drive or gain root access.

> It's also important that any of your exposed machines be running up-to-date versions of all software and applications. Security holes are found in programs all the time, and if you don't keep your machines patched, you may be leaving a gaping hole in your network.

Balancing Security Requirements and Usability

As we have already mentioned, and will many more times throughout the book – a "secure" system is a series of compromises that require an understanding of the intrinsic value of the data being protected and the people, hardware, and software involved.

The key is making the right compromises. One of those is the balance between protection of the integrity of the system and ease of use for the users who participate in the system. Again, we come back to people. While people can be a threat through malice, much more often they breach security through carelessness. For this reason it is extremely important to provide users with a system that is easy to use, one that they use by default, or even better, one they will use without even noticing it's there.

Having a system of complex passwords that cannot be broken with a password-cracking tool isn't worth much if the users tape their passwords to their monitors. If a security system is too complicated, users are encouraged to find mechanisms to bypass the security for their own convenience. Achieving a successful balance between usability and security is one of the hardest parts of creating a secure system.

Because it is impossible to make a system completely impervious to breaches of security it is also important to have contingency plans for those rare instances when data is compromised or damaged. Of course, the most common way to deal with the problem is to make frequent and regular backups, encrypted if necessary. This of course does not provide any assistance in the case of compromised data.

The violation of the integrity of your private data is a much more difficult problem. Generally the strategy should be to minimize the damage. If the time of the breach can be verified and *every* access to the data is logged, it may be possible to figure out which data has been compromised and then make sure that further data isn't at risk. Logging is a very important aspect of computer security that's often overlooked.

Depending on the type of system you are running these steps may or may not be sufficient. Some systems may simply require you to change your passwords or re-encrypt stored data with a new private key. Others may require you to ensure the attack hasn't left your system with new breaches or backdoors.

Implementing Security

Once you have figured out what you have to secure and to what degree, you have choose the tools for each item. We've chosen the Java programming language because we believe that it is the best tool for the job. This book is meant to be a cookbook of sorts, to teach you how to use cryptography and the Java security model to secure your application. This is not a reference book. The JavaDoc provided by Sun provides an excellent source of information on APIs and packages. Instead, we'll be teaching you high-level use of these libraries.

We'll start by discussing the basic cryptographic primitives such as message digests and ciphers, and then move on to more advanced topics, such as network encryption with SSL. Finally, we'll compose a reasonably complete security-sensitive banking application to demonstrate how you can use the various Java security libraries and tools together.

Obviously Java security isn't the entire picture, so before we discuss Java security we're going to go over several additional technologies that can be used to help secure your applications. These do not so much compete with Java as support it.

Security Technologies and Tools

Here we'll quickly mention:

- Operating Systems
- IP Security
- Virtual Private Networks
- Firewalls
- Intrusion Detection Tools

These obviously are only a sample of the other areas within the security spectrum, but they will serve to give a better understanding of how application security fits into the wider scheme of computer system security. Our goal with this section is not to provide a detailed insight into network security but merely to highlight other topics you should be aware of.

Let's begin by taking a look at Operating Systems.

Operating Systems

The operating system you're using will greatly affect the security of your applications. If your OS is breached, an attacker will be able to replace any part of your application by changing the class files that compose it. It won't matter how secure you've programmed your application to behave if someone can change the way that it works.

Some operating systems cannot be easily secured, such as Windows 95/98/Me and versions of MacOS prior to X. These are consumer-oriented and written without security in mind. If you need security, you should use a more robust operating system such as Linux, Solaris, or Windows NT/2000.

Once you've installed an operating system, it's important to apply the latest security patches that the vendor supplies. Also, make sure that no extraneous services are running, such as FTP and telnet. In addition, file permissions should be set appropriately so that users are not granted access to files they do not need.

On some operating systems, it's possible to configure which network connections are allowed. This can be extremely useful for applications such as databases and RMI servers because it can allow you to configure who should be allowed to connect to a service. Used in conjunction with a well-configured java.policy file (which will be covered in Chapter 7), this would provide a great deal of protection against unauthorized use of a server.

Information on securing an operating system could easily fill an entire book. If possible, you should have an experienced system administrator install, and configure, any server operating systems you're going to use.

IP Security

Network traffic is not encrypted by default. The current protocol for handling network traffic, called **IPv4**, does not support encryption. **IPsec**, part of the new IPv6 protocol, adds support for protecting network communication over IP. It's similar to **Secure Socket Layer** (**SSL**), which we'll discuss in Chapter 9, except that it's completely transparent to the application using it. Communication can be automatically encrypted and authenticated, depending on the configuration. Performance is also typically better than when using SSL, as the operating system and routers handle it, rather than a Java-based application.

If your network uses IPsec, then there would be little use in using RMI over SSL, as the traffic would be unreadable by anyone not involved in the direct communication. IPsec is somewhat new, but is slowly gaining ground in corporate networks. Hopefully it will achieve widespread use in the near future. If you're interested in reading more about IPsec, take a look at the charter at http://www.ietf.org/html.charters/ipsec-charter.html.

Virtual Private Networks

Usually referred to as **VPNs**, these are a method for tunneling secure communication over an unsecured medium, such as the Internet provides. VPNs are typically used to connect two different networks transparently. The communication on each network is unencrypted, but a proxy that sits between the network and the transmission medium encrypts any traffic sent between the two networks.

The proxies handle the encryption and decryption requirements transparently, so that the end user sees no difference between the local network and the remote network despite the addition of a security layer between the two. VPNs are becoming quite popular, especially for employees working remotely.

Firewalls

A firewall restricts network traffic between two points. They are most often used to separate a private network from the Internet. You can usually configure a firewall to allow certain types of traffic through to the private network, such as only allowing traffic on port 80 to have access to the network. That way, no one could send messages bound for any non-public services that might be running on those boxes, such as a database.

There are several forms of firewalls available. In brief, these are:

- ❑ **Origin/Destination Firewalls** – Firewalls that filter packets based on the origin and/or the destination of the packet.

- ❑ **Gateway Firewalls** – Usually used in a **bastion host** (**dual homed**) system with two network cards. One card is connected to the Internet, and one to the intranet. The gateway would be implemented to allow Internet traffic restricted access to the intranet.

- ❑ **Client-side Firewalls** – Most commonly seen in corporate environments where access to specific sites is restricted to employees, and the company is also protected from external attacks.

- ❑ **Server-side Firewalls** – Sometimes known as a **Demilitarized Zone** (**DMZ**), these create a safe area where the servers are protected from both the Internet and the intranet, but can be accessed by both.

Firewalls are complex, multi-purpose beasts. You should have an experienced network administrator install and configure your firewall(s), based on the needs of your particular application. Once your firewall is installed and functioning, it will add security to your network, thus adding security to your application.

Intrusion Detection Tools

There are a number of tools that you can use to detect attackers. The most common is a **packet sniffer**. A packet sniffer allows you to view all the traffic on your network. You can see if odd activity is taking place, or if machines are attempting to send messages they should not be. There are several commercial packet sniffers available, but our favourite is a free one: Ethereal, from http://www.ethereal.com. It works on both UNIX and Windows.

Another common type of intrusion detection tool detects if someone has altered any of the files on your machine without your knowledge. The most widely used of these is called **Tripwire**, and is available in two flavours: a commercial one at http://www.tripwire.com and a non-commercial version at http://www.tripwire.org.

There are many more tools available for network protection, as well as authentication systems such as Kerberos, which we won't cover in this book (for more information on Keberos see for example http://web.mit.edu/kerberos/www/). Instead, we'll be focusing on issues directly relating to application security, such as:

- ❑ Executable code protection
- ❑ Protecting your data on the server
- ❑ Protecting your data in transit
- ❑ Access control

As we mentioned earlier, the medium we have selected is the Java programming language, so let's take a brief look at it now.

Java Security

Java as a language has a number of security features that set it apart from its predecessors like C++. We're going to briefly discuss these here, although we will be coming into contact with them in greater detail over the course of this book. The most well known of the security features is Java's ability to run code in a **sandbox**.

A sandbox is essentially a collection of safe resources that a piece of code is allowed to access. Applets run in a sandbox by default in Java. They are given access only to the CPU and a chunk of memory, as well as the ability to make a network connection back to the server that the applet originated from. Because of this, applets are typically safe to run, even if you are not certain what they are doing.

The sandbox prevents a malicious applet from reading your e-mail password off your hard drive and sending it to someone else, for example. Starting with Java 2 (JDK 1.2), a sandbox can be defined to allow access to specific resources, like file access to a certain directory.

Furthermore the Java language also provides support for security – Java doesn't have pointers, which makes it impossible for direct access to memory. Also, every time an array is accessed, the virtual machine checks the index to be sure that it is within the defined length of the array. If it is not, an exception is thrown. These two features eliminate the most common security hole occurring with software written in C and C++: **buffer-overrun**. For those of you unfamiliar with the term, the following example may help to clarify the situation.

Let's say you have a mail server that accepts a username and a password to allow access to e-mail. You allocate 100 bytes to each of those inputs, assuming that no username or password will exceed these boundaries. Unfortunately, these will be written to the memory, and if the input value exceeds these boundaries, the overflow of information may write directly into memory past the space that you allocated. In fact, it is sometimes possible to begin writing over executable code, allowing an attacker to insert arbitrary binary commands into the program. Java is immune to this attack, as array bounds are checked, and the Virtual Machine throws an exception if the program attempts to access memory beyond the end of the array.

Our next chapter will highlight general areas of Java coding practice that will aid the development of secure code.

While we're covering the very basic features of Java that contribute to its intrinsic security, we should also mention the **byte code verifier** and the **class loader**.

The Byte Code Verifier

Java can also protect against potentially dangerous code by verifying byte code before running it. By verifying the byte code, the VM ensures that code being run can't perform certain dangerous operations, like use variables that haven't been initialized, or pop too many items off the stack.

The Class Loader

The purpose of the class loader is to load the specified classes into the VM. It works with the security manager and the access controller to ensure that the classes being loaded comply with the local security policy in force.

We'll be discussing the Java security manager and access control when, in Chapter 7, we investigate the fine-grained policy-based security approach taken by Java 2

Java and Cryptography

Java also provides easy access to **cryptography**, both in the core libraries, and in a standard extension (`java.security` and `javax.crypto`). Cryptography is the "science of secret writing" and we'll make extensive use of cryptography throughout this book as we show how to develop secure applications where data is obscured (to prevent eavesdropping), and identity can be proved. The use of complex mathematical functions in cryptography allows us to develop encryption routines and digital signatures, which each have a great variety of uses in computer security.

> *Indeed, while this book does discuss the intrinsic aspects of security offered by the Java language, we will spend a great deal of time dealing with the use of cryptography in developing secure applications.*

The Java language and the Java platform are continually evolving. Our aim, within this book has been to provide practical, working examples and illustrations using the architecture and extensions available at the time of writing with JDK 1.3. It is very likely that JDK 1.4 will have changes in the architecture; however, the fundamental concepts of cryptography, and the use of cryptography in secure applications will still be applicable.

We'll dig into basic cryptography, and how cryptography is supported in Java, in Chapter 3. Details of what software we've used throughout the book are contained in the Introduction.

Illustrating the Need for Security – Hamlet!

When describing security protocols, it's often necessary to use examples to illustrate the point. For this book, we're going to use characters and situations from the classic Shakespeare play *Hamlet* to underscore the need for good security.

Throughout the play, Hamlet, the famous Danish hacker, wanders about the castle antagonizing Claudius, the King of Denmark, kills or threatens to kill, various residents of the castle and generally makes a nuisance of himself. Finally, Claudius decides to rid the royal family of Hamlet once and for all, so he sends him "with fiery quickness" to England. He also sends his trusted agents Rosencrantz and Guildenstern along bearing a note which requests that Hamlet be immediately executed on arrival. Unfortunately for Claudius, as well as Rosencrantz and Guildenstern, the king neglected to take the necessary precautions to ensure that:

1. Hamlet could not read the message

2. He could not alter it

As a result, Hamlet was able to stealthily slip into the cabin while Rosencrantz and Guildenstern slept and read the message. Upon seeing that he was to be executed, the devious Dane hacked the message, replacing the request for his own execution with one for the death of those unfortunate civil servants, Rosencrantz and Guildenstern. He affixed to the message the seal of his father, the former King of Denmark and escaped in an unlikely plot twist involving pirates.

As faithful servants to Claudius, Rosencrantz and Guildenstern never thought to sneak a peek at the contents of the message and were summarily executed on arrival in England.

Throughout the course of this book we will examine ways Claudius could have secured the transmission to the English King and how the King could have verified that the content was in fact the original message Claudius had sent.

Summary

This chapter has provided some perspective on computer security. We started by considering the need, when developing a computer application, to protect sensitive data, control access to resources, and track activity within the application.

From there we moved on to highlighting how these areas of concern can be addressed by resolving issues related to the importance of the application, and identifying the most vulnerable areas of the application.

As we pointed out at the start of the chapter, this book is aimed at discussing security for Java applications. Applications themselves sit in a wider computing context, however, so a brief section of the chapter highlighted other areas of computer security like operating systems, communication protocols, and tools that can help secure a system. We then moved on to mention some of the core attributes of the Java language and platform to whet your appetite for later chapters.

Finally we introduced the scenario from Hamlet, which will give us a great basis for introducing and discussing difficult cryptographic approaches.

Now we've provided some context let's get down to business and look into the nuts and bolts of Java security, by taking a look at how to approach writing secure Java code.

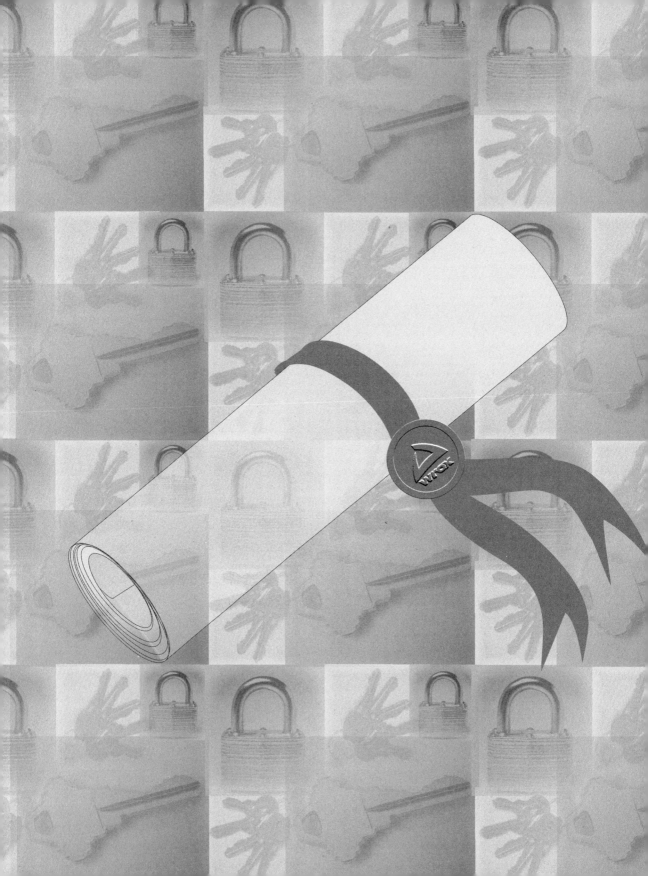

Secure Java Code

Security experts tell us that there is no such thing as secure code – code that is truly free of all possible security holes. This is true of most complex computer applications: there are too many factors to consider to ever be certain that *all* possible avenues of attack are closed. In the real world, we want to write code that is both free from all known security holes and unlikely to contain new ones.

The Java security model (which we'll discuss in far more detail later) is designed to protect users from malicious code, but it is possible to write **trusted code** that accidentally allows other code to bypass some of these security mechanisms. Some code accesses sensitive information and resources, such as files and passwords. There should be no holes in the software that you write that would allow someone to access those resources without permission.

In this chapter, we'll go over a number of hints and tips that should help you to recognize these holes and close them before they become a problem. We'll start with the most common situations and gradually move on to somewhat more esoteric situations and will cover the following topics:

- ❑ Accessibility
- ❑ Serialization
- ❑ Packages
- ❑ Privileged Code
- ❑ Native Methods

Accessibility

When writing Java code, it is important to make a conscious decision about the accessibility of all methods, classes, and member variables. The different levels are, in order of descending accessibility: `public`, `protected`, package-private, and `private`. Package-private has no declaration, but is the level granted by default when accessibility is not explicitly declared. Package-private is sometimes also referred to as "default" or "friendly". Here are the definitions of the various levels of accessibility and how they relate to the class that defines them:

❑   `Public` – Any class can access an entity.

❑   `Protected` – The class itself, any subclasses, and any classes inside the same package can access the entity.

❑   Package-private – This is the default accessibility, which is used when no accessibility is declared. It defines that only the class itself and any classes in the same package can access the entity.

❑   `Private` – Only the class itself can access the entity.

Assuming that byte code verification is turned on, it will be impossible to reach restricted fields and methods. You should therefore strive to reduce the accessibility of these entities as much as possible. If a method only needs to be called from within a single class, then that method should be declared `private`. If a variable only needs to be accessed from within a single method with no persistence, then it should be a local variable and not a member variable at all.

Member variables should be private whenever possible, with access provided through **accessor/mutator methods** such as `getX()` and `setX()`. These are commonly referred to collectively as accessor methods, although this isn't technically correct. Here's an example of using accessor methods to protect a private member variable:

```java
public class Account {

  private float accountBalance;

  public float getBalance() {
    return accountBalance;
  }

  public void setAccountBalance(float balance) {
    accountBalance = balance;
  }
}
```

This is standard Java programming practice for writing JavaBeans, and for good reason. If security checks are required, then they can be centralized in those accessor methods, rather than recoding all classes that access those member variables. It's also possible to provide only a getter or a setter method, allowing for read-only and write-only variables.

Accessibility and Security

In languages such as C++, the accessibility modifiers (`public`, `private`, `protected`, and `friend`) are checked at compile time, but not during run time. This means that it's possible for a malicious class to get access to a private member variable belonging to a different class. In Java, the byte code verifier ensures that a class cannot access entities it is not allowed to. The byte code verifier is turned on by default when running applets, but not applications. In order to turn the verifier on, you need to pass the `-verify` option to the Virtual Machine upon instantiation.

> By default, it is possible for objects to access private member variables in other objects. If you are using code that you wish to restrict with the security model, you should *always* use the **-verify** switch to ensure that the accessibility rules in Java are being enforced.

Let's take a look at an example. We'll define two classes: Victim and Perpetrator, to demonstrate access to private member variables. Victim will contain a private member variable, secret, and Perpetrator will attempt to access it. To begin, we'll need to define Victim to contain a public member variable to enable compilation. Here's the first draft of Victim.java:

```java
public class Victim {

  public String secret;

  public Victim() {
    secret = "squeamish ossifrage";
  }
}
```

And Perpetrator.java:

```java
public class Perpetrator {

  public static void main (String[] args) {
    Victim victim = new Victim();
    System.out.println(victim.secret);
  }
}
```

Now we can compile them with:

```
C:\>javac Victim.java Perpetrator.java
```

To run the example, type:

```
C:\>java Perpetrator
```

It runs with no difficulty, displaying **squeamish ossifrage**. Now we want to change the accessibility of Victim.secret to private. Here's our updated Victim.java:

```java
public class Victim {

  private String secret;

  public Victim() {
    secret = "squeamish ossifrage";
  }
}
```

Recompile Victim.java (and only Victim.java) with:

```
C:\>javac Victim.java
```

Run the test again with:

```
C:\>java Perpetrator
```

You get the same output as before: **squeamish ossifrage**. But how can this be? Victim.secret is defined as a private member variable, but Perpetrator was able to get access to it. The reason for this behavior is that it's the byte code verifier's job to determine if a class attempts to access restricted entities. And by default, byte code loaded from the filesystem is not verified. To turn on the byte code verifier, execute

```
C:\>java -verify Perpetrator
```

and you should see the following output:

```
Exception in thread "main" java.lang.IllegalAccessError: try to access field
        Victim.secret from class Perpetrator at Perpetrator.main(Perpetrator.java:4)
```

This example shows that it is important to instantiate Java applications with the -verify switch in any situation in which secret data is being kept in private variables and non-trusted classes are running.

Final Classes, Methods, and Variables

The final keyword labels a class, method, or variable, as a constant. That is, a final entity should always remain the same. Classes defined as final cannot be subclassed, final methods cannot be overridden, and final variables cannot be reassigned.

Note that a final variable cannot be reassigned, but that doesn't mean that it can't be modified. For example, imagine that we have a Hashtable, h, which has been labeled as final. We cannot change h itself to point to a new Hashtable, but we can call its put() methods. The same is true of arrays. A final variable holding an array cannot be reassigned, but the contents of the array can be changed as desired.

By making a class final, and providing no way to change its contents (no set() methods, for instance), you can create objects that are immutable, such as String.

Static Fields

Static variables are assigned to a class, rather than an object. There is only one instance for a given class, regardless of how many objects of that class are instantiated. These are often used to define constants within a class, by adding the final modifier. If static variables need to be declared public so that other classes can read them, they should also be declared final so that they cannot be modified, because otherwise, the class's behavior could be modified by outside code. If you need a publicly accessible static variable that needs to change, it would be best to use a private variable that is static, and return a copy of it from a get() method, and create a set() method to perform the actual changes on it. That way, modifications can be managed from within your class, as mentioned earlier.

Clear Sensitive Information

When storing sensitive information in an object, it's important to know what happens to that information when the object is no longer in use. Typically, the garbage collector will free that memory up for use later, but there is no guarantee that the memory will get cleared until it is actually re-allocated by another request for more memory. In certain situations, it might be possible for someone to get read access to that memory after the application has exited, or even during execution if there is some way of reading memory directly in the operating system your application is running under.

For instance, imagine that you have a private key object like the following (we'll be discussing keys a lot from the next chapter onwards):

```
public class PrivateKey {
  private byte[] keyContents;

  // Methods here

}
```

You use it to decrypt some messages, and then exit the VM. Then a C application starts up and allocates a huge chunk of memory. By searching through that allocated memory, it may be able to find your private key, which is just an array of bytes.

Ideally, when handling sensitive information, it is best to clear out the data when you are finished with it. For our `PrivateKey` class, we might add a method, `clear()`, that does just that:

```
public class PrivateKey {

  private byte[] keyContents;

  public void clear() {
    for (int i=0;i<keyContents.length;i++) {
      keyContents[i] = (byte) 0x00;
    }
  }

  // Other methods go here

}
```

Our `clear()` method zeroes out the actual byes of the `keyContents` bytes array, so that no one else can read them. Depending on your underlying data structures, clearing objects can be somewhat difficult. Note that it's not sufficient to simply set them to `null`. You need to actually get down to the level that the primitives are stored and changed those primitives to new, zeroed out values.

When you're done using that `PrivateKey`, you should call `clear()` to ensure that the sensitive data is cleared. You could place a call to `clear()` in the `finalize()` method, but this doesn't guarantee that the memory will be cleared before the VM exits. It's much better to call `clear()` manually.

Immutable Classes

A number of classes in Java are immutable, such as `String` and `BigInteger`. Since they cannot be changed, they also cannot be cleared. The solution, in this case, would be not to use `Strings` or `BigIntegers` to store data that you need to zero out. Instead, you should store passwords and private keys in arrays, and provide clear methods in your classes for those arrays.

Most cryptographic implementations in Java store their private keys in `BigIntegers`. This means that it is theoretically possible for someone to search memory to find private keys, since there is no way to zero them out. We stress the "theoretically" part. It would be extremely difficult to actually steal private keys in this fashion, but it can't be completely ruled out. If you are writing a program that handles private keys, you need to evaluate your particular circumstance and decide if you need to worry about the immutability of `BigInteger`.

For the truly paranoid, the Operating System paging mechanism may need to be taken into consideration. While your program is running, the OS may swap out parts of memory to disk, including sensitive information like passwords and private keys. There's really nothing you can do about this in Java, except try to clear information as quickly as possible to reduce the possibility of it being swapped out. If your application needs this level of security, you probably need to look at using native code, which can lock segments of memory and prevent them from being swapped out.

As always, security is a continuum. There are always going to be potential weaknesses for any application. What you must do is determine your acceptable risk. If you have the time and money, you can buy or create a provider that doesn't use `BigInteger`, or write code that doesn't allow your passwords to be swapped out to disk, but it's not typically required of most applications.

Storing and Returning Objects and Arrays

When returning objects and arrays, it's important to realize that it might be possible for the calling object to modify what you've returned. Here's an example:

```
public class Example {

  private String[] internalData;

  public String[] getData() {
    return internalData;
  }
}
```

Note that we could modify `internalData` with the following lines in some other code, assuming `example` is an instance of `Example`:

```
String[] array = example.getData();
array[0] = "This is a new String.";
```

Now the first element of the private array `internalData`, belonging to `example`, has been changed. This is probably not the behavior intended. Instead, a copy should be made of the array before returning it. That way, even if the array returned gets modified, it won't alter the internal state of the original object.

As a corollary, when a mutable object or array gets passed in to an object to be used as an internal variable, it's important to make a copy. Here's another example object:

```
public class Example {

    private String[] internalData;

    public Example(String[] data) {
        internalData = data;
    }
}
```

Again, there is a possible vulnerability if we run the following code:

```
String[] someData = {"String1","String2"};
Example example = new Example(someData);
someData[0] = "New String";
```

At this point, the `internalData` array in example has been modified without going through the example object. Again, the solution is to make a copy of the array. This should be done in the constructor, like so:

```
    public Example(String[] data) {
        internalData = new String[data.length];
        System.arraycopy(data,0,internalData,0,data.length);
    }
```

If you're storing something other than an array, the `clone()` method could be used. If `clone()` isn't available, you may need to create a new object and copy over the values from the original object with `get()` and `set()` methods.

You can also call `clone()` on an array, but you need to realize that each object in the array will not be cloned, but only the top level array. If you want to do a deep copy, you need to take care of it manually like in our example above.

Note that if you're storing immutable data types, you don't need to worry about them being modified after the fact. A `String`, for instance, cannot be changed once it's instantiated, so you don't need to make a copy of it before returning it, even if it's being used as an internal variable.

Now that we've covered accessibility, let's take a look at the issues arising from serialization.

Serialization

Serialization allows storage and transmission of an object's state. It's typically used to transfer objects between VMs and to save an object's state between instances of a VM. Special care needs to be taken when serializing and deserializing, and creating objects that are serializable. Once an object is serialized, it is outside of the control of the Java security system. It is possible that someone who would normally be unable to modify an object could alter the serialized form of it.

By default, serialization stores all internal variables to whatever output stream is provided. This includes even private variables, so be careful when implementing the `Serializable` interface. Also realize that subclasses may implement the `Serializable` interface, allowing for serialization when it was not intended. You can avoid this by declaring your class `final`, or implementing the `private` methods `readObject(java.io.ObjectInputStream input)` and `writeObject(java.io.ObjectOutputStream output)` and having them throw a `NotSerializableException` like so:

```
private void readObject(ObjectInputStream input)
    throws IOException, ClassNotFoundException {
    throw new NotSerializableException("This class is not serializable");
}

private void writeObject(ObjectOutputStream output)
    throws IOException, ClassNotFoundException {
    throw new NotSerializableException("This class is not serializable");
}
```

This prevents the VM from serializing or deserializing an instance of the class this code appears in.

Transient

The `transient` keyword is used to specify variables that shouldn't remain the same from one instantiation to the next. For instance, if you have a reference to a file handle, that should be declared `transient`, as it would not be valid upon deserialization in a different VM. You also wouldn't want your application reading or writing to the wrong file.

If a variable is declared `transient`, it will not be serialized. If you're storing sensitive information that you don't want to be exposed to serialization, you can declare it `transient`. Typically, however, one would not declare a sensitive class to be serializable at all, but there are occasions when it might be necessary.

Validation

There are times when it is necessary to validate the fields in an object when it is deserialized. It is a good idea to validate any fields that need to be internally consistent. You'll need to override two methods: `readObject()` and `writeObject()`. Details can be found in the classes `java.io.ObjectInputStream` and `ObjectOutputStream`.

The streams call the methods `readObject()` and `writeObject()` in your class when serializing and deserializing an object of that type. It is in those methods that you should perform your validation, like checking that a balance is non-zero, or that an account number falls into the correct range.

Encryption

It is also possible to encrypt an object on serialization, but there is no built-in support for key management. It's probably easier to serialize and then encrypt the serialized object at the application layer instead. Alternatively, you could use `javax.crypto.SealedObject`, which accomplishes a similar function. Again, the key management is still somewhat problematic. We'll discuss this topic further in Chapter 4, but now we'll take a look at packages.

Protecting Packages

By default, your Java code can be in any package it wishes, which can expose certain methods and variables, since a malicious class might join a pre-existing package and thus gain access to protected and package-protected methods and variables. You could create your own class, for instance, `MaliciousFileOutputStream`, and place it in the `java.io` package. It would then have access to any of the previously unreachable protected methods of all the classes in `java.io`. There are three ways to protect against this:

- ❑ Sealed JAR files
- ❑ A `package.definition` entry in `java.security`
- ❑ Restricting package access

Although we'll encounter much more on these topics later, let's take a brief look at each of these in turn:

Sealed JAR Files

A sealed JAR indicates to the VM that all classes defined in a package in the JAR must come from that JAR. That is, no one can join a package in the JAR from the outside. To seal a JAR, you need to add a `Name` and a `Sealed` entry to the `MANIFEST.MF` file for each package you want sealed. Let's say we wanted to seal `com.isnetworks.*`, so that no one could define a class in that package. We would add the following two lines to the `MANIFEST.MF` file before signing it:

```
Name: com/isnetworks/
Sealed: true
```

For an example of signing a JAR file, see Chapter 7.

Using package.definition Entries

You could also add a `package.definition` entry to your `java.security file`, restricting anyone from creating a class in that package unless they had the proper permission.

The `java.security` file defines security defaults for a Virtual Machine. It's located inside your Java installation, in `$JAVA_HOME/jre/lib/security/java.security`. If you're running on Windows, you likely have two VMs installed, one in `C:\JDK1.3` and the other in `C:\Program Files\JavaSoft\JRE`. It's not important for you to understand exactly how the file defines the security properties of the VM, as we'll discuss it in more detail later.

Let's say we wanted to restrict defining classes in `com.isnetworks.private.*` and `com.isnetworks.crypto.*`. We would add the following line to the `java.security` file:

```
package.definition=com.isnetworks.private,com.isnetworks.crypto
```

Then you'll need to grant some permissions to the `codeBase` that actually defines your `com.isnetworks.private.*` and `com.isnetworks.crypto.*` classes. This can be done in the `java.policy` file:

```
RuntimePermission("defineClassInPackage.com.isnetworks.private");
RuntimePermission("defineClassInPackage.com.isnetworks.crypto");
```

The java.policy file is found in the same directory as the java.security file we mentioned earlier and it defines permissions that code will be assigned in the VM. We'll talk in detail about permissions in Chapter 7.

Restricting Package Access

You can also restrict which classes are allowed to access a package. The sun.* packages, for instance, are restricted from being used when a security manager is installed. Add the following line to your java.security file to restrict package access to com.isnetworks.*:

```
package.access=com.isnetworks.*
```

Then you will need to grant the following permission in the java.policy file to whatever codeBases you want to grant access to the com.isnetworks.* packages:

```
RuntimePermission("accessClassInPackage.com.isnetworks");
```

Privileged Code

We'll talk in detail about **privileged code** in Chapter 7, but we need to briefly mention it here for completeness. Essentially privileged code allows you to temporarily grant permission to run a small section of code to a caller that would normally not have that permission. The archetypical example is that of an applet using a font, which requires the VM to open a font file on the user's machine. While an applet is not normally allowed to open a file, in this case it is allowed.

It is very rare that you will need to write privileged code. Typically it's only required for system-level tasks, which will already have the permissions required, as in the font example we mentioned. If you find that you need privileged code, however, here are a few guidelines:

❑ **Be careful when passing parameters** – If your privileged code takes input parameters, be aware that they may not always be what you expect. For instance, let's say that you want to provide some privileged code that reads the java.version system property. One way to implement it (the wrong way) would be the following:

```
public String getProperty(final String property) {
  return (String) AccessController.doPrivileged(new PrivilegedAction() {
  public Object run() {
    return System.getProperty(property);
  }
  });
}
```

Then one might expect the calling class to call getProperty("java.version"), and all would be well. But it could also call getProperty("username") and find out the user's login name. The proper way to write such a privileged block is the following:

```
public String getJavaVersion() {
  return (String) AccessController.doPrivileged(new PrivilegedAction() {
    public Object run() {
      return System.getProperty("java.version");
    }
  });
}
```

By removing the parameters passed to the privileged block, we remove the possibility of them being used improperly.

❑ **Make privileged code as short as possible** – By keeping your code short, you reduce the possible avenues of attack, and make it easier to be sure that your code cannot be exploited.

❑ **Really try not to use privileged code** – Since privileged code is somewhat risky, it's best not to use it unless it's absolutely necessary.

Before we conclude this chapter, however, we really ought to mention native methods.

Native Methods

Making a call to a native method from within Java is restricted by the Java security manager. Once a native method is executing however, it is outside the control of the security manager and can do whatever it is allowed to by the underlying operating system. Be careful to restrict access to potentially dangerous code, and be sure to restrict what can be passed as an argument to a native method and what can be returned.

Native methods can access and modify Java objects without having their actions checked by the Java security manager. This means, for instance, that if you pass a `String` to a native method, it could modify that object, despite the fact that you would normally expect all strings to be immutable in a VM. Not only can immutable objects be modified by native methods, but member variables and methods that would normally be inaccessible due to being declared private, will be accessible to native code if those objects are passed in.

Summary

We've mentioned a number of potential avenues of attack in this chapter – accessing private member variables improperly, snooping memory, and so on. Many of these you are unlikely to face in real life, depending on the scale of your applications. Nonetheless, it's important to be aware of the security implications of Java code, and to write your code to be as secure as your requirements dictate.

We've also talked about a number of programming techniques that you should always use that add security to your applications, such using private member variables and using immutable objects when useful. We've also discussed the importance of clearing out your variables once they've been used so that there's no possibility of something sensitive being captured.

It is also important to remember that your packages must be protected, by using one of the three methods discussed in that section (sealing your JAR files, using a `package.definition` in your `java.security` file, or restricting package access through the security manager). We also briefly discussed both privileged code and native methods as potential problem areas when writing secure code.

Now that we understand how we should structure our applications, we're going to introduce the subject of cryptography, and look at how it can be used to give applications greater security.

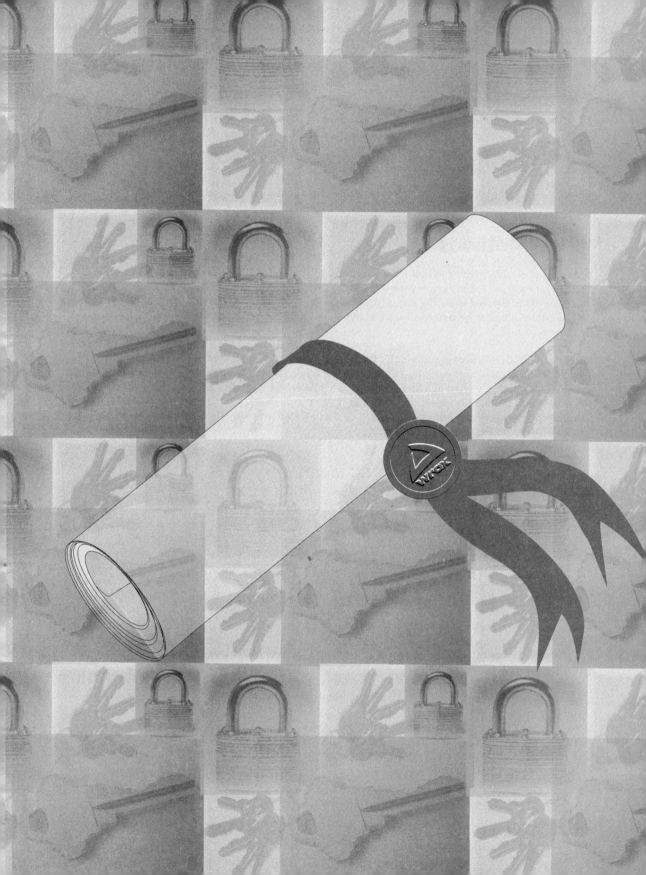

Introduction to Cryptography and Cryptography Services in Java

Now that we've discussed some of the requirements of secure applications, we need to discuss the most powerful weapon in the developers' arsenal for enforcing those requirements – **cryptography**. In this chapter we're going to describe cryptography itself and cover the basics of using cryptography in Java programming.

Cryptography, from the Greek, is the science of secret, or hidden, writing and in this chapter we'll be looking at the two important services it can offer, along with the support Java provides for cryptography. So we'll be looking at:

- ❑ **Encryption** – the practice of hiding messages so that they cannot be read by anyone other than the intended recipient

- ❑ **Authentication** – the process of determining authenticity – that a message has not been surreptitiously altered, or that a person is who they claim to be

- ❑ The **Java Cryptography Architecture** (**JCA**) and the **Java Cryptography Extension** (**JCE**)

This chapter is intended to set the scene for the rest of the book, where we'll talk in more detail about many of the cryptographic principles outlined here, and provide detailed code examples illustrating their practical implementation.

Encryption

In order to illustrate encryption, we're going to call on the time-honored example of the Caesar cipher. While expanding the Roman Empire, Julius Caesar was concerned that his messengers were reading orders sent to his soldiers. To prevent this, he created a cipher to encrypt those messages. A **cipher** is a method for encrypting messages.

The Caesar cipher is a simple one: rotate each letter in the message three letters ahead in the alphabet. That is, A becomes D, B becomes E, and so on. One could create a table to encrypt messages like so:

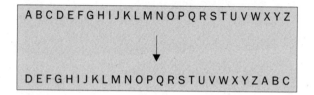

The message "ATTACK AT DAWN" becomes "DWWDFN DW GDZQ". To return the message to its readable state, the recipient would rotate each letter three places back in the alphabet, thus **decrypting** the message. The Caesar cipher is an example of a **symmetric cipher**, as the same information is required to encrypt and decrypt.

At this point, we need to define some key terms that we'll be using throughout this book when discussing cryptography. Encryption is the process of turning a **plaintext message** into its corresponding **ciphertext**. In the Caesar example above, the plaintext is "ATTACK AT DAWN" and the ciphertext is "DWWDFN DW GDYQ". An **algorithm** and a **key** must be defined in order to encrypt or decrypt messages.

The algorithm in this example is the rotation of letters and the key is 3, for the number of places to rotate.

Diagrammatically we can represent the encryption process by:

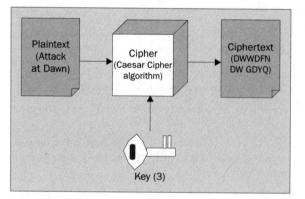

Similarly the decryption process looks like this:

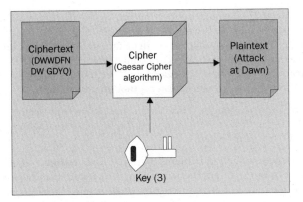

Notice that the key for encryption and decryption is the same: 3. This is what makes the Caesar cipher symmetric, the fact that the same key is used for both activities.

Modern symmetric cryptographic algorithms are much more advanced than the Caesar cipher, but they operate in a similar fashion – one passes a plaintext message into a cipher with a given key and out comes the ciphertext. The same procedure in reverse produces the original message.

Symmetric Encryption Algorithms

Symmetric ciphers come in two types: **block ciphers** and **stream ciphers**. A block cipher encrypts data one chunk at a time – typically 64 bits, but some algorithms use 128 bits. A stream cipher encrypts a stream of data one bit or one byte at a time. A block cipher can be used to create a stream cipher, and vice-versa, but it is more efficient to use the appropriate type of cipher for your application. If you need to encrypt a single message, use a block cipher. If it's a constant stream of information, like a socket, it's probably best to use a stream cipher.

The strength of a symmetric algorithm is determined for the most part by the size of the key. The longer the key, the more difficult it is to crack. Key length is expressed in bits, with typical key sizes varying between 40 and 448 bits. In order to crack an encrypted message, an attacker could attempt to determine the key that was used by brute-force, that is they could try every possible key and see if the message decrypts.

The set of possible keys that work with a cipher is termed the **key space**. Now for a 40-bit key, there are 2^{40} possible keys while 128 bits means 2^{128} potential keys. Each additional bit added to the key length doubles its security.

While it's possible for a supercomputer to break a 56-bit key in well under 24 hours, a 128-bit key will take 2^{72} times longer to crack by brute force, longer than the age of the universe!

Let's look at some common symmetric algorithms in use today:

❑ **DES and TripleDES** – Perhaps the best-known symmetric encryption algorithm is DES, or the **Data Encryption Standard**. It was invented in the 1970s at IBM, and was originally known as "Lucifer". DES was the first encryption algorithm to become a national standard in the United States and has often been used to secure bank transactions. As DES is getting a bit long in the tooth, the National Institute of Standards and Technology in the United States (NIST) is trying to replace DES with the **Advanced Encryption Standard** (**AES**).

DES keys are 56 bits in length. This is a bit short to be truly secure, as modern computers can crack a 56-bit key in a reasonable amount of time, so to deal with this, a variation on DES called TripleDES was invented.

TripleDES, sometimes called **DESede**, is simply three rounds of DES applied with different keys. The first round is an encryption round; the second round decryption; and the third round is another round of encryption. Hence the name DES**ede** – encryption, decryption, encryption. Two or three keys can be used, increasing the total number of key bits from 56 to 112 or 168. If two keys are used, the first key is used for the first and third rounds, and the second key for the second round. If three keys are used, each one is used for a different round.

These keys are then combined into a single key for transport, which is 112 or 168 bits long. TripleDES is considerably more secure than DES due to its increased key length.

❑ **Blowfish** – Blowfish is a block cipher invented by Bruce Schneier in 1993 as a faster and more secure replacement for DES. It allows for keys of greater length than in DES or TripleDES, up to 448 bits.

❑ **RC4** – RC4 stands for "Rivest's Code 4", and was created by Ron Rivest of RSA Data Security, Inc. in 1987. RC4 is a stream cipher, and is used in most implementations of SSL, for securing TCP/IP connections. Its keys are typically either 40 or 128 bits in length.

❑ **AES** – The Advanced Encryption Standard was chosen in October 2000 by the National Institute of Standards and Technology (NIST). They selected an algorithm called **Rijndael** (pronounced "Rhine-dahl"), developed by Joan Daemen and Vincent Rijman. AES allows key lengths of 128, 192, and 256 bits, and block sizes also of 128, 192, and 256 bits.

Limitations of Symmetric Encryption

These symmetric algorithms all work in roughly the same fashion: the same key is used to both encrypt and decrypt messages. This means that in order to send a secret message to someone you must both agree on a key beforehand. To help explain what this means, let's go over an example using our situation borrowed from Hamlet:

Let's say that Claudius, wary of subterfuge, decides to secure his orders of execution so that Hamlet's erstwhile friends Rosencrantz and Guildenstern can't read it. To do this, Claudius will send his message inside a locked box. Before sending the box, he makes a copy of the key and sends it to the King of England, so that the King will be able to open the box.

Claudius puts his message in that box, locks it with the key and gives the box to Rosencrantz and Guildenstern to deliver to the King of England. When Hamlet sneaks into their room to steal the message, he is incapable of reading, or meaningfully altering, the message because he can't get it out of the box. The message is delivered to the King of England who opens it with the key he had been previously sent and reads the message. The tragedy is averted. Or is it...?

What if Claudius asks Horatio to deliver the key to the King of England? Horatio, who is a friend of Hamlet, can make a copy of the symmetric key, which, remember, can lock and unlock the box. Before Hamlet leaves for England, Horatio gives him a copy of that key. On the boat, when the message is supposedly secure in its locked box, Hamlet opens it with his key, alters the message, puts it back in the box, re-locks it and escapes with some pirates. On delivery of the message, Rosencrantz and Guildenstern are wrongfully executed and any future communications between Claudius and the King of England run the risk of being similarly compromised. What Hamlet and Horatio just did is known as an **eavesdropping attack**. They stole a copy of the key as it was transmitted from Horatio to the king.

This is the problem with symmetric, or **secret-key** encryption – the key needs to be kept secret, and any exposure of the key compromises the secrecy of any **ciphertext**, such as the encrypted execution order, created with that key.

So the question is, how can Claudius send a message to the King without risking that someone will read the message contents or compromise the key?

Asymmetric Encryption

Asymmetric Encryption, also known as **Public-Key Encryption**, solves the problem of needing a pre-established secret key before sending messages. Rather than using a single key for encryption and decryption, asymmetric encryption uses *two* keys, one for each function: the **public key**, for encryption, and the **private key**, for decryption. Using them works as follows:

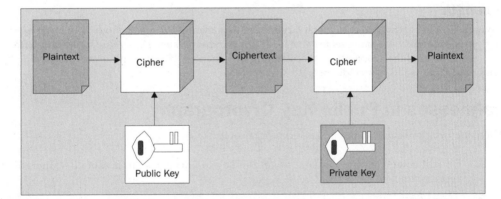

Messages encrypted with the public key can only be decrypted by the corresponding private key. Also, knowing the public key doesn't give you any knowledge of the private key, so the public key can actually be published so that *anyone* can read it with no danger of compromising any messages. A person wishing to use asymmetric encryption keeps their private key private and only publishes their public key for others to use. Then anyone can use the public key to encrypt messages to this person and only that specific person, having the private key, can decrypt them.

Returning to our previous example, Claudius can now prevent the messenger from reading the message or copying the key. In order to secure the message with an asymmetric algorithm, Claudius would need a different kind of box. This box would have a special lock with two kinds of keys, one that could only lock the box and another that could only unlock the box. Claudius would then need the King of England to send him the box, unlocked, and the key for locking it.

Claudius sends Horatio to the King of England to get such a box and Horatio returns bearing the box and the key to lock it. Claudius drops his message into the box and locks it with the locking key. Now neither he, nor Rosencrantz and Guildenstern, nor Hamlet can get into the box. Even if Horatio gives Hamlet a copy of the locking key, Hamlet is unable to get the message because that key will not unlock the box.

Asymmetric Encryption Algorithms

There are two main asymmetric encryption algorithms to consider here:

❑ **RSA** – RSA is the most common and well-known encryption algorithm. It was invented by Ron Rivest, Adi Shamir, and Len Adleman at MIT in 1977. RSA was patented in the United States, but that patent was released to the public domain on September 6, 2000, two weeks before it was to expire. Expect a large number of U.S. software products to begin incorporating RSA into their products, as they no longer need to pay royalties to RSA Security Inc. to use the RSA algorithm. RSA is probably the most elegant pubic-key algorithm. We will be implementing RSA as a Java extension later in this book.

RSA keys have the interesting quality of being interchangeable. That is, both the public key and the private key can be used to encrypt data. Whatever one encrypts, only the other can decrypt. This is especially useful for digital signatures, which we will discuss later.

❑ **ElGamal** – ElGamal was invented by Taher ElGamal. It was the first public-key algorithm to be free of patent restrictions in the United States, as of April 29, 1997. ElGamal is used in some versions of both PGP and SSL (see later).

Key Length

Asymmetric encryption requires much larger keys than symmetric encryption. A 1024-bit asymmetric key supplies roughly the same security as a 128-bit symmetric key. This is due to the structure of the key, and is beyond the scope of our discussion in this chapter. If you're interested in knowing how RSA works, see Chapter 12, which dissects RSA in detail.

Weaknesses in Public Key Cryptography

There are two drawbacks to public-key cryptography:

1. It's still somewhat problematic to get the key to encrypt with, making it vulnerable to certain attacks.

2. Asymmetric encryption is slow compared to symmetric encryption.

Let's go over the problems with getting the key. The situation is definitely improved over symmetric key encryption because we don't have to be worried about someone eavesdropping on the key exchange. But we can't be certain that the key we get hasn't been tampered with.

Let us return to metaphor: imagine that the King of England sends Horatio back with his locking box to deliver it to Claudius. Horatio decides that Hamlet will want to know what Claudius and the King are up to, so he substitutes his own two-keyed locking box in place of the king's. Claudius receives the box, thinking it's the King of England's, drops in the message, and locks the box with the locking key that Horatio provided. Horatio gives Hamlet the unlocking key to his box. Later, on the ship, Hamlet opens the box, reads, and alters the message. He then replaces Horatio's box with the King of England's box, and no one is the wiser. Rosencrantz and Guildenstern deliver the locked box and are summarily executed when the King opens the box and reads the message, since no one realizes that the message has been compromised. This is known as the **man-in-the-middle attack**. It is not an attack on the locked box (or the encryption) per se, but on the method we are using for the exchange.

There are solutions to this problem of sending the key, and these are to use **certificates** to verify the public key. We'll discuss these in detail later, but the gist of it is this: information is attached to each person's public key, indicating who owns it.

The second problem with asymmetric encryption is speed. Symmetric encryption is much faster than asymmetric, up to 1000 times faster in fact. In many applications, this speed difference is going to be a serious issue. What we'd like is a type of encryption that gives us the speed of symmetric encryption with the flexibility of asymmetric encryption. And that's what we get in **session-key** or **hybrid cryptosystems**.

Session-key Encryption

Session-key encryption is a way of using both symmetric and asymmetric encryption together to get the best of both worlds. In the examples we've given so far, speed hasn't really been discussed. We passed an entire message through an asymmetric algorithm without indicating how long that might take. On a device with a feeble CPU, like a smart card or a Palm Pilot, asymmetric encryption of an entire message might take entirely too long to be practical.

A **session-key** can be used for encrypting the message instead. This is a symmetric key that will encrypt the message, and then the key itself will be encrypted using a public key.

To extend our Hamlet metaphor to almost absurd lengths, let's say that an asymmetric locking box big enough to hold an entire message would be very cumbersome. The King of England, therefore, sends a smaller box. Fortunately it is big enough to hold a key. Instead of putting the whole message into the King's special locking-box, Claudius gets his own simple (symmetric) box and puts the message in it. He locks the box with his simple key (called the **session-key**), and then puts that key into the King's box and locks it with the King's public key. Because the King's box only comes with the key to lock the box, neither Claudius, nor Rosencrantz and Guildenstern, nor Hamlet, can open either box.

Even if Horatio manages to intercept the King's public key and give a copy to Hamlet, when Hamlet tries to open the boxes, he will find the key doesn't open either one. On delivery of both boxes, the King opens the second box containing the *session-key* with his own **private** key, takes out the session-key and opens the box containing the message.

> *This may not seem worthwhile in the physical world, where it would be much easier to just build a bigger box, but in the digital world, the CPU cycles saved by not asymmetrically encrypting an entire message can be critical in the usability of an application. This is a major advantage to using session keys.*

In addition, session-key encryption offers some additional security. Some asymmetric key algorithms such as RSA can be susceptible to text analysis attacks when used in a certain manner. Because text has recurring patterns, repeated cipher-texts can be analyzed to break the encryption contextually. However, if you encrypt the random-looking binary data of the session-key with an asymmetric algorithm it is virtually impossible to contextually analyze it due to the way in which asymmetric encryption works.

When sending a message with session-key encryption, you do not encrypt the message with your key, but rather you encrypt the message with a symmetric session-key, and then encrypt the session-key with the public key of the intended recipient.

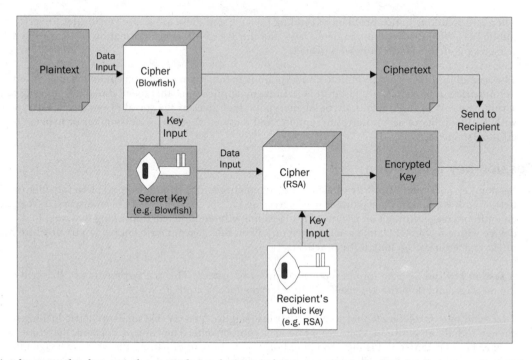

As shown in the diagram, the secret key is being used twice – once as the key for the encryption of the message, and once as input for encryption by the RSA algorithm. We now need to send the secret key to our intended recipient, but we do so once it's been encrypted with their public key.

Once the recipient receives the message and the encrypted session-key, he or she can decrypt the key with his or her private key, and then decrypt the message with that decrypted session-key.

> *Session-key encryption is still susceptible to the man-in-the-middle attack. We will address solutions for that particular attack later.*

Examples of session-key encryption protocols are:

- ❑ **PGP** – PGP was invented by Phil Zimmermann in 1991. PGP stands for "**Pretty Good Privacy**", which is an understatement of its effectiveness. PGP is used to encrypt e-mail using session-key encryption. It combines a number of algorithms, including RSA, TripleDES, and many others and provides an easy way to secure personal e-mail from eavesdropping.

- ❑ **S/MIME** – S/MIME stands for **Secure/Multipurpose Internet Mail Extension**. It was invented by RSA to secure e-mail, similar to PGP. It has the backing of three major corporations: Microsoft, RSA, and AOL (through Netscape).

- ❑ **SSL and TLS** – **Secure Socket Layer** and its successor, **Transport Layer Security**, are attempts to secure TCP/IP traffic. Mostly designed for web use, SSL and TLS can also provide security for any other form of Internet traffic. We will discuss SSL and TLS in detail in a later chapter.

Key Agreement

Like asymmetric encryption, **key agreement** is another way to send secure messages without exchanging a secret key. Key agreements rely on public-private key pairs, just like asymmetric encryption. However, these keys cannot be used for encryption. They can only be used to create a **shared secret**. The shared secret can then be used to construct a session-key, as in the previous section. The primary difference in the case of a key agreement is that the session-key is *never* sent at all, while under normal session-key encryption the session-key is sent, but it is sent encrypted.

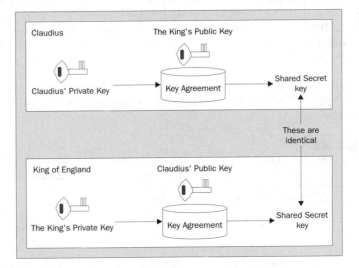

Let's return to the Hamlet story to for an example of a key agreement in action.

Claudius wants to send the King another secret message. Unfortunately for him, if he wants to use a key agreement, he is going to have to wait several hundred years for the invention of **Diffie-Hellman**, which is a key agreement algorithm that allows two parties to independently generate a shared secret key (see below). Key agreement doesn't really have an obvious physical equivalent because it relies on an attribute of the encryption algorithm, so we are going to bring our Hamlet story into the present for the time being.

Claudius happens to have access to the King of England's Diffie-Hellman public key. Using the King's public key, and his own private key, Claudius generates a shared secret, which he then uses to generate a TripleDES secret key. He encrypts his message with this secret key and sends the message to the King. When the King receives the message, he uses Claudius' public key and his own private key to generate the same shared secret that Claudius had previously used. He creates a TripleDES key from that secret and uses it to decrypt the message.

The Diffie-Hellman Key Agreement Algorithm

Diffie-Hellman was created by Whitfield Diffie and Martin Hellman in 1976. It was the first algorithm to have separate public-private key pairs, and changed the world of cryptography forever. It is only through public-key cryptography that messages can be exchanged without needing to have previously shared some secret information. Before the development of Diffie-Hellman, if you wanted to share secret data with someone, you would have to meet them in private and exchange keys. Public-key cryptography added the ability to exchange keys in the open.

Summary of Encryption Algorithms

Typically the strength of an encryption algorithm is based on two things:

❑ The algorithm used

❑ The size of the key

For symmetric algorithms, a basic rule of thumb is that 128-bit keys are adequate for most uses. For asymmetric algorithms, 1024-bit keys will provide roughly the same level of security. RSA keys, for instance, should be 1024 bits in length in any applications requiring a high level of security, including e-commerce. This is because public-private key pairs have a particular mathematical requirement that makes the key space smaller than just the bit size of the key.

Here is a list of some of the most commonly used algorithms. The symmetric ciphers have varying levels of security based on their key length. The asymmetric ciphers are considered secure when using 1024-bit keys or greater.

Symmetric Ciphers

Algorithm	Type	Key size	Notes
DES	Symmetric block cipher	56 bits	Most common encryption algorithm in current use. Too weak for good security however.
TripleDES	Symmetric block cipher	168 bits (112 effective)	Good incremental improvement over DES. Provides acceptable security for a modern system.
Blowfish	Symmetric block cipher	Variable (up to 448 bits)	Long key length provides excellent security.
RC4	Symmetric stream cipher	Variable (usually 40 or 128 bits)	Fast stream cipher. Used in most SSL implementations. Good security when used in 128-bit configurations.
AES	Symmetric block cipher	Variable (128, 192, or 256 bits)	Relatively new cipher. Replacement for DES. Likely to have excellent security, though it has not been around long enough to be sure.

Asymmetric Ciphers

Algorithm	Type	Key size	Notes
RSA	Asymmetric block cipher	Variable (usually 512, 1024, or 2048 bits)	Most popular public key algorithm. U.S. patent expired in September 2000, making it free to implement.
El Gamal	Asymmetric block cipher	Variable (usually 512, 1024, or 2048 bits)	Less common than RSA, but used in some protocols like PGP.

Key Agreement Algorithms

Algorithm	Type	Key size	Notes
Diffie-Hellman	Key agreement	Variable (usually 512 or 1024 bits)	First public-key cryptographic algorithm. Still used in certain variations of popular protocols, including SSL and PGP.

Additional Methods for Hiding Data

Now that we've discussed the most common symmetric and asymmetric algorithms, we're going to discuss some other ways of hiding information.

Steganography

Steganography is the practice of hiding messages inside another message. For example, making the first letter of every word in a paragraph spell out a message.

Steganography isn't cryptography per se, but it allows secret transmission of information. It's pretty easy to hide extra information in computer files. A digital photograph, for instance, can hold an enormous amount of hidden data in the least significant bits of the pixels. The human eye isn't sensitive enough to notice the difference between a 24-bit pixel with the value of (in **big-endian** format):

```
011010101101111010101100
```

and this one:

```
011010101101111010101101
```

*Big-endian is a format where the most significant bits are stored in the first byte – the leftmost; if the rightmost byte stored the most significant bits it would be referred to as **little-endian**.*

If a picture is 1024x768 pixels in size, there are 786,432 pixels. If we use that last bit to store information, we get one bit of extra information per pixel, giving us 96K of hidden info in a 2.25 MB file. The problem with a scheme such as this is that if someone figures out that you're sending hidden messages, they can be easily read.

Steganography combined with cryptography could be useful in certain situations, mainly if you don't want an eavesdropper to be aware that there is a hidden exchange of information taking place in addition to a public one.

Codes

Another form of secret messaging is **codes**. A code is a word, or phrase, that stands for another word or phrase that wouldn't be understandable through context. For instance, Claudius could tell the king that a message containing the text, "The crow flies at midnight", meant to kill Hamlet. Upon reading this message about a crow, there's no way that Hamlet could know what it meant.

Codes can be extremely difficult to break, but they have a very limited number of expressions. Encryption allows a full message to be sent, with no limitation on length or complexity. Codes also have the same liability that symmetric encryption does – some secret information needs to be exchanged ahead of time, namely the meaning of each possible code. Codes are almost never used in computer security due to their limitations.

One-Time Pads

The most secure form of encryption is the **one-time pad**. In fact, the one-time pad is the only form of encryption to be proven completely unbreakable if done properly. It involves creating a completely random key that is exactly as long as the message. Then both parties need to have the key in order to encrypt and decrypt the message. The key must be used only once, and it must be completely random, otherwise it is possible to break the encryption.

Let's run through an example of a one-time pad:

1. Write out the message with no spaces or punctuation: CLAUDIUSDIDIT

2. Now produce a random letter for each letter in the message. This is the pad:
   SYQJOWJQGBOEF

3. Now combine those two sets of characters by adding their character values together, and rotating around the alphabet where necessary. So for instance in the message the first L in CLAUDIUS has a value of 12, the random letter it's mapped to – Y – a value of 25 giving a combined value of 37. Wrapping round the alphabet leaves a value of 11 corresponding to K. Thus the ciphertext produced from using the pad is: VKRESFEJKKSNZ

4. In order to get the original plaintext once again, we need to subtract the pad from the ciphertext as so:

   VKRESFEJKKSNZ - SYQJOWJQGBOEF = CLAUDIUSDIDIT

The beauty of the one-time pad system is that there is no way for an attacker to know if they've managed to crack the key, because the ciphertext could be any plaintext message of equal length. The ciphertext VKRESFEJKKSNZ could decrypt to TWASBXVVWUTKL, THEGHOSTDIDIT, or even to LEMONSAREGOOD, depending on the pad one tried to use.

The problem with one-time pads is in the transmission of the key. The key must be transferred completely securely before the message can be sent. This means that, like symmetric encryption, you must have arranged for the secret communication beforehand. But one-time pad encryption requires a much larger key than does symmetric – in fact the key must be at least as long as the message. And a key can never be reused, unlike in symmetric encryption.

The most obvious use for one-time pad encryption is for a single message that must be entirely secure. One-time pads were used during World War II for some of the communications that spies sent back to their agencies. Most communications, however, were encrypted via some other method, due to the difficulty of managing all the keys that one-time pads require. One-time pads are rarely used in computer security.

Elliptic Curve Cryptography (ECC)

Elliptic curve cryptography (**ECC**) is a variant of public-key cryptography. It has a different mathematical basis from RSA, the current public-key standard. This basis makes it somewhat faster and possibly more secure than RSA, but it hasn't been around long enough to be tested as thoroughly as RSA. Once ECC has been around for a few more years, it may very well surpass RSA in use at some point, but it is too early to tell for certain.

We're not going to get into the mathematics of encryption algorithms here, apart from pointing out that the security of RSA is based on the difficulty of factoring large integers. It is theorized that no easy way to do this will ever be found, but, if there were such a shortcut, RSA would crumble. ECC is based on the elliptic curve logarithm problem instead, so is not vulnerable to a factoring shortcut.

We will be focusing on proven methods of encryption, such as RSA, and will not be utilizing elliptic curve cryptography in this book. Nonetheless, the protocols used in cryptography remain very similar, whether one is using RSA or elliptic curve, and so most of the examples could be easily converted if one had access to an ECC library. If you're interested in learning more about elliptic curve cryptography, see the ECC FAQ at http://cryptoman.com/elliptic.htm.

That concludes our overview of encryption; now let's look at the second major use of cryptography – authentication.

Authentication

Authentication is the process of determining the authenticity of a message or user. It can be used to verify the identity of a user, or that a message hasn't been tampered with.

Message Digests

A message digest, sometimes called a **hash**, is a fingerprint for a document and it's purpose is to provide proof that the data hasn't been altered or tampered with.

Let's go back to ancient Denmark again to see where a message digest would be useful. Assume Claudius is paranoid about the possibility of his message being altered. He could secretly give Rosencrantz a document with a sum of all the characters in the original document, where a equals 1, b equals 2, etc. When the King of England receives the message, he can add up all the characters himself to see if they add up to the right number. If not, he knows the message has been corrupted and Rosencrantz and Guildenstern's lives will be spared.

Needless to say, modern hashing algorithms, such as the ones we are going to be using below are much more sophisticated and harder to circumvent than a simple sum of the characters, which would allow letter transposition, for instance.

> *The principle is the same, however – the same message put through a particular algorithm should always produce the same hash.*

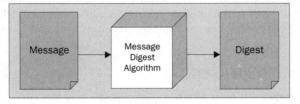

Message digests are small, usually 16 or 20 bytes in length. Since it is very, very unlikely for two documents to have the same message digest, unless they are the same message, this provides a way of checking that one document is the same as another one. For instance, if you download a file, you would like some assurance that it is the file you requested and that it has not been damaged in transit. If the message digest were posted along with the file, it would be possible to compare the two.

Once you receive the file and the digest, you can run the message through the message digest algorithm and compare it with the digest you downloaded. If the digests do not match, then the file has been changed. This indicates that the download must have introduced some errors.

Another use for message digests is password authentication. Most operating systems store passwords as hashed versions of themselves, rather than the original text of the password. When someone tries to log in, their password is hashed, and then those hashes are compared. This means that the original password isn't stored anywhere on the machine, making it difficult to steal someone else's password. Message digests are one-way functions, so it isn't possible to decrypt the hash to find the password; the only option for deducing the password is to try guessing it.

Two of the more commonly used message digest algorithms are:

- ❑ **MD5** – MD5 was written by Ron Rivest of RSA Security Inc. MD5 is a 128-bit message digest that is quite common. It is used in a number of password storage mechanisms, including many modern UNIX systems.

- ❑ **SHA and SHA-1** – SHA stands for **Secure Hash Algorithm** and was developed by NIST and published in 1993. SHA-1 was a revision to SHA. In general, when people speak of SHA, they are referring to SHA-1. SHA is a 160-bit hashing algorithm. It is somewhat more secure than MD5, due to its longer digest.

Message Authentication Codes

A **message authentication code**, or **MAC**, is a message digest created with a key. This adds security to the message digest, by requiring a secret key to be possessed by both parties in order for the receiver to validate the message.

Returning to our earlier example, when Hamlet steals Claudius' message, he may also be able to steal the digest for that message and replace both the message and its corresponding digest. While the new, corrupted message would not match the original digest, it would match the new one Hamlet provides in its place and the King would think the message was unaltered.

If, however, Claudius locks the digest for the message in a box, Hamlet cannot steal it or alter it. Claudius would not even have to lock the message itself in a box to ensure its integrity. The King could unlock the box and remove the digest. When he compared it to the digest of the original document, he would know immediately whether it had been altered.

The same message and key always produces an identical message authentication code.

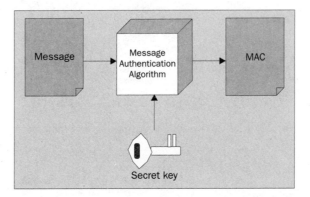

A MAC is typically used in a scenario where a secure connection is already available. SSL, for example, uses MACs to verify the data received, using a secret key that is exchanged at the beginning of the session. If some data is mangled or altered during transmission, checking the MAC will expose the problem.

The most common MACs in use are **Hashing Message Authentication Codes** (**HMACs**). They function identically to MACs, except that internally they use a hashing algorithm like MD5 or SHA-1 to compute the MAC. Examples of MAC Algorithms are:

❏   **HmacMD5** – HmacMD5 is a message authentication code using the MD5 digest algorithm, along with a key

❏   **HmacSHA1** – HmacSHA1 is similar to HmacMD5, but uses SHA-1 as an algorithm

Digital Signatures

Digital signatures provide two things:

❏   A guarantee of the source of the data

❏   Proof that the data has not been tampered with

A digital signature is computed with a person's private key and verified with their public key. Generation of a digital signature requires a public-private key pair. As in asymmetric encryption, the public key can be distributed freely. Only the private key needs to be kept secret. Again though, it is essential that the private key remain private, as anyone who managed to get a copy could impersonate the original owner.

The first algorithm we need to consider here is RSA. In addition to being used for encryption, RSA can also be utilized as a signature algorithm. To create a digital signature, the user simply creates a message digest of the document to be signed, and then encrypts it using their private key.

47

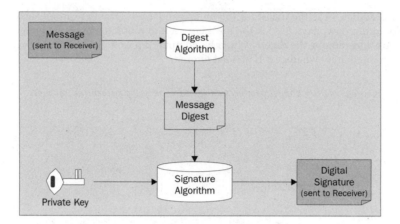

It can then be decrypted only with their public key, proving that they encrypted the message digest:

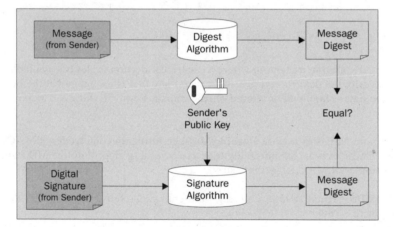

A second procedure uses the **Digital Signature Algorithm** (**DSA**), which is part of NIST's **Digital Signature Standard** (**DSS**). DSS is an attempt to provide digital signatures without using encryption, unlike RSA. When using DSA, technically the message digest is not encrypted with the private key, but rather a different mathematical algorithm is used to produce a signature with the message digest and the private key. Verification is also not technically decryption. Essentially, however, DSA and RSA function similarly for digital signatures.

Digital Certificates

There is an inherent problem in using public keys to authenticate. How can you know that a public key you have belongs to a certain person? Let's go back to the example of Claudius and the King of England. Claudius wants to send an encrypted message to the King. In order to do so, he needs the King's special box and the locking key for it. But how can we be sure that it's truly the King's and not someone else's, like Hamlet's or Horatio's?

A digital certificate is essentially a signed statement by one party that another party's public key belongs to them. It's similar in concept to a passport, where an authority (the government) is signing a statement of identity for you. They are in essence vouching that you are who your passport says you are.

A certificate is essentially a person's public key and some identifying information, signed by an authority's private key verifying the first person's identity. It can then be verified using that authority's public key.

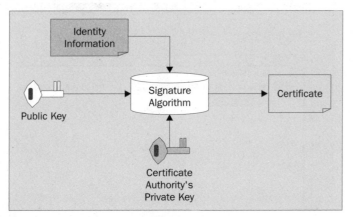

Claudius wants to get the King of England's message box, and he wants to be assured that it really belongs to the king. He's received the King's box and key via a messenger, and wants to be sure that the box hasn't been tampered with.

What Claudius needs is a trusted third party to guarantee that the box and key are valid. This third party would put an official seal on the King's box and the King would send it to Claudius, who could check the third party's signature to determine authenticity.

Presumably, at this point in Danish and English history, the Church is the only authority to which kings would defer, so the Church will serve as the **Certificate Authority** (**CA**), the trusted third party, in our metaphor. In order to ensure the integrity of the box and keys, Claudius would make sure that the King's box has the official seal of the church, which we assume, for the sake of the metaphor, cannot be forged.

Certificates can also contain some extra information besides just the public key and the digital signature. SSL certificates contain the hostname that the certificate was created for. If a browser attaches to an SSL web server and the certificate doesn't match its URL, it will display an error message alerting the user to the discrepancy. Certificates can also be used for signing and encrypting e-mail. Those certificates would have the user's e-mail address embedded in them.

Certificate Chaining

Certificates are often **chained**. Chaining is the practice of signing a certificate with another private key that has a certificate for its public key. This allows one certificate authority to be authorized by a different certificate authority, often referred to as a **root CA**.

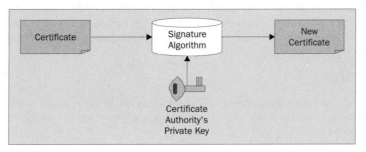

A certificate chain, when viewed in Windows, might appear like so:

Here the VeriSign Class 1 Primary CA (Certificate Authority) validates the second-tier CA, which in turn validates Jess Garms' certificate.

The top certificate in a chain must be self-signed. There is no ultimate authority for certificates, no government agency at the top that determines who can be a CA. Anyone can self-sign their own certificates and thus become a certificate authority. The difficult part is getting anyone else to accept your self-signed certificate as valid.

Verisign is accepted due to the fact that it has been in business for a while and has brokered deals with major security vendors to have its certificates included in various software packages. Both Internet Explorer and Netscape Communicator, for instance, include certificates from Verisign in their install. They then automatically accept those certificates when making an SSL connection. If you want to connect to a site that presents a certificate that hasn't been signed by a well-known CA, both IE and Netscape will warn you of this fact and ask if you are certain that you want to continue connecting.

Cryptanalysis

Cryptanalysis is the practice of analyzing and breaking cryptography. There are a number of different ways to foil cryptography if it is improperly used, and it is important to be aware of those when designing a secure system.

As we've previously indicated, the strength of cryptography is in part dependent on the size of the key. We've already discussed how various algorithms and implementations have different key sizes, and thus different resistance to cryptanalysis. Recently, an Internet project – Distributed.net – harnessing the power of thousands of distributed computers was able to crack DES in less than 24 hours. (DES has a 56-bit key length – so that's 2^{56}, or 72,057,594,037,927,936 possible keys!).

But, as we pointed out earlier each bit added to the length of the key would double the size of the **key space**, thus doubling the time it would take to search through all those keys. TripleDES with a key size of 112 bits then, does not take twice as long to crack, but 2^{56} times longer. Even assuming that computers will continue to get faster and faster, a TripleDES-encrypted message is going to take quite a while to crack.

Beyond Brute Force

Just using long enough keys isn't enough to foil cryptanalysis. Besides brute-force cracking of the key, a common attack is to determine how the key was created. Keys are created through the generation of random numbers. That's what makes them impossible to guess – the fact that they were created through a process that can't be predicted. Unfortunately, computers are notoriously bad at creating random numbers. There are some algorithms, called **Pseudo Random Number Generators** (**PRNGs**), which attempt to solve that problem. They haven't been entirely successful however. There have been a number of cases of cracked PRNGs, the most recent of which occurred in Netscape Navigator. It was determined that the stream of random numbers it generated could be predicted and thus the keys it was using could be determined.

An ideal source of random numbers requires specialized hardware. No algorithm is going to be capable of generating true randomness without some sort of random information to seed it with. Several companies make random-number generating hardware, as well as cryptography accelerators that perform that function in addition to increasing the speed of calculation.

There are a number of other ways to do cryptanalysis besides brute-force and determining how the random numbers were generated. These attacks vary, but they can be classified based on how the attacker attempts to glean information about the key. If an attacker can gain access to large amounts of encrypted data, or plaintext and ciphertext versions of the same data, they may be able to break your security more easily than if they didn't have access to that data. Using session-key cryptography can reduce the risk of such attacks.

It's also important to watch for instances where your cryptographic resources could be abused. For instance, you should never make publicly available a service for encrypting data with your privately held key. An attacker could mount what is known as an **adaptive-chosen-plaintext** attack where any data the attacker chooses is encrypted with your private key and the resulting ciphertext is used to determine what your key is.

> It's also important that the cryptographic algorithms you use be resistant to cryptanalysis. We have tried to recommend only well-known and accepted algorithms in this book, algorithms such as RSA, Blowfish, AES, and the like. Nonetheless, it's a good idea to check the literature every once in a while and make sure that the algorithms you're planning on using continue to be safe.

Key Management

Key storage is a major consideration in any secure system. Since all the security of an encrypted piece of data is contained within the keys, those keys become the primary targets of most attacks. Yet the keys must remain accessible to the user. This is a difficult problem. Usually the keys are stored encrypted with a password that only the appropriate user knows, and then protected with native file-system permissions. That means that an attacker will have to compromise the machine the key is stored on and then crack the password. This is almost certainly easier than brute-force cryptanalysis, so it is important to be ready for such attacks.

Smart cards are one attempt to solve the key management problem. A smart card is a tiny computer that can be stored in a form-factor the size of a credit card. This computer stores a private key and a certificate, and can be used to encrypt and decrypt information. The key, however, is never exposed, and can't be copied off the card. The card itself is tamper-resistant, and typically has a quick-erase function that is invoked if the card is probed. Unfortunately, there is no built-in support for smart cards in Java. Companies that sell smart cards are working on building drivers, but no standard has yet emerged.

Protocols

Cryptography isn't simply the mathematical algorithms involved in encryption and authentication. Cryptography must also be put to use in an organized fashion. This is especially true when using multiple algorithms in multiple steps, such as session-key encryption. Protocols determine the exact order and way in which each algorithm must be used in order to maximize security. In certain cases, if a protocol is incorrect, it can expose secure information even though none of the algorithms has been broken.

For instance, imagine a scenario in which Claudius wants to send messages to the King of England, and vice-versa. They exchange their specialized boxes, but unbeknown to them, Hamlet intercepts them and sends them each his own. Now Claudius sends a message to the King of England in what he thinks is the King's box. Hamlet intercepts the message, opens it with his key and then puts the message in this "dummy" box. Both Claudius and the King think that their communications are secure, when in fact they have been compromised.

In order to thwart protocol attacks, it's best to use well-established protocols, like SSL and S/MIME. These have been designed by experts, and evaluated and tested by other experts. There's no value in creating a new protocol that performs the same function as one of these pre-existing ones. If you can use them, you should.

Now that we've discussed the basics of cryptography, we're going to take a look at how to put this information to use in Java.

The Java Cryptography Architecture and the Java Cryptography Extension

The **Java Cryptography Architecture** (JCA) and the **Java Cryptography Extension** (JCE) were designed to provide an implementation-independent API for cryptographic functions in Java. The JCA is part of the Java 2 run-time environment, while the JCE is an **extension** (an addition to the Java environment that has the same privileges as the core Java classes) to the JCA not included with the JDK. The JCE adds simple encryption and decryption APIs to the JCA.

We will be using the JCA and the JCE throughout this book, whenever we need to use a cryptographic function. By using these APIs, our applications will be portable to different environments using different Java libraries.

> **Here we're going to generally discuss the JCA and the JCE from a fairly high level – JavaDoc is available for all the classes we discuss, and thus we won't be repeating the API documentation. In later chapters we'll investigate detailed use of the classes we'll introduce in this section.**

The JDK ships with only certain cryptographic functions enabled, namely those defined by the JCA. These include digital signatures and message digests, but no ciphers, which can be used to encrypt and decrypt data. Due to export restrictions in force at the time the architecture was created, Sun had to separate out those parts from the JDK proper and place them in a separate product, the Java Cryptography Extension.

Our first task is to discuss the JCA.

The Java Cryptography Architecture (JCA)

The Java Cryptography Architecture is composed of a number of classes in the `java.security` package and its sub-packages. These classes provide generic APIs for functions like digital signatures and message digests. The important classes include:

- ❑ `MessageDigest`
- ❑ `Signature`
- ❑ `KeyPairGenerator`
- ❑ `KeyFactory`
- ❑ `CertificateFactory`
- ❑ `KeyStore`
- ❑ `AlgorithmParameters`
- ❑ `AlgorithmParameterGenerator`
- ❑ `SecureRandom`

Each one is used in a similar manner, via a **factory pattern** (a pattern that defines an interface for creating an object but lets the subclasses decide which class to actually instantiate). An instance is obtained with a call to `getInstance()` on the class, with a `String` argument indicating the name of the algorithm requested. For instance, to get a SHA-1 message digest use:

```
MessageDigest myMessageDigest = MessageDigest.getInstance("SHA-1");
```

The resulting instance can then be used normally. Note that the new keyword is rarely called on any of the classes in the JCA. In fact, many of the classes we're looking at do not even have public constructors. The reason for this is that it allows the underlying implementation to be easily swapped out without needing to alter any of the code that relies on these services.

Cryptographic Service Providers

A **Cryptographic Service Provider**, usually abbreviated **provider**, is a collection of implementations of various algorithms. Sun ships its Java 2 VM with at least one provider – the SUN provider, class name sun.security.provider.Sun.

It contains implementations of the following algorithms:

- ❑ MD5 message digest
- ❑ SHA-1 message digest
- ❑ DSA digital signature signing and verification
- ❑ DSA key pair generation
- ❑ DSA key conversion
- ❑ X.509 certificate creation
- ❑ Proprietary keystore implementation
- ❑ DSA algorithm parameters
- ❑ DSA algorithm parameter generation
- ❑ Proprietary random number generation

JDK1.3 ships with a second provider, the RSAJCA provider, class name com.sun.rsajca.Provider. It provides the following algorithms:

- ❑ RSA key pair generation
- ❑ RSA key conversion
- ❑ RSA signatures using SHA-1 or MD5 message digests

When getting an instance of one of the JCA classes, you can specify a provider if you like, or allow the VM to determine which provider it will use for the underlying engine. Then the JCA classes delegate calls to that internal engine, which must extend the **Service Provider Interface** (**SPI**) for that class. This design is based on the **strategy pattern**, which is commonly used in OO programming. This pattern defines a family of algorithms, encapsulates each one, and makes them interchangeable, allowing us to swap out algorithms from different providers easily.

Here's a diagram of how the JCA works using the MessageDigest class as an example:

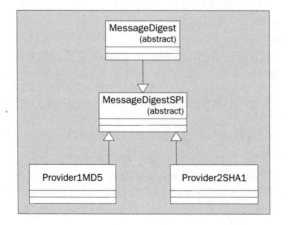

`MessageDigest` has a delegate, which is a subclass of `MessageDigestSPI`. In the example above, it could be either `Provider1MD5` or `Provider2SHA1`. `MessageDigest` decides which one to instantiate and delegate to based on what algorithm was requested and what providers are installed. The other classes, like `Signature`, work in an identical fashion.

We don't need to be overly concerned with the SPI classes right now, as only the provider utilizes them. Application code just accesses the top-level abstract class, in this case, `MessageDigest`.

Let's go through a quick example of how you would access the JCA in code using a message digest as our desired algorithm.

Accessing the JCA

As we mentioned previously, a message digest provides a sort of fingerprint for a set of data. This fingerprint is called either the digest or a hash of the data. The two most commonly used algorithms are MD5 and SHA-1. We'll use MD5, which produces a 16-byte byte array given any set of data:

To get the instance of an MD5 hash algorithm, we make a call to `MessageDigest`'s `getInstance()` method:

```
MessageDigest myMessageDigest = MessageDigest.getInstance("MD5");
```

If we wanted to specify the Sun provider, we could do so by passing an argument to `getInstance()` like so:

```
MessageDigest myMessageDigest = MessageDigest.getInstance("MD5","Sun");
```

Once we have the message digest, we can give it data to digest with its `update()` method. Note that each `update()` *appends* to the data already updated, and does not replace it. Assuming our data was stored in a byte array called `myData`, we would call:

```
myMessageDigest.update(myData);
```

Once we've supplied all the data, we can actually get the digest by calling the `digest()` method, which returns a byte array:

```
byte[] signatureBytes = myMessageDigest.digest();
```

What's actually happening behind the covers is that the JCA is proxying requests to `MessageDigest` to a class specified by the provider. If we were using the Sun provider, then the digest operations would be handled by the class `sun.security.provider.MD5`. A different provider would cause a different underlying class to be instantiated and called – it would still use the same algorithm, MD5, but might do so in a different fashion. For instance, you might have a provider that implemented all its algorithms in native code.

Now that we've discussed the basics of the JCA, we want to move on to the JCE, which adds encryption to Java.

The Java Cryptography Extension (JCE)

The JCE is very similar in design to the JCA. It uses factory methods to create instances of classes, which then delegate their actual cryptographic functions to underlying engines configured by a provider.

The JCE itself is just the classes in the `javax.crypto` package and its sub-packages. It includes the following classes and interfaces, among others:

- ❑ Cipher
- ❑ KeyAgreement
- ❑ KeyGenerator
- ❑ Mac
- ❑ SecretKey
- ❑ SecretKeyFactory

We will be discussing in detail exactly how to use these various classes in Chapters 4 and 5 on encryption. For now, we'll go through a quick example of using `KeyGenerator`, `SecretKey`, and `Cipher` to indicate how we can encrypt some data. We need to create a key, and then we will use it to initialize a cipher and perform the encryption.

First of all, we need to get an instance of `KeyGenerator` of the appropriate type. The type of key is the same as the algorithm desired, and for this example, we're going to use the Blowfish encryption algorithm. The algorithm to use is specified with a string:

```
KeyGenerator keyGenerator = KeyGenerator.getInstance("Blowfish");
```

Then we can generate a key with that key generator:

```
Key key = keyGenerator.generateKey();
```

Finally, to perform the encryption, we need to create a cipher and initialize it with the key we just created. When we fetch an instance of `Cipher`, we need to specify the algorithm, the mode and the padding. We're going to use ECB mode with PKCS5 padding. We haven't discussed modes and paddings yet, but we will do so in detail in the next chapter. They're somewhat complicated, so for now, all you need to know is that they must be specified.

So to obtain a `Cipher` instance, we use the following:

```
Cipher cipher = Cipher.getInstance("Blowfish/ECB/PKCS5Padding");
cipher.init(Cipher.ENCRYPT_MODE, key);
```

Assuming our data to encrypt is a byte array in the variable `myData`, we can encrypt that data and put it in the byte array `cipherText`:

```
byte[] cipherText = cipher.doFinal(myData);
```

> **In order to actually use encryption in Java, you need to have the proper classes that perform these functions. You need both a JCE *and* a Provider installed for your VM.**

Installing a JCE

In order to use the JCE, you need to install it. You can use any of a number of possible implementations of the JCE itself, many of which come with a provider containing implementations of various algorithms. A short list follows:

Name	URL	License	Notes
Bouncy Castle	http://www.bouncycastle.org	Open Source Apache-style	Most complete, freely available JCE provider.
BeeJCE	http://www.virtualunlimited.com/products/beejce/	Open Source LPGL	Good JCE implementation but lacks RSA support.
OpenJCE	http://www.openjce.org	Open Source Apache-style	Defunct project but supports JCE 1.2 API.
Cryptix JCE	http://www.cryptix.org	Open Source Apache-style	Appears defunct.
SunJCE	http://java.sun.com/products/jce	Java license (free for use)	Reference implementation, but doesn't function with other providers, and lacks RSA encryption support.

We recommend the Bouncy Castle JCE provider for most uses, though the different JCE implementations should all produce compatible results when using the same algorithms.

For basic information, here are two lists of the basic algorithms supported by Bouncy Castle and Sun:

Bouncy Castle Algorithms

- Blowfish
- DES
- DESede (TripleDES)
- IDEA
- RC2
- RC4
- RC5
- RC6
- Rijndael (AES)
- Skipjack
- Twofish
- RSA
- MD2
- MD5
- RipeMD160
- SHA-1
- Diffie-Hellman
- DSA

Sun's JCE

- ❑ DES
- ❑ TripleDES
- ❑ Blowfish
- ❑ Diffie-Hellman

> **Most people's first instinct will be to download and use Sun's JCE. We recommend strongly *against* that, unless you have some requirement that you use that specific provider. In gaining exportability for its provider, Sun has placed code in its JCE that prevents other providers from being used once its JCE is installed. This means, for instance, that you can't use the AES algorithm from Bouncy Castle while using the Diffie-Hellman algorithm from Sun. Sun's JCE provides only a few algorithms, and RSA encryption is noticeably lacking. As many of the programs in this book use RSA, they will *not* function with Sun's JCE.**

To install the JCE and a provider, you should perform the following steps:

- ❑ Download the provider
- ❑ Copy the JAR files to an appropriate location
- ❑ Configure your `java.security` file
- ❑ Test your installation

Let's look at each of these more closely. We'll also provide a detailed example of installing the Bouncy Castle provider and JCE, as it will enable you to run the code examples in this book (all the code contained in the book can be downloaded from www.wrox.com).

Downloading the Provider

After downloading one of the free providers from the above list extract it and read any installation documents that come with it, in case there are special instructions.

> *Bouncy Castle can be downloaded from www.bouncycastle.org – pick up the JCE with Provider and Lightweight API.*

Copying the JAR Files

In order to have the JCE classes available to all Java applications, including tools like `javac` and `keytool`, we'll install the JAR files as extensions. If you're going to be running pre-compiled applications, you don't necessarily need the JCE classes installed as an extension though. They may be placed on the CLASSPATH instead. Unfortunately this latter approach seems to give problems in certain environments.

> *We recommend installing the JCE as an extension.*

Extensions are placed inside the Java Run-time Environment's lib/ext directory or directories, depending on your environment. You need to copy the necessary JAR files into that directory or directories. Read the documentation that comes with the provider to determine which JAR files you should use for your environment.

The Bouncy Castle provider does not come with JAR files for installing as an extension, but they can be easily built. Extract the file you downloaded earlier (named `jce-jdk13-104.zip` or similar). CD into the directory `classes` and run the following command, which will JAR up the necessary files:

```
C:\> jar cvf bouncycastle.jar javax org
```

A new JAR file will be created, called `bouncycastle.jar`. That file can now be installed as an extension. The location of extensions varies by operating system.

- ❑ **UNIX** – If you're using UNIX, this is typically a single location, `$JAVA_HOME/jre/lib/ext`. `$JAVA_HOME` is likely to be something like `/usr/local/jdk1.3`. It will vary according to how you installed your JDK. Copy the necessary JARs into that `lib/ext` directory.

- ❑ **Windows** – Java is typically installed into two locations in windows. One location is for development and includes all the tools of the JDK, and the other is solely a run-time environment. The JDK itself is usually in `C:\jdk1.3` or the like, while the run-time environment is typically in `C:\Program Files\JavaSoft\JRE\1.3`. Each one has a `lib/ext` directory. For the two examples above, they would be:

  `C:\jdk1.3\jre\lib\ext`

  and

  `C:\Program Files\JavaSoft\JRE\1.3\lib\ext`

  Copy the necessary JARs into those two directories on your machine.

Configuring java.security to Enable the Provider

Parallel to the `lib/ext` directory is a directory `lib/security`. In it is a file, `java.security`, which defines what cryptographic providers are enabled. In it you will see one or more lines like the following:

```
security.provider.1=sun.security.provider.Sun
security.provider.2=com.sun.rsajca.Provider
```

This indicates to the VM that there are two cryptographic service providers, what their **precedence** is, and what class names should be used to access them. When asked for an implementation of a cryptographic algorithm, the VM will query each of the listed providers in order, looking for such an implementation. It will use the first one it finds, based on that precedence.

We can edit the list to add our new provider by adding a line like the following:

```
security.provider.3=org.bouncycastle.jce.provider.BouncyCastleProvider
```

The specific class name that you need to add will vary with your provider. Here is the full list of providers for our VM, which uses the built-in JDK providers and Bouncy Castle:

```
#
# List of providers and their preference orders (see above):
#
security.provider.1=sun.security.provider.Sun
security.provider.2=com.sun.rsajca.Provider
security.provider.3=org.bouncycastle.jce.provider.BouncyCastleProvider
```

Again there will be slight differences according to operating system:

❑   Windows – the modification will need to be done to *both* java.security files, the one in your JDK directory and the one in your JRE directory. On our test system, their locations were as follows:

```
C:\jdk1.3\jre\lib\security\java.security
```

```
C:\Program Files\JavaSoft\JRE\1.3\lib\security\java.security
```

❑   On UNIX, there is only one copy of java.security. On our test system it was:

```
/usr/local/jdk1.3/jre/lib/security/java.security
```

Testing Your Installation

Now let's try running a simple program that will attempt to use some of the classes in the JCE. If this fails, then something needs to be adjusted in your setup. The test will attempt to generate a secret key for the Blowfish algorithm, using the javax.crypto classes. Remember all the programs listed in the book are available from the Wrox web site (**www.wrox.com**).

```java
import javax.crypto.*;

public class JCEInstallTest {

  public static final String stringToEncrypt = "This is a test.";

  public static void main(String[] args) throws Exception {

    // Generate a Blowfish key

    System.out.print("Attempting to get a Blowfish key...");
    KeyGenerator keyGenerator = KeyGenerator.getInstance("Blowfish");
    keyGenerator.init(128);
    SecretKey key = keyGenerator.generateKey();
    System.out.println("OK");

    // Attempt to encrypt some text

    System.out.print("Attempting to get a Cipher and encrypt...");
    Cipher cipher = Cipher.getInstance("Blowfish/ECB/PKCS5Padding");
    cipher.init(Cipher.ENCRYPT_MODE, key);
    byte[] cipherText = cipher.doFinal(stringToEncrypt.getBytes("UTF8"));
    System.out.println("OK");

    System.out.println("Test completed successfully.");
  }
}
```

You can compile and run it as normal using:

```
C:\> javac JCEInstallTest.java
```

and

```
C:\> java JCEInstallTest
```

After a short delay (10 - 30 secs) while the key is being generated, you should see the following output:

```
Attempting to get a Blowfish key...OK
Attempting to get a Cipher and encrypt...OK
Test completed successfully.
```

Troubleshooting

If you run into any problems compiling or running the example, try looking through the following table, which contains some possible solutions:

Problem	Explanation and Possible Solution(s)
Compile-time error: `package javax.crypto does not exist`	The JCE classes are not accessible by the compiler. Make sure that the JAR file containing the `javax.crypto` classes is in the `lib/ext` directory. If you're running Windows, make sure it is in both `lib/ext` directories, especially the one under the JDK (typically `c:\jdk1.3\jre\lib\ext`). Check to make sure there are no extra Java installations on your machine. If there are, either remove them, or add the JARs to their `lib/ext` directories.
Compiles, but the following error obtained when running: `Exception in thread "main" java.lang.NoClassDefFoundError: javax/crypto/KeyGenerator`	The JCE classes are not accessible by the run-time environment. Check that the JAR file containing the `javax.crypto` classes is in the `lib/ext` directory. If you're running Windows, make sure it is in *both* `lib/ext` directories, especially the JRE under `Program Files`. Check to make sure there are no extra Java installations on your machine. If there are, either remove them, or add the JARs to their `lib/ext` directories.
Compiles, but the following error obtained when running: `Exception in thread "main" java.security.NoSuchAlgorithmException: Algorithm Blowfish not available`	The provider is probably not registered properly. Check your `java.security` files and make sure that you have created an entry for the provider you installed. Make sure there are no extra `java.security` files on your hard drive that are being used by your runtime to configure your providers. If there are, make sure to add the providers to them as well. Perhaps the JCE is installed, but the algorithm JAR is not installed properly. Check that *all* the required JARs are in the `lib/ext` directory.

Table continued on following page

Problem	Explanation and Possible Solution(s)

Compiles, but fails to run with an error referencing
 	
`Cannot set up certs for trusted CAs`
 	
or
 	
`unsigned jar`
	Sun's JCE may be installed. Make sure you do not have any of the following files in `lib/ext` or on your classpath:
	
	`local_policy.jar`
	
	`sunjce_provider.jar`
	
	`US_export_policy.jar`
	
	`jce1_2_1.jar`
	
	Also check that your `java.security` file is properly configured as described earlier.

Sun's JCE

Sun provides a reference implementation of the JCE, which at the time of writing was version 1.2.1. As we pointed out previously, there are no asymmetric encryption algorithms provided in this version. It would seem likely that, as the RSA patent is now in the public domain, Sun will add RSA support to the JCE in the future.

Provider signing

As of version 1.2.1, Sun's JCE added an interesting requirement to any providers of encryption: all cryptographic service providers must be signed by Sun Microsystems. In order to get Sun to sign your provider, you must seek permission from the United States government. To date, Sun has yet to sign any alternative providers.

Fortunately, there are a number of alternative JCE providers that exist, which provide the same services that Sun's does, and are open source and freely useable, as they were written outside the United States. Check our previous list earlier in this chapter. Again, we've found Bouncy Castle's to be the most usable.

Sun added their signing requirement so that the U.S. government would allow them to export the JCE to other countries. This has been successful, but has the unfortunate side effect that it is unlikely that people will want to use Sun's JCE due to that signing requirement. For instance, we've written an Open Source JCE provider for RSA signatures and encryption, which is featured in Chapter 12. Unfortunately we weren't able to get a response from Sun regarding getting this provider signed.

One of the algorithms missing from Sun's JCE is the ability to perform RSA encryption. It would be nice if we could add our provider to Sun's to create a complete solution. This, however, just isn't possible, as Sun's JCE classes throw an exception if someone requests an RSA algorithm from our provider.

Fortunately a user can easily forego Sun's JCE and use one of the alternatives.

Throughout this book we'll be using the JCA and JCE APIs in our code examples (though not Sun's provider). You can use any provider that supports the algorithms being used. It's easy to switch providers, and you can even have multiple providers installed at a given time, each providing different algorithms, or even the same algorithms with different underlying implementations.

Summary

This chapter has been aimed at providing the foundations for understanding the rest of the book.

We've given a brief introduction to cryptography, which is one of the core components of computer security facilitating encryption and authentication. As a basis for the forthcoming chapters we've investigated various cryptographic operations, including symmetric and asymmetric encryption, message digests, digital signatures, and digital certificates. While discussing these topics a number of commonly used (and proven) algorithms were highlighted.

Moving on from our general coverage we went on to introduce the Java Cryptography Architecture (JCA) and the Java Cryptography Extension (JCE), which provide implementation-independent APIs for using cryptography in Java. Here we showed how the architecture fits together and how the various classes may be accessed. More specifically we discussed the various JCE options available and how to install the Bouncy Castle provider and JCE, which the code in this book has been written to take advantage of.

In our next chapter we'll investigate symmetric encryption in depth using practical code examples.

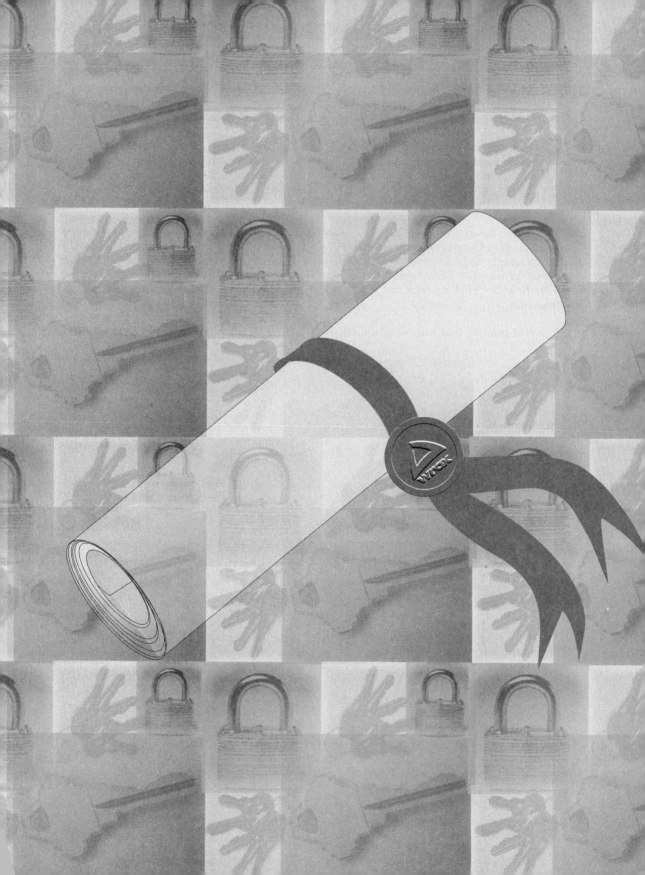

Symmetric Encryption

In Chapter 3 we introduced symmetric encryption, and in this chapter we're going to elaborate on the subject by describing how to use the JCE to perform symmetric encryption. To begin with, we will look at how we encrypt and decrypt using symmetric encryption. Then we discuss applications for symmetric encryption, followed by some examples, which deal with the following aspects of encryption:

- ❑ Basic encryption
- ❑ Encryption using Blowfish
- ❑ Password-based encryption

The main topics discussed in this chapter are:

- ❑ Key storage, including wrapping and unwrapping
- ❑ Modes
- ❑ Cipher streams and how to initialize ciphers with an initialization vector
- ❑ Sealed objects

Remember, before trying to run any of the code in the chapter you'll need an encryption engine installed. Here we'll be using the Bouncy Castle provider because it has support for many algorithms, and won't restrict us from using any other providers in the future (instructions for its installation are provided in the previous chapter).

Encryption and Decryption

Symmetric encryption, also known as **secret-key** encryption, is the simplest type of encryption. A single key is used, which must be kept secret, hence the name. In order to encrypt data, we take the key and use it to initialize a cipher. The cipher can then be used to encrypt data passed to it. Decryption is similar – a cipher gets initialized with the same key, and the data passed in is decrypted.

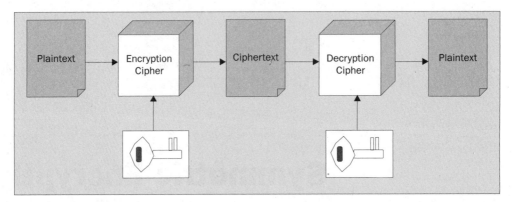

The strength of encryption is based on the length of the key. For symmetric encryption, that key length is typically between 40 and 128 bits, but some algorithms can have even longer keys. DES, which is probably the most commonly used symmetric algorithm, has a key length of 56 bits, which is really not enough for a secure system, as we discussed in Chapter 3. We should use at least 128 bit keys if we're going to use symmetric encryption.

Applications

Symmetric encryption can be applied in quite a number of areas. It is much faster than asymmetric, or public-key encryption (sometimes by a factor of 1000) and for that reason it is recommended in situations where lots of data must be transformed. File encryption, network encryption, and database encryption are all good places to employ symmetric encryption. Its main weakness is the symmetry of the key. That same key must be used to encrypt and decrypt, so anyone with the ability to encrypt also has the ability to decrypt. If you are sending a symmetrically encrypted message, both sender and receiver must agree on a key in advance. For that reason, it is often best to use symmetric encryption to encrypt a large amount of data, and then encrypt the symmetric key with asymmetric encryption. We will investigate that further in the next chapter. For now, let's begin with a simple example – encrypting and decrypting a string.

The only JCE classes our code will use are the (`javax.crypto.*`) classes, which are used to handle cryptography. This makes the programs portable to any provider that supports the algorithms we use. We've discussed some of these classes in the previous chapter, but now let's investigate them in more depth along with the `java.security.Key` class.

javax.crypto.Cipher

The cipher is essentially the engine that performs the encryption and decryption of data. The `Cipher` class has four methods that we're interested in right now: `getInstance()`, `init()`, `update()`, and `doFinal()`. Let's go over them one by one:

getInstance()

As we've mentioned before, most of the classes in the JCE use factory methods instead of normal constructors. Rather than create an instance with the new keyword, we make a call to the class's getInstance() method, with the name of the algorithm and some additional parameters like so:

```
Cipher cipher = Cipher.getInstance("DESede/ECB/PKCS5Padding");
```

The first parameter is the name of the algorithm, in this case, "DESede". The second is the mode the cipher should use, "ECB", which stands for Electronic Code Book. The third parameter is the padding, specified with "PKCS5Padding". We'll go into more detail about the mode and padding later. For now, just be aware that even though it is possible to skip the declaration of the mode and padding they should be declared anyway. If the mode and padding are skipped, the provider picks a mode and padding to use, which is rarely what you want, and prevents the code from being ported to other providers.

init()

Once an instance of Cipher is obtained, it must be initialized with the init() method. This declares the operating mode, which should be either ENCRYPT_MODE or DECRYPT_MODE, and also passes the cipher a key (java.security.Key, described later). Assuming we had a key declared, initialized, and stored in the variable myKey, we could initialize a cipher for encryption with the following line of code:

```
cipher.init(Cipher.ENCRYPT_MODE, myKey);
```

The JCE 1.2.1 specification adds two more possible operating modes, WRAP_MODE and UNWRAP_MODE. These modes set up a cipher to encrypt or decrypt keys. We'll use these modes later, when we use asymmetric encryption.

update()

In order to actually encrypt or decrypt anything, we need to pass it to the cipher in the form of a byte array. If the data is in the form of anything other than a byte array, it needs to be converted. If we have a string called myString and we want to encrypt it with the cipher we've initialized above, we can do so with the following two lines of code:

```
byte[] plaintext = myString.getBytes("UTF8");
byte[] ciphertext = cipher.update(plaintext);
```

Ciphers typically buffer their output. If the input is large enough that it produces some ciphertext, it will be returned as a byte array. If the buffer has not been filled, then null will be returned.

Note that in order to get bytes from a string, we should specify the encoding method. In most cases, it will be UTF8.

> If you don't specify the encoding type, you will get the underlying platform's default encoding. This is almost never what you want, and can cause bizarre errors when encryption takes place on one platform, and decryption on another. Always specify the encoding.

doFinal()

Now we can actually get the encrypted data from the cipher. doFinal() will produce a byte array, which is the encrypted data.

```
byte[] ciphertext = cipher.doFinal();
```

A number of the methods we've talked about can be overloaded with different arguments, like start and end indices for the byte arrays passed in. We're not going to go into detail covering them, as they are presented clearly in the JCE's JavaDoc.

java.security.Key

Key is an interface that defines a key to be used for cryptographic functions. A key object cannot be instantiated directly with new, but rather is created by a factory method in a class like javax.crypto.KeyGenerator or java.security.KeyFactory. Key defines three methods: getAlgorithm(), getEncoded(), and getFormat(). They are all concerned with transporting keys, which we'll describe later in this chapter.

javax.crypto.KeyGenerator

KeyGenerator allows us to create new keys for use in symmetric encryption. There are three methods that we're interested in at this point: getInstance(), init(), and generateKey().

getInstance()

As in Cipher, we cannot construct a KeyGenerator with new. Instead we need to call getInstance() with the name of the algorithm. An optional second parameter can be used to define the provider we wish to use. The following line of code will create a key generator that will generate DESede keys:

```
KeyGenerator keyGenerator = KeyGenerator.getInstance("DESede");
```

init()

Instances of KeyGenerator need to be initialized with the size of the key to be generated. With some algorithms, like TripleDES, this is always the same (168 bits). Other algorithms, like Blowfish, have variable key lengths as shown in Chapter 3.

The following line will initialize the key generator created above:

```
keyGenerator.init(168);
```

generateKey()

This method actually generates the Key object that can be used by an instance of Cipher. There are no arguments, so the call is quite simple:

```
Key myKey = keyGenerator.generateKey();
```

Simple Encryption Example

Now that we've gone over some of the classes and methods we'll need for symmetric encryption, we're going to create a simple program that utilizes them. Our program will create a DESede key, and then encrypt a string with it. We'll then decrypt the encrypted string and display it along with the plaintext and ciphertext bytes as and when we use them.

Here we're using the name DESede rather than TripleDES since that's the term used in the Bouncy Castle provider. You may have to change this if you using a different provider.

```java
import java.security.*;
import javax.crypto.*;

/**
 *  SimpleExample.java
 */

public class SimpleExample
{
  public static void main (String[] args)
                          throws Exception
  {
    if (args.length != 1) {
      System.err.println("Usage: java SimpleExample text");
      System.exit(1);
    }
    String text = args[0];

    System.out.println("Generating a DESede (TripleDES) key...");

    // Create a TripleDES key

    KeyGenerator keyGenerator = KeyGenerator.getInstance("DESede");
    keyGenerator.init(168);  // need to initialize with the keysize
    Key key = keyGenerator.generateKey();

    System.out.println("Done generating the key.");

    // Create a cipher using that key to initialize it

    Cipher cipher = Cipher.getInstance("DESede/ECB/PKCS5Padding");
    cipher.init(Cipher.ENCRYPT_MODE, key);

    byte[] plaintext = text.getBytes("UTF8");

    // Print out the bytes of the plaintext

    System.out.println("\nPlaintext: ");
    for (int i=0;i<plaintext.length;i++) {
      System.out.print(plaintext[i]+" ");
    }

    // Perform the actual encryption

    byte[] ciphertext = cipher.doFinal(plaintext);

    // Print out the ciphertext

    System.out.println("\n\nCiphertext: ");
    for (int i=0;i<ciphertext.length;i++) {
      System.out.print(ciphertext[i]+" ");
    }

    // Re-initialize the cipher to decrypt mode

    cipher.init(Cipher.DECRYPT_MODE, key);

    // Perform the decryption

    byte[] decryptedText = cipher.doFinal(ciphertext);

    String output = new String(decryptedText,"UTF8");

    System.out.println("\n\nDecrypted text: "+output);

  }
}
```

To run the example, enter the following:

```
C:\> javac SimpleExample.java
C:\> java SimpleExample "HelloWorld!"
```

The string "HelloWorld!" will then be converted to a byte array, encrypted, and then decrypted and converted back to a `String`. Here's what the output should look like bearing in mind that the actual ciphertext will be different each time you run the example, because the key is generated anew on every execution:

```
Generating a DESede key...
Done generating the key.

Plaintext:
72 101 108 108 111 87 111 114 108 100 33

Ciphertext:
78 78 -43 -52 -12 -87 112 -68 24 -16 -49 -88 101 -44 -66 122

Decrypted text: HelloWorld!
```

Blowfish Example

Now we're going to modify the previous example to use Blowfish instead of DESede. Thanks to the architecture of the JCE, this is a very simple task. We just change the arguments passed to the `KeyGenerator` and `Cipher` initializations, and a few comments. Blowfish keys can be any bit size from 8 to 448, as long as the number is divisible by 8. We'll use 128 for our example.

The changes from the DESede example are highlighted below:

```
import java.security.*;
import javax.crypto.*;

/**
 * BlowfishExample.java
 *
 * This class creates a Blowfish key, encrypts some text,
 * prints the ciphertext, then decrypts the text and
 * prints that.
 *
 * It requires a JCE-compliant Blowfish engine.
*/

public class BlowfishExample
{
  public static void main (String[] args)
                          throws Exception
  {
    if (args.length != 1) {
      System.err.println("Usage: java BlowfishExample text");
      System.exit(1);
    }
    String text = args[0];

    System.out.println("Generating a Blowfish key...");

    // Create a Blowfish key
```

```
KeyGenerator keyGenerator = KeyGenerator.getInstance("Blowfish");
keyGenerator.init(128);  // need to initialize with the keysize
Key key = keyGenerator.generateKey();

System.out.println("Done generating the key.");

// Create a cipher using that key to initialize it

Cipher cipher = Cipher.getInstance("Blowfish/ECB/PKCS5Padding");
cipher.init(Cipher.ENCRYPT_MODE, key);

byte[] plaintext = text.getBytes("UTF8");

// Print out the bytes of the plaintext

System.out.println("\nPlaintext: ");
for (int i=0;i<plaintext.length;i++) {
  System.out.print(plaintext[i]+" ");
}

// Perform the actual encryption

byte[] ciphertext = cipher.doFinal(plaintext);

// Print out the ciphertext

System.out.println("\n\nCiphertext: ");
for (int i=0;i<ciphertext.length;i++) {
  System.out.print(ciphertext[i]+" ");
}

// Re-initialize the cipher to decrypt mode

cipher.init(Cipher.DECRYPT_MODE, key);

// Perform the decryption

byte[] decryptedText = cipher.doFinal(ciphertext);

String output = new String(decryptedText,"UTF8");

System.out.println("\n\nDecrypted text: "+output);

  }
}
```

Of course, if you run this program, you'll see the following output:

```
Generating a Blowfish key...
Done generating the key.

Plaintext:
72 101 108 108 111 87 111 114 108 100 33

Ciphertext:
21 -74 -74 12 32 103 -72 -18 -19 -51 67 28 31 -91 -26 -104

Decrypted text: HelloWorld!
```

Now let's look at a different method of encryption.

Password-Based Encryption (PBE)

The examples that we've given so far have used binary keys. These keys need to be stored in some fashion – on a hard drive or floppy disk for instance. **Password-based encryption** (PBE) uses a password as the key. This is convenient because the security then rests with the user rather than in a physical medium. Unfortunately, password-based encryption in general isn't as secure as algorithms with binary keys like TripleDES or Blowfish. To demonstrate this, let's say we use Blowfish with a key size of 128 bits. That gives us a **keyspace** of 2^{128}. Password-based encryption typically uses ASCII characters. An average user's password might be 6 characters in length. If it's entirely lowercase, there are only 26^6 possible keys, or roughly 2^{28}. Adding capital characters and symbols helps quite a bit, but it cannot even approach the keyspace of a good symmetric algorithm.

To add to their insecurity, most passwords are simple everyday words. If an attacker were trying to crack a password, they would likely try every English word, which could be done rather quickly on a fast computer. This is known as a dictionary attack and is surprisingly successful. There are a number of tools out there that will automate a dictionary attack – some even test combinations of words, differing capitalization, and the use of numbers and some symbols. It's quite interesting to try one of these tools out and see how secure a password is. A good password should be at least 8 characters long and use capitalization, numbers, and symbols, like "m1Nnes0+a". It's important that the password be simple enough to memorize, however, as you should never write a password down.

Password encryption uses a combination of hashing and normal symmetric encryption. The password is hashed using a message digest algorithm like SHA-1 (we'll discuss this topic more in Chapter 6), and then the resulting hash is used to construct a binary key for an algorithm like Blowfish as shown in the following diagram:

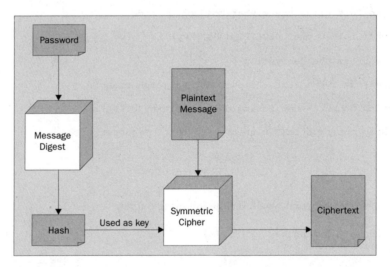

As we mentioned, one of the problems with password-based encryption is that it is possible to create a precompiled list of passwords, hash them, and have a set of keys ready to try on encrypted data. This allows an attacker to try all normally used keys very quickly, and so determine if any of them decrypt the data. There are two techniques used to combat this attack: **salting** and **iteration counts**. A salt is a random value appended to the password before it is hashed to create a key, and the iteration count is the number of times the salt and password are hashed. Let's examine each of these in some detail and see how they improve security.

Salt

By adding a random piece of data to the password before hashing it, we greatly increase the number of possible keys created from a single password. Without a salt, the word "sasquatch" hashes to a specific value. If we add 8 bytes of random data before hashing it, then "sasquatch" can hash to 2^{64} possible values. That means that it is effectively impossible to create a precompiled-key list dictionary, as it would be far too large. Instead, the attacker is forced to perform a hashing computation rather than a simple lookup on the data, which will take quite some time.

The salt is stored with the data that is encrypted. Each time a new piece of data is encrypted, a new salt is generated. This means that the same phrase will encrypt to a different value each time it is encrypted, even if the same password is used every time. To decrypt, the salt must be extracted from the encrypted data, and then combined with the password to create the decryption key.

An example of the use of a salt is the password checking system in Linux. Typically passwords are MD5-hashed with a random salt. The salt is then prepended to the resulting hash. That salt and hash are then written to the password file. The first few characters are the salt and the remaining characters are the password hashed with the salt. When someone tries to log in, the operating system reads the password they type in and their entry in the password file. It then hashes the user's typing along with the first characters of their password entry. If the resulting hash is equal to the remaining characters in their entry, their password is correct.

In just a moment we'll show an example of using salt and password-based encryption that should help make this process clearer.

Iteration Count

The iteration count is an attempt to increase the time that an attacker will have to spend to test possible passwords. If we have an iteration count of a thousand, we need to hash the password a thousand times, which is a thousand times more computationally expensive than doing it just once. So now our attacker will have to spend 1000 times more computational resources to crack our password-based encryption.

Password-Based Encryption Example

Let's write a simple class that does password-based encryption and decryption. We'll use an iteration count of 1000, and a random 8-byte or 64-bit salt. When we write the ciphertext out, the first 64 bits will be the salt that we need to use to create the key to decrypt it. When we decrypt, we'll use those 64 bits as the salt and we'll only decrypt the ciphertext that begins after the 64th bit. Note that the salt isn't being kept secret – it's just different for each batch of text that we're going to encrypt.

We want the output of the example to be displayable on the screen. To accomplish that, we're going to BASE 64 encode the output, which transforms binary data into ASCII characters.

BASE64 Encoding

Binary data is typically stored in bytes of 8-bits. Standard ASCII is only 7 bits though, so if we want to display binary as ASCII, we're going to lose at least one bit per byte. BASE64 encoding is a way of overcoming this problem. 8-bit bytes are converted to 6-bit chunks and then into characters. Six bits are used so that some control characters can be used indicating when the data ends. The encoded characters can then be displayed on the screen and converted back into binary with no difficulty. Of course, since we're moving from an 8-bit chunk to a 6-bit chunk, we're going to have more chunks – 3 bytes becomes 4 characters and vice-versa.

There is a BASE64 encoder and decoder in the `sun.misc` package. Since this is not included in a `java.*` package, its location could change in a future release of Java.

For that reason, we have provided a BASE64 encoder and decoder in Appendix C of this book.

We can use it as a drop-in replacement for the `sun.misc` implementation, by changing the import statement in `PBE.java` from:

```
import sun.misc.*;
```

to

```
import com.isnetworks.base64.*;
```

and include the BASE64 classes in the classpath.

Our code example will have two options: encryption and decryption. Encryption will require a password and some plaintext, and decryption a password and some encrypted data. We'll create a salt for the encryption and prepend it to the ciphertext after it's been encrypted, like so:

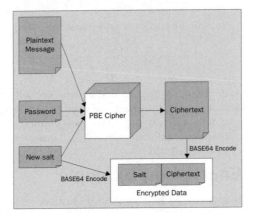

When decrypting, we'll take that block of encrypted data and separate it into the salt and the ciphertext. Then we can use the password and the salt to initialize a cipher that can decrypt the ciphertext into the original plaintext message like this:

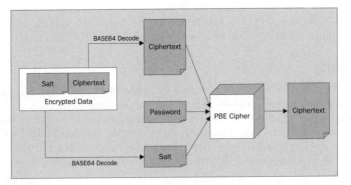

Password-based encryption in Java requires that we use two new classes in the `javax.crypto.spec` package, PBEKeySpec and PBEParameterSpec, as well as `javax.crypto.SecretKeyFactory`.

PBEKeySpec

We use PBEKeySpec to create a key based on a password, using an instance of SecretKeyFactory. This is one of the few classes in the JCE that we can actually call the standard constructor on. It takes a char array as an argument due to the fact that passwords are typically not stored as strings, since strings are immutable in Java, and there are times when you would like to be sure that a password is cleared out when you're done using it. For more information, see Chapter 2 on writing secure code.

```
char[] password = "sasquatch".toCharArray();
PBEKeySpec keySpec = new PBEKeySpec(password);
```

SecretKeyFactory

In order to actually use the PBEKeySpec as a key, we need to run it through a SecretKeyFactory, which will generate the key given a key specification, by calling generateSecret().

We create an instance of SecretKeyFactory by calling getInstance() with the name of the algorithm we need. Here's an example of creating a SecretKey from a PBEKeySpec:

```
SecretKeyFactory keyFactory =
   SecretKeyFactory.getInstance("PBEWithSHAAndTwofish-CBC");
SecretKey theKey = keyFactory.generateSecret(keySpec);
```

PBEParameterSpec

To create a cipher that uses PBE, we need to pass the salt and the iteration count to the cipher on instantiation. PBEParameterSpec is a wrapper for that salt and iteration count. It is given to the cipher on initialization, along with the key. Assuming the salt and iterations are already defined, here's how we would get a cipher, using PBEParameterSpec:

```
PBEParameterSpec paramSpec = new PBEParameterSpec(salt, iterations);
Cipher cipher = Cipher.getInstance("PBEWithSHAAndTwofish-CBC");
cipher.init(Cipher.ENCRYPT_MODE, theKey, paramSpec);
```

PBE Algorithm Names and Providers

You may have noticed the strange name for the algorithm that we used to initialize our key factory and cipher above, PBEWithSHAAndTwofish-CBC. This specifies password-based encryption using SHA as a message digest and Twofish in CBC mode as the symmetric encryption algorithm. There are a great number of possible password-based encryption algorithms, including but not limited to:

- ❑ PBEWithMD5AndDES
- ❑ PBEWithSHAAndBlowfish
- ❑ PBEWithSHAAnd128BitRC4
- ❑ PBEWithSHAAndIDEA-CBC
- ❑ PBEWithSHAAnd3-KeyTripleDES-CBC

Most of the above algorithms are equivalently secure. The only possible exception is PBEWithMD5AndDES. Since DES uses a 56-bit key, it's possible that a password would be more secure than the DES key it creates. We recommend using one of the other algorithms if you have a choice in your application.

Unfortunately, no crypto provider supports all PBE algorithms and here we'll use the Bouncy Castle provider to get support for PBEWithSHAAndTwofish-CBC.

Now let's take a look at our complete example of PBE. It uses SHA-1 and Twofish to encrypt or decrypt some text using a password. The iteration count is set to 1000 and the salt is randomly chosen on encryption. The salt is then written to the first 8 bytes of the output text.

PBE Example Code

When decrypting, this program will read the first 8 bytes of the ciphertext and use that as the salt:

```
import java.security.*;
import javax.crypto.*;
import javax.crypto.spec.*;
import java.util.*;

// This is for BASE64 encoding and decoding

import sun.misc.*;

/**
 *  PBE.java
 */
```

If you're not using a Sun-based VM, comment out the import sun.misc.* line shown above, and uncomment the following line. This will switch to our BASE64 encoders:

```
// import com.isnetworks.base64.*;

public class PBE
{
  private static int ITERATIONS = 1000;

  private static void usage()
  {
    System.err.println("Usage: java PBE -e|-d password text");
    System.exit(1);
  }

  public static void main (String[] args)
                           throws Exception
  {
    if (args.length != 3) usage();

    char[] password = args[1].toCharArray();
    String text = args[2];
    String output = null;
```

```java
    // Check the first argument: are we encrypting or decrypting?

    if ("-e".equals(args[0])) output = encrypt(password, text);
    else if ("-d".equals(args[0])) output = decrypt(password, text);
    else usage();

    System.out.println(output);
}

private static String encrypt(char[] password, String plaintext)
                          throws Exception
{
    // Begin by creating a random salt of 64 bits (8 bytes)

    byte[] salt = new byte[8];
    Random random = new Random();
    random.nextBytes(salt);

    // Create the PBEKeySpec with the given password

    PBEKeySpec keySpec = new PBEKeySpec(password);

    // Get a SecretKeyFactory for PBEWithSHAAndTwofish

    SecretKeyFactory keyFactory =
        SecretKeyFactory.getInstance("PBEWithSHAAndTwofish-CBC");

    // Create our key

    SecretKey key = keyFactory.generateSecret(keySpec);

    // Now create a parameter spec for our salt and iterations

    PBEParameterSpec paramSpec = new PBEParameterSpec(salt, ITERATIONS);

    // Create a cipher and initialize it for encrypting

    Cipher cipher = Cipher.getInstance("PBEWithSHAAndTwofish-CBC");
    cipher.init(Cipher.ENCRYPT_MODE, key, paramSpec);

    byte[] ciphertext = cipher.doFinal(plaintext.getBytes());

    BASE64Encoder encoder = new BASE64Encoder();

    String saltString = encoder.encode(salt);
    String ciphertextString = encoder.encode(ciphertext);

    return saltString+ciphertextString;
}

private static String decrypt(char[] password, String text)
                          throws Exception
{
    // Below we split the text into salt and text strings.

    String salt = text.substring(0,12);
    String ciphertext = text.substring(12,text.length());

    // BASE64Decode the bytes for the salt and the ciphertext
```

```
      BASE64Decoder decoder = new BASE64Decoder();
      byte[] saltArray = decoder.decodeBuffer(salt);
      byte[] ciphertextArray = decoder.decodeBuffer(ciphertext);

      // Create the PBEKeySpec with the given password

      PBEKeySpec keySpec = new PBEKeySpec(password);

      // Get a SecretKeyFactory for PBEWithSHAAndTwofish

      SecretKeyFactory keyFactory =
        SecretKeyFactory.getInstance("PBEWithSHAAndTwofish-CBC");

      // Create our key

      SecretKey key = keyFactory.generateSecret(keySpec);

      // Now create a parameter spec for our salt and iterations

      PBEParameterSpec paramSpec =
        new PBEParameterSpec(saltArray, ITERATIONS);

      // Create a cipher and initialize it for encrypting

      Cipher cipher = Cipher.getInstance("PBEWithSHAAndTwofish-CBC");
      cipher.init(Cipher.DECRYPT_MODE, key, paramSpec);

      // Perform the actual decryption

      byte[] plaintextArray = cipher.doFinal(ciphertextArray);

      return new String(plaintextArray);
   }
}
```

Running the Example

After compiling, we can run the example. For example, to encrypt we could type:

```
C:\> java PBE -e sasquatch "Hello World!"
```

This will encrypt the string "Hello World!" using PBE with the password of "sasquatch". We should see output similar to the following:

```
+xeivHEOb1M=AT/VYJ1YI1JoQSMfKryaKw==
```

We can decrypt the output with:

```
C:\> java PBE -d sasquatch "+xeivHEOb1M=AT/VYJ1YI1JoQSMfKryaKw=="
```

and of course, we get our original message returned to us:

```
Hello World!
```

Key Storage

One of the primary difficulties in establishing good security through cryptography is key storage. In order for a key to be useful, it must be persistent. But by keeping the key around, we risk it being compromised. Let's imagine that we want to encrypt some personal files on our computer so that no one can read them. We create a 448-bit Blowfish key and encrypt our files with it, thinking that our files will now be secure. But if someone were to get into our machine, they'd be able to read the key and decrypt the files. In order for the files to be safe, we have to protect the key that we used to encrypt those files.

One way to protect the key is to keep it on a floppy disk and only use it when a file needs to be encrypted or decrypted. Another possibility is to use a smart card, which is a tiny computer, the size of a credit card. Its purpose is to store keys and perform cryptographic operations directly on the card, without ever exposing the key. Smart cards and floppy disks are somewhat inconvenient, however, because they require some external physical medium to store the key.

Let's return to the idea of keeping the key on our computer in the filesystem. Anyone with read access could decrypt our files. One way to work around this is to encrypt the keys using password-based encryption, using a good strong password that no one is likely to guess. This is what Netscape Communicator does when storing private certificates for encrypted e-mail.

Storing the keys in the filesystem reduces their security, even if they're encrypted: they're now protected by PBE, which is almost always going to be less strong than the keys the key store contains. It's a good idea to protect any key storage mechanism in additional ways, like setting file permissions and physically securing the box the keys are on. Let's discuss encrypting keys for storage and transmission.

Key Wrapping and Unwrapping

JCE 1.2.1, which some providers implement, provides an easy means of encrypting a key. As we mentioned earlier, `javax.crypto.Cipher` has a method `wrap()`, which takes a key as an argument and returns a byte array, which is the encrypted value of the key. We need to initialize the cipher in `WRAP_MODE` instead of `ENCRYPT_MODE`. If we had a PBE cipher, just like in the previous example, we could wrap a secret key like so:

```
cipher.init(Cipher.WRAP_MODE, passwordKey, paramSpec);
byte[] encryptedKeyBytes = cipher.wrap(secretKey);
```

To decrypt the key, we initialize it in `UNWRAP_MODE`, and then call `cipher.unwrap()` with the algorithm of the wrapped key and the type `SECRET_KEY`, because that's the type of key that was wrapped:

```
cipher.init(Cipher.UNWRAP_MODE, passwordKey, paramSpec);
Key key = cipher.unwrap(encryptedKeyBytes, "Blowfish", Cipher.SECRET_KEY);
```

Key Encryption without Wrapping

If we don't have `wrap()` and `unwrap()` in our provider's cipher implementation, then we'll need to perform the encryption and decryption using `java.security.Key`'s `getEncoded()` method and `javax.crypto.SecretKeySpec`.

java.security.Key

Once we have a key, getEncoded() will return an encoded form of the key as a byte array. We can then encrypt that byte array with a PBE cipher, like so:

```
byte[] keyBytes = myKey.getEncoded();
cipher.init(Cipher.ENCRYPT_MODE, passwordKey, paramSpec);
byte[] encryptedKeyBytes = cipher.doFinal(keyBytes);
```

Those encrypted key bytes can then be written to more permanent storage, like a file or a database.

SecretKeySpec

To decrypt a key, we need to use the class SecretKeySpec. SecretKeySpec implements SecretKey, but can be constructed from a byte array. We decrypt the key bytes using the PBE cipher, and then we construct an instance of SecretKeySpec with the decrypted bytes and the name of the algorithm:

```
cipher.init(Cipher.DECRYPT_MODE, passwordKey, paramSpec);
byte[] keyBytes = cipher.doFinal(encryptedKeyBytes);
SecretKeySpec myKey = new SecretKeySpec(keyBytes; "Blowfish");
```

We'll show an example of encrypting a key with PBE and storing it for future use later in this chapter (in the example using cipher streams). In order to understand how stream ciphers work, we need to first examine in more detail how ciphers themselves work, specifically their mode and padding. Let's begin by looking at padding.

Padding

Block ciphers, like most of the ciphers we've been discussing so far, operate on distinct chunks of data – usually 64 bits. Some newer block ciphers like AES operate on 128 bits or more at a time. But the plaintext data to be encrypted won't always be a multiple of the block size. So before encrypting, padding needs to be added to the data. There are a number of different ways padding can be added, but most symmetric algorithms use one of two types of padding:

❑ No padding

❑ PKCS#5 padding

No padding is exactly that, no padding. It requires that the data we are encrypting end on a block exactly, with no extra data. PKCS#5 is more commonly used. **PKCS** stands for **Public Key Cryptography Standard**, and there are a number of PKCS standards created for use in various cryptographic functions, like key exchange and certificate requests. Along with those broad protocol definitions, they also define some padding methods. Of these methods, PKCS#5 is the most commonly used for symmetric encryption.

PKCS#5 padding works as follows: the bytes remaining to fill a block are assigned a number, which is the number of bytes that were added to fill the block. For instance, if we have an 8-byte block, and only 3 bytes are filled, then we have 5 bytes to pad. Those 5 bytes are all assigned the value "5", for the 5 bytes of padding. The illustration opposite should help clarify this:

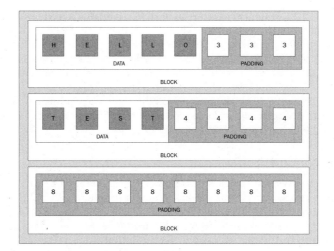

If we have data that ends on an even multiple of 8 bytes, we need to add an entire block of padding. This way, we know that there is *always* padding that must be removed after decryption.

Mode

In addition to specifying the padding, we also need to specify the mode for a block cipher before using it. The mode defines how a cipher should apply an encryption algorithm. Changing the mode can allow a block cipher to function as a stream cipher. Block ciphers operate on data a block at a time, where a block can be any number of bits, usually 64 or 128. A stream cipher, on the other hand, can encrypt or decrypt data a byte at a time, making it much more useful for streaming applications, like network communication.

We will discuss some of the more common modes below.

ECB (Electronic Code Book)

ECB is the simplest mode: the same plaintext block will always encrypt to the exact same ciphertext block. This is fine for sending single chunks of data, like a key, but not good for implementing an encrypted stream of information. This is because if the same plaintext is sent multiple times, the same ciphertext will also be sent.

Let's say we're sending the following message in a chat application, "meet me later", and we're sending it one character at a time. The following might be our ciphertext if we were using DES:

```
mD8hEmbih6E=        m
TRw+doCp3EQ=        e
TRw+doCp3EQ=        e
Dj3lTDsRkxw=        t

mD8hEmbih6E=        m
TRw+doCp3EQ=        e

xXyJjiHigk8=        l
x26P5lw+XyM=        a
Dj3lTDsRkxw=        t
TRw+doCp3EQ=        e
XIoLD1MHGO4=        r
```

Notice that 'e' always encrypt to the exact same ciphertext. If an attacker knew that we were sending text messages, then a frequency analysis would quickly indicate that e's were encrypted to "TRw+doCp3EQ=". With some time and a complete encrypted session transcript, it wouldn't be difficult to crack the code, as the use of ECB in this application has reduced the strength of the encryption from 2^{56} bits to less than 100 characters. This is only as secure as a simple character-by-character replacement.

The real weakness here is that each block is encrypted the same way. If our key or data keeps changing, ECB is perfectly safe. But if similar blocks keep getting sent with the same key, it is possible to gain some information from those blocks that we might not want broadcast.

CBC (Cipher Block Chaining)

CBC mode changes the behavior of the cipher so that the same plaintext block no longer necessarily encrypts to the same ciphertext block, thus solving the main problem with ECB. CBC uses information from the previous block to encrypt the current block, thus changing it from ECB. A problem with this method is that identical messages will still encrypt identically, because all of the blocks that would alter future blocks are the same. To fix this, we need to use an **initialization vector** or **IV**. The IV is just a block of random data used to initialize the cipher. It need not be kept secret, but it should be different for every message. That way, even if we send two identical messages, as long as they have different IVs, they will encrypt differently. In that sense, an initialization vector is a lot like salt used in password-based encryption.

CBC is suitable for transmitting text, but it requires transmitting a full block of data at a time – usually 8 characters. This is fine for a complete message, but not for a talk application, which needs to send a single character at a time.

CFB (Cipher FeedBack)

CFB works similarly to CBC, except that it can operate on smaller chunks of data – typically 8 bits. This is perfect for encrypting something like a chat session, where single byte chunks of data need to be sent.

CFB also requires an IV that must be unique for each message sent with the same key.

OFB (Output FeedBack)

OFB is similar to CFB, except that it provides better protection against data being lost in transit. A single bit error in the ciphertext produces a single bit of error in the plaintext. Other modes cause the entire block to get lost.

Like CFB and CBC, OFB also requires an IV.

CipherStreams

Some of the most useful classes that the JCE provides are the two `CipherStream` classes in the `javax.crypto` package: `CipherInputStream` and `CipherOutputStream`. They provide convenient wrappers around standard input and output streams that automatically encrypt and decrypt. You can use them anywhere you use a normal `InputStream` or `OutputStream`, like network programming or file IO.

`CipherInputStream` and `CipherOutputStream` are both constructed by a call to `new()` with the stream to wrap and the cipher to use. If we have a cipher prepared, we could encrypt a file with:

```
FileInputStream input = new FileInputStream("plaintext_filename");
FileOutputStream output = new FileOutputStream("ciphertext_filename");
CipherOutputStream cipherOutput = new CipherOutputStream(output, cipher);
int r = 0;
while (r=input.read() != -1) {
  cipherOutput.write(r);
}
cipherOutput.close();
output.close();
input.close();
```

Decrypting is similar to this – we simply place the cipher in DECRYPT_MODE, and use the cipher streams in the same fashion.

When using cipher streams, it is important to set the mode properly. ECB mode, as we mentioned, isn't a good idea for large chunks of data that are non-random, like a text file. Instead, we'll need to use a mode like CBC, which requires an initialization vector. We'll show setting the mode in the code example coming up.

Initializing a Cipher with an IV

javax.crypto.spec.IVParameterSpec encapsulates an initialization vector in the JCE. One is constructed with a byte array and a call to new() for IVParameterSpec.

To create the bytes for the IV, we should use java.security.SecureRandom to generate a byte array equivalent to the block size for the cipher we are using. Most block ciphers have a block size of 64 bits (8 bytes). AES has a variable block size, either 128, 192, or 256 bits, but is typically set to 128-bit (16 bytes).

SecureRandom

SecureRandom is easy to use. We can construct one normally, with the default constructor, and then pass byte arrays to it with nextBytes() and receive them back filled with random data. For instance, to create an 8-byte array using secure random we could do the following:

```
byte[] randomBytes = new byte[8];
SecureRandom random = new SecureRandom();
random.nextBytes(randomBytes);
```

As an aside, you may have noticed a delay during the running of the examples we have seen so far and wondered what causes it. Well, it's not the encryption that's so slow; it's the initialization of java.security.SecureRandom. Sun's implementation of SecureRandom creates a great number of threads and checks their interaction over a period of time. It then uses that to initialize a **Pseudo-Random Number Generator** (**PRNG**). It's the thread creation and interaction that takes so long.

To combat this, a couple of providers have created implementations of SecureRandom that are at least partially native, giving a huge speed increase in the seeding of the random number generator. Cryptix (http://www.cryptix.org) provides an implementation that runs on Linux and the various BSDs, and Virtual Unlimited (http://www.virtualunlimited.com) provides one for Windows.

Also, the initialization of SecureRandom is only expensive the first time it's done in a single Java VM instance. If you have a long-running program or a server, you can initialize SecureRandom on startup and all later operations will run quite quickly. You may also want to try to architect your programs so that they run for a longer period of time rather than starting and stopping often. This would allow you to amortize the cost of initialization.

Creating and Using an IV

To create the IV with those random bytes, just construct a new instance of IVParameterSpec:

```
IVParameterSpec iv = new IVParameterSpec(randomBytes);
```

Now we can use the IV to initialize a cipher, like so:

```
Cipher cipher = Cipher.getInstance("Blowfish/CBC/PKCS5Padding");
cipher.init(Cipher.ENCRYPT_MODE, key, iv);
```

And we're ready to use that cipher in a cipher output stream.

Keeping Track of the IV

It's important to realize that that same IV needs to be used to initialize a cipher for decrypting as well. It's a lot like the salt used with password-based encryption. Just like the salt, it doesn't need to be hidden like the key does. We can safely expose it along with the ciphertext that we've encrypted.

A common way to handle this is to place the initialization vector at the beginning of the ciphertext. That's exactly what we're going to do in the next example, which will encrypt and decrypt a file, and also keep a symmetric key stored in the filesystem encrypted with a password.

CipherStream Example – FileEncryptor

We're going to write a program that encrypts and decrypts files using cipher streams. We'll use AES (sometimes known as Rijndael) as the algorithm to encrypt the file. In order to decrypt it, we'll need to use the same key, so we'll store the key encrypted in a file with password-based encryption.

We'll offer three options when running our little application: key creation, file encryption, and file decryption. Each of those options will cause a different method to get called: createKey(), encrypt(), or decrypt().

```
import java.security.*;
import javax.crypto.*;
import javax.crypto.spec.*;
import java.io.*;

/**
 *  FileEncryptor.java
 *
 *  This class encrypts and decrypts a file using CipherStreams
 *  and a 256-bit Rijndael key stored in the filesystem.
 */

public class FileEncryptor
{
  private static String KEY_FILENAME="rijndaelkey.bin";
  private static int ITERATIONS=1000;
```

```
public static void main (String[] args)
                         throws Exception
{
  if ((args.length < 2) || (args.length > 4))
  {
    System.err.println("Usage: java CipherStreamExample -c|-e|-d password
                       [inputfile] [outputfile]");
    System.exit(1);
  }

  // Convert the password into a char array

  char[] password = args[1].toCharArray();

  if ("-c".equals(args[0])) createKey(password);
  else if ("-e".equals(args[0])) encrypt(password, args[2], args[3]);
  else if ("-d".equals(args[0])) decrypt(password, args[2], args[3]);
  else (System.out.println("Usage: java CipherStreamExample -c|-e|-d password
                           [inputfile] [outputfile]");
}
```

Now let's write the `createKey()` method. The first thing we need to do is generate an AES key. Since AES is also known as Rijndael, we'll use that as an algorithm name to create a key generator.

```
/**
 *  Creates a 256-bit Rijndael key and stores it to
 *  the filesystem as a KeyStore.
 */

private static void createKey(char[] password)
                              throws Exception
{
  System.out.println("Generating a Rijndael key...");

  // Create a Rijndael key

  KeyGenerator keyGenerator = KeyGenerator.getInstance("Rijndael");
  keyGenerator.init(256);
  Key key = keyGenerator.generateKey();

  System.out.println("Done generating the key.");
```

Now we want to encrypt the key with a password. We'll create an 8-byte salt and create a PBE cipher with the password:

```
  // Prepare key encryption cipher using the password

  byte[] salt = new byte[8];
  SecureRandom random = new SecureRandom();
  random.nextBytes(salt);
  PBEKeySpec pbeKeySpec = new PBEKeySpec(password);
  SecretKeyFactory keyFactory = SecretKeyFactory.getInstance(
    "PBEWithSHAAndTwofish-CBC");
  SecretKey pbeKey = keyFactory.generateSecret(pbeKeySpec);
  PBEParameterSpec pbeParamSpec = new PBEParameterSpec(salt, ITERATIONS);
  Cipher cipher = Cipher.getInstance("PBEWithSHAAndTwofish-CBC");
  cipher.init(Cipher.ENCRYPT_MODE, pbeKey, pbeParamSpec);
```

Now we can use the cipher to encrypt the encoded form of the key:

```
// Encrypt the key

byte[] encryptedKeyBytes = cipher.doFinal(key.getEncoded());
```

In order to be able to decrypt the key, we need to have the salt. We'll write the salt that we generated to the first 8 bytes of the file, and then we'll write the encrypted key and close the file.

```
// Write out the salt, and then the encrypted key bytes

FileOutputStream fos = new FileOutputStream(KEY_FILENAME);
fos.write(salt);
fos.write(encryptedKeyBytes);
fos.close();
}
```

Before we can do any file encryption or decryption, we'll need to have access to the key. We're going to write a method called `loadKey()` that will load a key, with a password specified as an argument. This is essentially the reverse of the `createKey()` method: we read in the salt, and the encrypted key bytes, and then decrypt the key with a PBE cipher. We'll use `javax.crypto.spec.SecretKeySpec` to create a key from the decrypted key bytes.

```
/**
 *   Loads a key from the filesystem
 */

private static Key loadKey(char[] password)
                        throws Exception
{
    // Load the bytes from the encrypted key file.

    FileInputStream fis = new FileInputStream(KEY_FILENAME);
    ByteArrayOutputStream baos = new ByteArrayOutputStream();
    int i = 0;
    while ((i=fis.read()) != -1) {
      baos.write(i);
    }
    fis.close();
    byte[] saltAndKeyBytes = baos.toByteArray();
    baos.close();

    // Get the salt, which is the first 8 bytes

    byte[] salt = new byte[8];
    System.arraycopy(saltAndKeyBytes,0,salt,0,8);

    // get the encrypted key bytes

    int length = saltAndKeyBytes.length - 8;
    byte[] encryptedKeyBytes = new byte[length];
    System.arraycopy(saltAndKeyBytes,8,encryptedKeyBytes,0,length);

    // Create the PBE cipher
    PBEKeySpec pbeKeySpec = new PBEKeySpec(password);
    SecretKeyFactory keyFactory = SecretKeyFactory.getInstance(
      "PBEWithSHAAndTwofish-CBC");
    SecretKey pbeKey = keyFactory.generateSecret(pbeKeySpec);
    PBEParameterSpec pbeParamSpec = new PBEParameterSpec(salt, ITERATIONS);
    Cipher cipher = Cipher.getInstance("PBEWithSHAAndTwofish-CBC");
    cipher.init(Cipher.DECRYPT_MODE, pbeKey, pbeParamSpec);
```

```
    // Decrypt the key bytes

    byte[] decryptedKeyBytes = cipher.doFinal(encryptedKeyBytes);

    // Create the key from the key bytes

    SecretKeySpec key = new SecretKeySpec(decryptedKeyBytes, "Rijndael");
    return key;
}
```

Now we can write the encrypt method. We start by loading the key with the `loadKey()` method we just wrote. Next we need to create an initialization vector that is 16 bytes long, equal to the block size of Rijndael.

```
/**
 *  Encrypt a file using Rijndael. Load the key
 *  from the filesystem, given a password.
 */

private static void encrypt(char[] password, String fileInput, String
                            fileOutput)
                    throws Exception
{
    System.out.println("Loading the key.");
    Key key = loadKey(password);
    System.out.println("Loaded the key.");

    // Create a cipher using that key to initialize it

    Cipher cipher = Cipher.getInstance("Rijndael/CBC/PKCS5Padding");

    System.out.println("Initializing SecureRandom...");

    // Now we need an Initialization Vector for the cipher in CBC mode.
    // We use 16 bytes, because the block size of Rijndael is 256 bits.

    SecureRandom random = new SecureRandom();
    byte[] iv = new byte[16];
    random.nextBytes(iv);
```

Now we'll open the files for reading and writing. We'll write the IV bytes to the output file unencrypted, as we'll need to use it later to decrypt the file. Then we'll create an `IVParameterSpec` object that we will use to create a cipher.

```
    FileInputStream fis = new FileInputStream(fileInput);
    FileOutputStream fos = new FileOutputStream(fileOutput);

    // Write the IV as the first 16 bytes in the file

    fos.write(iv);
    IvParameterSpec spec = new IvParameterSpec(iv);

    System.out.println("Initializing the cipher.");

    cipher.init(Cipher.ENCRYPT_MODE, key, spec);
```

Now we want to wrap a `CipherOutputStream` around the `FileOutputStream` using the cipher we just created:

```
    CipherOutputStream cos = new CipherOutputStream(fos, cipher);
```

Now we simply read the bytes from the input stream and write them to the cipher stream. This will encrypt the entire file. When we're done, we close the input and output.

```java
System.out.println("Encrypting the file...");

int theByte = 0;
while ((theByte = fis.read()) != -1)
{
    cos.write(theByte);
}
fis.close();
cos.close();
}
```

Decrypting the file is just the opposite. We read in the IV, initialize a cipher, and create a `CipherInputStream` and use it to decrypt the file.

```java
/**
 *  Decrypt a file using Rijndael. Load the key
 *  from the filesystem, given a password.
 */

private static void decrypt(char[] password, String fileInput, String fileOutput)
                            throws Exception
{
    System.out.println("Loading the key.");
    Key key = loadKey(password);
    System.out.println("Loaded the key.");

    // Create a cipher using that key to initialize it

    Cipher cipher = Cipher.getInstance("Rijndael/CBC/PKCS5Padding");

    FileInputStream fis = new FileInputStream(fileInput);
    FileOutputStream fos = new FileOutputStream(fileOutput);

    // Read the IV from the file. It's the first 16 bytes.

    byte[] iv = new byte[16];
    fis.read(iv);

    IvParameterSpec spec = new IvParameterSpec(iv);

    System.out.println("Initializing the cipher.");
    cipher.init(Cipher.DECRYPT_MODE, key, spec);

    CipherInputStream cis = new CipherInputStream(fis, cipher);

    System.out.println("Decrypting the file...");

    int theByte = 0;
    while ((theByte = cis.read()) != -1)
    {
        fos.write(theByte);
    }
    cis.close();
    fos.close();
}
}
```

Running the Application

Now let's run the application. We'll begin by creating a key, protected with the password "sasquatch".

```
C:\> java FileEncryptor -c sasquatch
```

This will print out a few messages like this:

```
Generating a Rijndael key...
Done generating the key.
```

Next we can encrypt a file. Create a file called test.txt in your current directory, and place some text in it. We can then encrypt it to testEncrypted.txt with the following command:

```
C:\> java FileEncryptor -e sasquatch test.txt testEncrypted.txt
```

This will give the following output:

```
Loading the key.
Loaded the key.
Initializing SecureRandom...
Initializing the cipher.
Encrypting the file...
```

You can now view the testEncrypted.txt file to check that it has been encrypted. If we wish, we can decrypt this file with the following command:

```
C:\> java FileEncryptor -d sasquatch testEncrypted.txt testDecrypted.txt
```

The output we get from this is:

```
Loading the key.
Loaded the key.
Initializing the cipher.
Decrypting the file...
```

We can now view the file testDecrypted.txt to verify that it has been properly decrypted.

CipherStreams with Other Algorithms

There's no requirement that we use Rijndael when encrypting files in the example above. It could easily be done with any other block cipher without changing anything besides the algorithm name and the bit size of the key. To use DESede for instance, just change "Rijndael" to "DESede" and the bit size from 256 to 168.

Sometimes we'll want to use a stream cipher, like RC4. RC4 is very fast, and would probably be the best choice for encrypting extremely large files, like audio or video files. RC4 is not quite as strong as AES, but as we've mentioned, 128 bits is enough strength for almost any application. Also, if we feel it's necessary, we can change the keysize we're using for RC4, as it can accept keys of up to 1024 bits.

RC4 doesn't use an initialization vector, as it's built into the algorithm. So we no longer need to create the IV, store it to the output file, or read it from the input file. There are only two lines that need alterations in both encrypt() and decrypt(). For encrypt() they are highlighted as shown below:

```
// Create a cipher using that key to initialize it

Cipher cipher = Cipher.getInstance("RC4");

System.out.println("Initializing SecureRandom...");

// Now we need an Initialization Vector for the cipher in CBC mode.
// We use 16 bytes, because the block size of Rijndael is 256 bits.

SecureRandom random = new SecureRandom();
byte[] iv = new byte[16];
random.nextBytes(iv);

FileInputStream fis = new FileInputStream(fileInput);
FileOutputStream fos = new FileOutputStream(fileOutput);

// Write the IV as the first 16 bytes in the file

fos.write(iv);
IvParameterSpec spec = new IvParameterSpec(iv);

System.out.println("Initializing the cipher.");

cipher.init(Cipher.ENCRYPT_MODE, key);
```

and for decrypt(), they are:

```
// Create a cipher using that key to initialize it

Cipher cipher = Cipher.getInstance("RC4");

FileInputStream fis = new FileInputStream(fileInput);
FileOutputStream fos = new FileOutputStream(fileOutput);

// Read the IV from the file. It's the first 16 bytes.

byte[] iv = new byte[16];
fis.read(iv);

IvParameterSpec spec = new IvParameterSpec(iv);

System.out.println("Initializing the cipher.");
cipher.init(Cipher.DECRYPT_MODE, key);

CipherInputStream cis = new CipherInputStream(fis, cipher);

System.out.println("Decrypting the file...");
```

Now we should be able to encrypt and decrypt files using RC4 instead of Rijndael/AES.

We've finished our discussion of cipher streams, and are going to move on to a new class that uses symmetric encryption: SealedObject.

Sealed Objects

The JCE provides a way to encrypt objects one at a time with a given cipher or key. The encrypted objects are then called **sealed objects**. Sealed objects can be useful for storing or transferring an encrypted version of an object, although the object to be encrypted needs to be serializable.

When constructing the sealed object, we need to use a fully initialized cipher. When decrypting, we can use either a cipher or just the key, and the sealed object will remember the settings for the cipher used to encrypt the object. Let's try an example of sealing an object with a DESede key. This example doesn't really do anything interesting externally, but rather simply expresses the syntax of using a `SealedObject` to seal a `String` object:

```java
import java.io.*;
import javax.crypto.*;
import java.security.*;

public class SealedObjectExample
{
  public static void main (String[] args)
                        throws Exception
  {
    String creditCard = "1234567890";

    KeyGenerator keyGenerator = KeyGenerator.getInstance("DESede");

    System.out.println("Creating a key.");

    Key key = keyGenerator.generateKey();
    Cipher cipher = Cipher.getInstance("DESede");
    cipher.init(Cipher.ENCRYPT_MODE, key);

    System.out.println("Encrypting the object.");
    SealedObject so = new SealedObject(creditCard, cipher);

    System.out.println("Unencrypting the object.");
    String unencryptedCreditCard = (String)so.getObject(key);

    System.out.println("Credit card number: "+unencryptedCreditCard);
  }
}
```

There is a bug, err, feature in the JDK1.2 that prevents extensions from using the class loader to create classes that are neither standard objects nor extensions. This means that if we create a custom object, say, a `CreditCard` object, as opposed to a simple `String`, we won't be able to decrypt it. Instead, we'll need to build our own implementation of `SealedObject` to accomplish that.

We've written an `EncryptedObject` class to do exactly that. It's functionally equivalent to `SealedObject`, but can be used with custom classes. We just need to have it in our classpath to use it. It's called `EncryptedObject` to avoid namespace collision with `SealedObject`, but they are otherwise identical, and you can use this `EncryptedObject` class as a drop-in replacement for `SealedObject` because its method signatures are exactly the same. It is provided for you in Appendix D of this book.

Summary

Symmetric encryption is a valuable tool for security. It provides us with the ability to hide data from prying eyes in various formats. Symmetric-key encryption has one big problem though: key distribution. In order to send encrypted messages to someone, we need to share a key with them. As we demonstrated in Chapter 3 with our Hamlet examples, this can be very difficult to do properly. In essence, we need to have a shared secret at some point in order to share secret messages in the future.

What's really needed is some way to bootstrap the process, some way to create a shared secret by exchanging purely public information. **Asymmetric-key** encryption, or **public-key** encryption does exactly that. In the next chapter, we'll show how to incorporate public-key encryption into our Java programs.

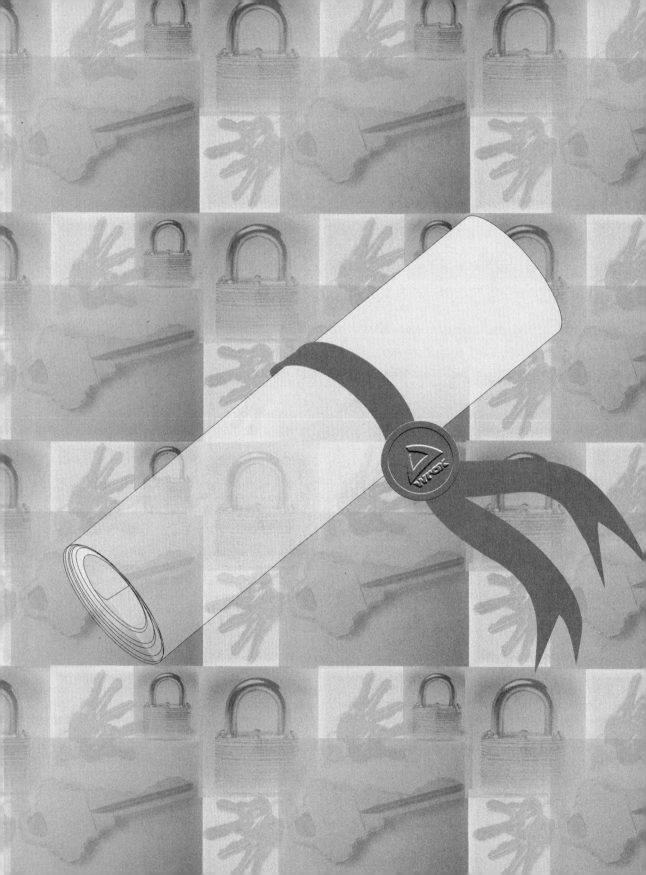

Asymmetric Encryption and Key Agreement

Both asymmetric encryption and key agreements solve the same problem: how to share secret data when any exchange of information could be eavesdropped upon. When using symmetric encryption, the key to encrypt and the key to decrypt were exactly the same. In order for two people to exchange a secret message, they first had to agree upon a secret key. Asymmetric, or public-key, encryption splits that key into two halves: the **public key** and the **private key**. Together they are referred to as a **key pair**. The two keys are complementary, so what one does, only the other can undo. We can encrypt a message with the public key, and then only the corresponding private key will decrypt it. In some algorithms, the private key can also be used to encrypt and then only the public key will decrypt that message. This is used to authenticate a message's origin and guarantee that the content was not altered.

In this chapter, we'll be covering the following areas:

❑   Ciphers, mode, and padding for asymmetric encryption

❑   Asymmetric encryption in Java

❑   Session key encryption

❑   File encryption using RSA Key Pairs

❑   Key agreements

We'll start by going into more detail on asymmetric encryption.

Asymmetric Encryption

Here's a diagram you may remember from Chapter 3:

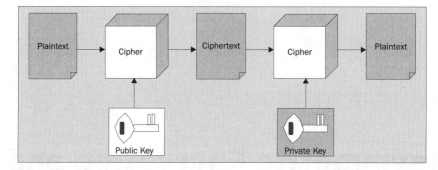

Plaintext is passed into a cipher that is initialized with a public key. That cipher then encrypts the plaintext, producing ciphertext. The ciphertext is then passed into a cipher initialized with the corresponding private key. That cipher then decrypts the ciphertext, returning a message identical to the original plaintext.

There is an enormous advantage to using public-key cryptography in that we no longer need to have a pre-existing secure communications channel in order to exchange a secret message.

RSA is the most common form of asymmetric encryption. It is used in protocols such as SSL for securing web traffic (described in detail in Chapter 9), and S/MIME, for securing e-mail (covered in Appendix A).

Asymmetric Ciphers, Mode, and Padding

We discussed mode and padding in the last chapter on symmetric encryption. As you will recall, mode defines how a cipher applies an encryption algorithm to plaintext and padding defines how plaintext is lengthened to fit the size that a cipher requires to operate. These are affected by the change to asymmetric encryption as follows.

Mode

The simplest mode is ECB (Electronic Code Book) where plaintext is encrypted a block at a time, and each block can stand on its own, with no relation to the blocks around it. Asymmetric ciphers are almost always used in ECB mode, and typically an asymmetric cipher is only used to encrypt a single block of plaintext data. Usually that block size is almost equal to the size of the key. 1024-bit RSA, for instance, can encrypt a block of data that is up to 117 bytes in length. If you need to encrypt more data than this, you will need to use session-key encryption, which we will discuss shortly.

Padding

Asymmetric encryption uses a very different form of padding from symmetric encryption. We defined PKCS#5 padding in the last chapter, which worked by padding blocks with bytes, each equal to the number of bytes of padding that were added. RSA, which is the only form of asymmetric encryption we're going to cover in detail, can use two forms of padding: PKCS#1 and **OAEP** (**Optimal Asymmetric Encryption Padding**). Both of these are defined by RSA Laboratories' PKCS#1 documentation (http://www.rsasecurity.com/rsalabs/pkcs/pkcs-1/index.html).

It's not really important to understand exactly how PKCS#1 and OAEP padding function, but if you want more info, you can find it in Chapter 12, when we implement an RSA provider using those two forms of padding. For now, here's what you need to know:

❏ PKCS#1 is the standard form of padding when using RSA. It unfortunately has some security holes in it when it is used for encrypting anything but random-looking binary data, like symmetric encryption keys. That makes it perfect for using in session-key encryption (described soon), but not good for directly encrypting data. PKCS#1 padding, however, is the most commonly used form of padding, and few RSA encryption programs handle any other type of padding.

❏ OAEP is an improvement on PKCS#1. It allows any kind of data to be encrypted, even if that data has obvious patterns in it, like English text. Unfortunately, OAEP is new, and has not been completely finalized by RSA Laboratories. Once the specification has been finalized, expect it to slowly work its way into the marketplace and replace PKCS#1.

Asymmetric Encryption in Java

For the most part, using asymmetric encryption in Java is the same as using symmetric encryption; you initialize a cipher with a key, and use it to encrypt or decrypt. The main difference is that there are two keys, a public key and a private key. Java has several classes that you'll need to use to create and manage these key pairs: KeyPair, PublicKey, PrivateKey, and KeyPairGenerator.

java.security.KeyPair

KeyPair encapsulates a public and private key pair. It has only two methods: getPublic(), which returns the public key of the pair, and getPrivate(), which returns the private key.

java.security.PublicKey

PublicKey is an interface for public keys. It's a sub-interface of Key, but doesn't add any methods. It's merely a signifier.

There is a commonly used sub-interface of PublicKey, in the java.security.interfaces package: RSAPublicKey. This interface defines public keys for the RSA algorithm. It adds extra methods for accessing information stored in RSA keys.

java.security.PrivateKey

PrivateKey is nearly identical to PublicKey, except that it signifies a private key.

Similar to PublicKey, there are sub-interfaces of PrivateKey, also in the java.security.interfaces package: RSAPrivateKey and RSAPrivateCrtKey. These classes contain extra methods for getting at parameters in those keys. RSAPrivateCrtKey is a sub-interface of RSAPrivateKey. It is nearly the same, except that the CRT variant stores extra information about the key to speed up computation.

java.security.KeyPairGenerator

Public and private keys are always generated together. KeyPairGenerator provides the means of generating key pairs from scratch. It's the asymmetric equivalent of KeyGenerator. Once a KeyPairGenerator is initialized, you can create a key pair by calling genKeyPair() on it. Repeated calls to this method will return a new key pair each time.

Before we get started using asymmetric encryption, we need to describe how asymmetric encryption is usually used: in session-key encryption.

Session-key Encryption

The greatest value in using asymmetric encryption is, oddly enough, in encrypting symmetric keys. Asymmetric encryption is slow, as much as 1000 times slower than symmetric. To make up for this inefficiency, session-key encryption is typically used. The message is encrypted with a symmetric key, and then the symmetric key is encrypted with the recipient's public key. Then the encrypted symmetric key is attached to the encrypted message, as in the following illustration from Chapter 2:

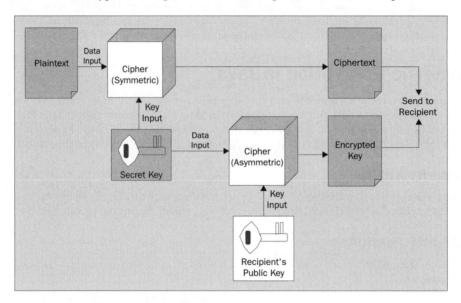

The user keeps their public-private key pair for a long time – usually a year or so. Each message sent to them is encrypted with a new symmetric key and that symmetric key is encrypted with their public key, which (as we mentioned) stays the same for an extended period of time. Since only a small amount of information is encrypted with the public key, the private key remains resistant to cryptanalysis. This also speeds up encryption, as only a small amount of data (the symmetric key) is encrypted using asymmetric encryption. The majority of the message is encrypted with a symmetric algorithm, which is much faster.

Session-Key Encryption Example

Let's take a look at some code that just encrypts and decrypts a session key with a public-private key pair. We'll use the RSA and Blowfish algorithms. Most implementations of RSA implement only one mode: ECB, and one of two forms of padding: either PKCS#1 or OAEP. Here we'll be using ECB mode and PKCS#1 padding. This should be available in any JCE implementation that has support for RSA encryption. Again we'll be using the Bouncy Castle JCE (note Sun's JCE won't work as it does not contain support for RSA encryption).

We're going to create a symmetric encryption key, create an RSA key pair, and encrypt the symmetric key with the public half of the RSA key pair. We're not actually doing anything with the symmetric key in this example besides encrypting it, as we're just illustrating how you could use RSA to encrypt a session key.

```java
import java.security.Key;
import java.security.KeyPair;
import java.security.KeyPairGenerator;
import javax.crypto.Cipher;
import javax.crypto.KeyGenerator;
import javax.crypto.SecretKey;
import javax.crypto.spec.SecretKeySpec;

// BASE 64 encoder from Sun. See Chapter 4 for notes on custom BASE64 encoders

import sun.misc.BASE64Encoder;

/**
 *  SimpleRSAExample.java
 *
 *  This is an example of using RSA to encrypt
 *  a single asymmetric key.
 */

public class SimpleRSAExample
{
   public static void main (String[] args)
                            throws Exception
   {
```

We'll start by creating the symmetric key we're going to encrypt. We'll use the Blowfish algorithm, and generate a 128-bit key:

```java
System.out.println("Generating a symmetric (Blowfish) key...");
KeyGenerator keyGenerator = KeyGenerator.getInstance("Blowfish");
keyGenerator.init(128);
Key blowfishKey = keyGenerator.generateKey();

System.out.println("Format: "+blowfishKey.getFormat());
System.out.println("Generating an RSA key...");
```

Now we generate our RSA key pair, with a size of 1024 bits:

```java
KeyPairGenerator keyPairGenerator = KeyPairGenerator.getInstance("RSA");
keyPairGenerator.initialize(1024);
KeyPair keyPair = keyPairGenerator.genKeyPair();

System.out.println("Done generating the key.");
```

Next we create a cipher using the public key to initialize it. We'll use Electronic CodeBook mode and PKCS1Padding. ECB is good for encrypting small blocks of random data, like a key. PKCS1Padding is the standard padding used in most implementations of RSA.

```java
Cipher cipher = Cipher.getInstance("RSA/ECB/PKCS1Padding");
cipher.init(Cipher.ENCRYPT_MODE, keyPair.getPublic());
```

We get the bytes of the symmetric key by calling getEncoded() on the key itself. This returns a byte array, which we will shortly encrypt using RSA:

```
byte[] blowfishKeyBytes = blowfishKey.getEncoded();
```

Now we'll encrypt those bytes with our RSA cipher:

```
byte[] cipherText = cipher.doFinal(blowfishKeyBytes);
```

Next we'll illustrate decrypting with RSA, using the private key. We can re-initialize the same cipher we used earlier for encryption, setting it to decrypt mode and passing in the private half of the key pair:

```
cipher.init(Cipher.DECRYPT_MODE, keyPair.getPrivate());

// Perform the decryption

byte[] decryptedKeyBytes = cipher.doFinal(cipherText);
```

We've got the decrypted bytes, so we can re-create the key by creating a SecretKeySpec with the decrypted key bytes and the algorithm name, "Blowfish". The SecretKeySpec class implements the Key interface, so could be used to initialize a symmetric cipher for encryption or decryption.

```
SecretKey newBlowfishKey = new SecretKeySpec(decryptedKeyBytes, "Blowfish");
    }
}
```

You can run the example after compiling with:

C:\>java SimpleRSAExample

You should see output like the following:

```
Generating a symmetric (Blowfish) key...
Format: RAW
Generating an RSA key...
Done generating the key.
```

If you get an exception, it's likely that your JCE provider is installed incorrectly. Check Chapter 3 for information on troubleshooting your provider.

Now that we've gone through a simple example, let's move on to something a little more useful: a short application that encrypts and decrypts files.

FileEncryptor with RSA

Now we're going to write a Java class that encrypts and decrypts files with RSA public and private keys, using an AES session key to encrypt the file itself. This is almost identical to the CipherStream example, using the FileEncryptor code, which we saw in the previous chapter, but this one will use asymmetric encryption to store the symmetric key inside the file, using a different symmetric key for each file. This enhances security by limiting the amount of ciphertext created with any one key. It also adds the ability to encrypt files with someone's public key, without needing to know their private key. This might be useful if you need to send files to someone; they could give you their public key, allowing you to encrypt files and send them.

`FileEncryptorRSA` will offer three functions:

- ❏ Create an RSA key pair
- ❏ Encrypt a file with a public key
- ❏ Decrypt a file with a private key

Let's look at each one in detail.

Creating an RSA Key Pair

This is a fairly simple operation. We want to create an RSA key pair, and then save the two halves, public and private, to the filesystem.

The public key is safe to expose to anyone, so we'll just write it directly to the filesystem unencrypted. You should set file permissions though so that no one can modify it. Unfortunately there's no way to do that in Java in a platform-independent manner, so we'll have to leave it up to the user. If you're using UNIX, you could use the command chmod 544 keyFilename. If using Windows, you can right-click on the file and set permissions so that only the owner can modify the file.

The private key, on the other hand, needs to be kept secret. So we're going to password-encrypt it before writing it to the filesystem, just like we did in the `FileEncryptor` in the previous chapter.

Here's the beginning of `FileEncryptorRSA.java`, up to the key generation. Much of this code we'll be going over is repeated from the `FileEncryptor` class in the last chapter. Important changes have been highlighted:

```
import java.security.*;
import java.security.spec.*;
import javax.crypto.*;
import javax.crypto.spec.*;
import java.io.*;
import java.util.*;

/**
 *  FileEncryptorRSA.java
 *
 *  This class encrypts and decrypts a file using CipherStreams
 *  and a 256-bit Rijndael key. The key is then encrypted using
 *  a 1024-bit RSA key, which is password-encrypted.
 */

public class FileEncryptorRSA {

/**
 *  When files are encrypted, this will be appended to the end
 *  of the filename.
 */

private static final String ENCRYPTED_FILENAME_SUFFIX=".encrypted";

/**
 *  When files are decrypted, this will be appended to the end
 *  of the filename.
 */
```

```
private static final String DECRYPTED_FILENAME_SUFFIX=".decrypted";

/**
 * Number of times the password will be hashed with MD5
 * when transforming it into a DESede (TripleDES) key.
 */

private static final int ITERATIONS = 1000;

/**
 * FileEncryptor is started with one of three options:
 *
 * -c:  create key pair and write it to 2 files
 * -e:  encrypt a file, given as an argument
 * -d:  decrypt a file, given as an argument
 */
public static void main (String[] args) throws Exception {
  if ((args.length < 1) || (args.length > 2)) {
    usage();
  } else if ("-c".equals(args[0])) {
    createKey();
  } else if ("-e".equals(args[0])) {
    encrypt(args[1]);
  } else if ("-d".equals(args[0])) {
    decrypt(args[1]);
  } else {
    usage();
  }
}

private static void usage() {
  System.err.println("Usage: java FileEncryptor -c|-e|-d [filename]");
  System.exit(1);
}
```

Our createKey() method will create an RSA key pair rather than a Rijndael key and store it as two files, one for the private, one for the public half of the key.

```
private static void createKey() throws Exception {
  BufferedReader in = new BufferedReader(new InputStreamReader(System.in));
  System.out.print("Password to encrypt the private key: ");
  String password = in.readLine();
  System.out.println("Generating an RSA keypair...");
```

We generate the RSA key pair using a KeyPairGenerator:

```
KeyPairGenerator keyPairGenerator = KeyPairGenerator.getInstance("RSA");
keyPairGenerator.initialize(1024);
KeyPair keyPair = keyPairGenerator.genKeyPair();

System.out.println("Done generating the keypair.\n");
```

We'll prompt the user for a filename to use to store the public key, and then store the bytes of the public key that we get by calling `getEncoded()` on the public half of the key.

```
System.out.print("Public key filename: ");
String publicKeyFilename = in.readLine();

// Get the encoded form of the public key so we can
// use it again in the future. This is X.509 by default.

byte[] publicKeyBytes = keyPair.getPublic().getEncoded();

// Write the encoded public key out to the filesystem

FileOutputStream fos = new FileOutputStream(publicKeyFilename);
fos.write(publicKeyBytes);
fos.close();
```

Now we want to write the private key out to a file, but this time we want to encrypt it.

```
System.out.print("Private key filename: ");
String privateKeyFilename = in.readLine();

// Get the encoded form. This is PKCS#8 by default.

byte[] privateKeyBytes = keyPair.getPrivate().getEncoded();
```

We'll encrypt the bytes of the private key with a `passwordEncrypt()` method, which we'll write shortly.

```
byte[] encryptedPrivateKeyBytes =
   passwordEncrypt(password.toCharArray(),privateKeyBytes);

fos = new FileOutputStream(privateKeyFilename);
fos.write(encryptedPrivateKeyBytes);
fos.close();
}
```

Here's `passwordEncrypt()`. Given a password and some plaintext, it will return the appropriate ciphertext. A salt is used, and will be the first 8 bytes of the array returned. (For more information on salt, see the previous chapter.) This code is almost identical to the password-encryption section of the `createKey()` method in last chapter's file encryptor example, but we have moved it into its own method here.

```
/**
 * Utility method to encrypt a byte array with a given password.
 * Salt will be the first 8 bytes of the byte array returned.
 */

private static byte[] passwordEncrypt(char[] password, byte[] plaintext)
                                  throws Exception {

   // Create the salt.
```

```
        byte[] salt = new byte[8];
        Random random = new Random();
        random.nextBytes(salt);

        // Create a PBE key and cipher.

        PBEKeySpec keySpec = new PBEKeySpec(password);
        SecretKeyFactory keyFactory =
          SecretKeyFactory.getInstance("PBEWithSHAAndTwofish-CBC");
        SecretKey key = keyFactory.generateSecret(keySpec);
        PBEParameterSpec paramSpec = new PBEParameterSpec(salt, ITERATIONS);
        Cipher cipher = Cipher.getInstance("PBEWithSHAAndTwofish-CBC");
        cipher.init(Cipher.ENCRYPT_MODE, key, paramSpec);

        // Encrypt the array

        byte[] ciphertext = cipher.doFinal(plaintext);

        // Write out the salt, then the ciphertext and return it.

        ByteArrayOutputStream baos = new ByteArrayOutputStream();
        baos.write(salt);
        baos.write(ciphertext);
        return baos.toByteArray();
    }
```

In order to continue this application, we need to first go over how we're going to encrypt a file with our public key.

Encrypt a File with a Public Key

When we encrypt a file, we need to read in the public key from a file and instantiate it. To do the same thing with a symmetric key, we used the class javax.crypto.SecretKeySpec. It isn't quite as easy as with public and private keys. Symmetric keys are encoded by simply spitting out the random data bytes that they are composed of. Asymmetric keys have a more complicated composition, and their encoding contains meta-information that is used to re-instantiate them. Exactly what a key encoding contains isn't terribly important to us, as Java provides us with classes for encoding and decoding keys transparently.

Encoding and Decoding RSA Keys

Public keys are encoded using X.509, which is a public specification for the transfer of public keys and certificates. Private keys are encoded using PKCS#8, which is a standard simply for encoding private keys. When you call getEncoded() on either a public or a private key, it automatically encodes it using the appropriate encoding mechanism.

To decode a key, you need to create an encoded key spec object and use a KeyFactory to instantiate an instance of the appropriate key type.

Given a byte array representing the encoded form of a public key, you create an X509EncodedKeySpec object from the bytes and use a KeyFactory to get the key:

```
X509EncodedKeySpec keySpec = new X509EncodedKeySpec(keyBytes);
KeyFactory keyFactory = KeyFactory.getInstance("RSA");
PublicKey publicKey = keyFactory.generatePublic(keySpec);
```

Decoding a private key is almost the same, but you use `PKCS8EncodedKeySpec` rather than `X509EncodedKeySpec`:

```
PKCS8EncodedKeySpec keySpec = new PKCS8EncodedKeySpec(keyBytes);
KeyFactory keyFactory = KeyFactory.getInstance("RSA");
PrivateKey privateKey = keyFactory.generatePrivate(keySpec);
```

Encrypted File Format

We're going to be creating a different symmetric key for each file that we encrypt. We'll then store the key, encrypted with RSA, in the encrypted file itself like so:

In the previous, symmetric, `FileEncryptor`, all we needed was the initialization vector (IV). Now we need the key as well as the IV. In order to separate the key from the IV, we'll write the length of the key before the key itself.

Now we'll return to our `FileEncryptorRSA` code, and add an `encrypt()` method:

```
/**
 *  Encrypt the given file with a session key encrypted with an
 *  RSA public key, which will be read in from the filesystem.
 */

private static void encrypt(String fileInput)
                            throws Exception {

  BufferedReader in = new BufferedReader
  (new InputStreamReader(System.in));
  System.out.print("Public Key to encrypt with: ");
  String publicKeyFilename = in.readLine();
```

We read in the bytes of the file into a byte array, `keyBytes`:

```
FileInputStream fis = new FileInputStream(publicKeyFilename);
ByteArrayOutputStream baos = new ByteArrayOutputStream();

int theByte = 0;
while ((theByte = fis.read()) != -1)
{
  baos.write(theByte);
}
fis.close();

byte[] keyBytes = baos.toByteArray();
baos.close();
```

Now we want to turn those bytes, which represent the encoded key, into an instance of an RSA public key. We do this with the X509EncodedKeySpec class, and a KeyFactory, as we mentioned earlier in this section.

```
X509EncodedKeySpec keySpec = new X509EncodedKeySpec(keyBytes);
KeyFactory keyFactory = KeyFactory.getInstance("RSA");
PublicKey publicKey = keyFactory.generatePublic(keySpec);
```

Now we can open up the file that we'll use to write out our encrypted content:

```
String fileOutput = fileInput + ENCRYPTED_FILENAME_SUFFIX;
DataOutputStream output = new DataOutputStream
(new FileOutputStream(fileOutput));
```

Since we're using session-key encryption, we'll need two ciphers: one for RSA-encrypting the session key, and one to use the session key to encrypt the file contents.

```
Cipher rsaCipher = Cipher.getInstance("RSA/ECB/PKCS1Padding");
rsaCipher.init(Cipher.ENCRYPT_MODE, publicKey);

// Now create a new 256 bit Rijndael key to encrypt the file itself.
// This will be the session key.

KeyGenerator rijndaelKeyGenerator = KeyGenerator.getInstance("Rijndael");
rijndaelKeyGenerator.init(256);
System.out.println("Generating session key...");
Key rijndaelKey = rijndaelKeyGenerator.generateKey();
System.out.println("Done generating key.");
```

We'll use the RSA cipher to encrypt the bytes of the symmetric key and write those bytes to the file:

```
byte[] encodedKeyBytes= rsaCipher.doFinal(rijndaelKey.getEncoded());
output.writeInt(encodedKeyBytes.length);
output.write(encodedKeyBytes);
```

We need an initialization vector to use our symmetric cipher in CBC mode. Rijndael uses a 16-byte IV.

```
SecureRandom random = new SecureRandom();
byte[] iv = new byte[16];
random.nextBytes(iv);

// Write the IV out to the file.

output.write(iv);
IvParameterSpec spec = new IvParameterSpec(iv);
```

Now we can actually encrypt the file data and write it out:

```
Cipher symmetricCipher = Cipher.getInstance("Rijndael/CBC/PKCS5Padding");
symmetricCipher.init(Cipher.ENCRYPT_MODE, rijndaelKey, spec);

CipherOutputStream cos = new CipherOutputStream(output, symmetricCipher);

System.out.println("Encrypting the file...");
```

```
      FileInputStream input = new FileInputStream(fileInput);

      theByte = 0;
      while ((theByte = input.read()) != -1)
      {
        cos.write(theByte);
      }
      input.close();
      cos.close();
      System.out.println("File encrypted.");
      return;
}
```

We're still not quite finished, as we need to write a decrypt() method. First, however, we'll discuss two of the classes we use in this example, which are not strictly crypto-related, but are quite useful: ByteArrayInputStream and ByteArrayOutputStream.

ByteArrayInputStream and ByteArrayOutputStream

Since the JCE operates almost entirely on byte arrays, we'll need the ability to manipulate those arrays effectively. Two of the most useful classes are java.io.ByteArrayInputStream and java.io.ByteArrayOutputStream. These allow us to read and write large arrays of bytes easily.

ByteArrayInputStream is a wrapper around a byte array. The constructor requires a byte array to create it. Once created, we can use the ByteArrayInputStream just like any other InputStream. An obvious use for the ByteArrayInputStream is to concatenate several byte arrays. We do just that in the passwordDecrypt() method of FileEncryptor.

ByteArrayOutputStream serves, not surprisingly, the opposite purpose to ByteArrayInputStream. We write bytes to it, and when we're finished, call to ByteArray() to get the actual byte array. This is useful for reading in a byte array from a file when we don't know the size of the array.

Decrypt a File with a Private Key

The last feature we want to add to our application is the ability to decrypt files that we've encrypted. In order to do this, we need to decrypt the symmetric key embedded into the file, and in order to do that, we need to decrypt the private RSA key, which is stored in a different file. Don't worry if this isn't perfectly clear right now, because we'll go over an example with a diagram shortly.

The RSA private key was encrypted with a password when the key was created. The key is just an array of bytes, so we'll write a passwordDecrypt() method that will decrypt those bytes with a given password. We'll need to use the salt, which was stored as the first 8 bytes of the file. This code is very similar to the key decryption in our FileEncryptor in the last chapter.

Note that our password-encryption uses 8 bytes of salt, but our symmetric file encryption (Rijndael) uses a 16-byte salt.

```
private static byte[] passwordDecrypt(char[] password, byte[] ciphertext)
                                 throws Exception {

    // Read in the salt.
```

```
    byte[] salt = new byte[8];
    ByteArrayInputStream bais = new ByteArrayInputStream(ciphertext);
    bais.read(salt,0,8);

    // The remaining bytes are the actual ciphertext.

    byte[] remainingCiphertext = new byte[ciphertext.length-8];
    bais.read(remainingCiphertext,0,ciphertext.length-8);

    // Create a PBE cipher to decrypt the byte array.

    PBEKeySpec keySpec = new PBEKeySpec(password);
    SecretKeyFactory keyFactory =
      SecretKeyFactory.getInstance("PBEWithSHAAndTwofish-CBC");
    SecretKey key = keyFactory.generateSecret(keySpec);
    PBEParameterSpec paramSpec = new PBEParameterSpec(salt, ITERATIONS);
    Cipher cipher = Cipher.getInstance("PBEWithSHAAndTwofish-CBC");

    // Perform the actual decryption.

    cipher.init(Cipher.DECRYPT_MODE, key, paramSpec);
    return cipher.doFinal(remainingCiphertext);
}
```

The first 8 bytes of the data passed in is the salt, just as we wrote it out in the `passwordEncrypt()` method earlier. Once we have that salt, we use it along with the password to initialize a cipher using password-based encryption.

Once we've got the private key, we can work on decrypting the session key embedded in the file we're trying to decrypt. The first chunk of the file is the length of the key, and the second chunk is the key itself. We'll read those in and decrypt them using our private RSA key.

After decrypting the session key, we need the IV to initialize a cipher. That's the next 16 bytes of the file. We read those in and create a cipher.

Here's a diagram detailing decryption:

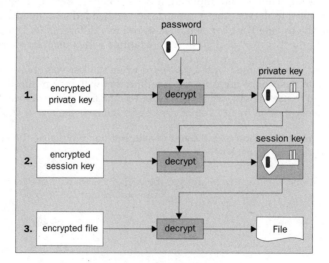

Now we just read in the remaining bytes of the file and decrypt them using that session key.

Our `decrypt()` method will load an RSA private key, and decrypt the session key that we've stored at the beginning of our encrypted file. We'll then use that session key to decrypt the remainder of the file.

```
private static void decrypt(String fileInput)
throws Exception {

  BufferedReader in = new BufferedReader(new InputStreamReader(System.in));
  System.out.print("Private Key to decrypt with: ");
  String privateKeyFilename = in.readLine();

  System.out.print("Password for the private key: ");
  String password = in.readLine();
```

Now we need to load the private key from the file system. We start by simply loading in the bytes of the file, which are encrypted.

```
FileInputStream fis = new FileInputStream(privateKeyFilename);
ByteArrayOutputStream baos = new ByteArrayOutputStream();

int theByte = 0;
while ((theByte = fis.read()) != -1)
{
  baos.write(theByte);
}
fis.close();

byte[] keyBytes = baos.toByteArray();
baos.close();
```

Now we decrypt the encrypted key bytes using the password the user entered:

```
keyBytes = passwordDecrypt(password.toCharArray(), keyBytes);
```

Now that we've got the bytes to the key, we need to create an instance of an RSA private key. As you may remember, private keys are stored in PKCS#8 format, so we need to use the class PKCS8EncodedKeySpec to create our private key.

```
PKCS8EncodedKeySpec keySpec = new PKCS8EncodedKeySpec(keyBytes);
KeyFactory keyFactory = KeyFactory.getInstance("RSA");
PrivateKey privateKey = keyFactory.generatePrivate(keySpec);
```

We'll create a cipher using the private key, which we'll use to decrypt the session key.

```
Cipher rsaCipher = Cipher.getInstance("RSA/ECB/PKCS1Padding");
```

We'll read in the encrypted bytes of the session key from our encrypted file.

```
DataInputStream dis = new DataInputStream(new FileInputStream(fileInput));
byte[] encryptedKeyBytes = new byte[dis.readInt()];
dis.readFully(encryptedKeyBytes);
```

Now we decrypt those bytes using our RSA cipher:

```
rsaCipher.init(Cipher.DECRYPT_MODE, privateKey);
byte[] rijndaelKeyBytes = rsaCipher.doFinal(encryptedKeyBytes);
```

Using the `SecretKeySpec` class, we can transform the decrypted session key bytes into a `SecretKey`.

```
SecretKey rijndaelKey = new SecretKeySpec(rijndaelKeyBytes, "Rijndael");
```

To decrypt the contents of the file, we need our original initialization vector, which we stored as the next 16 bytes in the file. This is identical to how we decrypted the file with our `FileEncryptor` from the previous chapter.

```
byte[] iv = new byte[16];
dis.read(iv);
IvParameterSpec spec = new IvParameterSpec(iv);

Cipher cipher = Cipher.getInstance("Rijndael/CBC/PKCS5Padding");
cipher.init(Cipher.DECRYPT_MODE, rijndaelKey, spec);
CipherInputStream cis = new CipherInputStream(dis, cipher);

System.out.println("Decrypting the file...");
FileOutputStream fos = new FileOutputStream(fileInput +
DECRYPTED_FILENAME_SUFFIX);

// Read through the file, decrypting each byte.

theByte = 0;
while ((theByte = cis.read()) != -1)
{
  fos.write(theByte);
}
cis.close();
fos.close();
System.out.println("Done.");
return;
}
```

Let's try running the example.

Our application has three functions:

1. Creating a key pair

2. Encrypting a file

3. Decrypting a file.

Each of these options is accessed by specifying a switch to the application:

❑   `-c` to create a key pair

❑   `-e` to encrypt

❑   `-d` to decrypt

After compiling the application, we want to create our RSA key pair:

```
C:\> java FileEncryptorRSA -c
```

The application will ask you for a password to encrypt the private key. Pick a good one that no one is likely to guess, as it will be protecting your private key. If anyone gets access to that key, they could decrypt encrypted data sent to you.

> *Remember, if you have any trouble compiling, or running the application, Chapter 3 has a JCE troubleshooting section.*

Once a password has been chosen, an RSA key pair will be generated. This can take some time – approximately 10-15 seconds on a 266 MHz Pentium II. When the keys have been created, you will be asked for a filename for the public key and then a filename for the private key.

If no exceptions are thrown, the keys have been created. If you like, you can look at them with any editor that can view hex.

To encrypt a file, we need access to two things: the file to be encrypted and a public key. Create a file test.txt and put some data in it. It doesn't really matter what kind of data you put in: text, binary, or anything else will be fine. Once it's created, you can encrypt that file with:

```
C:\> java FileEncryptorRSA -e test.txt
```

You will be prompted for the filename of the public key. Enter the one that you provided in the key creation step earlier. The application will now generate a 256-bit AES key. Again this takes a while (about 5-10 seconds on a 266 MHz Pentium II).

Now the applicaton will encrypt the file, producing a new file with .encrypted appended to the end of the filename.

To decrypt the file, we need two things: the private key and the password it was encrypted with. Let's decrypt:

```
C:\> java FileEncryptorRSA -d test.txt.encrypted
```

You will be asked for the private key filename and the password for that private key. That key is then used to decrypt the session key embedded in the encrypted file, which is then used to decrypt the file. The new file will be called test.txt.encrypted.decrypted, and should be identical to the original test.txt.

Why You Should Use Session-Key Encryption

When people are first introduced to session-key encryption, the first question they always have is, "Is it really necessary to use all those keys? Can't we just encrypt the file with RSA and be done with it?" Technically, yes, we *could* encrypt the entire file with an RSA public key and then decrypt it with the private key. But we really shouldn't, for three reasons:

1. When storing the private key, we really need to encrypt it, in case anyone manages to get into our filesystem. By encrypting it with a good password, we provide an extra layer of protection around our private key. Also, keep in mind that if our private key is compromised, every single message encrypted with its corresponding public key is compromised as well.

2. The use of a session key speeds up the process greatly. As we've said before, symmetric cryptography can be orders of magnitude faster than asymmetric.

3. It's more secure. RSA has some weaknesses that can be exploited with certain messages. Symmetric keys, which appear to be random data, do not expose any of these weaknesses. If we were to encrypt large chunks of predictable data, like text files, with RSA directly, we might be at greater risk of having our plaintext recovered from the ciphertext.

In short, session key encryption is the right way to use public-key encryption. It's faster and it's more secure. Now that we've covered asymmetric encryption, we're going to talk about another cryptographic technology using public-private key pairs to share encrypted information: key agreement.

Key Agreement

In addition to asymmetric encryption, there is an alternative way to exchange secret data over an insecure channel. A key agreement provides a method to create a shared secret key by exchanging only public keys. Diffie-Hellman is the standard algorithm for performing a key agreement. There are no others in common use. Key agreement is not used as commonly as asymmetric encryption, like RSA, but it is used in some protocols and applications, such as alternative forms of PGP and SSL.

To explain how a key agreement works, we'll return to our Hamlet examples and imagine Claudius and the King of England attempting to exchange a secret message. There is a diagram on the next page that should help elucidate how Diffie-Hellman works. Let's walk through it step-by-step:

❑ Claudius sends the King of England Claudius' public key.

❑ The King sends Claudius the King's public key.

❑ Claudius performs a key agreement using his private key and the King's public key and creates a shared secret, which can be transformed into a session key. You can see this illustrated in the top half of the diagram.

❑ The King performs a key agreement as well, using his private key and Claudius' public key. The resulting shared secret is exactly the same as the one that Claudius came up with. This half of the exchange takes place in the bottom half of the diagram.

Now the King and Claudius could use a symmetric algorithm like Blowfish to encrypt messages to each other.

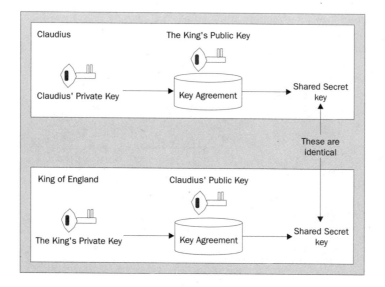

Key Agreement in Java

Key agreement in Java uses one new class that we haven't yet talked about: `javax.crypto.KeyAgreement`. A `KeyAgreement` object is created with a call to `KeyAgreement.getInstance()`, with the name of the algorithm passed in (DH for Diffie-Hellman).

Once we have a `KeyAgreement` object, we can initialize it with our private Diffie-Hellman key. These keys are very similar to the RSA keys we've been dealing with: they are stored as a `KeyPair` object, which contains a `PrivateKey` and a `PublicKey`. We use the private key to initialize the key agreement object by calling `init()` on that `KeyAgreement`.

Once the key agreement is initialized, other people's public keys are passed in with the `doPhase()` method, which takes a public key and a `Boolean`, `lastPhase`, that indicates whether we are finished passing in keys or not. Diffie-Hellman allows any number of public keys to be added to perform a key agreement.

Once all the keys have been passed in with `doPhase()`, a call to `generateSecret()` will perform the actual key agreement and return a byte array that is the shared secret. That shared secret can then be used to create a session key and encrypt communication to the other party.

In the next section, we're going to write an example of using Diffie-Hellman to secure communication in a chat application.

Using Diffie-Hellman

A chat application is an ideal example to illustrate key agreements, because both clients are active simultaneously, allowing for easy key exchange. This won't be a full-fledged chat implementation, because we don't want to obfuscate the important issue, which is creating the shared secret key and encrypting and decrypting data with it.

Our chat application will be one-sided. That is, there will be a client that sends messages and a server that receives them. Everything sent from the client will be encrypted. We'll use 1024-bit DH and 168-bit DESede (TripleDES).

Here is a diagram of how the communication between client and server will be handled:

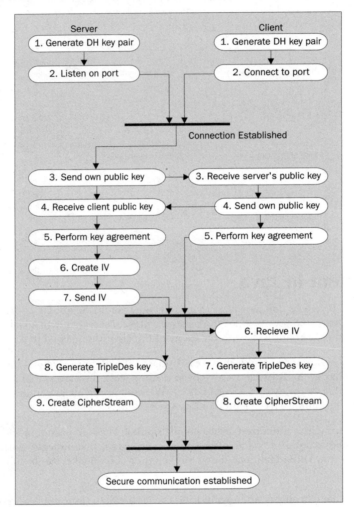

Note that the communication takes place synchronously, with some work being done by server and client separately in-between communication.

In order to perform a key agreement, both client and server must have Diffie-Hellman key pairs so that they can exchange public keys. Those public keys must have some matching information – namely the modulus and base used to create those keys. There is a standard for that modulus and base, known as **SKIP** (the **Simple Key management for Internet Protocols**).

SKIP has established values for 512, 1024, and 2048-bit keys. We're going to use 1024-bit DH keys, so we'll use the 1024-bit SKIP spec. It's not important to know anything about SKIP besides the fact that it defines a way for Diffie-Hellman parameters to match. We'll highlight the use of SKIP in the code when we get to it.

Let's start writing the code. We'll have two classes: `KeyAgreementServer` for the server and `KeyAgreementClient` for the client. We'll begin with the server.

The Server

Let's start by taking a look at the actual code for the server. We'll start by defining a static variable that defines the bytes for our SKIP modulus. If you use Diffie-Hellman in your own applications, you can just copy out this static block and use it.

```java
import java.io.*;
import java.net.*;
import java.math.*;
import java.security.*;
import java.security.spec.*;
import javax.crypto.*;
import javax.crypto.spec.*;
import javax.crypto.interfaces.*;

public class KeyAgreementServer {

  private static final byte SKIP_1024_MODULUS_BYTES[] = {
    (byte)0xF4,   (byte)0x88,   (byte)0xFD,   (byte)0x58,
    (byte)0x4E,   (byte)0x49,   (byte)0xDB,   (byte)0xCD,
    (byte)0x20,   (byte)0xB4,   (byte)0x9D,   (byte)0xE4,
    (byte)0x91,   (byte)0x07,   (byte)0x36,   (byte)0x6B,
    (byte)0x33,   (byte)0x6C,   (byte)0x38,   (byte)0x0D,
    (byte)0x45,   (byte)0x1D,   (byte)0x0F,   (byte)0x7C,
    (byte)0x88,   (byte)0xB3,   (byte)0x1C,   (byte)0x7C,
    (byte)0x5B,   (byte)0x2D,   (byte)0x8E,   (byte)0xF6,
    (byte)0xF3,   (byte)0xC9,   (byte)0x23,   (byte)0xC0,
    (byte)0x43,   (byte)0xF0,   (byte)0xA5,   (byte)0x5B,
    (byte)0x18,   (byte)0x8D,   (byte)0x8E,   (byte)0xBB,
    (byte)0x55,   (byte)0x8C,   (byte)0xB8,   (byte)0x5D,
    (byte)0x38,   (byte)0xD3,   (byte)0x34,   (byte)0xFD,
    (byte)0x7C,   (byte)0x17,   (byte)0x57,   (byte)0x43,
    (byte)0xA3,   (byte)0x1D,   (byte)0x18,   (byte)0x6C,
    (byte)0xDE,   (byte)0x33,   (byte)0x21,   (byte)0x2C,
    (byte)0xB5,   (byte)0x2A,   (byte)0xFF,   (byte)0x3C,
    (byte)0xE1,   (byte)0xB1,   (byte)0x29,   (byte)0x40,
    (byte)0x18,   (byte)0x11,   (byte)0x8D,   (byte)0x7C,
    (byte)0x84,   (byte)0xA7,   (byte)0x0A,   (byte)0x72,
    (byte)0xD6,   (byte)0x86,   (byte)0xC4,   (byte)0x03,
    (byte)0x19,   (byte)0xC8,   (byte)0x07,   (byte)0x29,
    (byte)0x7A,   (byte)0xCA,   (byte)0x95,   (byte)0x0C,
    (byte)0xD9,   (byte)0x96,   (byte)0x9F,   (byte)0xAB,
    (byte)0xD0,   (byte)0x0A,   (byte)0x50,   (byte)0x9B,
    (byte)0x02,   (byte)0x46,   (byte)0xD3,   (byte)0x08,
    (byte)0x3D,   (byte)0x66,   (byte)0xA4,   (byte)0x5D,
    (byte)0x41,   (byte)0x9F,   (byte)0x9C,   (byte)0x7C,
    (byte)0xBD,   (byte)0x89,   (byte)0x4B,   (byte)0x22,
    (byte)0x19,   (byte)0x26,   (byte)0xBA,   (byte)0xAB,
    (byte)0xA2,   (byte)0x5E,   (byte)0xC3,   (byte)0x55,
    (byte)0xE9,   (byte)0x2F,   (byte)0x78,   (byte)0xC7
  };
```

In order to use SKIP, we need a `BigInteger` representation of that modulus:

```
private static final BigInteger MODULUS = new BigInteger
                                  (1,SKIP_1024_MODULUS_BYTES);
```

We also need a base for Diffie-Hellman, which SKIP defines as 2:

```
private static final BigInteger BASE = BigInteger.valueOf(2);
```

Now we can wrap those two SKIP parameters into one `DHParamaterSpec`, which we'll use to initialize our `KeyAgreement` later.

```
private static final DHParameterSpec PARAMETER_SPEC =
                             new DHParameterSpec(MODULUS,BASE);
```

Now let's get into the actual code. We begin by initializing a key pair generator with the SKIP parameters we specified, and generating a key pair. This corresponds to step 1 on the server side of the diagram.

```
public static void main (String[] args) throws Exception {

  if (args.length != 1) {
    System.err.println("Usage: java KeyAgreementServer port");
    System.exit(1);
  }

   int port = Integer.parseInt(args[0]);

  // Create a public key pair.
  // This will take a while: 5-15 seconds.

  System.out.println("Generating a Diffie-Hellman KeyPair...");
  KeyPairGenerator kpg = KeyPairGenerator.getInstance("DH");
  kpg.initialize(PARAMETER_SPEC);
  KeyPair keyPair = kpg.genKeyPair();
```

Once the key pair has been generated, we want to listen on a given port for a connection to come in. Once we get a connection, we'll get two streams: one for input, one for output. This is step 2 in the diagram.

```
// Open a port and wait for a connection

  ServerSocket ss = new ServerSocket (port);
  System.out.println("Listening on port "+port+"...");
  Socket socket = ss.accept();
  DataOutputStream out = new DataOutputStream(socket.getOutputStream());
```

Now, looking at the diagram we've presented, the next thing to do is send our public key and receive the client's. This corresponds to server steps 3 and 4 in the diagram.

```
System.out.println("Sending my public key.");
    byte[] keyBytes = keyPair.getPublic().getEncoded();
    out.writeInt(keyBytes.length);
    out.write(keyBytes);

    // Receive the client's public key

    System.out.println("Receiving client's public key...");
    DataInputStream in = new DataInputStream(socket.getInputStream());
    keyBytes = new byte[in.readInt()];
    in.readFully(keyBytes);
    KeyFactory kf = KeyFactory.getInstance("DH");
    X509EncodedKeySpec x509Spec = new X509EncodedKeySpec(keyBytes);
    PublicKey clientPublicKey = kf.generatePublic(x509Spec);
```

We can now use the client's public key and our own private key to perform the key agreement as shown in step 5.

```
System.out.println("Performing the KeyAgreement...");
    KeyAgreement ka = KeyAgreement.getInstance("DH");
    ka.init(keyPair.getPrivate());
    ka.doPhase(clientPublicKey,true);
```

In a chat application, each character is sent over the wire, separately encrypted. Because of this, we don't want to use ECB mode, where a character gets encrypted the same way every time. If every 'e' became the value 197, it would be easy for an eavesdropper to see a pattern after a short while, just by analyzing the frequency with which certain codes came up. Instead of using ECB then, we're going to use CFB, with a block size of 8 bits (1 byte) to send each character. CFB will encrypt the same character in a different way each time. But in order to use CFB8, we need an initialization vector of 8 bytes. We'll create that IV randomly and send it to the client, who will need to know the value in order to initialize its own cipher in CFB8 mode. It doesn't matter if someone eavesdrops on the IV when it's sent over the wire. It's not sensitive information.

Creating the IV and sending it corresponds to steps 6 and 7.

```
byte[] iv = new byte[8];
    SecureRandom sr = new SecureRandom();
    sr.nextBytes(iv);
    out.write(iv);
```

Next we actually generate the secret byte array we share with the client and use it to create the session key (step 8).

```
byte[] sessionKeyBytes = ka.generateSecret();

    // Create the session key

    SecretKeyFactory skf = SecretKeyFactory.getInstance("DESede");
    DESedeKeySpec DESedeSpec = new DESedeKeySpec(sessionKeyBytes);
    SecretKey sessionKey = skf.generateSecret(DESedeSpec);
```

Now we use that session key and the IV we created earlier to create a `CipherInputStream`. We'll then use it to read all the characters that are sent to us by the client (step 9).

```
System.out.println("Creating the CipherStream...");
Cipher decrypter = Cipher.getInstance("DESede/CFB8/NoPadding");
IvParameterSpec spec = new IvParameterSpec(iv);
decrypter.init(Cipher.DECRYPT_MODE, sessionKey, spec);
CipherInputStream cipherIn = new CipherInputStream(socket.getInputStream(),
                              decrypter);
```

Now we just keep reading the input and printing it to the screen, until a −1 is sent over the wire, signaling the end of transmission.

```
int theCharacter=0;
theCharacter = cipherIn.read();
while (theCharacter != -1) {
   System.out.print((char)theCharacter);
   theCharacter = cipherIn.read();
}
```

Once the −1 is received, we want to close up our streams and exit.

```
cipherIn.close();
in.close();
out.close();
socket.close();
   }
}
```

Now that we've covered the server, let's move on to the client.

The Client

The client is nearly identical to the server, with two small exceptions: it receives the IV rather than generating and sending it. It also sends characters through a `CipherOutputStream`, rather than receiving them through a `CipherInputStream`.

```
import java.io.*;
import java.net.*;
import java.math.*;
import java.security.*;
import java.security.spec.*;
import javax.crypto.*;
import javax.crypto.spec.*;

public class KeyAgreementClient {
```

Once again, we start with the SKIP modulus and base so our keys will agree. This is the same as the server code.

```
    private static final byte SKIP_1024_MODULUS_BYTES[] = {
      (byte) 0xF4,  (byte) 0x88,  (byte) 0xFD,  (byte) 0x58,
      (byte) 0x4E,  (byte) 0x49,  (byte) 0xDB,  (byte) 0xCD,
      (byte) 0x20,  (byte) 0xB4,  (byte) 0x9D,  (byte) 0xE4,
      (byte) 0x91,  (byte) 0x07,  (byte) 0x36,  (byte) 0x6B,
      (byte) 0x33,  (byte) 0x6C,  (byte) 0x38,  (byte) 0x0D,
      (byte) 0x45,  (byte) 0x1D,  (byte) 0x0F,  (byte) 0x7C,
      (byte) 0x88,  (byte) 0xB3,  (byte) 0x1C,  (byte) 0x7C,
      (byte) 0x5B,  (byte) 0x2D,  (byte) 0x8E,  (byte) 0xF6,
      (byte) 0xF3,  (byte) 0xC9,  (byte) 0x23,  (byte) 0xC0,
      (byte) 0x43,  (byte) 0xF0,  (byte) 0xA5,  (byte) 0x5B,
      (byte) 0x18,  (byte) 0x8D,  (byte) 0x8E,  (byte) 0xBB,
      (byte) 0x55,  (byte) 0x8C,  (byte) 0xB8,  (byte) 0x5D,
      (byte) 0x38,  (byte) 0xD3,  (byte) 0x34,  (byte) 0xFD,
      (byte) 0x7C,  (byte) 0x17,  (byte) 0x57,  (byte) 0x43,
      (byte) 0xA3,  (byte) 0x1D,  (byte) 0x18,  (byte) 0x6C,
      (byte) 0xDE,  (byte) 0x33,  (byte) 0x21,  (byte) 0x2C,
      (byte) 0xB5,  (byte) 0x2A,  (byte) 0xFF,  (byte) 0x3C,
      (byte) 0xE1,  (byte) 0xB1,  (byte) 0x29,  (byte) 0x40,
      (byte) 0x18,  (byte) 0x11,  (byte) 0x8D,  (byte) 0x7C,
      (byte) 0x84,  (byte) 0xA7,  (byte) 0x0A,  (byte) 0x72,
      (byte) 0xD6,  (byte) 0x86,  (byte) 0xC4,  (byte) 0x03,
      (byte) 0x19,  (byte) 0xC8,  (byte) 0x07,  (byte) 0x29,
      (byte) 0x7A,  (byte) 0xCA,  (byte) 0x95,  (byte) 0x0C,
      (byte) 0xD9,  (byte) 0x96,  (byte) 0x9F,  (byte) 0xAB,
      (byte) 0xD0,  (byte) 0x0A,  (byte) 0x50,  (byte) 0x9B,
      (byte) 0x02,  (byte) 0x46,  (byte) 0xD3,  (byte) 0x08,
      (byte) 0x3D,  (byte) 0x66,  (byte) 0xA4,  (byte) 0x5D,
      (byte) 0x41,  (byte) 0x9F,  (byte) 0x9C,  (byte) 0x7C,
      (byte) 0xBD,  (byte) 0x89,  (byte) 0x4B,  (byte) 0x22,
      (byte) 0x19,  (byte) 0x26,  (byte) 0xBA,  (byte) 0xAB,
      (byte) 0xA2,  (byte) 0x5E,  (byte) 0xC3,  (byte) 0x55,
      (byte) 0xE9,  (byte) 0x2F,  (byte) 0x78,  (byte) 0xC7
    };

    private static final BigInteger MODULUS = new BigInteger
    (1, SKIP_1024_MODULUS_BYTES);

    private static final BigInteger BASE = BigInteger.valueOf(2);

    private static final DHParameterSpec PARAMETER_SPEC =
    new DHParameterSpec(MODULUS, BASE);
```

Now we get into the application itself. We start by generating a key pair, corresponding to the client-side step 1 of the diagram.

```
public static void main (String[] args) throws Exception {

   if (args.length != 2) {
     System.err.println("Usage: java KeyAgreementClient host port");
     System.exit(1);
   }

   String host = args[0];
   int port = Integer.parseInt(args[1]);
```

```
        // Generate a key pair

        System.out.println("Generating a Diffie-Hellman key pair...");
        KeyPairGenerator kpg = KeyPairGenerator.getInstance("DH");
        kpg.initialize(PARAMETER_SPEC);
        KeyPair keyPair = kpg.generateKeyPair();
```

Next we open up a socket and connect to the server (shown in client step 2):

```
        System.out.println("Trying to connect to "+host+", port "+port+".");
        Socket s = new Socket (host,port);
        DataOutputStream out = new DataOutputStream(s.getOutputStream());
        DataInputStream in = new DataInputStream(s.getInputStream());
```

We receive the server's public key as in step 3:

```
        System.out.println("Receiving the server's public key.");
        byte[] keyBytes = new byte[in.readInt()];
        in.readFully(keyBytes);
        KeyFactory kf = KeyFactory.getInstance("DH");
        X509EncodedKeySpec x509Spec = new X509EncodedKeySpec(keyBytes);
        PublicKey serverPublicKey = kf.generatePublic(x509Spec);
```

We send our public key to complete step 4:

```
        System.out.println("Sending my public key.");
        keyBytes = keyPair.getPublic().getEncoded();
        out.writeInt(keyBytes.length);
        out.write(keyBytes);
```

We perform the actual key agreement (step 5):

```
        System.out.println("Performing the KeyAgreement...");
        KeyAgreement ka = KeyAgreement.getInstance("DH");
        ka.init(keyPair.getPrivate());
        ka.doPhase(serverPublicKey,true);
```

We need to receive the IV from the server (step 6):

```
        byte[] iv = new byte[8];
        in.readFully(iv);
```

Now we generate the DESede key from a Diffie-Hellman generated shared secret, which would be step 7:

```
        byte[] sessionKeyBytes = ka.generateSecret();

        // Create the session key

        SecretKeyFactory skf = SecretKeyFactory.getInstance("DESede");
        DESedeKeySpec DESedeSpec = new DESedeKeySpec(sessionKeyBytes);
        SecretKey sessionKey = skf.generateSecret(DESedeSpec);
```

Next we create the cipher stream that we'll be using to write to the server as shown in step 8.

```
System.out.println("Creating the CipherStream...");
Cipher encrypter = Cipher.getInstance("DESede/CFB8/NoPadding");
IvParameterSpec spec = new IvParameterSpec(iv);
encrypter.init(Cipher.ENCRYPT_MODE, sessionKey, spec);

CipherOutputStream cipherOut = new CipherOutputStream(s.getOutputStream(),
                                                      encrypter);
```

We're connected securely. We can now send data to the server, which we gather from the keyboard.

```
String testString = "Established Connection.\n\n";
byte[] byteArray = testString.getBytes();
cipherOut.write(byteArray);

System.out.println("Established Connection.\n");

// Now send everything the user types

int theCharacter=0;
theCharacter = System.in.read();
while (theCharacter != '~') // The '~' is an escape character to exit
{
  cipherOut.write(theCharacter);
  theCharacter = System.in.read();
}

// Clean up

cipherOut.close();
in.close();
out.close();
s.close();
  }
}
```

Running the Example

Compile the code and let's try running it. It can be run from two separate machines, or from the same machine. For this example, we'll run it using two virtual machines on a single box.

Begin by running the server in the first VM window:

```
C:\> java KeyAgreementServer 8001
```

That will cause the server to start up and listen on port 8001. It will take a few seconds for the key pair to be generated, so be patient. Once it's ready to go, we can start the client on the other VM with:

```
C:\> java KeyAgreementClient localhost 8001
```

The client should start up and generate its key pair. Once that's finished, it will attach to the machine named "localhost" on port 8001. The client and server will then exchange public keys and perform their key agreements. Once that's finished and you see the message, "Established Connection", you can type into the client and everything you enter will be sent to the server encrypted. Upon receiving it, the server will decrypt each character and display it on the screen.

It's interesting to fire up a packet sniffer (such as Ethereal, which can be downloaded for free from http://www.ethereal.com) and check out exactly what gets sent from client to server. Then try using a standard talk application and examine the difference.

Summary

Asymmetric encryption is extremely powerful, but limited in scope. It is normally used almost entirely for key management – data is typically encrypted with a symmetric algorithm and only that key is encrypted asymmetrically. But just by being able to encrypt that key, we now have the ability to store and send messages without needing to exchange an initial secret, as we would have with a standard symmetric algorithm.

In this chapter, we've covered asymmetric encryption and key agreements, both of which are very useful for enabling the sharing of secret information without exposing a secret in the process. We've written a couple of applications demonstrating the use of session-key encryption, and creating session keys with RSA and Diffie-Hellman.

However, asymmetric encryption does not establish the source of any data, or prove that it has not been altered in transit. For those functions, we'll have to look at message digests, digital signatures, and digital certificates, which we'll cover in the chapter.

Message Digests, Digital Signatures, and Certificates

So far when discussing cryptography, we've restricted ourselves to encryption, the process of translating messages into a secret format so that an interloper cannot read them. In this chapter we're going to talk about using cryptography for **authentication**.

Authentication is the process of validating the identity of a user or the integrity of a piece of data. As you'll discover in this chapter, there are three technologies that provide different types of authentication: **message digests**, **digital signatures**, and **certificates**. This chapter will cover a lot of ground as we discuss these three areas in detail, which will involve looking at:

❑ Using message digests in Java, password authentication for message digests and **message authentication codes** (**MAC**)

❑ How Java implements digital signatures and identity authentication

❑ Digital certificate contents, the X.509 standards and versions, digital certificates in Java, keystores, certificate chaining, and **Public Key Infrastructure** (**PKI**)

Luckily, there is a natural progression from one to the other, as digital signatures use message digests, and certificates use digital signatures. Because of this dependency, we'll begin by talking about message digests and lead into the other sections afterwards.

Message Digests

As we saw previously, a message digest is essentially a fingerprint for a piece of data. The purpose of a message digest is to provide proof that data has not been altered. For instance, when downloading a file, you may wish to know that data hasn't been lost in transit. If you have a message digest of the file computed before the download, you could compare it to a digest computed after the download. If they match, the file is unaltered.

The process of getting a message digest from some data is often referred to as **hashing**. The advantage of using a message digest over comparing it to a copy of the original data itself is size: a message digest is typically 16 or 20 bytes long, no matter how long the data itself is. Computing a message digest is simple: you pass data into a message digest algorithm, and out pops the message digest itself. You may remember this diagram from Chapter 3:

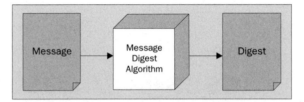

One use for message digests is in FTP file validation. Occasionally during a large file transfer an error could occur. If the server offers a message digest of the file, you could compare it to the file downloaded to make sure that no data was altered during the transfer.

Using Message Digests in Java

Java 2 provides a class that encapsulates computing a message digest: `java.security.MessageDigest`.

java.security.MessageDigest

`java.security.MessageDigest` is quite easy to use. As was the case with `Cipher`, rather than create instances with `new()`, the method `getInstance()` is used, with a string containing the algorithm required and, optionally, the provider. The two main algorithms we will use are MD5 and SHA-1, as they are the most common message digest algorithms in popular use.

Once we have a `MessageDigest` object, there are two methods that we will use to actually hash some data: `update()` and `digest()`.

update()

Data to be hashed is passed to the message digest by calling the `update()` method with a byte or an array of bytes. A very large amount of data can be hashed, up to 2^{64} bits, depending on the underlying algorithm.

digest()

`digest()` actually returns the hash in the form of a byte array. Once you've passed all of the data you want to hash to the message digest object, `digest()` will process it.

If you have a small amount of data to hash, `update()` can be skipped, and you can pass your data to be hashed to `digest()` directly, as it can optionally accept a byte array to digest.

Let's go over an example of computing a message digest for a file.

Computing a Message Digest on a File

We're going to write a simple application to take the MD5 message digest of a file and display that message digest to the screen. Then we'll change one character in the file and take a look at the resulting message digest.

```java
import java.security.MessageDigest;
import java.io.*;
import sun.misc.*;

/**
 *  DigestFile.java
 *
 *  This class creates an MD5 message digest from a file
 *  and displays it to the screen BASE64 Encoded.
 */

public class DigestFile {

  /**
   *  The only argument is the name of the file to be digested.
   */

  public static void main (String[] args) throws Exception {

    if (args.length != 1) {
      System.err.println("Usage: java DigestFile filename");
      System.exit(1);
    }

    // Create a message digest

    MessageDigest md = MessageDigest.getInstance("MD5");

    BufferedInputStream in = new BufferedInputStream(new
                             FileInputStream(args[0]));

    int theByte = 0;
    while ((theByte = in.read()) != -1)
    {
      md.update((byte)theByte);
    }
    in.close();

    byte[] theDigest = md.digest();

    System.out.println(new BASE64Encoder().encode(theDigest));
  }
}
```

There are only three lines of code that are specific to the message digest. The first one creates a `message digest` using a factory method. In this case we're asking for one implementing the MD5 algorithm:

```
MessageDigest md = MessageDigest.getInstance("MD5");
```

Once we've got the `MessageDigest` object, we need to send it the bytes that we want it to use in computing the digest. We pass these with the `update()` method, which can accept bytes either one at a time, as we're doing, or an array at a time with `update(byte[] bytearray)`. The `MessageDigest` object buffers the input and processes it on the fly, so updating a byte at a time is reasonably efficient.

Once we've passed all the data, we call `digest()` to get a byte array of the message digest. MD5 will return a 128-bit array. SHA-1 (Secure Hash Algorithm) would return a 160-bit array. We can easily convert the above program to SHA by just changing the "MD5" to "SHA" when we request a `MessageDigest` object.

Let's run the example on a file to see how using a message digest can determine if a file has been modified. Start by creating a file, say, `test.txt`. Put some text in there, such as "Hello World". Next compile the example above and run it.

```
C:\> java DigestFile test.txt
```

The output we get is "sQqNsWTgdUEFt6mb5y4/5Q==". This is a 128-bit message digest that has been BASE64-encoded for our viewing. For more information on BASE64, see Chapter 4. Now let's change one character, changing "Hello World" to "Hello World!" Our new message digest is "7Qdih1MuhjZehB6Sv8UNjA==", which is different from the first one. If you change the file back to its original state, you should get the original message digest.

Note that if you change the algorithm used, the hash produced will be different as well.

Now that we've looking at a simple example of using a message digest, let's move on to more advanced use.

Using Message Digests with Streams

The `java.security` packages contains two classes that facilitate the creation of message digests: `DigestInputStream` and `DigestOutputStream`. They are both filters around a stream that enable you to automatically get the digest of all the data passed through them. You simply construct them around an existing stream like this (assuming you have an `OutputStream` called `existingOutputStream`):

```
MessageDigest messageDigest  = MessageDigest.getInstance("SHA");
DigestOutputStream output = new
                DigestOutputStream(existingOutputStream, messageDigest);
```

Then every byte you write to output will automatically get included in the computation of the message digest. When you're done writing, just call `output.getMessageDigest()` and it will return a `MessageDigest` object. You can then call `digest()` on that and get the byte array of the digest itself.

Digest Stream Example

Let's alter our previous code, `DigestFile`, to use a digest stream. Since we're already using a `FileInputStream`, all we need to do is wrap that stream inside a `DigestInputStream`. Then we read through all the data, and our message digest will automatically be updated.

```java
import java.security.MessageDigest;
import java.security.DigestInputStream;
import java.io.*;
import sun.misc.*;

/**
 * DigestStreamExample.java
 *
 * This class creates an MD5 message digest from a file
 * and displays it to the screen BASE64 Encoded.
 */

public class DigestStreamExample {

    /**
     * The only argument is the name of the file to be digested.
     */

    public static void main (String[] args) throws Exception {

        if (args.length != 1) {
            System.err.println("Usage: java DigestStreamExample filename");
            System.exit(1);
        }

        // Create a message digest

        MessageDigest md = MessageDigest.getInstance("MD5");

        BufferedInputStream in = new BufferedInputStream(new
                                      FileInputStream(args[0]));

        // Create a DigestInputStream

        DigestInputStream digestIn = new DigestInputStream(in, md);

        // Now read all the data, which will automatically be digested

        while (digestIn.read() != -1);

        byte[] theDigest = md.digest();

        System.out.println(new BASE64Encoder().encode(theDigest));
    }
}
```

You can run the example with the same arguments you used for the last example:

```
C:\> java DigestStreamExample test.txt
```

You'll then see a BASE64-encoded message digest, just like in the previous example. The only thing we've changed is the way we're reading the data.

You may note that we're not actually doing anything with the data we're reading in. If we wanted to, we could use that data, for example write it to another file, or process it into some other format. Let's say you wrote an application that compressed data, and you wanted to add a message digest to it to ensure that the data isn't altered after compression and decompression. You could wrap a DigestInputStream around your FileInputStream before compression. Then you'd automatically get a message digest without needing to read the data twice.

Now that we've covered two different ways to compute message digests on a file, let's move on to a different use for message digests: storing and authenticating passwords.

Password Authentication

A common use for message digests is for password authentication. Since a message digest is a one-way transformation of data, it can't be converted back into the original data that was used to create the digest. We can store a hash of the pasword, and know that there's no chance of someone decrypting the stored password, as there is no way to decrypt a message digest directly. We should point out that this doesn't mean that storing your passwords as hashes makes them completely secure, but it's significantly better than storing them in the clear.

Let's say an attacker wants to discover your password, and he's been able to get a hold of your computer's password store. If your passwords are kept in the clear, he now knows your password. If they're hashed, he'll be unable to decrypt them, but will instead have to try hashing every potential password he can think of and see if the hashes match.

To make it harder for an attacker to discover your password even if he has the hashed version, you need to use salt (as we discussed in Chapter 4) to store these passwords, so that it isn't possible for an attacker to create a pre-compiled list of common passwords' message digests.

Storing passwords is different from encrypting data with a password though. We need to store the password itself, not data encrypted with it. The goal is to have a password defined that the user knows, and that a server can validate, without the server needing to actually know the password.

Password Storage

First we need to have the user pick a password, so we can check it again in the future. Then we have a three-step process as illustrated:

1. Create a new, random, salt and prepend it to the password

2. Hash the resulting data (salt and password)

3. Prepend the same salt to the hash and store the result, so that later we can use the salt to hash whatever password is entered, to determine if the passwords match

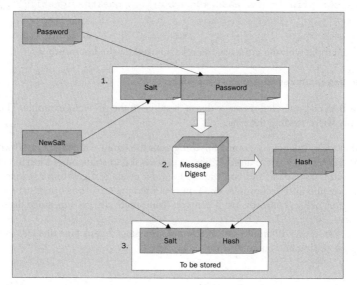

It is common to BASE64-encode the result so that it can be stored in ASCII format.

Password Authentication

Authenticating that password is similar – we need to hash the password that the user enters and compare that to the password hash on file. In order for the hashes to be equal, we need to use the same salt that we did before, which we have stored as well:

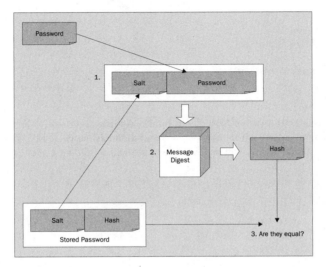

Again we can consider three distinct steps:

1. Prepend the salt from the stored password to the password that the user types in.

2. Hash that salt and password.

3. Compare the resulting hash with the one stored in the file. If they are equal, the password matches. Note that we never actually compare passwords themselves, only the hashes.

Password Storage Example

Let's write a short application that illustrates password authentication. The example will perform two functions: creation of a digest version of the password and validation of the password. Essentially, this example code performs what we've just described above for storing passwords.

We'll write a class, `PasswordAuthenticator`, that will hash and store passwords and authenticate them. By passing a –c switch to the application we'll indicate that the password is to be created, and a –a switch indicates that it should be authenticated.

```
import java.security.*;
import java.io.*;
import java.util.*;

// PasswordAuthenticator.java:

public class PasswordAuthenticator {
```

```
    public static void main (String[] args)
    throws Exception {

      if (args.length != 2) {
        System.err.println("Usage: java PasswordAuthenticator -c|-a
                           password");
        System.exit(1);
      }

      if ("-c".equals(args[0])) {
        createPassword(args[1]);
      } else {
        authenticatePassword(args[1]);
      }
    }
```

Now we'll write a `createPassword()` method. It takes a string argument, which will be the password to hash. We will prepend a 12-byte salt to the password and then hash it with MD5. Then we'll store the salt and the hash in cleartext, so that the salt will be available to use when validating later.

```
   private static void createPassword(String password)
    throws Exception {

      // Create a new salt

      SecureRandom random = new SecureRandom();
      byte[] salt = new byte[12];
      random.nextBytes(salt);
```

We now get an instance of a message digest and use it to digest the salt and password.

```
      MessageDigest md = MessageDigest.getInstance("MD5");
      md.update(salt);
      md.update(password.getBytes("UTF8"));
      byte[] digest = md.digest();
```

Next we open up a file, called password, and write the bytes of the salt and the hash of the password to it. That's really all that our `createPassword()` method does.

```
      FileOutputStream fos = new FileOutputStream("password");
      fos.write(salt);
      fos.write(digest);
      fos.close();
    }
```

Now we'll write the method that uses that stored password to check a password that the user enters. That method is `authenticatePassword()`. We begin by reading in the contents of the password file into a byte array using a `ByteArrayOutputStream`. We'll place the resulting array into `hashedPasswordWithSalt`, as the array contains both the password and the salt, with the salt being the first twelve bytes of the array.

```
  private static void authenticatePassword(String password)
throws Exception {

   // Read in the byte array from the file "password"

   ByteArrayOutputStream baos = new ByteArrayOutputStream();
   FileInputStream fis = new FileInputStream("password");
   int theByte = 0;
   while ((theByte = fis.read()) != -1)
   {
     baos.write(theByte);
   }
   fis.close();
   byte[] hashedPasswordWithSalt = baos.toByteArray();
   baos.reset();
```

The salt will be the first 12 bytes of the array we just read in, so we can copy it out into a new byte array:

```
   byte[] salt = new byte[12];
   System.arraycopy(hashedPasswordWithSalt,0,salt,0,12);
```

We now have the salt, so we can use it to hash the password the user entered:

```
   MessageDigest md = MessageDigest.getInstance("MD5");
   md.update(salt);
   md.update(password.getBytes("UTF8"));
   byte[] digest = md.digest();
```

Now we want to compare that digest with the one in the file. That's the remaining bytes that we read in.

```
   byte[] digestInFile = new byte[hashedPasswordWithSalt.length-12];
   System.arraycopy(hashedPasswordWithSalt,12,
   digestInFile,0,hashedPasswordWithSalt.length-12);
```

We have both digests, the one from the file and the one we just created, and so we can compare them. If they are equal, the passwords match. If not, then the user entered a different password.

```
   if (Arrays.equals(digest, digestInFile)) {
     System.out.println("Password matches.");
   } else {
     System.out.println("Password does not match");
   }
  }
}
```

Running the Example

You can execute the example with:

```
C:\> java PasswordAuthenticator -c [password]
```

where [password] is some password you've chosen. It will create a password file, called, appropriately enough, password, in the working directory. That file will contain the salt and the hash of the salt and password. Here's what your password file might look like if you entered "sasquatch" as your password:

```
teF•Ús
²¬†Öœ+¡o<sðÉ,»|S,ÃyXá
```

You can check a password against it with:

```
C:\>java PasswordAuthenticator -a [password]
```

This will respond with either "Password matches" or "Password does not match", depending on whether you enter the correct password or not.

The creation of the password takes a while (5 to 30 seconds), as it must initialize a SecureRandom object. Authenticating, however, is quite fast. In a real-world application, you would probably want some way to store the state of the SecureRandom so that subsequent runs would be faster.

Message Authentication Codes (MAC)

A message authentication code (MAC), is essentially a keyed message digest. This is often used for authenticating data sent over an insecure network, such as the Internet. Two parties exchange secret keys and then use them to validate the data. As a cryptographically secure digest produced with a shared key, MACs solve one of the weaknesses of using message digests in an insecure environment. If you use a message digest normally, and send the digest in the clear, you risk leaving yourself open to a man-in-the-middle attack.

We can illustrate the process of creating a message authentication code by:

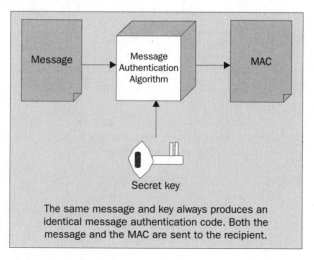

The same message and key always produces an identical message authentication code. Both the message and the MAC are sent to the recipient.

The verification process is quite straightforward:

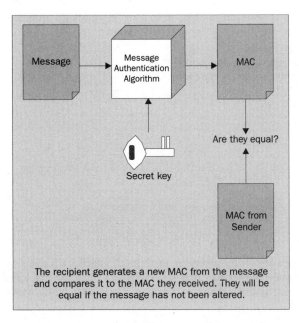

A MAC based on a cryptographic hash function is often referred to as a **HMAC** (**Hashed Message Authentication Code**). There are other types of MACs, based on block ciphers, but they are not used as often.

There are two HMAC functions in Sun's JCE: one using MD5, the other using SHA-1. You can request them with `HmacMD5` and `HmacSHA1` respectively. Other providers, like Bouncy Castle, support even more algorithms.

> There is a bug in Sun's JCE version 1.2. If you initialize a MAC with a key that is 64 bytes long, it will always hash the same way. This is a pretty serious security hole, so be sure that you are setting your key lengths manually, and that they are not set to 64 bytes. Provided you do that, there are no other known problems with the HMACs in Sun's JCE. JCE v1.2.1 fixes this problem.

Let's take a look at using a MAC in Java. We'll start with the class `javax.crypto.Mac`, which encapsulates a message authentication code.

javax.crypto.Mac

`javax.crypto.Mac` is essentially a cross between `Cipher` and `MessageDigest`. It digests data, like a message digest, but requires a key, like a cipher. You can create a key by passing the bytes you wish to use along with the algorithm name into the constructor for `SecretKeySpec`. Then pass that `SecretKeySpec` into the Mac object in its `init()` method. Data is passed to the MAC with the `update()` method, and the bytes of the MAC are generated with `doFinal()`.

We're going to take a look at an example of using a MAC (in order to execute this code, you'll need to install a JCE that has support for HMACs, like Bouncy Castle).

MAC Example

This is a simple example of generating a MAC from a text input using a random key.

```
import javax.crypto.Mac;
import javax.crypto.spec.SecretKeySpec;
import java.security.SecureRandom;
import sun.misc.*;

// MACExample.java

public class MACExample {

  public static void main (String[] args) throws Exception {

    if (args.length != 1) {
      System.err.println("Usage: java MACExample text");
      System.exit(1);
    }
```

We'll start by generating a key for the algorithm `HmacSHA1` which is a hashing MAC that uses SHA1 as its digest algorithm. We'll make the key size 20 bytes (160 bits), to match the bit length of the message digest. If we were using MD5 as our hashing algorithm, we'd want our key size to be 12 bytes (128 bits).

```
    SecureRandom random = new SecureRandom();
    byte[] keyBytes = new byte[20];
    random.nextBytes(keyBytes);
    SecretKeySpec key = new SecretKeySpec(keyBytes, "HMACSHA1");

    System.out.println("Key: " + new
                    BASE64Encoder().encode(key.getEncoded()));
```

Now that we have our key, we can get an instance of our MAC and initialize it with said key.

```
    Mac mac = Mac.getInstance("HmacSHA1");
    mac.init(key);
```

To create the message authentication code itself, we pass the bytes to the MAC with `update()`. Once we've done that, we can get the MAC with a call to `doFinal()`.

```
    mac.update(args[0].getBytes("UTF8"));
    byte[] result = mac.doFinal();
```

Now we display the MAC, BASE64-encoded so it's somewhat more human-readable.

```
    System.out.println("MAC: "+new BASE64Encoder().encode(result));
    }
}
```

To run the example, simply execute it with a `String` argument containing the text you want a MAC for:

```
C:\>java MACExample "This is some text"
```

You should see the key and the the message authentication code produced, like so:

```
Key: mySE98IqYb3YTe7oTgt0h29ogZg=
MAC: Tw3UFOEN9SJjNfvPv5e5g8RusUs=
```

Each time you run it you will get a different result, as the key is generated anew with each execution.

MACs are used in such protocols as SSL, to validate the data being sent across the wire. By using a MAC, one can be sure that no one changes the message in transit.

The problem with using a MAC is that you need to share a secret key. We can exchange secret keys easily enough using asymmetric encryption or we can use a key agreement algorithm like Diffie-Hellman, but it would be nice if we could authenticate data directly, without having to exchange secret keys. That's exactly what digital signatures offer us, which we'll discuss in the next section.

Digital Signatures

A digital signature is analogous to a physical signature in a number of ways, but they are not identical. A digital signature associates an individual with a particular piece of data, like a signed contract or an e-mail. Physical signatures attempt to do the same thing, but a physical signature on its own doesn't contain a reference to the document that was being signed. Forging a physical signature is easier than forging a digital signature: you just copy the signature from another document. Digital signatures usually provide a greater degree of security, as they are associated with the document signed, and are very difficult to forge without access to the key that was used to create them.

Digital signatures are often used to tie a particular piece of data to a person. For instance, you might digitally sign your outgoing e-mail, notifying anyone who reads it that it was written by you. Another possible use of digital signatures is signing legal documents, like contracts. Though this isn't common today, there is movement towards the use of digital signatures in legal transactions.

A digital signature is essentially a message digest that's been processed with someone's private key. You take the data that you wish to sign and pass it through a message digest algorithm. Then take that digest and your private key and pass it through a signature algorithm. The resulting data is a digital signature for that data, signed by that private key. The signature can then be passed around with the data, providing proof that whoever signed the data had access to the private key that signed it.

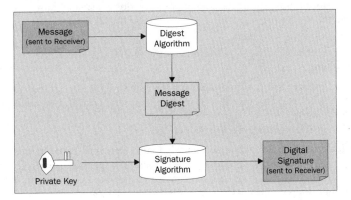

In order to validate that signature, you process the signature with the creator's public key and then compare the resulting digest to a digest of the data. If they match, you know that the private key was used to sign that data. You also get the added benefit of knowing that the data hasn't been altered since it was signed.

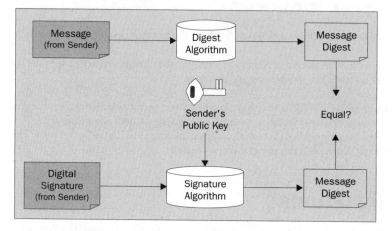

There are two main uses for digital signatures: guaranteeing integrity and guaranteeing identity:

❑ **Integrity** – Digital signatures provide a way of guaranteeing the integrity of data. Just like a message digest, you can check the signature against the data to determine that the data hasn't been changed since it was signed. One disadvantage of a message digest that we discussed is the possibility of someone tampering with both the data and the message digest. By signing the digest with a private key, we make it impossible for an attacker to recreate that signature with a new set of data unless that attacker has access to the signer's private key.

❑ **Authentication** – Digital signatures also establish the identity of the signer. As only the possessor of a private key can sign a piece of data, we can be assured that as long as that key hasn't been compromised, that user did indeed sign it. This provides us with a means of non-repudiation. Non-repudiation means that once someone signs something, they cannot in the future deny having done so.

Digital signatures enable us to do all sorts of interesting things, such as:

❑ Sign a contract – The United States passed a law in 2000 that legalized the use of "electronic signatures" for binding contracts. Though this law doesn't specify how an electronic signature needs to be created, it does provide a legal basis for using digital signatures to bind parties in a contract.

❑ Sign e-mail – Using S/MIME or PGP, you can sign your e-mail with a private key. Then the receiver can check the signature and be assured that the e-mail they just received was actually written by you.

❑ Create a timeserver that can timestamp and sign data – This is an interesting and not obvious use of digital signatures. Essentially a time stamp provides proof that some information existed at a specific point in time, by signing it with time produced by a trusted source. For more information on timestamping, see Appendix A.

❑ Authenticate to a server much more securely than a password-based login – By signing a request, a user can prove to a server that she or he possesses a specific private key. Since the signature doesn't contain any sensitive information, and a private key is extremely difficult to forge, a much higher degree of security is provided.

Because digital signatures are so difficult to forge, they provide much greater protection than do standard physical signatures. After physically signing a contract, it's possible that someone could alter that contract and present it as if you had signed it. With a digital signature, any alteration of the data invalidates the signature. The security of such a signature, however, rests entirely in the security of the private key. It is very important the key be protected, as compromise of the key means that a thief could pose as the owner of the key, signing data just as if he or she were the owner. Smart cards, which we'll discuss later, provide one means of protecting private keys.

In this section we'll be taking a look at the two following areas:

❑   Digital Signatures in Java

❑   Authenticating Identity

Before we get into the details of using digital signatures in Java, however, we should mention the two most common algorithms used to digitally sign: RSA and DSA.

RSA vs. DSA

We've already discussed using RSA for asymmetric encryption, but it can also be used to sign data. For encryption using RSA, we use the public key to encrypt and the private key to decrypt. Signing with RSA is exactly the opposite: we encrypt with the private key so that only the public key can decrypt it, as in the earlier diagram. This does nothing to hide the data, because everyone has access to the public key, but it does prove the identity of the signer, because only that specific private key could have encrypted data to be decrypted by the public key.

DSA (Digital Signature Algorithm) was designed by the US government to allow for digital signatures without any encryption capabilities. DSA works similarly to RSA signing in practice (data can be signed and signatures verified), but because of the lack of an encryption capability, DSA avoided some of the patent and export restrictions placed upon RSA. Those issues are less pertinent today because the RSA patent has expired and the United States is slowly easing its export restrictions.
Another important difference between RSA and DSA is speed: DSA is faster at generating signatures and RSA is faster at validating signatures. As most of the time a signature is validated many more times than it is generated, RSA is faster for most applications.

Sun's JDK v1.2 supports only DSA signatures out of the box. In order to get RSA signatures you'll need to download a provider that supports it, like Bouncy Castle. Alternatively, you can use JDK 1.3, which contains support for RSA signatures provided by RSA Security, Inc.

You may be asking yourself, "Which should I use? DSA or RSA?" The answer depends on your application. If you need to be compatible with a pre-existing application, your choice has been made for you: you're stuck with whatever algorithm that application uses. If you're creating a brand-new app though, you have a choice. We recommend RSA, as it is used most often and has the most flexibility. If you find that you need to have both encryption and digital signatures, you'll only have to manage one pair of keys, rather than two (one for RSA and one for DSA).

Digital Signatures in Java

The class `java.security.Signature` handles digital signatures in Java. The naming can be somewhat confusing, as `Signature` refers to the object used to create and verify digital signatures, but not the signatures themselves. Those signatures are simply manipulated as byte arrays, and do not have a Java object devoted to them.

java.security.Signature

There are six methods in `Signature` we'll be using: `getInstance()`, `initSign()`, `initVerify()`, `update()`, `sign()`, and `verify()`. Keys are generated using `KeyPairGenerator`, just like asymmetric encryption. Let's go over the methods in `Signature`.

getInstance()

This method works just like `getInstance()` in the rest of the JCA and JCE. You specify an algorithm, and optionally a provider, to get an instance of the object. The keyword `new()` is not used for `Signature` objects.

Algorithms must be specified by hash algorithm and signature algorithm. Typical RSA algorithm names are `MD5withRSA` and `SHA1withRSA`, while DSA is specified with `SHA1withDSA` or `MD5withDSA`.

initSign() and initVerify()

There are two ways to initialize a signature object, depending on whether you want to sign some data or validate a signature. `initSign()` takes a private key, and `initVerify()` takes a public key.

update()

Once your signature object is initialized, you pass data to it using the `update()` method. If you are signing, you pass it the data you want to sign. If you are verifying a signature, you pass it the data that was signed.

sign()

If you're signing data, the `sign()` method will return the bytes of the digital signature for the data you've passed in using the `update()` method.

verify()

If you're verifying data rather than signing it, call `verify()` with the bytes of the digital signature. It will return a `boolean` value indicating whether or not the signature is valid. If the signature is invalid, one of two things will happen: either `false` will be returned, or a `SignatureException` will be thrown. The exception is thrown if the byte array of the signature passed has an invalid format or if the signature object was not properly initialized. Be sure to catch this exception if testing for validity.

Let's go over a simple example of using signatures in Java.

Simple Digital Signature Example

We're going to write a short example of creating a key pair and using the private key to sign some data, then verifying the signature with the corresponding public key.

This code can be run using Sun's JDK1.3 or later, which includes support for RSA signatures. If you're using 1.2, you can install a JCE provider with RSA support (like Bouncy Castle) and you'll be able to use RSA signatures.

```
import java.security.Signature;
import java.security.SignatureException;
import java.security.KeyPair;
import java.security.KeyPairGenerator;
import sun.misc.*;

// SignatureExample.java
```

```
public class SignatureExample {

  public static void main (String[] args) throws Exception {

    if (args.length != 1) {
      System.err.println("Usage: java SignatureExample \"text to be"
                          + " signed\"");
      System.exit(1);
    }
```

We start by generating a 1024-bit RSA key pair:

```
System.out.println("Generating RSA key pair...");
KeyPairGenerator kpg = KeyPairGenerator.getInstance("RSA");
kpg.initialize(1024);
KeyPair keyPair = kpg.genKeyPair();
System.out.println("Done generating key pair.");
```

Now we fetch the data that we're going to sign. It's the first argument passed in.

```
byte[] data = args[0].getBytes("UTF8");
```

To sign the data, we need to get an instance of a `Signature` object with the name of the algorithm we wish to use. We're using MD5 with RSA for this example. Once we've got an instance, we initialize it for signing with our private key:

```
Signature sig = Signature.getInstance("MD5WithRSA");
sig.initSign(keyPair.getPrivate());
```

Now we pass it the data we want to sign:

```
sig.update(data);
```

To actually sign the data, we call `sign()`. This generates a byte array containing the digital signature. We'll display those bytes, BASE64-encoded.

```
byte[] signatureBytes = sig.sign();

System.out.println("\nSingature:\n" + new
                   BASE64Encoder().encode(signatureBytes));
```

Next we're going to verify the signature we just created. We'll start be re-initializing the signature object we created, this time for verification. We pass it the public key during initialization.

```
sig.initVerify(keyPair.getPublic());
```

Now we pass it the data that was signed, which will be used to verify the signature. If this data were altered in any way, the verification would fail.

```
sig.update(data);
```

We're ready to verify. We need to catch `SignatureException`, as `verify()` will throw that exception if the signature is in an invalid format (say, a byte had been lost).

```
boolean verified = false;
try {
   verified = sig.verify(signatureBytes);
} catch (SignatureException se) {
   verified = false;
}

if (verified) {
   System.out.println("\nSignature verified.");
} else {
   System.out.println("\nSignature did not match.");
}
    }
}
```

To run the example, type

```
C:\>java SignatureExample "text to sign"
```

It will take a few seconds to generate the key pair as `SecureRandom` is initialized. Once that's been done, the application will sign "text to sign" with the private key and display that digital signature in BASE-64 format. Then it will validate the signature and display that it was successful in validating:

```
Generating RSA key pair...
Done generating key pair.

Signature:
ZQA0OM4bsfXglTHG6ArILe5sqI7PqJ+u29kZpZyCZm76GHyqDUAiXqPtv2qQkDpwvos1P3lydFvX
YFswOeEXTOf9SVw+4I87Ef497AacHdli7hmonmPz7fJWYlNQoErq7j60xJKmYd13Ex4QjFrGdPTk
1l2bqvAcT6BwtzTJ/mg=

Signature verified.
```

The example above could easily be modified to use DSA instead of RSA. Just change the algorithm names and recompile. If you want to see signature validation fail, just change the data that you pass in during the validation phase.

Now that we've discussed the simple creation and use of digital signatures, let's move on to how to use digital signatures to authenticate identity.

Authenticating Identity

Because a digital signature cannot be easily forged for a document, it provides a way to validate a user's identity based on whether or not they can sign a given piece of data.

Let's say that we have a client-server application that requires restricted access, like a bank account management system. We want to establish something stronger than username and password, something cryptographically secure, something that prevents unauthorized users from logging in.

One mechanism we discussed in the last chapter uses public-private RSA keys and encryption to perform authentication. The server could encrypt some random data with the user's public key and if the user can decrypt it, they are allowed into the system. There are times when this is not a valid approach to the problem, however. Perhaps our client can't do encryption, for instance. There are systems for storing private keys that allow them to be used only for digital signatures for example. Instead of using encryption then, we can use digital signatures to perform authentication.

We have each client generate a key pair and give a copy of their public key to the server. Now when the client wants to access the server, we can perform the following steps to authenticate:

1. The server creates a timestamp and a large random number and sends them to the client.

2. The client signs that timestamp and the random number with its private key and sends the signature back to the server.

3. The server receives the signature and validates it. Since only the client's private key could sign that data, the server knows it is dealing with the proper client.

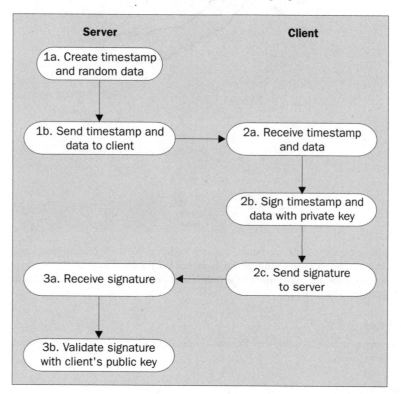

This approach has some drawbacks, however. It's important that your client-server communication be secure, as man-in-the-middle attacks are possible. If someone can place themselves between the client and server, they could intercept the authentication and pose as a valid user. This can be avoided by encrypting the communication or by using a physically secure medium, like a direct connection.

Despite its limitations, signature validation is sometimes used in the real world to perform authentication. We're going to write an example of just such an application.

Authentication Example

For this example, we'll create a server that reads a public key from the filesystem and authenticates users over a network connection, using the public key it's stored. In a real application, you'd probably want to store your public keys in a database or LDAP server. Just make sure that whatever you use is secure. As an aside, there isn't really a standard way for storing public keys. This, unfortunately, can make key management difficult, especially if you're using disparate systems. We'll discuss this problem in greater detail later in this chapter, when we cover certificates.

Our application will contain three classes: one to generate the key pairs, `GenerateKeyPair`; one for the server, `SignatureAuthenticationServer`; and one for the client, `SignatureAuthenticationClient`. We will discuss in detail what each one does, but essentially `GenerateKeyPair` generates RSA key pairs for use by the client and server. The server will wait on a port for authentication requests and the client will attempt to authenticate to that server using a digital signature. Here is a diagram describing from a high-level what we're going to do:

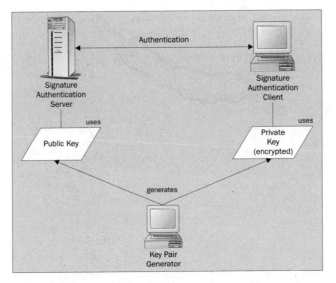

First, the application needs to generate public and private keys. We'll use code almost identical to that which we used in our asymmetric encryption examples in Chapter 5. We'll store the private key encrypted with a password. The user will be prompted for the names of the public and private key files, as well as for a password to use for encrypting the private key.

Key Pair Generator

Our key pair generator won't require any command-line arguments. Instead, it will prompt the user for filenames and a password.

```java
import java.io.*;
import java.security.*;
import javax.crypto.*;
import javax.crypto.spec.*;

// GenerateKeyPair.java

public class GenerateKeyPair {
```

First, we'll set the number of iterations to use when encrypting passwords:

```
private static final int MD5_ITERATIONS = 1000;

public static void main(String[] args) throws Exception {

    // Just call createKeyPair

    createKeyPair();

}

/**
 *   Creates a 1024 bit RSA key pair and stores it to
 *   the filesystem as two files.
 */
```

In the next part of the code, we'll create a 1024-bit RSA key pair and save it onto the filesystem as two separate files. Their names will be determined later on when we ask for the user to name them.

```
private static void createKeyPair()
throws Exception {
    BufferedReader in = new BufferedReader(new
                        InputStreamReader(System.in));
    System.out.print("Password to encrypt the private key: ");
    String password = in.readLine();
    System.out.println("Generating an RSA keypair...");

    // Create an RSA key

    KeyPairGenerator keyPairGenerator = KeyPairGenerator.getInstance("RSA");
    keyPairGenerator.initialize(1024);
    KeyPair keyPair = keyPairGenerator.genKeyPair();

    System.out.println("Done generating the keypair.\n");
```

Now that we've created the keypair, we'll write the public key to a file with a user-specified name:

```
    System.out.print("Public key filename: ");
    String publicKeyFilename = in.readLine();
```

We now get the encoded form of the public key so that we can use it again in the future. This is X.509 by default.

```
    byte[] publicKeyBytes = keyPair.getPublic().getEncoded();

    // Write the encoded public key out to the filesystem

    FileOutputStream fos = new FileOutputStream(publicKeyFilename);
    fos.write(publicKeyBytes);
    fos.close();
```

We now need to do the same thing for the private key, but we'll also need to encrypt this key:

```
System.out.print("Private key filename: ");
String privateKeyFilename = in.readLine();

// Get the encoded form. This is PKCS#8 by default.

byte[] privateKeyBytes = keyPair.getPrivate().getEncoded();
```

This is where the key is actually encrypted:

```
byte[] encryptedPrivateKeyBytes =
passwordEncrypt(password.toCharArray(),privateKeyBytes);

fos = new FileOutputStream(privateKeyFilename);
fos.write(encryptedPrivateKeyBytes);
fos.close();
}
```

This is a utility method to encrypt a byte array with a given password. Salt will be the first 8 bytes of the byte array returned.

```
private static byte[] passwordEncrypt(
        char[] password, byte[] plaintext) throws Exception {

// Create the salt.

byte[] salt = new byte[8];
SecureRandom random = new SecureRandom();
random.nextBytes(salt);

// Create a PBE key and cipher.

PBEKeySpec keySpec = new PBEKeySpec(password);
SecretKeyFactory keyFactory =
    SecretKeyFactory.getInstance("PBEWithSHAAndTwofish-CBC");
SecretKey key = keyFactory.generateSecret(keySpec);
PBEParameterSpec paramSpec = new PBEParameterSpec(salt, MD5_ITERATIONS);
Cipher cipher = Cipher.getInstance("PBEWithSHAAndTwofish-CBC");
cipher.init(Cipher.ENCRYPT_MODE, key, paramSpec);

// Encrypt the array

byte[] ciphertext = cipher.doFinal(plaintext);

// Write out the salt, then the ciphertext and return it.

ByteArrayOutputStream baos = new ByteArrayOutputStream();
baos.write(salt);
baos.write(ciphertext);
return baos.toByteArray();
}
}
```

To generate the key pair, just execute java GenerateKeyPair and it will prompt you for a password to encrypt the private key with and filenames for the public and private keys. Here's an example:

```
C:\>java GenerateKeyPair
Password to encrypt the private key: sasquatch
Generating an RSA keypair...
Done generating the keypair.

Public key filename: publicKey
Private key filename: privateKey
```

The public key is now stored in the file publicKey, and the private key in the file privateKey. Our server will need the public key file, and our client will require the private key.

Once we have the key pair generated, we need to write the server to handle the authentication.

Signature Authentication Server

Our server will follow the pattern illustrated in the previous diagram. Here's what the server needs to do:

1. Load the public key from the filesystem

2. Initialize SecureRandom, so that we do not need to wait while it is initialized during our first network connection

3. Listen on a port for a connection

4. When a connection comes in, create a timestamp and some random data and send it to the client; this is known as the **nonce**

5. Receive a signature from the client

6. Validate that signature

7. Return success or failure to the client

We use both a timestamp and a random value for the nonce to guarantee that the nonce never repeats. This approach is also used in HTTP-digest authentication, which we will discuss in Chapter 8. The use of nonces is also discussed in Appendix A.

Now let's take a look at the code for SignatureAuthenticationServer.java. Our class is going to extend Thread, so that we can handle multiple requests simultaneously. Each time a client connects, we will create a new instance of the SignatureAuthenticationServer and it will handle the client's request.

```
import java.io.*;
import java.net.*;
import java.util.*;
import java.security.*;
import java.security.spec.*;

// SignatureAuthenticationServer.java
```

```
public class SignatureAuthenticationServer extends Thread {

  private static final int PORT = 8001;

  private Socket mSocket;
  private PublicKey mPublicKey;
```

Our constructor takes a socket, which the request comes in on, and a public key, which is the public key of the client that we will allow to connect. In a real application, we would need to deal with multiple public keys, perhaps stored in a database.

```
public SignatureAuthenticationServer (Socket socket, PublicKey publicKey)
{
  mSocket = socket;
  mPublicKey = publicKey;
  this.start();
}
```

Our `run()` method handles the request. It will create our nonce, a 24-byte array holding an 8-byte timestamp and a 16-byte random number. Then we'll send that nonce to the client to be signed. The client will sign the data and return it to us.

```
public void run() {
  try {

    byte[] dataToBeSigned;

    // Get our input and output streams from the socket

    DataInputStream inputFromClient = new
                   DataInputStream(mSocket.getInputStream());
    DataOutputStream outputToClient = new
                   DataOutputStream(mSocket.getOutputStream());
```

We create the nonce from a timestamp and random value. We'll use a `ByteArrayOutputStream` to concatenate those values.

```
    long timestamp = System.currentTimeMillis();
    ByteArrayOutputStream baos = new ByteArrayOutputStream();
    DataOutputStream dos = new DataOutputStream(baos);
    dos.writeLong(timestamp);

    // Create a random value

    byte[] randomValue = new byte[16];
    SecureRandom random = new SecureRandom();
    random.nextBytes(randomValue);

    baos.write(randomValue);

    dataToBeSigned = baos.toByteArray();
```

Now we'll write our nonce to the client. We start by sending the length of the nonce, so the client knows how much data to read.

```
outputToClient.writeInt(dataToBeSigned.length);
outputToClient.write(dataToBeSigned);
outputToClient.flush();
```

The client will respond with the signature, length-first. We'll read that in and place it in a variable , signatureBytes.

```
byte[] signatureBytes = new byte[inputFromClient.readInt()];
inputFromClient.readFully(signatureBytes);
```

Now we can validate the signature:

```
Signature signature = Signature.getInstance("MD5WithRSA");
signature.initVerify(mPublicKey);
signature.update(dataToBeSigned);
boolean authorized = false;
try {
  authorized = signature.verify(signatureBytes);
} catch (SignatureException se) {
  // In case the signature is padded incorrectly
  // this can happen if the client is using the wrong key.
}
```

We'll write out to the client whether it succeeded or not:

```
outputToClient.writeBoolean(authorized);

if (authorized) {
  System.out.println("Client was authorized.\n");
} else {
  System.out.println("Access denied.\n");
}
} catch (Exception e) {
System.err.println("Exception: ");
e.printStackTrace();
}
}
```

Now we'll write our `main()` method, which will wait on a port and create a new `SignatureAuthenticationServer` to handle each request. We start by asking the user for the public key's filename, and then opening that file.

```
public static void main (String[] args) throws Exception {
  BufferedReader in = new BufferedReader
  (new InputStreamReader(System.in));
  System.out.print("Public Key of client: ");
  String publicKeyFilename = in.readLine();
```

We'll call `readPublicKey()`, a method we'll define later, to actually read in and instantiate a public key.

```
PublicKey publicKey = readPublicKey(publicKeyFilename);
```

Next we want to initialize an instance of `SecureRandom`. This takes a while, so we want to do it before any clients can connect. `SecureRandom` is lazy, so we need to actually generate some random bytes in order for `SecureRandom` to truly initialize.

```
System.out.println("Initializing SecureRandom...");
SecureRandom random = new SecureRandom();
byte[] randomBytes = new byte[20];
random.nextBytes(randomBytes);
```

Next we'll create a server socket and loop over connections coming in. Each time a connection comes in, we'll create a new `SignatureAuthenticationServer` to handle it. In a real application, it would be a good idea to have some sort of pool of threads or server instances to handle these requests, so that a new thread doesn't have to be spun off each time.

```
ServerSocket ss = new ServerSocket(PORT);
System.out.println("Listening on port "+PORT);

while (true) {
  SignatureAuthenticationServer sas =
  new SignatureAuthenticationServer
  (ss.accept(), publicKey);
  }
}
```

Finally, we need to write our `readPublicKey()` method, which reads a public key from the filesystem given a filename. We begin by simply reading the bytes out of the file.

```
private static PublicKey readPublicKey(String filename) throws Exception {

FileInputStream fis = new FileInputStream(filename);
ByteArrayOutputStream baos = new ByteArrayOutputStream();

int theByte = 0;
while ((theByte = fis.read()) != -1)
{
   baos.write(theByte);
}
fis.close();

byte[] keyBytes = baos.toByteArray();
baos.close();
```

Now that we've got the bytes, we need to turn the encoded key into a real RSA public key. Public keys are encoded in X.509 format, so we'll use the `X509EncodedKeySpec` class to create our key.

```
X509EncodedKeySpec keySpec = new X509EncodedKeySpec(keyBytes);
KeyFactory keyFactory = KeyFactory.getInstance("RSA");
PublicKey publicKey = keyFactory.generatePublic(keySpec);
return publicKey;
  }
}
```

As we mentioned, the server spins off a thread for each request that comes in. This way the server can handle multiple clients simultaneously.

Now let's look at the client.

Signature Authentication Client

The client must do the following:

1. Load the private key and decrypt it

2. Open a connection to the server

3. Read a byte array from the server to sign

4. Sign the byte array

5. Return the digital signature

6. Read a boolean value from the server indicating whether permission was granted or not

```
import java.io.*;
import java.net.*;
import java.security.*;
import java.security.spec.*;
import javax.crypto.*;
import javax.crypto.spec.*;

// SignatureAuthenticationClient.java:

public class SignatureAuthenticationClient {

  private static final int PORT = 8001;

  private static final int MD5_ITERATIONS = 1000;
```

All of the work takes place in our main() method. We'll start the client with an argument indicating the name of the host to connect to. Then we'll prompt the user for the filename of the file that holds the private key, and the password to use to decrypt it.

```
public static void main (String[] args) throws Exception {
if (args.length != 1) {
  System.err.println("Usage: java AuthenticationClient hostname");
  System.exit(1);
}

String hostname = args[0];

// Begin by asking for the private key's filename

BufferedReader in = new BufferedReader
(new InputStreamReader(System.in));
System.out.print("Private Key: ");
String privateKeyFilename = in.readLine();
System.out.print("Password: ");
String password = in.readLine();
```

We'll write a method `getPrivateKey()` that will load and decrypt the private key. We'll detail it later.

```
PrivateKey privateKey = getPrivateKey
                    (privateKeyFilename, password.toCharArray());
```

Now we'll open a connection to the server and get the input and output streams.

```
System.out.println("\nOpening a connection...");
// Open up a connection
Socket socket = new Socket(hostname, PORT);

DataInputStream inputFromServer = new
  DataInputStream(socket.getInputStream());
DataOutputStream outputToServer = new
  DataOutputStream(socket.getOutputStream());
```

We'll read in the data that we need to sign and place it in a byte array, `dataToBeSigned`:

```
byte[] dataToBeSigned = new byte[inputFromServer.readInt()];
inputFromServer.readFully(dataToBeSigned);
```

Now we'll sign that data:

```
Signature signature = Signature.getInstance("MD5WithRSA");
signature.initSign(privateKey);
signature.update(dataToBeSigned);
byte[] signatureBytes = signature.sign();
```

Then we write out the signature bytes to the server:

```
outputToServer.writeInt(signatureBytes.length);
outputToServer.write(signatureBytes);
outputToServer.flush();
```

We'll read a single boolean value from the server. This indicates whether our authentication was accepted or not.

```
boolean verified = inputFromServer.readBoolean();

if (verified) {
  System.out.println("We were authenticated.");
} else {
  System.out.println("Permission denied.");
  }
}
```

Now we need to write our `getPrivateKey()` method. This takes the filename for the private key and a `char` array containing the password. We've seen code just like this in Chapters 4 and 5, so we're not going to go into much detail about how this method works.

```
private static PrivateKey getPrivateKey(String privateKeyFilename,
                              char[] password)
                              throws Exception {

// Load the private key bytes

FileInputStream fis = new FileInputStream(privateKeyFilename);
ByteArrayOutputStream baos = new ByteArrayOutputStream();
```

```
      int theByte = 0;
      while ((theByte = fis.read()) != -1)
      {
        baos.write(theByte);
      }
      fis.close();

      byte[] keyBytes = baos.toByteArray();
      baos.close();

      keyBytes = passwordDecrypt(password, keyBytes);

      // Turn the encoded key into a real RSA private key.
      // Private keys are encoded in PKCS#8.

      PKCS8EncodedKeySpec keySpec = new PKCS8EncodedKeySpec(keyBytes);
      KeyFactory keyFactory = KeyFactory.getInstance("RSA");
      PrivateKey privateKey = keyFactory.generatePrivate(keySpec);
      return privateKey;
    }
```

Finally, we have a method to actually decrypt the bytes of the key (again, code like this was described in Chapters 4 and 5).

```
    private static byte[] passwordDecrypt(char[] password, byte[] ciphertext)
                              throws Exception {

      // Read in the salt.

      byte[] salt = new byte[8];
      ByteArrayInputStream bais = new ByteArrayInputStream(ciphertext);
      bais.read(salt,0,8);

      // The remaining bytes are the actual ciphertext.

      byte[] remainingCiphertext = new byte[ciphertext.length-8];
      bais.read(remainingCiphertext,0,ciphertext.length-8);

      // Create a PBE cipher to decrypt the byte array.

      PBEKeySpec keySpec = new PBEKeySpec(password);
      SecretKeyFactory keyFactory =
              SecretKeyFactory.getInstance("PBEWithSHAAndTwofish-CBC");
      SecretKey key = keyFactory.generateSecret(keySpec);
      PBEParameterSpec paramSpec = new PBEParameterSpec(salt, MD5_ITERATIONS);
      Cipher cipher = Cipher.getInstance("PBEWithSHAAndTwofish-CBC");

      // Perform the actual decryption.

      cipher.init(Cipher.DECRYPT_MODE, key, paramSpec);
      return cipher.doFinal(remainingCiphertext);
    }
  }
```

Running the Example

Once you've generated your keys using the `GenerateKeyPair` class, you should be able to run the server with:

```
C:\>java SignatureAuthenticationServer
```

It will request a public key filename, read it in, and begin listening on a port. Here's what the output will look like:

```
Public Key of client: publicKey
Initializing SecureRandom...
Listening on port 8001
```

You can then execute the client from that same machine with:

```
C:\>java SignatureAuthenticationClient localhost
```

It will request a filename from the user for their private key, and then the password that the key is encrypted with. Then it will establish a connection to localhost and attempt to prove its identity with a digital signature, as the above diagrams illustrate.

Here's what the output might look like:

```
Private Key: privateKey
Password: sasquatch

Opening a connection...
We were authenticated.
```

This short code example (`SignatureAuthenticationServer` and `SignatureAuthenticationClient`) could be extended to provide the front-end authentication for an entire process. As we mentioned, however, if you're using signatures for authentication you need to make sure that your interchange is encrypted.

Limitations of Digital Signatures

When validating a signature, you must do so with an entity's public key. But how do you know if the public key is correct? Unless you got it directly from them in a secure fashion, you can't be certain the public key is actually theirs. Digital certificates are an attempt to solve just that problem, to attach identity to a public key in an unforgeable way. In the following section, we'll show how to use certificates to validate identity.

Digital Certificates

A digital certificate is an assurance provided by a third party that a public key belongs to its purported owner. As we mentioned in Chapter 3, a certificate is analogous to a passport: a third party (the government) is providing an assurance that you are the person your passport indicates you to be. Certificates can be issued to subjects other than people, however, like companies or other organizations.

A certificate is essentially your public key and some other information signed by a third party's private key. That third party is known as the **certificate authority** (**CA**).

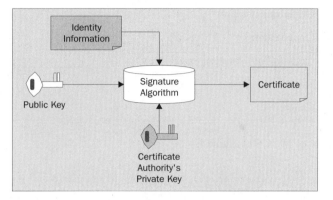

The two best-known certificate authorities are Verisign and Thawte (which is actually a subsidiary of Verisign). There are others, but they occupy only a few percent of the CA market. By signing your public key, the CA is indicating that it believes the subject to be the individual the certificate claims them to be.

> *The value of certificates is in establishing trust. If you trust a certificate authority, then you trust all the certificates it issues. As shipped by Sun, the JDK trusts Verisign and Thawte.*

Other trusted authorities can be added to your JDK with `keytool`, which we will describe later. First, we're going to discuss what data is stored in a certificate.

Certificate Contents

The JDK uses X.509 certificates by default. X.509 is the most widely used standard for digital certificates. They are defined in RFC 2459, which can be found at http://www.ietf.org/rfc/rfc2459.txt. There are three versions of X.509: v1, v2, and v3. The later versions add some optional features to certificates, which we'll discuss shortly. First let's go over the contents of an X.509v1 certificate, and discuss each field:

X.509v1 Certificate

The X.509v1 Certificate comprises the following areas:

- ❑ **Version** – This field defines the version of the certificate: v1, v2, or v3.

- ❑ **Serial Number** – The serial number is a large integer that is unique to the CA issuing the certificate.

- ❑ **Signature Algorithm** – This defines the algorithm that the CA used to sign this certificate.

- ❑ **Validity** – The validity defines the period of time for which the certificate is valid. The validity is defined as two dates: not before and not after. The certificate is valid between those dates.

- ❑ **Subject** – The subject indicates whom the certificate is issued to. Subjects are stored as X.500 names. X.500 is a standard for online directories, and an X.500 name defines what information defines the name of an individual. X.500 names contain the following information:

Attribute	Contents
CN	Common name
OU	Organizational Unit
O	Organization
L	Organization's location (usually city)
ST	Organization's state
C	Country

An example of an X.500 Name is:

```
CN=Jess Garms, OU=Development, O=ISNetworks, ST=Washington, C=US
```

❑ **Subject Public Key** – The subject public key is, not surprisingly, the public key of the subject of the certificate.

❑ **Signature** – The certificate authority signs the certificate, and stores the signature in this field. Checking this signature against the public key of the certificate authority can validate the certificate.

X.509v2 Certificate

Version 2 of X.509 adds two optional fields to the X.509 certificate: the Issuer Unique Identifier and the Subject Unique Identifier. These are rarely used, but we include them for completeness:

❑ **Issuer Unique Identifier** – If the same X.500 name is used for different certificate issuers, the issuer unique identifier can separate them.

❑ **Subject Unique Identifier** – If two subjects have the same X.500 name, the subject unique identifier can be used to keep them distinct.

Because these two fields are not in common use, version 2 certificates are also rare.

X.509v3 Certificate

Version 3 adds an important and somewhat complex field to certificates – **extensions**.

Extensions are optional in v3 certificates, but can provide the following: subject and issuer attributes, key usage and policies, and certification path constraints.

❑ **Subject and Issuer Attributes** – This field provides additional attributes of the subject and/or the issuer. It includes information like alternative names and directory attributes.

❑ **Key Usage and Policies** – X.509v3 certificates allow the CA to specify how a certificate and its associated keys can be used. A key or a certificate can be restricted to support only signing, or only encryption, for example.

❑ **Certification Path Constraints** – Some certificates can be used to validate other certificates. Certification path constraints let a CA specify what kind of certificates another certificate can create.

Viewing Certificates

Let's take a look at a sample certificate to see the information it contains. The example here is a Verisign certificate used for signing e-mail. We can open it directly in Windows by double-clicking on it, which displays the following:

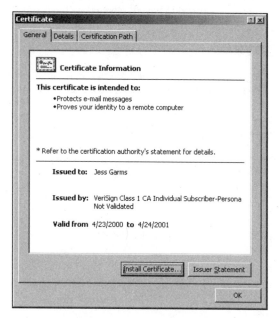

This view of the certificate indicates who the subject is (Jess Garms) and who the issuer is (Verisign). It also lists the validity (4/23/2000 to 4/24/2001) and the constraints (encrypt e-mail and establish identity).

We can take a look at some of the other attributes of the certificate by clicking on the "Details" tab:

Most UNIX variants don't have an easy way to view certificates, but later in this chapter we'll write a simple Java program for displaying certificate attributes.

It's important to note that the signature on a certificate covers the entirety of the certificate. If a single attribute is changed, the certificate will become invalid, as the signature on it will not match the contents. If you need to change an attribute in a certificate, you need to have it reissued by the certificate authority that created it.

Certificates in Java

There are three classes in the JDK that we'll be most interested in using to deal with certificates: `Certificate`, `X509Certificate`, and `CertificateFactory`. These are all found in the `java.security.cert` package.

java.security.cert.Certificate

This is an abstract class that encapsulates a certificate. The methods we'll use most often when dealing with certificates are `getPublicKey()` and `verify()`. Certificates are normally immutable, so there are no `set()` methods.

getPublicKey()

This method returns the public key of the subject of this certificate.

verify()

This method verifies the signature on this certificate. It requires that you pass in the public key of the certificate authority that signed it.

java.security.cert.X509Certificate

This is another abstract class that provides methods for dealing with X.509 certificates. It inherits from `Certificate` and has a number of extra `get()` methods for fetching X.509 attributes from a certificate, like the validity period and the serial number.

java.security.cert.CertificateFactory

A certificate factory generates certificate objects from an encoding of a certificate. `CertificateFactory` is an abstract class, so it cannot be instantiated directly, but `getInstance()` will fetch a `CertificateFactory` for you to use.

There is a deprecated class in the JDK, `java.security.Certificate`. It was used in JDK 1.1, but has been superceded in Java 2 by the classes in the `java.security.cert` package. It will eventually be removed. You should not use it in any Java 2 code.

None of the classes in the standard JDK support generating certificates, only reading them. In order to generate our own certificates, we're going to need to introduce two concepts: **keystores** and **keytool**.

Keystores

A keystore in Java is a collection of keys and certificates. A keystore is usually stored in a file, but it could be stored in another medium, such as a database or an LDAP server. Java uses the class `java.security.KeyStore` to represent an in-memory copy of a keystore. You can manipulate a keystore through this class, and load and store keys and certificates from it.

To load a keystore, you must first get an instance of it using `KeyStore.getInstance()`, passing the keystore type as an argument. The default keystore implementation is called "JKS", for Java KeyStore. There are other possible keystores available from other libraries, which we will cover later.

Keys and certificates are stored as entries in a keystore, referenced by a name, known as their alias. You can get a list of all the aliases in a keystore with the `aliases()` method, which returns an `Enumeration`.

There are two types of entries in a keystore:

❑ **Trusted certificates** – A trusted certificate is a certificate that you believe actually belongs to the subject that it claims. An example of a trusted certificate is a certificate from a CA like Verisign that will be used to validate other certificates. You can add a trusted certificate to a keystore with `setCertificateEntry()`.

❑ **Keys** – Keys are private or symmetric keys that can be used for digital signatures and/or encryption. A key in a keystore must be associated with a certificate for that key. This is not a trusted certificate, but simply a certificate that contains the subject that owns the private key. You can add a key entry with `setKeyEntry()`. According the JDK documentation, both private keys and symmetric keys can be stored in a keystore, but we have found storage of symmetric keys in the default keystore to be buggy and would not recommend actually using the keystore to hold symmetric keys. Instead they should be serialized and stored in some other fashion, (as we did in Chapter 4).

Keystores use passwords to control access to private keys. The default keystore doesn't actually encrypt any data with the password, but merely checks the password on loading to make sure it's the same. If you want to protect your keystore, you'll want to use another provider's keystore, such as Bouncy Castle's. Their keystore offers password-based encryption to protect the keys.

Before we show an example of using the `KeyStore` class, we need to talk about the default Java keystore, and how one can create certificates to store in it.

Default Keystore

There is a default keystore in Java, which is stored as a file, `.keystore`, in the current user's home directory. On a Windows 2000 machine, for instance, it might be found at the following location:

```
C:\Documents and Settings\garms\.keystore
```

On a Linux machine, that location might be something like:

```
/home/garms/.keystore
```

The default keystore is important when using `keytool` to manage keys and certificates. Let's discuss what `keytool` is and how to use it.

Keytool

`Keytool` is an application that ships with the JDK. It manages keystores and can create certificates. It replaces `javakey`, found in Java 1.1.

If a keystore isn't specified, `keytool` operates on the keystore in the user's home directory, with the filename of `.keystore`. It can also work with other files, with the `-keystore` option.

157

Running `keytool` on its own, yields a list of the available functions and options, like so:

```
C:\>keytool
keytool usage:

-certreq     [-v] [-alias <alias>] [-sigalg <sigalg>]
             [-file <csr_file>] [-keypass <keypass>]
             [-keystore <keystore>] [-storepass <storepass>]
             [-storetype <storetype>] [-provider <provider_class_name>] ...

-delete      [-v] -alias <alias>
             [-keystore <keystore>] [-storepass <storepass>]
             [-storetype <storetype>] [-provider <provider_class_name>] ...

-export      [-v] [-rfc] [-alias <alias>] [-file <cert_file>]
             [-keystore <keystore>] [-storepass <storepass>]
             [-storetype <storetype>] [-provider <provider_class_name>] ...

-genkey      [-v] [-alias <alias>] [-keyalg <keyalg>]
             [-keysize <keysize>] [-sigalg <sigalg>]
             [-dname <dname>] [-validity <valDays>]
             [-keypass <keypass>] [-keystore <keystore>]
             [-storepass <storepass>] [-storetype <storetype>]
             [-provider <provider_class_name>] ...

-help

-identitydb  [-v] [-file <idb_file>] [-keystore <keystore>]
             [-storepass <storepass>] [-storetype <storetype>]
             [-provider <provider_class_name>] ...

-import      [-v] [-noprompt] [-trustcacerts] [-alias <alias>]
             [-file <cert_file>] [-keypass <keypass>]
             [-keystore <keystore>] [-storepass <storepass>]
             [-storetype <storetype>] [-provider <provider_class_name>] ...

-keyclone    [-v] [-alias <alias>] -dest <dest_alias>
             [-keypass <keypass>] [-new <new_keypass>]
             [-keystore <keystore>] [-storepass <storepass>]
             [-storetype <storetype>] [-provider <provider_class_name>] ...

-keypasswd   [-v] [-alias <alias>]
             [-keypass <old_keypass>] [-new <new_keypass>]
             [-keystore <keystore>] [-storepass <storepass>]
             [-storetype <storetype>] [-provider <provider_class_name>] ...

-list        [-v | -rfc] [-alias <alias>]
             [-keystore <keystore>] [-storepass <storepass>]
             [-storetype <storetype>] [-provider <provider_class_name>] ...

-printcert   [-v] [-file <cert_file>]

-selfcert    [-v] [-alias <alias>] [-sigalg <sigalg>]
             [-dname <dname>] [-validity <valDays>]
             [-keypass <keypass>] [-keystore <keystore>]
             [-storepass <storepass>] [-storetype <storetype>]
             [-provider <provider_class_name>] ...

-storepasswd [-v] [-new <new_storepass>]
             [-keystore <keystore>] [-storepass <storepass>]
             [-storetype <storetype>] [-provider <provider_class_name>] ...
```

Let's go over each of these options:

- ❏ -certreq – Creates a certificate request to use to get a CA-signed certificate. Use this option to get a certificate from Verisign that you can use with keytool.
- ❏ -delete – Deletes an entry from a keystore.
- ❏ -export – Exports a certificate from a keystore, DER-encoded. BASE64 encoding can be added with the -rfc option. Note that private keys are not exportable.
- ❏ -genkey – Generates a key pair and a self-signed certificate. You can specify the algorithm with -keyalg, such as: -keyalg RSA.
- ❏ -help – Displays the possible options you can use with keytool.
- ❏ -identitydb – Converts a JDK1.1-style identity database to the new Java2-style keystore.
- ❏ -import – Imports a new certificate into the keystore. Useful for adding new certificates and adding a signed certificate to an existing alias.
- ❏ -keyclone – Copies an entry in the keystore.
- ❏ -keypasswd – Changes the password protecting a particular alias.
- ❏ -list – Lists all the aliases in the database.
- ❏ -printcert – Displays a certificate.
- ❏ -selfcert – Generates a self-signed certificate.
- ❏ -storepasswd – Changes the password of the keystore.

The -v option specifies verbose-mode for any of the commands and the -keystore option lets you specify what file to open.

Generating a Certificate with Keytool

The JDK on its own provides only one way to generate certificates: using keytool. We're going to go through an example of creating a certificate and storing it in a keystore.

> Note, keystores are linked to the provider, and that a .keystore file generated by one provider will not work with another.

In these examples, we'll be using the default Sun JCA provider as stated in Chapter 3, and you'll have to set up your java.security files with the security providers as stated in that chapter.

To generate a certificate using the default algorithm, which is DSA, just run the following command:

```
C:\>keytool -genkey -alias test
```

You can change the algorithm with the -keyalg switch. -keyalg RSA, for instance, will tell keytool to generate a certificate with RSA keys.

Keytool will open the default keystore in your home directory, .keystore. You can specify a keystore file to open or create by appending -keystore [filename] to the command.

You will then be asked for your keystore password. If you've not used the keystore before, just pick a password, which `keytool` will set to be the password for this keystore. Otherwise, you'll need to use the same password you used last time. After entering your password, you will be asked a series of questions about the subject of the certificate. Answer them as you'd like, since this is just an example.

```
C:\>keytool -genkey -alias test
Enter keystore password:  password
What is your first and last name?
  [Unknown]:  Jess Garms
What is the name of your organizational unit?
  [Unknown]:  Dev
What is the name of your organization?
  [Unknown]:  ISNetworks
What is the name of your City or Locality?
  [Unknown]:  Seattle
What is the name of your State or Province?
  [Unknown]:  Washington
What is the two-letter country code for this unit?
  [Unknown]:  US
Is <CN=Jess Garms, OU=Dev, O=ISNetworks, L=Seattle, ST=Washington, C=US> correct
?
  [no]:  yes
```

The last line, <CN=Jess Garms, OU=Dev, O=ISNetworks, L=Seattle, ST=Washington, C=US>, is an X.500 name. Keytool asks you to confirm that it is correct before generating your certificate. Answer yes, and `keytool` will create your certificate. This takes a few seconds, after which you'll be asked for a password to use for the key:

```
Enter key password for <test>
        (RETURN if same as keystore password):
```

You can just hit enter, which will use the keystore's password for the key.

We now have an entry in our keystore that you can view with `keytool -v -list`:

```
C:\>keytool -v -list
Enter keystore password:  password

Keystore type: jks
Keystore provider: SUN

Your keystore contains 1 entry:

Alias name: test
Creation date: Tue Mar 27 11:38:08 PDT 2001
Entry type: keyEntry
Certificate chain length: 1
Certificate[1]:
Owner: CN=Jess Garms, OU=Dev, O=ISNetworks, L=Seattle, ST=Washington, C=US
Issuer: CN=Jess Garms, OU=Dev, O=ISNetworks, L=Seattle, ST=Washington, C=US
Serial number: 38f3710f
Valid from: Tue Mar 27 11:38:07 PDT 2001 until: Mon Jun 25 11:38:07 PDT 2001
Certificate fingerprints:
        MD5:  2E:11:94:B3:47:7D:E8:8F:45:4B:A2:D2:89:B9:7E:66
        SHA1: 30:F5:27:69:40:BB:D6:A6:DE:80:16:DB:8E:47:46;06:1D:7A:F4:37


*******************************************
*******************************************
```

We'll use `keytool` again in later chapters when we create and manage certificates for SSL. For now, we're going to move on to an example of using the certificate classes in Java to read a certificate and examine it. Then we'll extend that example to talk directly to our keystore.

Using Certificates in Java

We're going to write a simple program for instantiating a `Certificate` object from a file and displaying some information about it. Our class will use `CertificateFactory` and `X509Certificate`.

We'll be reading a certificate from a file, which we'll export from our keystore using `keytool`. We'll give the exact commands for doing so after the code.

Our class will be called `PrintCertInfo`. We'll pass in the name of the file containing the cert when we execute the application.

```
import java.io.*;
import java.security.cert.Certificate;
import java.security.cert.CertificateFactory;

// PrintCertInfo.java

public class PrintCertInfo {

  public static void main (String[] args) throws Exception {
```

We need to start by getting an instance of a certificate factory that handles X.509 certificates:

```
    CertificateFactory certFactory =
                  CertificateFactory.getInstance("X.509");
```

Now we'll open our certificate file:

```
    FileInputStream fis = new FileInputStream (args[0]);
```

We generate a certificate object from the file using our certificate factory, and then close the file:

```
    Certificate cert = certFactory.generateCertificate(fis);
    fis.close();
```

Now we've got our certificate and we can call methods on it. To see general information, we can just print out what `toString()` gives us:

```
    System.out.println(cert);
  }
}
```

Now we need to export our certificate. Start by creating a certificate in your keystore. You can use the `keytool` commands we gave in the last section to do so. We'll assume you've created a certificate with the alias `"test"` in your default keystore.

You can export that certificate with the following command:

```
C:\>keytool -export -alias test -file test.cer
```

This will create a file, test.cer, containing your certificate.

Now we can run PrintCertInfo on the certificate like so:

```
C:\ >java PrintCertInfo test.cer
[
[
  Version: V1
  Subject: CN=Jess Garms, OU=Dev, O=ISNetworks, L=Seattle, ST=Washington, C=US
  Signature Algorithm: SHA1withDSA, OID = 1.2.840.10040.4.3

  Key:  Sun DSA Public Key
    Parameters:DSA
        p:      fd7f5381 1d751229 52df4a9c 2eece4e7 f611b752 3cef4400 c31e3f80 b6
512669
    455d4022 51fb593d 8d58fabf c5f5ba30 f6cb9b55 6cd7813b 801d346f f26660b7
    6b9950a5 a49f9fe8 047b1022 c24fbba9 d7feb7c6 1bf83b57 e7c6a8a6 150f04fb
    83f6d3c5 1ec30235 54135a16 9132f675 f3ae2b61 d72aeff2 2203199d d14801c7
        q:      9760508f 15230bcc b292b982 a2eb840b f0581cf5
        g:      f7e1a085 d69b3dde cbbcab5c 36b857b9 7994afbb fa3aea82 f9574c0b 3d
078267
    5159578e bad4594f e6710710 8180b449 167123e8 4c281613 b7cf0932 8cc8a6e1
    3c167a8b 547c8d28 e0a3ae1e 2bb3a675 916ea37f 0bfa2135 62f1fb62 7a01243b
    cca4f1be a8519089 a883dfe1 5ae59f06 928b665e 807b5525 64014c3b fecf492a

  y:
    ebad2508 b5ce642d dec3e95f 69eb00c7 127467e3 12555ad6 3955e5a1 51e63b2d
    e6d71087 c11aa32e 855fe04a 05649444 cdafa7ee 05df74c0 f81ccdd3 75f5d69f
    ef71ec46 7eb9d8a5 dcbee7e6 9e52c07d 80c230bf 77b5cc2b 045a505e 074e9d32
    a493addc 546cae53 10be36e0 a2ec009a 0e058781 706808cb 70a7402c 09ab6841

  Validity: [From: Tue Mar 27 11:38:07 PDT 2001,
               To: Mon Jun 25 11:38:07 PDT 2001]
  Issuer: CN=Jess Garms, OU=Dev, O=ISNetworks, L=Seattle, ST=Washington, C=US
  SerialNumber: [    38f3710f ]

]
  Algorithm: [SHA1withDSA]
  Signature:
0000: 30 2D 02 14 37 AC 4B 39   78 CE 78 64 2F E1 D3 E6  0-..7.K9x.xd/...
0010: C8 DF 54 3A 3C 0F 83 03   02 15 00 83 EF C0 C4 5C  ..T:<..........\
0020: 7A EA 64 AB 86 1C 35 5F   32 9A F9 D7 84 4A CC     z.d...5_2....J.

]
```

There's a lot of binary data in this display, but we can look through and pick out some interesting information:

- ❑ The version – V1. As we saw earlier there are three versions of X.509, with v1 and v3 being the most common. As we mentioned, v3 adds the ability to define uses for certificates, like code signing, e-mail signing, or certificate signing. Java supports all three versions, but the certificates generated by keytool will all be V1.

- ❑ The subject – In this case, it's a person: Jess Garms. There is some additional information here, like the physical location and company name.

- ❑ The signature algorithm – For default certificates generated by keytool, it's SHA1withDSA.

- ❑ The public key – This is probably the most important part of the certificate. When displaying it in this format, we see a bunch of parameters and their binary data.

- ❑ The validity – This is a pair of dates, before and after which the certificate will not be valid. Certificates are typically valid for a year, but this varies by application. CA certificates for instance, often last quite a bit longer, up to 30 years. The certificates that keytool creates are valid for 90 days by default, but this can be changed using the -validity option.

- ❑ The issuer – In this case, is the same as the subject. That's because this is a self-signed certificate. As we've said earlier, there's no easy way in Java 2 to create a certificate signed by someone other than the subject.

- ❑ The serial number – Serial numbers should be unique within a CA. That is, no two certificates signed by the same certificate authority should have the same serial number. This allows the CA to keep track of certificates and revoke them as needed based solely on the serial number.

- ❑ The algorithm and the signature – This is the signature on the certificate, made by the issuer. It's binary data, and in this case, it's a SHA1WithDSA signature.

Now that we've shown how to create a certificate from a file, let's move on to pulling one directly out of a keystore.

KeyStore Example

We're going to write another class that displays certificate information, but this time we're going to read that certificate from our keystore. We'll use the java.security.KeyStore class to do so. Our application will require two arguments to be passed in: the alias of the certificate to load, and the password of the keystore.

```
import java.io.*;
import java.security.cert.CertificateFactory;
import java.security.cert.Certificate;
import java.security.KeyStore;

// PrintCertFromKeyStore.java

public class PrintCertFromKeyStore {

  public static void main (String[] args) throws Exception {

    if (args.length != 2) {
      System.err.println(
        "Usage: java PrintCertInfo alias password");
      System.exit(1);
    }
```

The default keystore is in the user's home directory, so we need to build that path:

```
String userHome = System.getProperty("user.home");
String keystoreFilename = userHome +
                          File.separator + ".keystore";
```

The password is the second argument passed in, and the certificate alias is the first:

```
char[] password = args[1].toCharArray();
String alias = args[0];
```

We'll open the keystore file and get an instance of `KeyStore` to handle the data in that file:

```
FileInputStream fIn = new FileInputStream(keystoreFilename);
KeyStore keystore = KeyStore.getInstance("JKS");
```

To load the keystore, we pass in the input stream and the password into an instance of `KeyStore`:

```
keystore.load(fIn, password);
```

Now we can fetch our certificate from the keystore and display it:

```
Certificate cert = keystore.getCertificate(alias);

// Display general information about the certificate
System.out.println(cert);
    }
}
```

Running the Example

To run it, you will need to have created a keystore as we discussed in the section on `keytool`. If you have an alias called "`test`" in your keystore and your password is "`password`", you can view it by executing the class we just wrote like so:

```
C:\>java PrintCertFromKeyStore test password
```

This will display the certificate directly out of your keystore. The output should look identical to the last example, which displayed the certificate from a certificate file.

Now that we've discussed the basics of certificates and how to use them in Java, we're going to move on to some more advanced topics: certificate chaining and certificate revocation.

Certificate Chaining

As we've mentioned, a certificate essentially vouches for one public key with another public key. It's possible to extend this further, and chain the verification through multiple certificates. For instance, Verisign can use its root certificate to vouch for an e-mail authority certificate, which can in turn vouch for individual user's certificates:

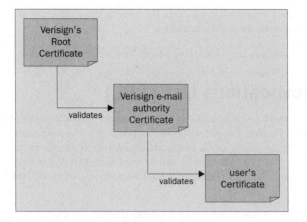

Notice that each entity in the certificate chain with the exception of the bottom one is functioning as a certificate authority. When a CA signs a certificate, they make a choice as to whether or not that entity itself can function as a CA. The certificate contains extensions that define what specifically it can and cannot be used for.

You can view the certificate chain of a certificate with Windows 2000 by double-clicking on a certificate. You will see information like this:

Because Verisign's Class 1 Primary CA certificate is trusted, their second-level certificate is also trusted, which then makes a personal certificate trusted, since it's been signed by that second-level CA.

Certificate chaining is used to manage certificates. By creating sub-certificates, it becomes easier to define the functions that individual certificates can be used for.

We've discussed how certificates are created and issued. Now we're going to go over how a certificate is revoked.

Certificate Revocations List (CRL)

Sometimes a certificate needs to be invalidated before it would normally expire. There are a number of reasons this would be necessary. Perhaps the private key corresponding to the public key in the certificate has been lost or compromised. Maybe the subject of the certificate is using the certificate for purposes the CA does not approve of, like signing viral code. Certificates can be used to control access to a corporate systems, so if an employee leaves the company, their certificate should be revoked so that they are no longer able to use that system.

Whatever the reason, the CA needs to be able to revoke a certificate. Certificate Revocation Lists provide the ability to do so. A CRL is essentially just a list of revoked certificate serial numbers that has been signed by the CA. Each CA has its own CRL that can be downloaded. If you want to know if a certificate is valid, you check the CRL to see if the certificate is in it. If the certificate is not listed in the CRL, then it has not been revoked.

`java.security.cert.X509CRL` provides an abstract class for dealing with CRLs. You can download a CRL from a CA and instantiate using the following code:

```
FileInputStream inStream = new FileInputStream("crl_filename");
CertificateFactory cf = CertificateFactory.getInstance("X.509");
X509CRL crl = (X509CRL)cf.generateCRL(inStream);
in.close();
```

You will then be able to use the `crl` object to test a certificate for validity with the following:

```
if (crl.isRevoked(certificate)) {
  System.out.println("Certificate has been revoked.");
} else {
  System.out.println("Certificate is okay.");
}
```

Note that a given CRL is only valid for certificates from that CA. The CRL is a list of serial numbers of certificates that have been revoked, so a revoked certificate from a different CA will not be in that list.

Typically, a CA will offer its CRLs for download on its web site. Verisign's, for instance, can be downloaded from http://crl.verisign.com. A revoked certificate will remain in a CA's CRL until the certificate itself would expire. Unfortunately, revocation checking is rarely done in most applications, due to the difficulty of downloading and checking a revocation list each time a check is required.

Now that we've covered some of the more complex components of certificate use, we're going to move on to the use of certificates to support a large system that establishes identity.

Public Key Infrastructure (PKI)

Public Key Infrastructure (**PKI**) is essentially a system for managing public-key cryptography. As we've seen so far, there are quite a number of algorithms, protocols, and security concerns involved in setting up even the beginnings of a secure system. PKI is an attempt to integrate a number of protocols and standards into a more unified system that will provide secure services.

PKI must provide at least the following services:

- ❏ Creation of certificates

- ❏ Revocation of certificates

- ❏ Validation of certificates

- ❏ Providing certificates to clients

Currently PKI is a moving target. There are attempts to define standards for the exchange of public keys and other information, including X.509 certificates. When defining your organization's security services, it is best to stick to well-established standards like X.509 and PKCS. You can find X.509 defined at http://www.ietf.org/rfc/rfc2459.txt. It contains references to the necessary PKCS standards.

Standards aside, different organizations will implement PKI differently. Some will be content with the PKI services provided by the large Certificate Authorities as defined in the browser. Other organizations may need more flexibility and control than can be provided by a standard CA. They may need to implement their own CA. Nonetheless, the standards used will be the same. The main difference is in who is the root and intermediate authority for your organization.

In the next section we're going to discuss how you can become your own CA using classes built into Sun's JDK.

Building Your Own CA

By creating your own CA, you gain the ability to control the certificates in your organization closely. You can define the rules for how a certificate gets created and how it can be validated, as well as how it can be revoked and how it can be obtained in the first place.

Let's look at a simple example. Imagine you have a large web site that takes online orders. Credit card data gets stored in a database, and access is provided by an application residing on your corporate intranet. You need to limit access to the credit card data to those who need it. One way to do that is to create a certificate that validates the certificates of clients who can access the database and sign it with the organization's root certificate. Additionally, you probably want to issue e-mail certificates to all your users so they can sign e-mail. Here is a diagram of one possible way of implementing the certificate chain:

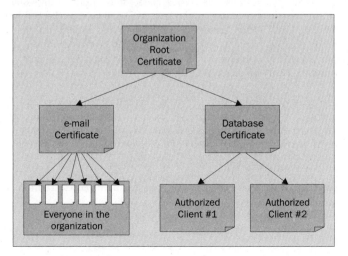

Now it would be possible for the application handling access to the credit card data to validate clients based on their certificates. If they are signed by the "Database Certificate," then they can be granted access to the data. Otherwise, they will be denied. SSL provides a way of doing this authentication quite easily in Java, and we will detail it in a later chapter.

For now, we need to cover a more difficult problem: how do we create those certificates in Java? We mentioned earlier that there was no programmatic way to create certificates exposed in the java classes. There are, however, a few options for signing certs in Java:

1. Purchase a product or library that will let you sign certificates – This works quite well, but will be expensive.

2. Write your own certificate signing code – This is a nice way to go, but will take a great deal of time.

3. Use the `sun.security.x509` classes to sign your certificates – This is quick and dirty, but will work, at least with the present version of the JDK from Sun.

To figure out how to sign certificates in Java, we looked at the JDK source to determine how `keytool` does its magic. It uses classes in `sun.security.x509` to self-sign certificates, but there's nothing in the X509 classes that require all certificates to be self-signed.

The sun.security.x509 Classes

We will be using a number of classes to create a new certificate. We're going to go over each of them, but first we should mention some of the issues when using `sun.*` classes.

The `sun.*` classes are a set of packages that Sun provides with their implementation of the Java 2 VM. They're essentially helper classes that enable functions that the VM must support. For instance, the `java.security.cert.CertificateFactory` can read a certificate from a BASE64-encoding, but there are no `java.*` classes that actually perform BASE64-decoding. There is, however, a `sun.*` class that does just that: `sun.misc.BASE64Decoder`. So the writers of `CertificateFactory` at Sun can just use that `BASE64Decoder` class to implement that part of `CertificateFactory`.

You may be asking yourself, "Should I use the `sun.*` classes in my apps?" Sun would answer that question with an unequivocal "No". In their documentation in the Java 2 SDK, they state that applications that use `sun.*` classes are not "100% pure Java". What this means in practice is that applications that rely on the `sun.*` classes won't necessarily run on non-Sun implementations of Java, or on newer versions of Java. Also, the default security configuration of the JDK won't let you access the `sun.*` classes if a security manager is instantiated. We'll talk more about the security manager in Chapter 7.

Even taking these problems into consideration, there are certain instances where using the `sun.*` classes makes sense. There are a number of classes in the `sun.security.x509` package that would take quite some time to re-implement from scratch, and if you just need quick access to certain functionality (and you don't need it to be portable) then using the `sun.*` classes is a reasonable solution (in fact, we're going to do exactly that in our certificate signer).

Now let's take a look at the classes we're going to be using. All these classes are from the `sun.security.x509` package:

X509CertImpl

Provides the underlying implementation of an X.509 certificate. We can use this class to create a new certificate, as it provides a method `sign()`, for signing the certificate.

X509CertInfo

Encapsulates the information stored in an X.509 certificate. This allows us to set all the necessary attributes for our new certificates.

X500Name

Represents an X.500 name.

AlgorithmId

Represents a cryptographic algorithm.

CertificateSubjectName

This is the X.500 name of the subject.

CertificateValidity

This is the validity period for the certificate.

CertificateSerialNumber

Represents the certificate serial number. This should be unique for a given CA.

CertificateIssuerName

This is the X.500 name of the issuer of the certificate.

CertificateAlgorithmId

The algorithm ID used to sign the certificate.

Now that we've introduced the classes we're going to use, let's start writing the code for creating a certificate.

Creating a Certificate in Java

For our example, we're going to use `keytool` to create a self-signed certificate and private key to be used for the certificate authority. Then our code will use that certificate and its private key to sign a different certificate, thus validating that certificate.

All the certificates will be stored in a keystore.

```
import java.io.*;
import java.security.*;
import java.security.cert.*;
import java.util.*;
import sun.security.x509.X509CertImpl;
import sun.security.x509.X509CertInfo;
import sun.security.x509.X500Name;
import sun.security.x509.AlgorithmId;
import sun.security.x509.CertificateIssuerName;
import sun.security.x509.CertificateSubjectName;
import sun.security.x509.CertificateValidity;
import sun.security.x509.CertificateSerialNumber;
import sun.security.x509.CertificateAlgorithmId;

// SignCertificate.java

public class SignCertificate {
```

We need to set two constants for our application:

- ❑ The algorithm to use to sign the certificate
- ❑ The validity period for the certificates

We'll use MD5WithRSA for the algorithm and we'll set the validity to one year.

```
private static final String SIG_ALG_NAME = "MD5WithRSA";
private static final int VALIDITY = 365;
```

We'll do all our work inside our main() method. We need to pass four arguments into the application: the keystore filename, the alias we want to use for our CA's certificate and private key, the alias of the certificate to sign, and the new alias we should store that certificate under.

```
public static void main (String[] args) throws Exception {

    if (args.length != 4) {
        System.err.println("Usage: java SignCertificate keystore "
                            + "CAAlias certToSignAlias newAlias");
        System.exit(1);
    }

    String keystoreFile = args[0];
    String caAlias = args[1];
    String certToSignAlias = args[2];
    String newAlias = args[3];
```

We need to get the passwords from the user to be used for the keystore and keys:

```
    BufferedReader in = new BufferedReader
    (new InputStreamReader(System.in));
    System.out.print("Keystore password: ");
    char[] password = in.readLine().toCharArray();
    System.out.print("CA (" + caAlias + ") password: ");
    char[] caPassword = in.readLine().toCharArray();
    System.out.print("Cert (" + certToSignAlias + ") password: ");
    char[] certPassword = in.readLine().toCharArray();
```

Now we'll load a keystore, using the password and keystore the user has provided:

```
    FileInputStream input = new FileInputStream(keystoreFile);
    KeyStore keyStore = KeyStore.getInstance("JKS");
    keyStore.load(input, password);
    input.close();
```

Load the CA's private key and certificate from the keystore:

```
    PrivateKey caPrivateKey =
            (PrivateKey)keyStore.getKey(caAlias, caPassword);
    java.security.cert.Certificate caCert =
            keyStore.getCertificate(caAlias);
```

Now we're going to start using the sun.* classes. We'll create an X509CertImpl from the encoded form of the CA's certificate. This will enable us to get the issuer of the certificate, which we'll need to create the new certificate.

```
byte[] encoded = caCert.getEncoded();
X509CertImpl caCertImpl = new X509CertImpl(encoded);
```

Now we'll create an X509CertInfo, which will hold the details of the CA certificate:

```
X509CertInfo caCertInfo = (X509CertInfo)caCertImpl.get
  (X509CertImpl.NAME + "." + X509CertImpl.INFO);

X500Name issuer = (X500Name)caCertInfo.get
  (X509CertInfo.SUBJECT + "." +
  CertificateIssuerName.DN_NAME);
```

Now we want to fetch the certificate to be signed, along with its corresponding private key. We need the private key in order to set a new entry in the keystore containing both the certificate and the private key. We're also going to create an X509CertInfo for our new certificate.

```
java.security.cert.Certificate cert =
  keyStore.getCertificate(certToSignAlias);
PrivateKey privateKey =
  (PrivateKey)keyStore.getKey(
  certToSignAlias, certPassword);
encoded = cert.getEncoded();
X509CertImpl certImpl = new X509CertImpl(encoded);
X509CertInfo certInfo = (X509CertInfo)certImpl.get
  (X509CertImpl.NAME + "." + X509CertImpl.INFO);
```

We need to set the validity for our new certificate:

```
Date firstDate = new Date();
Date lastDate = new Date(
  firstDate.getTime() + VALIDITY*24*60*60*1000L);
CertificateValidity interval = new
  CertificateValidity(firstDate, lastDate);

certInfo.set(X509CertInfo.VALIDITY, interval);
```

We'll create a new serial number from the current time. It's vital that certificates have unique serial numbers for a given CA. This method will work fine, provided we create no more than one certificate a second. If you need more than that, you'll need to change the code so that it keeps track of numbers issued and does not repeat.

```
certInfo.set(X509CertInfo.SERIAL_NUMBER,
  new CertificateSerialNumber((int)(firstDate.getTime()/1000)));
```

Now we'll set the issuer of the new certificate, which is our CA:

```
certInfo.set(X509CertInfo.ISSUER +
  "." + CertificateSubjectName.DN_NAME, issuer);
```

Next we'll put the algorithm information into the certificate:

```
AlgorithmId algorithm = new
  AlgorithmId(AlgorithmId.md5WithRSAEncryption_oid);
certInfo.set(CertificateAlgorithmId.NAME + "." +
  CertificateAlgorithmId.ALGORITHM, algorithm);
X509CertImpl newCert = new X509CertImpl(certInfo);
```

At last we'll sign the certificate with our CA's private key:

```
newCert.sign(caPrivateKey, SIG_ALG_NAME);
```

Finally, we want to store the new certificate to the keystore and write that keystore back out to the filesystem:

```
keyStore.setKeyEntry(newAlias, privateKey, certPassword,
  new java.security.cert.Certificate[] { newCert } );

// Store the keystore

FileOutputStream output = new FileOutputStream(keystoreFile);
keyStore.store(output, password);
output.close();

  }
}
```

Notice that the code is actually pretty short. What we're doing here is pretty simple: signing a certificate with a private key. Now let's try running it.

Running the Code

First, we need to create a self-signed certificate and private key for the CA and put it in a keystore. Here's the command we'll use, which will generate an RSA key pair and a certificate and store them in a file called keystore:

```
C:\>keytool -genkey -v -alias CA -keyalg RSA -keystore keystore
```

You will be asked to pick a password. Then you will need to answer the standard series of questions about the entity that the certificate will be associated with:

```
What is your first and last name?
  [Unknown]:  CA
What is the name of your organizational unit?
  [Unknown]:  Security
What is the name of your organization?
  [Unknown]:  ISNetworks
What is the name of your City or Locality?
  [Unknown]:  Seattle
What is the name of your State or Province?
  [Unknown]:  Washington
What is the two-letter country code for this unit?
  [Unknown]:  US
Is <CN=CA, OU=Security, O=ISNetworks, L=Seattle, ST=Washington, C=US> correct?
  [no]:  yes
```

```
Generating 1024 bit RSA key pair and self-signed certificate (MD5WithRSA)
        for: CN=CA, OU=Security, O=ISNetworks, L=Seattle, ST=Washington, C=US
Enter key password for <CA>
        (RETURN if same as keystore password):
[Saving keystore]
```

This is the key and certificate for the CA, so you should pick a good password for it.

Next we need to create the certificate that we want to sign with the CA's certificate:

```
C:\>keytool -genkey -v -alias myKey -keyalg RSA -keystore keystore
```

Answer the questions with the attributes you want your new certificate to contain.

This will also create a self-signed certificate, but our code is going to replace that certificate with one that we sign with the CA. Let's run that code:

```
C:\>java SignCertificate keystore CA myKey myKey_signed
```

We now have a third certificate in our keystore, "myKey_signed". You can view the certificates in your keystore with the following command:

```
C:\>keytool -list -v -keystore keystore
```

You should see a list containing all your keys and certificates. Among them should be your newly created certificate:

```
*******************************************
*******************************************


Alias name: mykey_signed
Creation date: Wed Mar 21 21:54:59 PST 2001
Entry type: keyEntry
Certificate chain length: 1
Certificate[1]:
Owner: CN=Jess Garms, OU=Dev, O=ISNetworks, L=Seattle, ST=Washington, C=US
Issuer: CN=CA, OU=Security, O=ISNetworks, L=Seattle, ST=Washington, C=US
Serial number: 3ab993b3
Valid from: Wed Mar 21 21:54:59 PST 2001 until: Thu Mar 21 21:54:59 PST 2002
Certificate fingerprints:
        MD5:  1C:76:E7:C8:A7:55:69:1E:BE:10:FD:FF:E5:62:B0:6C
        SHA1: 25:87:BA:4D:56:B3:1B:0B:7C:46:D0:28:C7:FA:4B:5A:61:A5:26:46


*******************************************
*******************************************
```

This certificate can be exported using keytool for use in other programs. The certificate will be exported DER-encoded by default; also BASE64-encoded if exported using the -rfc option. You can also export the CA certificate as well in the same fashion.

Note that pre-existing systems will not accept your new certificates by default. You'll need to import the CA as trusted in order for them to recognize your signed certificates. This is a sensitive operation, however, and should be done with care. Make sure you really want to trust all certificates issued by this CA.

By exporting the CA's certificate into a file, you will be able to import it into, say, a browser, and have it trusted. Here's an example:

Export the CA certificate:

```
C:\>keytool -export -alias CA -keystore keystore -file CA.crt
```

That file can now be opened in a browser and installed as a CA.

Summary

In this chapter we've covered a lot of ground. We discussed various ways to prove message authenticity and identity using message digests, digital signatures, and certificates. In particular, we covered the computation of message digests, password authentication codes, the use of digital signatures in authenticating identity, and how to chain certificates together (and revoke them).

We've also shown how to use these technologies in Java, and written several examples in order to demonstrate this. To be more specific, we've been able to demonstrate digest streams, password storage techniques, MACs, digital signatures, authentication, and keystores, and discussed their values and their limitations.

In the next chapter we're going to venture away from cryptography and start examining the Java security model and how it can be used to add security to your applications.

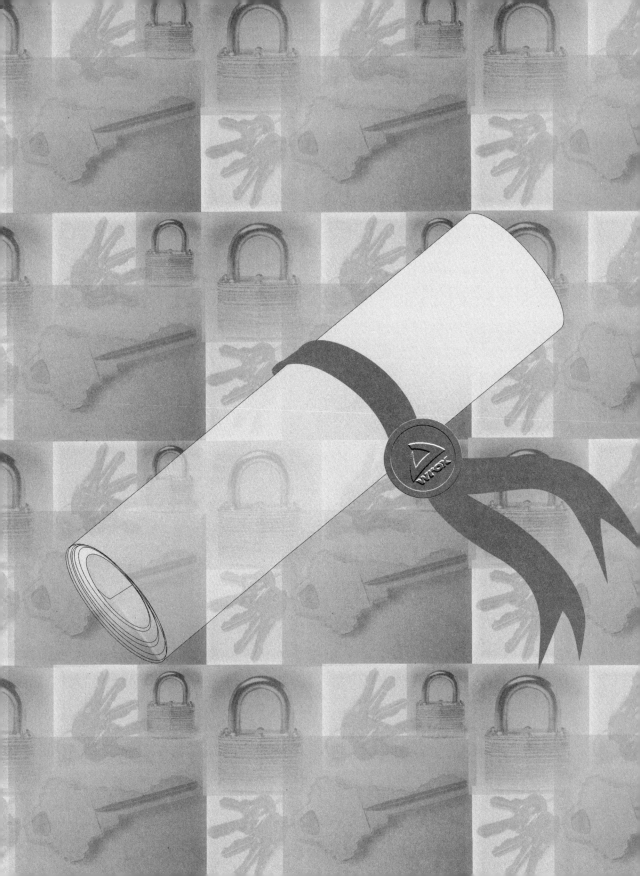

The Core Java Security Model and Applet Security

Now that we've covered some of the basic tools of security like encryption and digital signatures, we're going to talk about the security model built into Java itself. Java was designed to be a secure language from the start, and much thought was put into how to accomplish this. Java 1.0 had a very simple security model, and Java 1.1 improved on that slightly. Java 2 is when Sun finally added fine-grained security to Java.

Java 2 security is **policy-based**. That is, there is a security policy in effect that controls the resources that code has access to. This policy is defined in the `java.policy` file, which we will discuss in a moment. Permissions are granted based on two things – **codebase** and **signer**.

Codebase is the location that the code comes from. It could be a specific directory on the local hard drive, or the URL that mobile code was downloaded from. The signer is the entity that signed the code in question. Together, the codebase and the signer specify the codesource. A codesource, for example, might define code signed by Sun Microsystems and downloaded from http://java.sun.com. Permissions are then doled out to one or more of these codesources. Permissions are specific actions that are allowed, like reading a specific file, or connecting to a specific machine on the network.

As we look in detail at Java 2 security in this chapter, we'll be covering the following topics:

- ❑ Managing cryptographic signatures
- ❑ Permissions and the Java security manager
- ❑ Applets, and how to run them outside the sandbox
- ❑ How to sign applets and run them in both Netscape and Internet Explorer

Let's begin by taking a look at the first of these areas.

Managing Cryptographic Signatures

There are two tools that Sun provides for managing cryptographic signatures on Java code: `keytool` and `jarsigner`. We've discussed `keytool` in detail in Chapter 6 but we haven't yet mentioned the `jarsigner` (JAR signing and verification tool), which is for signing JAR files, thus attaching a specific signer to a specific set of code. Note that `keytool` and `jarsigner` replace `javakey`, a tool that shipped with JDK1.1. A third application, `policytool`, is for managing a security policy in Java 2.

As we've already discussed this in the previous chapter, let's take a look at the `jarsigner`.

Jarsigner

`Jarsigner`, an application shipped with the JDK, does two things: it signs JAR files, and verifies signatures on JAR files. JAR stands for **Java AR**chive. It's really just a `.zip` file that can support signatures. By signing a JAR file with `jarsigner`, you are vouching for the source of the contents of that file with a certificate. You must have a private key and a certificate in your keystore in order to sign JAR files. The certificate could be self-generated, but typically you'll want a CA to sign your certificate in order for other people to verify your identity.

Typically, signed JAR files are used to deliver signed applets. However, they can be used to deliver any code that can be trusted. A software developer could distribute signed JAR files that would allow the user to be certain that the code came directly from that developer and hadn't been modified by a third party. Sun does just that with the updates that you can download for its free IDE, Forte for Java. If you select an extra feature that the IDE doesn't by default support, it will download the necessary components from Sun. Once those components are downloaded, it will verify the signatures on them with a certificate it already contains, and then install them. If the signature cannot be verified, the IDE will not automatically install the code.

Signed Applets, Integrity, and Security

Applets are typically signed in order to grant them extra permissions, like reading and writing to the local filesystem. What happens if a file in the signed JAR has been modified? One would expect that a security exception would be thrown. Unfortunately, that's not always the case. In versions of Java before 1.2.1, if a class was loaded from a signed JAR, and that class' signature was invalid, the class would be allowed to run, but no extra permissions would be granted. What this means in practice is that it is possible to replace a number of classes in a signed JAR without causing any exceptions to be thrown. By replacing only those classes that don't actually step outside the sandbox, it's possible to significantly alter the behavior of an applet.

In Java 1.2.1, this bug was fixed, by requiring that every class within the same package inside a signed JAR needs to be signed by the same certificate. So how can we sign our JAR files?

Signing a JAR File

Let's give a quick example of using `keytool` and `jarsigner` to create and verify a JAR.

We need some content to place in that JAR, so we'll use `HelloWorld`, a time-honored example:

```
public class HelloWorld {
  public static void main (String[] args) {
    System.out.println("Hello World!");
  }
}
```

Compile that into `HelloWorld.class` and next we'll turn it into a JAR file with:

```
C:\> jar cvf HelloWorld.jar HelloWorld.class
```

You should now have a file called `HelloWorld.jar`. In order to sign it, we're going to need a private key and its corresponding certificate, which we can generate with:

```
C:\> keytool -genkey -alias exampleSig4257_ch3_2nd_ed_ib_inprog3IDX.docgKey
```

This will create an alias called `exampleSigningKey` in your default keystore using the default signature algorithm, which is DSA. You'll be asked for your keystore password in order to store the newly generated key and certificate. If you've never used `keytool` before (which is covered in detail in Chapter 6), you can make up a password. If you can't remember your keystore password, you may want to create a new one by moving the old one somewhere outside your home directory. The default keystore is called `.keystore`. Renaming it to `old.keystore`, for instance, will allow you to create a new one.

We now have a keypair with the alias `exampleSigningKey`. These aliases are used in keystores as handles to reference a particular entry. We'll use it when we sign the JAR:

```
C:\> jarsigner HelloWorld.jar exampleSigningKey
```

This signs `HelloWorld.jar` with the private key and certificate belonging to the alias `exampleSigningKey`. We can now verify it with the following:

```
C:\> jarsigner -verify -verbose HelloWorld.jar
```

The response we get tells us if the JAR has been signed, and if the signature is valid for that JAR. By specifying the verbose option, we'll also see if the certificate of the signer can be found in our keystore. Here are the results of running jarsigner verification. Note that we've added a `-certs` switch to give us information about what certificates the files were signed with.

```
C:\> jarsigner -verify -verbose -certs HelloWorld.jar

          190 Mon Apr 17 18:11:14 PDT 2000 META-INF/EXAMPLES.SF
         1042 Mon Apr 17 18:11:14 PDT 2000 META-INF/EXAMPLES.DSA
            0 Mon Apr 17 18:10:16 PDT 2000 META-INF/
smk       426 Sun Apr 16 16:34:12 PDT 2000 HelloWorld.class

     X.509, CN=Jess Garms, OU=Dev, O=ISNetworks, L=Seattle, ST=Washington, C=US
  (examplesigningkey)

   s = signature was verified
   m = entry is listed in manifest
   k = at least one certificate was found in keystore
   i = at least one certificate was found in identity scope

 jar verified.
```

Notice the `smk` next to the entry for `HelloWorld.class`. That specifies that the signature was verified, the entry is in the manifest, and the certificate was in the keystore. Also, we can see the information embedded in the certificate, which is in X.509 format.

Signed JAR Files

A JAR is simply a collection of files bundled into a single file. When a JAR is signed, it is not the JAR itself that is signed, but some or all of the files it contains. This means that a signed JAR doesn't always guarantee all of its content. Files can be added to a signed jar without necessarily invalidating the signature, with a tool like WinZip. In addition, modifying one file doesn't invalidate the signature of another. The signatures must then be stored in the JAR itself, along with some extra information, like message digests and signer information. This extra information takes the following forms:

- ❑ The manifest
- ❑ The signature file
- ❑ The digital signature file

We'll also take a quick look at the nature of the signed resources before we leave this subject. Let's start by taking a look at the manifest file.

The Manifest

All of that extra information goes into a directory in the JAR, named META-INF. In that directory is a file, MANIFEST.MF, typically known as the manifest. In a normal, unsigned JAR, its contents look something like this:

```
Manifest-Version: 1.0
Created-By: 1.3.0rc3 (Sun Microsystems Inc.)
```

When we sign a JAR, however, the names and hashes of the files are recorded in the manifest like so:

```
Manifest-Version: 1.0
Created-By: 1.3.0rc3 (Sun Microsystems Inc.)

Name: UsernameApplet.class
SHA1-Digest: Tqsr1dgU9cPxX1+qZZ+O348+dfQ=

Name: UsernameNetscapeApplet.class
SHA1-Digest: m5olpv90S83fOCxmno6/0BaSFGQ=
```

The Signature File

There is a second file in the META-INF directory, the **signature file**. This will be named something like SIGNER.SF, where SIGNER is the name of the alias used to sign the file. This is a human-readable file containing the digest of the manifest, and the digests of each of the manifest entries. Here's an example:

```
Signature-Version: 1.0
SHA1-Digest-Manifest: dtSHlvrX/vvDl+zC0V3vwc4JS60=
Created-By: 1.3.0rc3 (Sun Microsystems Inc.)

Name: UsernameApplet.class
SHA1-Digest: XMWl/rsSwfLRWgxQfNBrHiisRNE=

Name: UsernameNetscapeApplet.class
SHA1-Digest: uUolweCxIryMgYpUQh1E8n8OC74=
```

The Digital Signature File

The **digital signature file** is the alias of the signer followed by `.DSA` or `.RSA`, depending on the algorithm used to sign. It is a digital signature in PKCS#7 format of the `.SF` file. It's in binary format, and is not human readable.

Signed Resources

Sometimes it is necessary to have a guarantee of authenticity on a JAR, an assurance that none of the files within it have been tampered with. For instance, imagine you're distributing a document with your application. You can place it in a signed JAR and have a guarantee that it wasn't tampered with.

If you call `getResourceAsStream()` on a JAR (the typical way to get resources from a JAR file within an applet), the signature on that resource will be checked, and a security exception thrown if the signature is not valid.

In Java 1.1, this is not the case. The signature on a resource is not checked when it is loaded, so it is possible to alter the resource without the applet detecting it. If you're using Java 1.1, it's probably necessary to use SSL on the server to guarantee that no one can stage a man-in-the-middle attack.

Now that we've covered JAR files, let's move on to take a closer look at permissions.

Permissions

There are several elements to consider when talking about permissions in Java. In this section, we'll cover:

- ❑ The Java security manager
- ❑ The `java.policy` file
- ❑ Creating your own permissions
- ❑ The `java.security` file
- ❑ Trusted classes
- ❑ Privileged code

Let's begin by asking a question: what is the function of the Java security manager?

The Java Security Manager

The Java security manager handles the checking of permissions as needed. There is a default implementation in `java.lang.SecurityManager`, which can be sub-classed and replaced if necessary. Java enforces security by asking the security manager for permission to take any action that is considered potentially unsafe.

Here's how the security manager works:

1. Your code calls some code that requires permission, such as :

```
new FileInputStream("filename");
```

2. That code in turn calls the security manager to see if that permission is granted.

3. The security manager decides if the permission is allowed. This is usually delegated to `java.security.AccessController`, but that's not required. If the permission is denied, a run-time exception, `java.lang.SecurityException`, is thrown. If the permission is allowed, the call to the security manager returns with no exception. The security manager checks the entire thread of execution to make sure that every class on the stack has the desired permission.

4. If no exception was thrown, the permission was allowed and execution can continue normally.

Investigating the Security Manager

Let's take a closer look at the security manger with some example code. We'll write a class (`FileWriteTest`) that tries to write to a file, and see what happens.

```
import java.io.*;

public class FileWriteTest {
  public static void main (String[] args) throws Exception {
    FileOutputStream fos = new FileOutputStream("test.txt");
    fos.write("This is some test text.".getBytes());
    fos.close();
  }
}
```

If we run this class directly, with `java FileWriteTest`, it executes with no problems. By default, a Java application runs without a security manager. You can force the use of a security manager with a command line switch, `-Djava.security.manager`, or you can instantiate one programmatically in your application with `System.setSecurityManager()`.

Let's see what happens if we run our code with a security manager:

```
C:\> java -Djava.security.manager FileWriteTest
```

We'll get a security exception when we try to execute it:

```
C:\> java -Djava.security.manager FileWriteTest
Exception in thread "main" java.security.AccessControlException: access denied
(java.io.FilePermission test.txt write)
        at
java.security.AccessControlContext.checkPermission(AccessControlContext.java:195)
        at
java.security.AccessController.checkPermission(AccessController.java:403)
        at java.lang.SecurityManager.checkPermission(SecurityManager.java:549)
        at java.lang.SecurityManager.checkWrite(SecurityManager.java:958)
        at java.io.FileOutputStream.<init>(FileOutputStream.java:96)
        at java.io.FileOutputStream.<init>(FileOutputStream.java:62)
        at FileWriteTest.main(FileWriteTest.java:5)
```

Here's what happened:

1. Our code called new `FileOutputStream("test.txt");`

2. `FileOutputStream`'s code looks like this:

```
public FileOutputStream(String name, boolean append)
        throws FileNotFoundException {
  SecurityManager security = System.getSecurityManager();
  if (security != null) {
    security.checkWrite(name);
  }
  fd = new FileDescriptor();
  if (append) {
    openAppend(name);
  } else {
    open(name);
  }
}
```

It calls `SecurityManager.checkWrite()` with the name of the file in question.

3. At this point, `SecurityManager` calls `AccessController`, which in turn calls `AccessControllerContext`, which is where the exception is finally thrown. If there were no `SecurityManager` returned by the system in the `FileOutputStream`, it would have silently gone on about its business without checking permissions. That's what happens by default when you start an application from classes residing on the local hard drive.

Let's say that we wanted to enable some code to write to a file, specifically this example. How could we do that? We need to decide how we will identify the code in question. Will it be signed? Or will it be loaded from a particular place in the filesystem? Or both?

If we want the code to be identified with a signature, then we need to place the code in a JAR file, and sign that JAR. Then we need to make sure that the certificate it was signed with is in the keystore that the VM will be using when it loads the classes.

To assign a permission based on where a class comes from, we'll need to learn how to use the `java.policy` file, which defines what permissions are assigned to what classes.

The java.policy File

Somehow permissions must be assigned to classes. These assignments are stored in the `java.policy` file, which is stored in `$JAVA_HOME/jre/lib/security`. Let's take a look at that file as it is in a default installation:

```
// Standard extensions get all permissions by default

grant codeBase "file:${java.home}/lib/ext/*" {
  permission java.security.AllPermission;
};
```

```
// default permissions granted to all domains

grant {

    // Allows any thread to stop itself using the java.lang.Thread.stop()
    // method that takes no argument.
    // Note that this permission is granted by default only to remain
    // backwards compatible.
    // It is strongly recommended that you either remove this permission
    // from this policy file or further restrict it to code sources
    // that you specify, because Thread.stop() is potentially unsafe.
    // See "http://java.sun.com/notes" for more information.

    permission java.lang.RuntimePermission "stopThread";

    // allows anyone to listen on un-privileged ports

    permission java.net.SocketPermission "localhost:1024-", "listen";

    // "standard" properies that can be read by anyone

    permission java.util.PropertyPermission "java.version", "read";
    permission java.util.PropertyPermission "java.vendor", "read";
    permission java.util.PropertyPermission "java.vendor.url", "read";
    permission java.util.PropertyPermission "java.class.version", "read";
    permission java.util.PropertyPermission "os.name", "read";
    permission java.util.PropertyPermission "os.version", "read";
    permission java.util.PropertyPermission "os.arch", "read";
    permission java.util.PropertyPermission "file.separator", "read";
    permission java.util.PropertyPermission "path.separator", "read";
    permission java.util.PropertyPermission "line.separator", "read";
    permission java.util.PropertyPermission "java.specification.version", "read";
    permission java.util.PropertyPermission "java.specification.vendor", "read";
    permission java.util.PropertyPermission "java.specification.name", "read";
    permission java.util.PropertyPermission "java.vm.specification.version", "read";
    permission java.util.PropertyPermission "java.vm.specification.vendor", "read";
    permission java.util.PropertyPermission "java.vm.specification.name", "read";
    permission java.util.PropertyPermission "java.vm.version", "read";
    permission java.util.PropertyPermission "java.vm.vendor", "read";
    permission java.util.PropertyPermission "java.vm.name", "read";
};
```

There are two entries in this file: one for all code under the directory ${java.home}/lib/ext/*, and one for everything. Let's take a look at the first entry:

```
grant codeBase "file:${java.home}/lib/ext/*" {
    permission java.security.AllPermission;
};
```

This specifies that all the Java extensions get full permissions. You may remember that in previous chapters, we installed JCE providers in that directory.

The java.security.AllPermission is a dangerous permission to grant, and should be used with care. Only use it for trusted classes that truly need to have access to all resources on a machine, as any code with AllPermission will not have any restrictions when running.

The next entry is a little more verbose. It starts with the following line:

```
grant {
```

This means that all classes will be granted this permission. Unless a codebase or a signer is specified, the permission applies to everything. The next lines are a number of permissions, for instance:

```
permission java.util.PropertyPermission "java.vm.name", "read";
```

There is a specific class, `java.util.PropertyPermission`, that defines this permission. Note that the permission itself does not define security. It is up to the code that uses that permission, like the security manager, to do so. The next argument, `java.vm.name` is a target name, and is interpreted by the `PropertyPermission` class itself. The last argument, `read`, is an action, and again, is interpreted by the `PropertyPermission` class. This means that the code in question (which is everything in this case) has been given the permission to read the property `java.vm.name`.

Developing Policy Files

Let's take a look at a more generic format for the policy file, as given in the Sun documentation, found in the `docs/guide/security` directory of the JDK documentation. We will comment throughout, and give a short example of writing your own policy file.

```
keystore "some_keystore_url", "keystore_type";
```

This we haven't mentioned before. It is possible to define a keystore inside the policy file. All you need to define is the keystore URL and the type. This could be quite useful in defining a system-wide keystore on a server that could be used to validate code that will be given permission. Here's an example of a keystore entry in a policy file, which defines a JKS keystore called `.keystore`:

```
keystore ".keystore", "jks";
```

Next we have the syntax for permission grants:

```
grant signedBy "signer_names", codeBase "URL" {
  permission permission_class_name "target_name", "action",
          signedBy "signer_names";
  ....
  permission permission_class_name "target_name", "action",
          signedBy "signer_names";
};
```

These lines define grants, based on the signer and the codebase. The `signer_names` are a list of signers, separated by commas, which must match certificate aliases in your keystore. If multiple signers are listed, code must be signed by all of the signers. The URL that defines a codebase is just a standard URL. It could define a local file or a web address. Note that both the `signedBy` and the `codeBase` are optional. You could use both, either one, or neither when defining a codesource.

The permissions entry is fairly straightforward. A permission class is named, which is literally the class that represents the permission, such as `java.util.PropertyPermission`. Then a `target_name` is specified. This would be something like a filename, a hostname, or a property name. Next is the action, which is optional. Some permissions require an action, some don't. A `FilePermission`, for instance, needs to know whether permission is being granted for reading, writing, or deleting. You can also add a signer on the end, which would allow a codesource to be defined a little more specifically without needing to define an entire extra grant entry.

Let's take a look at some examples to see how this might work in practice:

```
grant {
  permission java.util.PropertyPermission "java.version", "read";
}

grant codeBase "http://www.isnetworks.com/-" {
  permission java.io.FilePermission "${/}isnetworks_files${/}-", "read";
  permission java.io.FilePermission "${/}isnetworks_files${/}-",
    "read, write, delete", signedBy "garms";
}
```

Note that the "${/}" is a platform-independent directory separator. "-" is a recursive form of a wildcard. An "*" can also be used as a wildcard, but it is non-recursive.

This defines a security policy as follows: First, *all* code can read the java.version system property, because the grant does not have any codesource defined. Next, all code downloaded from http://www.isnetworks.com can read files in /isnetworks_files/. All code from http://www.isnetworks.com that is signed by "garms" can read, write, and delete files in /isnetworks_files.

Note that the last entry could also have been written as two separate entries like so:

```
grant codeBase "http://www.isnetworks.com/-" {
  permission java.io.FilePermission "${/}isnetworks_files${/}-", "read";
}

grant codeBase "http://www.isnetworks.com/-" signedBy "garms" {
  permission java.io.FilePermission "${/}isnetworks_files${/}-",
    "read, write, delete";
}
```

Policy files can be stored on remote machines, provided that they are accessible via an HTTP URL from the client machine. You can specify a URL with the -Djava.security.policy= switch when starting a VM.

FileWriteTest Revisited

Let's try modifying our java.policy file so that our earlier example of writing out to a file will be allowed. First of all we'll assign a permission to write the specific file by codebase by adding a grant entry to our java.policy file. We have two options for where we can grant this permission: either in the default java.policy file, or in the user's home directory, in .java.policy. For this example, let's create a .java.policy file specific to a user. Note that the same permissions that we are about to grant could just as easily go in the default system java.policy, which is located in $JAVA_HOME/lib/security.

The example was written on a Windows 2000 machine with a username of garms, so the home directory is C:\Documents and Settings\garms. This is the directory in which the .java.policy file will be created (on Windows NT, the home directory would be C:\WINNT\Profiles\garms).

Here's our `.java.policy` file:

```
// Grant code in c:\test_code ability to read and write to a file "test.txt"

grant codeBase "file:${/}test_code${/}*" {
  permission java.io.FilePermission "${/}test_code${/}test.txt", "read, write,
          delete";
};
```

Now any code in `C:\test_code` has full access to the file `C:\test_code\test.txt`. If you copy our previous `FileWriteTest.class` file to the directory `C:\test_code`, you can try running it in that directory:

```
C:\test_code> java -Djava.security.manager FileWriteTest
```

Now a file should exist in that directory called `test.txt`. Let's try signing some code now and granting permissions based on the signer.

Signing Code and Granting Permissions

The first task is to remove the `test.txt` file, so we know that if it gets created the permission was granted. Next, let's edit our `.java.policy` file (again, in the home directory) and add a requirement for signer:

```
keystore ".keystore";

// Grant code signed by examplesigningkey the ability to read and write
// to a file "test.txt"

grant signedBy "examplesigningkey" {
  permission java.io.FilePermission "${/}test_code${/}test.txt",
          "read, write, delete";
};
```

Notice that the first line defines the location of our keystore. This is necessary if we want to verify signatures, which in this case, we most certainly do. It's also worth noting that the `signedBy` and codebase declarations are case-insensitive, but the permission names, being Java classes, are case-sensitive.

Next we need to JAR and sign our `FileWriteTest` class. We'll use the `exampleSigningKey` we created earlier. From the directory `c:\test_code`, run the following command:

```
C:\test_code> jar cvf FileWriteTest.jar FileWriteTest.class
C:\test_code> jarsigner FileWriteTest.jar exampleSigningKey
```

Now that the JAR has been signed, we can run the example like so:

```
C:\test_code> java -Djava.security.manager -cp FileWriteTest.jar FileWriteTest
```

And it should work normally. If the signature is invalid, or isn't in your keystore, you should get an `AccessControlException`.

Troubleshooting

We noticed some strange behavior with the JCEKS keystore provided with Sun's JCE when trying this example. In particular, the VM couldn't find an implementation of that JCEKS keystore, despite the fact that `keytool` and `jarsigner` worked just fine with JCEKS.

The only solution we were able to find was to run the example using the JKS keystore implementation provided by default in Java 2. This is a confirmed bug in JDK 1.2 and 1.3. Hopefully it will be fixed in a maintenance release of JDK 1.3.

policytool

Another way to edit the `java.policy` file or a `.java.policy` file is with the `policytool`, which is a graphical tool for editing security policies. You can run it by typing **policytool** at the command-line. Here's a screenshot:

This is the policy that we built by hand in the last example. You can see that the policy file is in the home directory, and the keystore is specified with `.keystore`. The bottom half of the window contains a list of codesources that are declared in this policy file. In this case, we have only one, which is code that has been signed by `exampleSigningKey`. We can edit it by double-clicking on it and we get the following dialog:

This lets us look at the permissions assigned to this particular codesource, as well as the definition of the codesource itself. If we edit the permission we have, we get another screen allowing us to select a permission:

You can select permissions, targets, actions, and a signer in this fashion.

`policytool` can sometimes be useful for figuring out why a policy file doesn't seem to be working the way you expect. There is a warning log accessible through the File menu that can provide some useful information if the file it's trying to open can't be parsed.

Permissions Included in Java

There are quite a number of permissions built into Java. The top-level classes include:

❑　`java.security.AllPermission` – Full permission to everything

❑　`java.security.BasicPermission` – Superclass for most simple permissions

❑　`java.io.FilePermission` – Permissions for reading and writing to files

❑　`java.net.SocketPermission` – Permission to open sockets to remote machines and resolve hostnames with DNS

`BasicPermission` is then subclassed into a number of other permissions including:

❑　`javax.sound.sampled.AudioPermission` – Permission to access underlying audio functions like playing and recording

❑　`java.awt.AWTPermission` – Permission for graphics-related activity like accessing the clipboard or reading AWT events

❑　`java.net.NetPermission` – Permission to alter the handling of URLs, like adding a password authenticator

❑　`java.util.PropertyPermission` – Permission to read and write to system properties

❑　`java.lang.reflect.ReflectPermission` – Permission to use reflection

❑　`java.lang.RuntimePermission` – Permission to certain run-time elements like setting the classloader or the security manager

❑　`java.security.SecurityPermission` – Permission to security elements like the security policy and cryptographic service providers

❑　`java.io.SerializablePermission` – Permission to read and write objects that are serializable

❑　`java.sql.SQLPermission` – Permission to set logging of SQL

You can find more information on configuring each of the above permissions in their JavaDoc.

Creating Your Own Permissions

There are times when it would be nice to create your own permissions. Let's say you want to restrict access to certain classes based on the caller's codesource. This would protect the user from untrusted code calling some sensitive installed classes.

We're going to code up an example of a protected resource that you must have a permission for, to be able to read it. We'll call it `SecretWord`, and it will contain one method: `getSecretWord()`. In order to read the secret word, which is a string, the class in question needs to have the appropriate permission granted to it, in this case, a `SecretWordPermission` with a name of `AccessPermission`.

To do this, we need to extend one of the abstract `Permission` classes in `java.security`. We have a couple of choices: we can use `Permission` itself or `BasicPermission`. The difference between the two is that `Permission` can use names as well as actions to define permissions, like giving permission to read and write (the action) a specific file (the name). `BasicPermission` supports only a name, like `queuePrintJob`. The constructor can also take an action, but `BasicPermission` does not use that action. We'll use `BasicPermission` in this case, as we don't need an action. We place this code in the file `SecretWordPermission.java`:

```
import java.security.*;

// SecretWordPermission.java

public class SecretWordPermission extends BasicPermission {

  public SecretWordPermission(String name) {
    super(name);
  }

  public SecretWordPermission(String name, String action) {
    super(name);
  }
}
```

Next we need to define a class that will check this permission before granting access to some sort of function. This is analogous to the FileOutputStream above. Here's SecretWord.java:

```
import java.security.*;

// SecretWord.java

public class SecretWord {

  private static final String mTheSecretWord = "ossifrage";

  public SecretWord() {
    super();
  }

  public String getWord() {

    // Try to get the SecurityManager

    SecurityManager security = System.getSecurityManager();
    if (security != null) {

      // Check to see if we have permission to read the word

      security.checkPermission(new
        SecretWordPermission("AccessPermission"));
    }
    return mTheSecretWord;
  }
}
```

Now we will write a class that actually uses SecretWord and attempts to get the secret word string from it. This is SecretWordTest.java:

```
public class SecretWordTest {
  public static void main (String[] args) {
    SecretWord secret = new SecretWord();

    // We try to access the secret word. This will
    // throw a SecurityException if we don't have permission

    String theSecretWord = secret.getWord();

    System.out.println("The secret word is: "+theSecretWord);
  }
}
```

Compile all of the `.java` files and let's try running the test. First we'll execute it without a security manager. `SecretWordTest` should be able to access the secret word with no difficulty:

```
C:\> java SecretWordTest
The secret word is: ossifrage
```

Now we'll try it with a security manager:

```
C:\> java -Djava.security.manager SecretWordTest
Exception in thread "main" java.security.AccessControlException: access denied
(SecretWordPermission   )
        at
java.security.AccessControlContext.checkPermission(AccessControlContext.java:195)
        at
java.security.AccessController.checkPermission(AccessController.java:403)
        at java.lang.SecurityManager.checkPermission(SecurityManager.java:549)
        at SecretWord.getWord(SecretWord.java:16)
        at SecretWordTest.main(SecretWordTest.java:7)
```

We get an exception because we don't have the `SecretWordPermission`. We need to grant that in a policy file. We're going to create one specifically for this application. Let's start by creating a JAR of the classes we need and then signing it This assumes you still have the `examplesigningkey` we used earlier. If not, you can regenerate it.

Start by creating a JAR containing the files we need:

```
C:\> jar cvf SecretWordTest.jar SecretWord*.class
```

That should put all three classes together in a JAR, which we can sign. Sign the JAR with:

```
C:\> jarsigner SecretWordTest.jar exampleSigningKey
```

Now the JAR has been signed. This doesn't actually give us any extra permissions though, as you can see by running the example with a security manager:

```
C:\> java -Djava.security.manager -cp SecretWordTest.jar SecretWordTest
```

So now we need to create a policy file that grants us the permissions we need. Let's create a file called `SecretWord.policy` that will grant us the required permission:

```
keystore "file:${user.home}${/}.keystore";

// Grant code signed by examplesigningkey
// the ability to read the secret word

grant signedBy "examplesigningkey" {
  permission SecretWordPermission "AccessPermission";
};
```

The first line defines the keystore as being `.keystore` in the user's home directory. This is the standard place for a keystore, but we need to define it regardless so that the security manager can find the alias that the signature is attached to.

Okay, so now we've got a signed JAR and we've granted it permission. Here's how we can run it with the appropriate permissions (all on the same line):

```
C:\> java -cp SecretWordTest.jar -Djava.security.manager
    -Djava.security.policy=SecretWord.policy SecretWordTest
```

This should produce the output we want with no exceptions. If you'd like to get an idea what the security manager is doing, you can run it with `security.debug` turned on like so:

```
C:\> java -cp SecretWordTest.jar -Djava.security.manager
    -Djava.security.policy=SecretWord.policy
    -Djava.security.debug=policy SecretWordTest
```

Let's have a look at what `security.debug` can do for us.

java.security.debug

By setting the system property `java.security.debug`, you can get a better idea of what's happening in your security-related code. It can be set to a few different values, which can be seen by running the command:

```
C:\> java -Djava.security.debug=help
```

which produces the following output:

```
all        turn on all debugging
access     print all checkPermission results
jar        jar verification
policy     loading and granting
scl        permissions SecureClassLoader assigns

The following can be used with access:

stack      include stack trace
domain     dumps all domains in context
failure    before throwing exception, dump stack
           and domain that didn't have permission
```

If you're trying to figure out why your code isn't getting the permission you expect, for instance, pass the option `-Djava.security.debug=access.failure` to the VM, and you will get the stack trace and domain that was denied permission. These options can be quite verbose, but will allow you to find problems much more quickly.

java.security.policy

By setting the system property `java.security.policy`, you can override or add to the default system security policy. By setting it with a single equals sign, you will add to the existing policy. If you set it with a double equals sign, you will replace the policy:

```
C:\> java -Djava.security.policy=SecretWord.policy
```

adds the policy `SecretWord.policy` to the system, while

```
C:\> java -Djava.security.policy==SecretWord.policy
```

Replaces the existing policy with the one defined in `SecretWord.policy`.

The java.security File

The `java.security` file is in `$JAVA_HOME/lib/security/`. This is where security properties are set for the VM. Here you define your security providers, your policy provider, your keystore type, and a number of other options. Let's go through them starting with the security provider definitions (which you may remember from Chapter 3):

```
security.provider.1=sun.security.provider.Sun
security.provider.2=com.sun.rsajca.Provider
security.provider.3=org.bouncycastle.jce.provider.BouncyCastleProvider
```

Next we have the policy provider definition:

```
policy.provider=sun.security.provider.PolicyFile
```

The default here is the provider that reads the policy files that we've just been using to describe security policies. Next:

```
policy.url.1=file:${java.home}/lib/security/java.policy
policy.url.2=file:${user.home}/.java.policy
```

This defines where the VM should look for policy files. It first tries the standard policy file, then looks in the user's home directory. Notice that you can use a URL, allowing you to place policy files on a web server for use throughout an organization. Note that SSL is not supported.

```
policy.expandProperties=true
```

This enables the expansion of properties like `${java.home}` to `C:\jdk1.2\jre`. By default it is set to `true`, to enable cross-platform property files. If it is set to `false`, all properties must be written out in their entirety.

```
policy.allowSystemProperty=true
```

Enables or disables the ability to override or add to the default property file(s). This is done with `java -Djava.security.policy=`, like we did in the example in the last section.

```
policy.ignoreIdentityScope=false
```

This entry is here for compatibility with the security model in Java 1.1, much of which has been deprecated in Java 2. If set to `false`, The VM remains compatible with 1.1. It is safest to change this to `true` if you know you do not need to support 1.1.

```
keystore.type=jks
```

This defines the keystore type. `jks` (Java KeyStore) is the Sun keystore provider. Another option would be `jceks` (Java Cryptography Extension KeyStore).

```
system.scope=sun.security.provider.IdentityDatabase
```

This is the class to instantiate as the system scope. It is here for 1.1 compatibility.

```
package.access=sun.
```

These are packages that will throw an exception if they are accessed without the appropriate permission (`RuntimePermission`, `"accessClassInPackage."+package`).

```
#package.definition=
```

If defined, this should cause a security exception to get thrown if you were to define a package with the name specified on this line if no such permission (`"defineClassInPackage."+package`) were granted. Note that the default policy file comments out the definition. The JDK's classloaders, however, do not actually check for this when loading classes. So unless you've written your own classloader, this won't have much effect.

Security Providers

The `java.security` file lets you define security providers. When a provider is added to the VM, either through the `java.security` file or programmatically, it registers itself with the `Security` class. Later, when someone requests a particular algorithm, let's say, "MD5", the `Security` class runs through its list of providers and returns the first implementation that matches the request.

The providers are ordered by their priority in the `Security` class itself, as defined in your `java.security` file. You can also modify this programmatically if you have the permissions to do so.

Sun includes a default security provider in Java 2, as defined by the line `security.provider.1=sun.security.provider.Sun`. It can perform MD5, SHA-1, and DSA for hashing and signing. In order to perform more cryptographic functions, you need to have an additional provider, like the Bouncy Castle or the JCE. Additionally, in Chapter 12, we'll show you how to write your own provider.

Trusted Classes

In Java 1.0, classes were either trusted or untrusted, and the distinction was easy to make: classes loaded from the local filesystem were trusted, and those from the network were untrusted. In 1.1, with the addition of signed applets, this distinction became a little less clear, but not too bad: classes loaded from the local filesystem or signed were trusted and unsigned classes loaded from the network were untrusted.

Java 2 added a finely-grained security mechanism that removed this clear distinction between trusted and untrusted. There are essentially three classpaths that define various levels of trust:

- ❑ The boot classpath
- ❑ Extensions
- ❑ The standard classpath

The Boot Classpath

The boot classpath is where all the java.* classes are stored, along with all of the other classes that are in the JDK, like javax.swing.* and the sun.* packages. These are typically stored in rt.jar and i18n.jar in $JAVA_HOME/lib.

> *Classes on the boot classpath are automatically fully trusted and have no security restrictions.*

By default, anything in $JAVA_HOME/classes is also on the boot classpath. Notice that this directory does not automatically exist, but can be created.

You can change the value of the boot classpath with an argument to the VM on instantiation. The –bootclasspath option will set the boot classpath for compiling, and the –Xbootclasspath will set the boot classpath during run time. Here's an example:

```
C:\> javac -bootclasspath C:\jdk1.1.8\lib\classes.zip MyClass.java
```

This will compile MyClass.java using the JDK 1.1 classes, with no 1.2 classes. If you wanted to then run the compiled class file, you could use:

```
C:\> java -Xbootclasspath C:\jdk1.1.8\lib\classes.zip MyClass
```

which would replace the default boot classes in 1.2 with the 1.1 classes.

Extensions

Extensions are additional class libraries that can be added to the Java run-time environment for extra functionality. The JCE is a perfect example of an extension. Extensions are stored in $JAVA_HOME/lib/ext. Any JAR files dropped into that directory are automatically installed and can be accessed from any Java program.

The default security policy in Java 2, located in $JAVA_HOME/lib/security/java.policy, gives classes in the extension directory all permissions. The following entry appears in the java.policy file:

```
// Standard extensions get all permissions by default

grant codeBase "file:${java.home}/lib/ext/*" {
  permission java.security.AllPermission;
};
```

You can change this if you like, restricting extension permission by signer or changing the permissions altogether.

The Standard Classpath

The standard classpath is defined by the environmental variable $CLASSPATH. If it is not defined, then it defaults to ".", the current working directory.

Classes on the standard classpath are not given many permissions by default. They have the ability to stop their own threads, open network connections on ports higher than 1024, and read a number of system properties. Those permissions are enumerated explicitly in the java.policy file and can be changed if desired.

As we have mentioned before, however, those security checks will not be in place unless the VM is started with a security manager, with the `-Djava.security.manager` option, or a security manager is installed programmatically with `System.setSecurityManager()`.

Reading the Classpaths

From within Java, if your code has permission, you can access the values of the three classpaths by making calls to `System.getProperty()`, like so:

```
// The boot classpath

System.getProperty("sun.boot.class.path");

// Extensions

System.getProperty("java.ext.dirs");

// The Standard Classpath

System.getProperty("java.class.path");
```

Privileged Code

When the security manager checks to see if an action is allowed, it checks that every class on the current execution stack has the required permission. This is to prevent someone from getting access to a forbidden resource through a trusted class. In essence, the most restrictive set of permissions for all the classes on the stack is in effect at a given time for a single thread.

Let's take a look at the `FileOutputStream` class, which other classes require a permission (`java.io.FilePermission`) to access. Consider a class, say, `MyUntrustedClass`, which attempts to access a `FileOutputStream` without that permission. From within the `FileOutputStream`, which is in `java.io`, the security manager is called.

The security manager then checks all the classes on the stack, which include the security manager, `java.io.FileOutputStream`, and `MyUntrustedClass`. Since one of them, `MyUntrustedClass`, does not have the necessary permissions to write to a file, an exception is thrown. Note that `java.io.FileOutputStream` *would* have permission to write to a file on its own, because it would normally be on the boot classpath. But, since it is being called by an untrusted class, the action is not allowed.

There are times, however, when it is necessary to circumvent this restriction, where all classes in the stack need to have a permission in order to perform a restricted action. For instance, let's say that we want to allow anyone to write an entry to a log file, but not to change anything in the file. We also want to make sure that the date is given for each entry. Here's an example of a first draft of that class, `Log.java`:

```
import java.io.*;
import java.util.*;

/**
 *  Log.java
 *
```

```
 *  This class logs entries to a file "log.txt" in the user's home directory.
 *  It stores the date along with whatever String the caller requests.
 */

public class Log {

  private static final String FILENAME = "log.txt";

  /**
   *  Add an entry to the log file, along with a
   *  timestamp of the current time.
   */

  public static void logAction(String text) {

    // File should go in the user's home directory

    String home = System.getProperty("user.home");
    String filename = home+File.separator+FILENAME;

    // Need to log date

    Date date = new Date();
    String textToBeWritten = date + ": " + text;

    // Open file for appending

    FileOutputStream fos = null;
    try {
      fos = new FileOutputStream(filename, true);
      PrintWriter out = new PrintWriter(fos);
      out.println(textToBeWritten);
      out.close();
    } catch (FileNotFoundException fnfe) {
      System.err.println("Log: could not create file: "+filename);
    } catch (IOException ioe) {
      ioe.printStackTrace();
    }
  }
}
```

Now let's create a test application that will call `Log.logAction`. We'll call it `TestLog.java`:

```
public class TestLog {
  public static void main (String[] args) {
    Log.logAction("This is a test.");
  }
}
```

If we run `TestLog` with a security manager installed, we'll get a security exception thrown when `Log` tries to access the file, since at present we haven't given either one any permissions. If we give permission to `Log` to write to a file, though, we'll still get a security exception thrown when `TestLog` calls `Log.logAction()`. This is because the security manager checks the entire stack of execution before allowing an action. At the time of the call, the stack looks like this:

```
TestLog
  -> calls Log
```

TestLog does not have the permission to open the file `log.txt` in the user's home directory, so the action is not allowed. One solution to this problem would be to give TestLog, and every other class that wants to call `Log.logAction()`, permission to write to that same file. But we don't really want that, because we can't control everyone else's actions, and one of them might overwrite the file, not add the date, or add the date improperly. We want *all* access to `log.txt` to go through `Log.logAction()`, so that we can control exactly what gets written to that file.

Privileged code allows us to assign a permission to a chunk of code that doesn't require the entire stack to have permission to access the resource. Instead, just the final class in the stack needs that permission. Privileged code is required, for instance, to let the VM open font files on the host machine on behalf of user code. We don't want to require the user code to have that permission, so just the VM has `AllPermission`, and calls privileged code to open the font file. Unfortunately, these privileged sections of code can be dangerous if not properly coded, so it's important to minimize the amount of code in a privileged block.

In the previous stack trace, just `Log` would need to have permission to the resource, and then it doesn't matter what class is calling `Log.logAction()` – access to the file would be allowed. In this way, untrusted applications can use trusted code in a limited way, like writing to a log.

Writing Privileged Code

In order to write privileged code, we need to implement one of two interfaces: `java.security.PrivilegedAction` or `java.security.PrivilegedExceptionAction`.

Which one to use depends on whether or not you need to be able to throw checked exceptions in your privileged code. In `Log`, we do not throw exceptions, so we'll implement `PrivilegedAction`.

`PrivilegedAction` and `PrivilegedExceptionAction` both return an `Object`, which can be `null` if you do not need to return anything from your privileged code. In our case, we do not need to return anything, so we'll just return `null`.

`PrivilegedAction` is usually implemented as an inner class, often anonymously. Since it's a little more clear when it's not being used as an anonymous inner class, we'll actually create a named inner class instead. We need to implement the `run()` method of `PrivilegedAction`, which is where we will actually access the file `log.txt`.

Let's write a new version of `Log.java`. This one will have to be in a package, as we need to grant it separate permissions from `TestLog`.

```
package logexample;

import java.io.*;
import java.util.*;
import java.security.*;

/**
 *  Log.java
 *
 *  This class logs entries to a file "log.txt" in the user's home directory.
 *  It stores the date along with whatever String the caller requests.
 */

public class Log {
```

```java
    private static final String FILENAME = "log.txt";

    /**
     * Add an entry to the log file, along with a
     * timestamp of the current time.
     */

    public static void logAction(String text) {

        /**
         * Inner class implementing PrivilegedAction
         * allows us to have file permission for writing to a logfile.
         */

        class LogPrivilegedAction implements PrivilegedAction {

            // Need an internal variable so we can access it with no args

            private String mText;

            public LogPrivilegedAction (String textArgument) {
                this.mText = textArgument;
            }

            public Object run() {

                // File should go in the user's home directory

                String home = System.getProperty("user.home");

                String filename = home+File.separator+FILENAME;

                // Need to log date

                Date date = new Date();
                String textToBeWritten = date + ": " + mText;

                // Open file for appending

                FileOutputStream fos = null;
                try {
                    fos = new FileOutputStream(filename, true);
                    PrintWriter out = new PrintWriter(fos);
                    out.println(textToBeWritten);
                    out.close();
                } catch (FileNotFoundException fnfe) {
                    System.err.println(
                        "Log: could not open file: "+filename);
                } catch (IOException ioe) {
                    ioe.printStackTrace();
                }
                return null;
            }
        }

        // End of LogPrivilegedAction definition

        AccessController.doPrivileged(new LogPrivilegedAction(text));
    }
}
```

This new version of Log.java is quite a bit more complicated than our earlier draft, but it accomplishes what we need: a block of code that has access to a resource without requiring all callers to also have access to that resource.

Running the Example

Now let's test it out. This is going to take a few steps, as we need to JAR it and sign it, and assign it permissions. Let's begin by compiling with the –d option, which will allow us to put the class files into their necessary destination directory matching their package description.

```
C:\> javac -d . Log.java
```

Now we should have a directory, logexample, that contains our class files. Let's JAR that up and sign it with examplesigningkey we created earlier:

```
C:\> jar cvf Log.jar logexample
C:\> jarsigner Log.jar examplesigningkey
```

Now that we have a JAR with the necessary classes, we need to modify TestLog.java to reflect the new package:

```
public class TestLog {
   public static void main (String[] args) {
      logexample.Log.logAction("This is a test.");
   }
}
```

Recompile TestLog:

```
javac -classpath Log.jar TestLog.java
```

Now we need to write a policy file that will have the correct permissions for classes signed by examplesigningkey. This is Log.policy:

```
keystore "file:${user.home}${/}.keystore";

// Grant code signed by examplesigningkey
// the ability to write to the file log.txt
// in the user's home directory

grant signedBy "examplesigningkey" {
   permission java.io.FilePermission "${user.home}${/}log.txt", "write";
   permission java.util.PropertyPermission "user.home", "read";
};
```

Note that we need the ability to write to the file log.txt, as well as the ability to read the property user.home, which will tell us the location of the user's home directory in the filesystem.

Here's how to run the example, now that we've created the necessary files:

```
java -cp Log.jar;. -Djava.security.manager
     -Djava.security.policy=Log.policy TestLog
```

This should run without throwing any exceptions, and create and write to a file called log.txt in your home directory. If you have any trouble with it, try running with the option -Djava.security.debug=policy, which will show what the security manager is doing as it parses the security policy and puts it into effect.

Now that we've discussed the Java security model in general, it's time to move on to more specific uses of Java security. We'll begin with applets.

Applets

Many developers are introduced to Java security when writing applets. Applets run in a sandbox by default, which offers very little access to the resources of the machine it's running on. No file access is allowed, and the only network connections that can be made must go back to the server from which the applet was loaded. In Java 1.0, there was no way for an applet to break out of this sandbox.

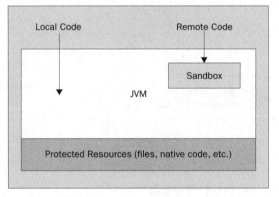

It was quickly recognized that this restrictive form of security, though great for some applications, didn't cover all requirements. There were times when an applet really did need access to some protected resource, in order to accomplish a certain task, such as printing or file storage. But how could this be accomplished without compromising security?

Java 1.1 introduced signed applets. If an applet was digitally signed, it was given full permission to system resources, as if it were running as an application on the user's machine.

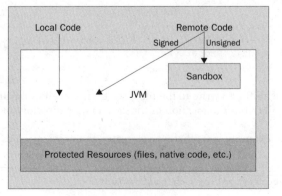

With 1.1, it was possible to use regular applets for most cases, and signed applets for those few scenarios where it was necessary to access protected resources. There was still a problem however. If an applet were signed, it was given full, unrestricted access to the local machine. If you downloaded an applet to print something, there was no guarantee that it wasn't also accessing your e-mail or password files.

To solve this problem, the primary browser manufacturers, Netscape and Microsoft, implemented different security policies in their browsers. Unfortunately, they are incompatible with each other and with the security policy of Java 1.1.

Java 2 introduced a comprehensive, fine-grained security model that covers applications and applets. By placing an entry for a particular piece of code in their `java.policy` file, a user can define very specific permissions for a given applet. While this sounds like a nice idea in theory, in practice it was recognized to be nearly impossible to get users to edit their `java.policy` files themselves. The Java environment provides no automatic way to edit this policy file on the fly, so an applet cannot ask for permission to, for instance, read from the filesystem.

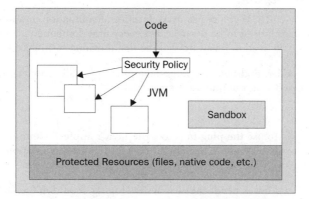

A number of developers were quite frustrated at this new situation. In Java 1.1, if you needed access to a resource, you signed your applet and you had access. In Java 2, you signed your applet and you had to somehow edit the user's `java.policy` file to get access. In response to these deployment issues, JavaSoft introduced **RSA signed applets** in JDK and JRE 1.2.2. These are applets that, once signed, are given full permission to protected resources. These are really just a return of signed applets circa Java 1.1.

Stepping Outside the Sandbox

There are a number of reasons you might need your applets to step outside the sandbox. A talk applet, for instance, might want to connect directly to other talk applets on the network, rather than go indirectly through a server. A number of applets might want the ability to print, especially a word processor or spreadsheet applet. It's also common to need some scratch space on the local file system to store state between sessions. There are even scenarios that require the use of native code from an applet.

In this section, we're going to create a small applet that tries to access some resources outside the sandbox. We're just going to write to a file on the hard drive in the user's home directory. This sounds pretty simple, but we're going to need to do it a number of different ways for the various browser and run-time combinations.

We'll start with the Java plug-in, and then move on to using applets in Netscape and then Internet Explorer.

The Java Plug-in

Java's original promise of "write once, run anywhere" was proving to be impractical around the time Java 1.1 was gaining ground. The major browsers, Netscape Navigator and Microsoft Internet Explorer, while ostensibly providing compatible Java runtimes, were in fact quite incompatible with each other. They were slow to support 1.1 in its entirety, and both were buggy.

JavaSoft introduced the Java plug-in with Java 2 in an attempt to improve the situation by providing a universal Java run-time environment for any browser. The Java plug-in runs inside the browser with a JRE supplied by JavaSoft. It supports everything that the Java environment would support on a developer's machine, and is consistent across browsers and, hopefully, platforms.

The JDK and the JRE as supplied by JavaSoft both come with the Java plug-in. By default, it will be installed and configured to run with your existing browsers.

Why Not Always Use the Plug-in?

It's a big download: 5 to 6 MB. If you're just using Java for an animation or a navigating tool, it's probably overkill. The plug-in doesn't need to be downloaded every time someone views the applet though, just the first time. Nonetheless, you need to be aware that the first download will take some time.

Also, HTML pages must be modified to use the Java plug-in for all browsers other than Netscape 6, which can be downloaded with the plug-in preinstalled.

Why Use the Plug-in?

The most obvious reason to use the plug-in is to write Java 2 applets. Neither Netscape 4.x or IE supports Java 2 at all, so if you want to use any of Java 2's features in an applet, you're pretty much stuck with the plug-in.

The plug-in also gives you fewer headaches when developing. You don't need to be worried about your code working differently in different browsers.

More importantly for this book, the plug-in inherits the Java 2 security model, so that we have fine-grained control over the actions of the applets. We can specify an applet's permissions based on where the code was downloaded from, who the digital signer is, or both. Let's take a look at an example.

A Sample Applet Requiring Permissions

We need to start by creating an applet that requires some extra permissions. Let's code up something that reads the name of the user and displays it. This requires access to information that is normally protected by the security manager, specifically, the system property `user.name`.

Here's `UsernameApplet.java`:

```
import java.applet.*;
import java.awt.*;

/**
 *  UsernameApplet.java
 *
 *  This applet requests the system property "user.name"
 *  and displays it. It should throw a security exception
 *  in most environments unless it has been given special
 *  permissions
 */
```

```
public class UsernameApplet extends Applet {

  String mUsername;

  public void init() {
    try {
      mUsername = System.getProperty("user.name");
    } catch (SecurityException e) {
      mUsername = null;
    }
  }

  public void paint(Graphics g) {
    if (mUsername != null) {
      g.drawString("Hello, " + mUsername + ".", 5, 25);
    } else {
      g.drawString("Couldn't get the username.", 5, 25);
    }
  }
}
```

Now we need an HTML file to actually see the applet in action. Here's UsernameApplet.html:

```
<HTML>
  <HEAD>
    <TITLE>
      Username Applet
    </TITLE>
  </HEAD>
  <BODY>
    <APPLET CODE="UsernameApplet.class" WIDTH=300 HEIGHT=200>
    </APPLET>
  </BODY>
</HTML>
```

To run the applet, compile it and type in the following command from the directory that both files are in:

```
C:\> appletviewer UsernameApplet.html
```

You should see the following applet:

In order to actually get the username, we're going to need to use a policy file to assign permission to read user.name. Let's assign all code in the directory of our applet that permission. Here's UsernameApplet.policy:

```
// Grant code in /test_code/ the ability to read the username.

grant codeBase "file:${/}test_code${/}*" {
  permission java.util.PropertyPermission "user.name", "read";
};
```

Copy all the files to c:\test_code or /test_code and run the following command:

```
C:\> appletviewer -J-Djava.security.policy=UsernameApplet.policy
                  UsernameApplet.html
```

This starts appletviewer with the new security policy we just defined, granting access to the user.name property. Here's what you should see:

Or rather, you should see your own username, rather than mine.

Getting the Plug-in to Work Inside a Browser

If you try running this example directly inside a browser, you'll notice that it fails. This is because the browser instantiates its own VM to handle the applet, rather than delegating to the Java Plug-in. In order to change this behavior, we need to edit the HTML that invokes the VM with the APPLET tag.

The easiest way to do this is using JavaSoft's HTMLConverter, which you can get from http://java.sun.com/products/plugin/1.2/features.html. Once you've downloaded the converter, you can start it with java HTMLConverter, provided it's on your CLASSPATH.

The HTMLConverter will then enable you to actually convert the APPLET tag in your HTML to a new OBJECT tag that can invoke the plug-in. Here's what the converted code looks like:

```
<HTML>
  <HEAD>
    <TITLE>
      Username Applet
    </TITLE>
  </HEAD>
  <BODY>
    <!--"CONVERTED_APPLET"-->
<!-- CONVERTER VERSION 1.0 -->
<OBJECT classid="clsid:8AD9C840-044E-11D1-B3E9-00805F499D93"
WIDTH = 300 HEIGHT = 200
codebase="http://java.sun.com/products/plugin/1.2/jinstall-12-
win32.cab#Version=1,2,0,0">
<PARAM NAME = CODE VALUE = "UsernameApplet.class" >

<PARAM NAME="type" VALUE="application/x-java-applet;version=1.2">
<COMMENT>
<EMBED type="application/x-java-applet;version=1.2" java_CODE =
"UsernameApplet.class" WIDTH = 300 HEIGHT = 200
pluginspage="http://java.sun.com/products/plugin/1.2/plugin-
install.html"><NOEMBED></COMMENT>

</NOEMBED></EMBED>
</OBJECT>

<!--
<APPLET  CODE = "UsernameApplet.class" WIDTH = 300 HEIGHT = 200 >

</APPLET>
-->
<!--"END_CONVERTED_APPLET"-->

  </BODY>
</HTML>
```

Now you should be able to run the example in IE or Netscape. Unfortunately, you'll almost certainly get a security exception, since the policy file we just wrote won't be used by default when the plug-in starts up. So in order to get the example to run inside a browser, we need to edit the `java.policy` file in `$JAVA_HOME/jre/lib/security`, or the user's `.java.policy` file in their home directory and add the entry that we had put in `UsernameApplet.policy`.

This is really the core difficulty when using the Java plug-in to enable an applet to step outside the sandbox: the end-user's policy file must be edited in order for the applet to get the permissions it needs.

As we mentioned earlier JavaSoft's response to this situation was to introduce the **RSA-signed applet** in JDK 1.2.2.

RSA-Signed Applets

Now let's take our applet from the last example and transform it into an RSA-signed applet. Note that real deployment would require a developer certificate from Verisign or Thawte, which costs about US$400 or US$200, respectively.

The application process for a developer certificate is somewhat involved. Your CA will require proof of your company's existence in some fashion. Expect it to take up to a week or two, depending on the type of bureaucracy you have to deal with in your organization. Look up developer certificates or code signing on either Verisign's or Thawte's web sites for more information (http://www.verisign.com and http://www.thawte.com).

You can sign applets with either Netscape's signtool or JavaSoft's jarsigner. Signtool is essentially Netscape's version of jarsigner. It can create and sign JAR files. For this example, we're going to use jarsigner because we've introduced it previously and it's easy to use. If you're interested in using signtool, we'll be covering it in the section on signing an applet for Netscape. The signing procedure is the same for an RSA-signed applet as for a Netscape-signed applet.

How Does It Work?

When the browser loads a web page with HTML including the Java plug-in tags that we mentioned earlier (OBJECT...), it starts the Java plug-in, which will then handle the loading and execution of the applet itself. The plug-in downloads the applet, and checks for a digital signature. If an RSA signature is found, the plug-in then checks the security policy as defined by java.policy and $USER_HOME/.java.policy. If there is an entry that matches the codesource (codebase and signer), then it checks to see if the permission java.lang.RuntimePermission usePolicy has been enabled. If so, it uses the permissions as defined in the policy. If not, it checks the certificate of the signer on the applet. If the signature can be traced back to a trusted CA, it asks the user if it should grant AllPermissions to the currently running applet.

Interestingly, the Java plug-in does not use the Java keystore to define a trusted CA. On Windows Netscape 3 or 4 and IE, it uses the Windows CryptoAPI to determine whether the CA is trusted. If the plug-in is running in Netscape 6, it uses the Netscape 6 CA database to determine trust.

The usePolicy Permission

By defining usePolicy as a permission, the VM is instructed to use the given policy for code in that codesource. An applet cannot override it, even if it is an RSA-signed applet. If you put the following entry in your java.policy file, no RSA-signed applet will be able to run with AllPermission, unless it is explicitly given that permission in a policy file.

```
grant {
   permission java.lang.RuntimePermission "usePolicy";
}
```

In other words, if the above appears in the user's policy file, there's no way to deploy an RSA-signed applet with full permissions to them unless they modify their policy. For better or for worse, the default policy file as shipped with the JRE does not include such an entry, allowing RSA-signed applets to have full permission.

Creating an RSA-signed Applet

We're going to use JDK 1.3 to sign this applet, because its keytool supports RSA signatures. Although signed by 1.3, the resulting applet will still run under 1.2.2.

Generate the Key

We begin by generating a key and certificate we're going to use to sign the applet. This is very similar to what we did in the last chapter to generate the "examplesigningkey" we used. In this case, however, we're going to use the RSA algorithm rather than the DSA algorithm, which is the default digital signature algorithm that Java uses. Here's how to generate the key:

```
C:\> keytool -genkey -alias appletsigningkey -keyalg RSA
```

You'll be asked for the password for your keystore, and then to enter some information about the owner of the key, like name, organization, and location. Fill these out and your key will be generated. Then you can assign a password to the key itself, if you want it to be different from the keystore password.

Get a Certificate

At this point, the procedure differs a bit if you're creating an applet for testing versus deploying. If you're testing, you need to import the certificate into your CA store. If you're deploying, you need to get your certificate signed by a CA like Thawte or Verisign.

Installing Your Own Certificate for Testing:

If you want to test your applet, you can export your certificate from the Java keystore and import it into the CA store. First, export the certificate to a file:

```
C:\> keytool -export -alias appletsigningkey -file appletsigningkey.cer
```

If you're using Windows, you need to import that certificate into the CryptoAPI keystore. Open appletsigningkey.cer by double-clicking on it. You should see something like the following:

Click on Install Certificate... and you can walk through the Certificate Import Wizard to install the certificate into your list of trusted CAs.

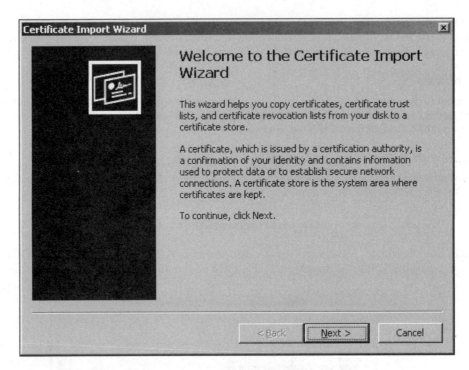

After the initial splash screen we are allowed to choose a certificate store:

Then we have a dialog showing the specified settings:

Followed by a dialog indicating where exactly the certificate will be stored:

Now that the certificate has been imported, the Java plug-in will recognize code signed with that certificate to be valid.

If you're using Solaris or Linux, you need to place the certificate in the cacerts file. This is stored in $JAVA_HOME/jre/lib/security/cacerts. Copy the certificate to that directory and CD to it. You can then import the certificate by running the following command:

```
C:\> keytool -import -alias appletsigningkey -keystore cacerts -file
            appletsigningkey.cer
```

The default password for cacerts is "changeit", but this, can and *should*, be changed with the keytool -storepasswd command.

Ordering a Signed Certificate from a CA:

If you want to deploy your applet, you need to buy a developer certificate from Thawte or Verisign. The first step you must take is exporting a **Certificate Signing Request** (**CSR**), from your keystore. Here's how to do that:

```
C:\> keytool -certreq -alias appletsigningkey -file appletsigningkey.csr
```

This will produce a file `appletsigningkey.csr`, which contains a BASE64-encoded CSR. It should look something like this:

```
-----BEGIN NEW CERTIFICATE REQUEST-----
MIIBrDCCARUCAQAwbDELMAkGA1UEBhMCVVMxEzARBgNVBAgTCldhc2hpbmd0b24xEDAOBgNVBAcT
B1NlYXR0bGUxEzARBgNVBAoTCklTTmV0d29ya3MxDDAKBgNVBAsTA0RldjETMBEGA1UEAxMKSmVz
cyBHYXJtczCBnzANBgkqhkiG9w0BAQEFAAOBjQAwgYkCgYEAxVRTqgCdjKQckukfGX9oHAWUFq1D
n7lizSgodgVZrYNI/5zGKdUi433NMVTFQ1ZooJi9qrtpBwxHiaAb54ZMo1B1VIlHziYntfxHS9Bk
bXegcVP/KDK8VQ6dKQArWLzl++o5HLdcUMwMk9w8YqcLPRmnIKjS5YVrCwWf51OtefUCAwEAAaAA
MA0GCSqGSIb3DQEBBAUAA4GBAGKgLsz6h3JKlSWVu6XZegkkpWK7IRfEgu7BkaA4CBre7kc918s5
TqF0u2m4a344zjmowMoPhdarnmkqRpxh4m78YQs8YxPZi4lJeW3EblXtd8iQZ/SY1dprR5F+wTER
OavXf+IXaN+fHDzxio7w2IvE49bPFECoh2101EUQV44s
-----END NEW CERTIFICATE REQUEST-----
```

You will need the content of that file, along with proof of your identity and $200-$400 to get a certificate from a CA. Go to their site and walk through the steps of requesting a cert. Eventually, they will e-mail you a BASE64-encoded certificate which can then be imported into your keystore to use for signing.

At this point, it might be a good idea to make a backup of your `.keystore` before proceeding. You're about to modify the certificate for the key you created earlier. You can import the new certificate into keystore with the following command, provided the new certificate is in the file `newcertificate.cer`:

```
C:\> keytool -import -alias appletsigningkey -file newcertificate.cer
```

At this point, the `appletsigningkey` entry in your keystore will be ready to be used to sign your applet.

Create and Sign the JAR

Create the JAR with the `jar` command:

```
C:\> jar cvf UsernameApplet.jar UsernameApplet.class
```

Sign it with `jarsigner`:

```
C:\> jarsigner UsernameApplet.jar appletsigningkey
```

We can now deploy it with the same HTML we used earlier for our Java plug-in example.

Now you should be able to run the example by opening that HTML file in a browser. Here's what you should see once the plug-in loads:

More Info will display the certificate information. Here's what my self-signed certificate displays:

Each of the Fields may be examined. Issuer here is grayed-out because this is a self-signed certificate. If a CA signed it, you would be able to view their certificate as well.

If the user decides to grant permission to the applet, it will run with AllPermissions inside the VM. That means it can read and write files, make network connections, and so on – anything a regular Java application can do when run without a security manager. As you can see, it was able to read the system property user.name:

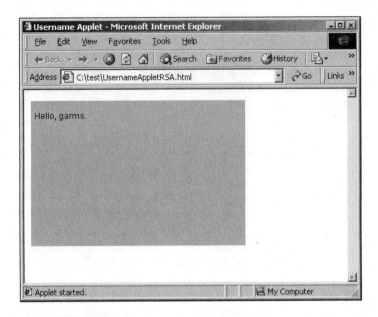

Signed Applets in Netscape

Sometimes, much to many a developer's chagrin, it's just not possible to deploy with the Java plug-in. User's may not be willing to wait for the 6 MB download, or risk the install. In those cases, you may want to use the VM built into Netscape itself. As of this writing, Netscape 4 supports Java 1.1, and Netscape 6 uses the Java plug-in. This could make your deployment a little tricky if you want your applet to work on both platforms.

If you just want to run under Netscape 6, you can create an RSA-signed applet as described in the previous section and you'll be all set. If, however, you want to run under Netscape 4 without using Java plug-in, you'll need to take some extra steps, which we will describe here (you're limited to Java 1.1 in Netscape, and only the subset of Java 1.1 that Netscape supports – this precludes anything in `java.security.*`, but most other packages from Java 1.1 should work).

Netscape's Java security model is a bit different from the standard 1.1 or 1.2 model. The code is granted permissions, similarly to under Java 2, but the applet itself can ask for permission. If it gets it, it can then execute restricted code that would, under normal circumstances, throw an exception. Netscape calls this its **Capabilities API**. There is documentation available at http://developer.netscape.com/docs/manuals/signedobj/. The capability classes can be downloaded from http://developer.netscape.com/docs/manuals/signedobj/capsapi.html.

> *In order to compile the following example, you'll need the Capabilities API classes, which you can download from Netscape at the URL above. The file is called* `capsapi_classes.zip`.

Making Use of the Capabilities API

To conform to the Capabilities API we're going to have to modify our applet. We need to make a call to the class `netscape.security.PrivilegeManager` in order to enable the ability to read a system property, and then disable it when we're done. Here's what our code will look like:

```java
import java.applet.*;
import java.awt.*;

// Import netscape class for security

import netscape.security.PrivilegeManager;

/**
 *  UsernameNetscapeApplet.java
 *
 *  This applet requests the system property "user.home"
 *  and displays it. It should throw a security exception
 *  in most environments unless it has been given special
 *  permissions
 */

public class UsernameNetscapeApplet extends Applet {

  String mUsername;

  public void init() {
    try {

      // Ask the PrivilegeManager for permission
      // to read system properties

      PrivilegeManager.enablePrivilege("UniversalPropertyRead");
      mUsername = System.getProperty("user.name");
      PrivilegeManager.revertPrivilege("UniversalPropertyRead");
    } catch (SecurityException e) {
      mUsername = null;
    }
  }

  public void paint(Graphics g) {
    if (mUsername != null) {
      g.drawString("Hello, " + mUsername + ".", 5, 25);
    } else {
      g.drawString("Couldn't get the username.", 5, 25);
    }
  }
}
```

The changes we made are highlighted. Here's how to compile the applet:

```
C:\> javac -classpath .;capsapi_classes.zip UsernameNetscapeApplet.java
```

Once again, we'll need an HTML file to execute the applet. Here's the code for
UsernameNetscapeApplet.html:

```html
<HTML>
  <HEAD>
    <TITLE>
      Username Netscape Applet
    </TITLE>
  </HEAD>
  <BODY>
    <APPLET CODE="UsernameNetscapeApplet.class" WIDTH=300 HEIGHT=200>
    </APPLET>
  </BODY>
</HTML>
```

Applet security in Netscape works differently if you're loading from the local filesystem versus a web server. If you load off the file system, you can try out your applet without signing it. Here's what we see when we load `UsernameNetscapeApplet.html` in Netscape:

The Details button will give some extra information about the permission that the applet is requesting. Here's the dialog box that appears:

If we grant the permission the applet is requesting, it will execute normally, just as it did before in the Java plug-in.

Deploying the Applet

If we want to deploy this applet, we're going to need to sign it. In order to do this, we'll need `signtool` from Netscape. You can download it for your platform from http://developer.netscape.com/software/signedobj/jarpack.html. You will also need a copy of Netscape Navigator v4.06 or higher to get a certificate that `signtool` can use. Again, you will need to go to a certificate authority to get that certificate, and it will cost somewhere between US$200 and US$400.

You use Netscape itself to generate your key pair, and request and receive the certificate. `Signtool` will then use the Netscape key and certificate database to sign your JAR. For this example, we'll show you how to generate a self-signed certificate and private key and use that to sign your applet. This is fine for testing, but for deployment you'll probably need to purchase a developer cert from a CA.

The key and certificate database are stored in your Netscape user profile. You'll need to know the location of these files in order to use signtool. Typically, they're stored in `~./netscape` on a UNIX machine, and in the Netscape user directory on Windows, which is a little harder to find. On my machine, it's `C:\Program Files\Netscape\Users\garms\`.

In order to use that certificate database, you need to initialize it in Netscape. If you've every created or imported a certificate, this has already been done. If not, we'll walk you through the initialization of your Netscape certificate database. There is no simple command for doing this, so instead we'll go through the steps for importing a certificate, and then cancel after the database is created.

First, open Netscape and click on the lock icon at the bottom left of the screen:

In the window that pops up, click on Certificates > Yours:

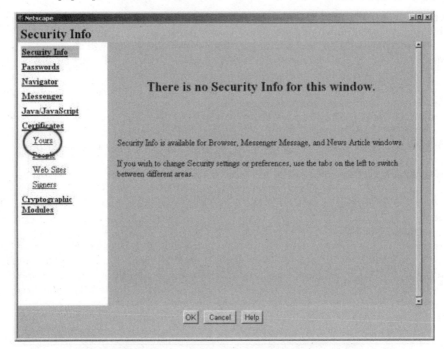

Next click on Import a Certificate...:

You will be asked to set a password for the database that is about to be created. Once you've done so, a file dialog box will pop up asking you to select the certificate to import. You can cancel the actual import, but the certificate database will remain created.

Now let's return to `signtool`. We'll begin by creating a self-signed certificate and private key. Be sure that you close any instances of Netscape you have running. Then run `signtool` with a `–G` option to specify key generation. You'll also need to include a `–d` option to specify the directory for the key database:

```
C:\> signtool -G"testsigner" -d "C:\Program Files\Netscape\Users\garms"
```

`Signtool` will then ask you a number of questions about the certificate you're about to create. When it's done, it will store the signing key in the Netscape certificate database.

You can list the keys available to use with the `–l` option, including a `–d` option to specify the directory in which your key database resides:

```
C:\> signtool -l -d "C:\Program Files\Netscape\Users\garms"
using certificate directory: C:\Program Files\Netscape\Users\garms

Object signing certificates
---------------------------------------
testsigner
    Issued by: testsigner (ISNetworks)
    Expires: Tue Jul 25, 2000
isnetworks internal
    Issued by: isnetworks internal (devcert)
    Expires: Wed Jul 12, 2000
---------------------------------------
```

We can now use either of these keys to sign our JAR. First, we need to create a directory that we will be jarring and signing. Unlike `jarsigner`, which could sign a JAR that already existed, `signtool` has to create a JAR as it signs. We'll create a directory called `jar_directory` in which we'll put the file `UsernameNetscapeApplet.class`.

Once that's been done we can create and sign the JAR file, `netscapeApplet.jar`:

```
C:\> signtool -d "C:\Program Files\Netscape\Users\garms" -k "testsigner" -Z
            "netscapeApplet.jar" jar_directory
```

The above should all be on one line. The `–d` directive tells signtool where to find the key and certificate files, the `–k` specifies the name of the signing certificate we want to use, `-Z` specifies the JAR file we want to create, and `jar_directory` is the directory whose contents we want to jar and sign.

Now we modify the HTML to reflect the name of the JAR file we've just created. This is `UsernameNetscapeAppletSigned.html`:

```
<HTML>
  <HEAD>
    <TITLE>
      Username Netscape Applet
    </TITLE>
  </HEAD>
  <BODY>
    <APPLET CODE="UsernameNetscapeApplet.class" ARCHIVE="netscapeApplet.jar"
          WIDTH=300 HEIGHT=200>
    </APPLET>
  </BODY>
</HTML>
```

If we open that file with Netscape, we get the following dialog:

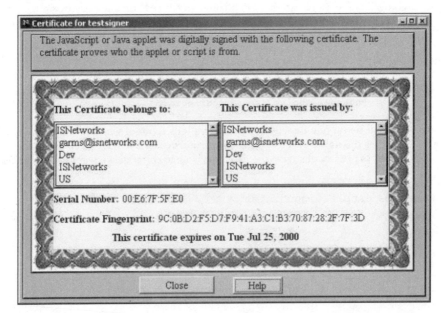

Note that it no longer claims that the code is not digitally signed and, in fact, there is some information at the bottom of the window, Identity verified by ISNetworks. This is because the particular certificate I used to sign this example code was self-generated. A CA-generated certificate would indicate the identity of the CA. If we click on the Certificate button, we get some information about the signer and the CA:

Again, in a CA-generated certificate, the issuer and the subject would be different.

If we grant the permission, our applet is able to read the system property user.name and display it for us:

Privileges in Netscape

The Netscape Capabilities API provides the ability for an applet to request extra permission and then use it. It works by calling the PrivilegeManager, like this line from our earlier example:

```
PrivilegeManager.enablePrivilege("UniversalPropertyRead");
```

There is a list of all properties available at:
http://developer.netscape.com/docs/manuals/signedobj/javadoc/netscape_security_Target.html.

The first time a privilege is requested, Netscape will pop up a dialog box asking the user if the privilege should be granted. If the user clicks Grant, then further privileges will be enabled without prompting, in the scope of that execution of the applet.

Once a privilege has been enabled with a call to PrivilegeManager.enablePrivilege(), it is available within the scope of that method. Because of this, you should only ask for privileges when you need them, and use them immediately. Otherwise you risk having the security manager throw an exception.

There is one exception though – applet start-up. It's usually nice to ask for everything you want up-front, so the user is confronted with all the security dialogs immediately. Then disable the privileged. Whenever a privilege is required for the applet, make a call to PrivilegeManager.enablePrivilege().

There is also another method in `PrivilegeManager` called `revertPrivilege()`, which can be used to terminate a given privilege within the context of a method. This helps to reduce the amount of code that runs with a given privilege, reducing the possibility of someone using your applet to mount an attack.

The applet security model is Netscape is somewhat bizarre. Because it requires Netscape classes to be called from within your applet, it is incompatible with any other applet security model. Thankfully, Netscape is abandoning its proprietary Java implementation and embracing Sun's Java plug-in in Netscape 6.0.

Signed Applets in Internet Explorer

Microsoft Internet Explorer introduced yet another Java security model. This one is a bit nicer than the Netscape security model in that you don't need to alter your code to create a signed applet. That being said, however, if it is possible to use the Java plug-in for your project rather than Microsoft's VM, we recommend you go with the Java plug-in.

IE recognizes four different security levels for signed applets: **high**, **medium**, **low**, and **custom**. Each one grants different permissions to the signed code:

❑ High security is the standard sandbox that you are used to in applets. No file I/O, no network I/O except to the server the applet was downloaded from, etc.

❑ Medium security is new. This allows certain additional functions, mostly revolving around providing some scratch space for the applet on disk, allowing it to store persistent information for future use.

❑ Low security is just like Java 2's `AllPermission`. Code that is run with the low security setting is free to do anything that a normal application would be allowed to do, including reading, writing, and deleting files, network access, registry access, and so on.

❑ Custom security is similar to Java 2's policy file. Specific permissions can be granted to do things like read a particular file, or connect to a certain machine.

When you sign your applet, you assign it a security level. That level will be displayed for the user when the applet is loaded and it will ask them if they want to allow the permission to be granted.

IE does not recognize signed JAR files, but rather signed `.cab` files. 'Cab' is short for Cabinet, and is very similar to a JAR file in that it can store multiple files and contain a signature.

In order to create and sign `.cab` files, you'll need Microsoft's SDK for Java. You can download it from http://www.microsoft.com/java/. At the time of this writing, the most current version was 4.0. Installing the SDK for Java will place a number of files in `C:\Program Files\Microsoft SDK for Java 4.0`, including all of the binary tools you will need to create and sign `.cab` files.

Running an Applet in IE

Once again, we're going to get our `UsernameApplet` to work in the browser, this time in IE 4 or 5. We will return to the code we used in the Java plug-in example, as IE doesn't require us to use any IE-specific code in our applet. We do need to modify it slightly, however, and move the sensitive code outside the `init()` method, due to a bug in Microsoft's Java implementation. Here's our new `UsernameApplet.java`:

```
import java.applet.*;
import java.awt.*;

/**
 *  UsernameApplet.java
 *
 *  This applet requests the system property "user.name"
 *  and displays it. It should throw a security exception
 *  in most environments unless it has been given special
 *  permissions
 */
public class UsernameApplet extends Applet {

    String mUsername;

    public void setUsername() {
        try {
            mUsername = System.getProperty("user.name");
        } catch (SecurityException e) {
            mUsername = null;
        }
    }

    public void paint(Graphics g) {
        if (mUsername != null) {
            g.drawString("Hello, " + mUsername + ".", 5, 25);
        } else {
            setUsername();
            g.drawString("Couldn't get the username.", 5, 25);
        }
    }
}
```

We can compile this file normally with

```
C:\> javac UsernameApplet.java
```

There's something that you should be aware of when using signed applets in Internet Explorer. Permissions are not necessarily assigned before the init() or start() method, so all actions requiring special permissions should go in a method that gets called later. In our example, we used the paint() method, but it would probably be better to have a separate method that gets called once from the paint() method if it has not been previously called.

Create a Signer

In order to sign the applet, we need a certificate. You can buy one from a CA for $200 or $400 as stated earlier, but for testing, you can generate a signing certificate with the following command, included in the Microsoft SDK for Java:

```
C:\> makecert -sk example -n "CN=Jess Garms" example.cert
```

This will create a certificate file, example.cert. In order to sign code, however, you need to convert it into a Software Publisher Certificate like so:

```
C:\> cert2spc example.cert example.spc
```

Create the Archive

Now we need to create a `.cab` file with the applet in it:

```
C:\> cabarc N UsernameApplet.cab UsernameApplet.class
```

Sign the Archive

Now we can sign the `.cab` file with "low" security, as this will give it access to read the system property `user.name`:

```
C:\> signcode -j JavaSign.dll -jp low -spc example.spc -k example
UsernameApplet.cab
```

The `-k` flag above specifies the private key to use to sign. In this case, we called it `"example"` when we created the certificate.

Create the HTML

We need to modify the HTML slightly to run the applet, because we need to specify the `.cab` file. We just add a `PARAM` tag `"cabbase"` set to the `.cab` filename. Here's `UsernameExplorerApplet.html`:

```html
<HTML>
  <HEAD>
    <TITLE>
      Username Explorer Applet
    </TITLE>
  </HEAD>
  <BODY>
    <APPLET CODE="UsernameApplet.class" WIDTH=300 HEIGHT=200>
      <PARAM NAME="cabbase" VALUE="UsernameApplet.cab">
    </APPLET>
  </BODY>
</HTML>
```

Running the Applet

Now we can execute the example by opening the HTML file in IE. We will be greeted with the following dialog box when the applet is loaded:

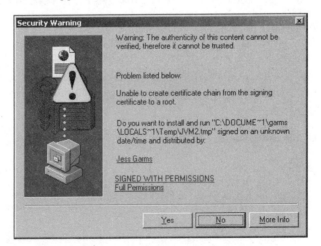

If you use a CA-signed certificate, you won't see the authenticity warning, but you will still see the dialog asking for permissions. If you click on the permission, you will get the following information:

If you grant the applet the permission it's requesting, it will run normally, and have access to read the user.name property.

Finely-Grained Permissions

Explorer also gives us the ability to sign an applet with specific permissions. These permissions can be set with a Permission INI Editor: piniedit. Here's a screenshot of what you should see if you execute piniedit:

For our applet, we want the ability to read the system property `user.name`, which we can specify like so:

Once that's been done, we can save the resulting file to `UsernameExplorerApplet.ini`. The contents of that file are as follows:

```
[com.ms.security.permissions.PropertyPermission]
Version=2
Unrestricted=false
AllowedSuffixes=
IncludedProperties=user.name
ExcludedProperties=

[com.ms.security.permissions.ThreadPermission]
Version=2
AllThreadGroups=false
AllThreads=false
```

The thread permissions are assigned to all applets by default.

Now that we have a permissions `ini` file, we can sign the `.cab` with those specific permissions with the following command (all on one line):

```
C:\> signcode -j JavaSign.dll -jp UsernameExplorerApplet.ini -spc example.spc
        -k example UsernameApplet.cab
```

Now if you open `UsernameExplorerApplet.html`, you should see the following dialog box:

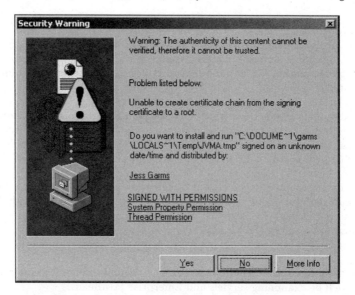

Note that now there are two permissions listed: System Property Permission and Thread Permission. You can click on these permissions to view more detail on them:

Now it's easy to make a decision about whether or not to run this applet. You can see that the only extra permission it's getting is the ability to read the `user.name` system property, and nothing else. Running with `AllPermissions` is a scary prospect, and it is best to avoid that if possible.

Summary

In this chapter we've covered a lot of ground. We've discussed the Java security model, and how it allows us to manage cryptographic signatures, as well as covering the `jarsigner` tool, which signs files within a JAR file. Over the course of that discussion, we learned that the JAR file contains a `META-INF` directory holding the manifest file, and the signature files so that the user downloading a JAR can ensure its integrity.

We also talked about permissions, and about how the Java Security manager allows us to both set existing permissions and create our own permissions for our files. This linked into the `java.policy` file and the `java.security` file, as well as use of the `policytool` in editing the `java.policy` file. We concluded that section with a discussion of classpaths and how these can affect security.

The main thrust of this chapter, however, was directed toward applets, and how to run them on different platforms (Netscape and Internet Explorer), and how to sign applets for use with these two browsers. We learned about the capability classes that Netscape needs to download before it can use signed applets, and about Microsoft's SDK for Java, which is needed to sign applets for use in Internet Explorer. We also covered the setting of finely-grained permissions with out discussion on `piniedit`.

Now that we've covered the Java security model and how applets interact with it, let's move to the next chapter, where we'll be examining servlets and Enterprise JavaBeans.

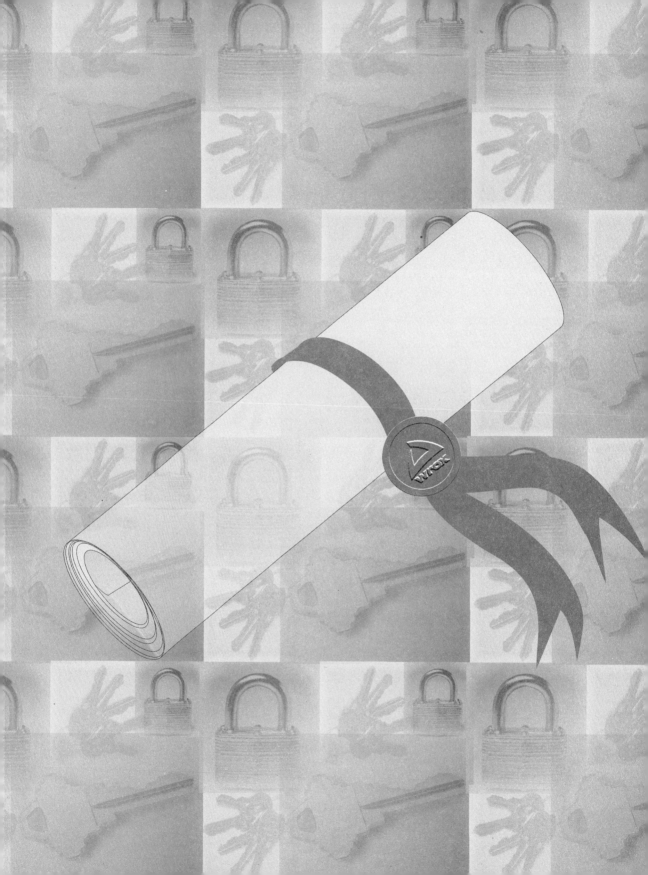

Additional Security Models in Java

Now that we've discussed the security models of applications and applets in Java 2, we're going to move on to discuss some additional security models in Java, such as the servlet security model and the Enterprise JavaBeans security model.

In particular, we'll be looking at the following areas:

- ❑ Servlet authentication
- ❑ Access controls (including declarative and programmatic security)
- ❑ Data integrity
- ❑ EJB architecture roles
- ❑ Defining roles and mapping roles to principals

We'll also discuss JAAS – the Java Authentication and Authorization Service – which will be included in JDK 1.4, and show how these models can be put into use in code. Let's begin this chapter by taking a closer look at servlets.

Servlets

Servlets are server-side Java components that dynamically generate web pages. They can be thought of as a server-side version of applets with no GUI. This book will not delve into the intricacies of servlets themselves, but instead we'll discuss the security model they support, as well as how to utilize them securely inside a larger application.

Users typically access web applications through a web browser, which establishes a connection to the web server, which can then call a servlet. Since servlets are meant for use in web applications, their security model is intended specifically to handle the requirements of web applications. Those requirements are:

❑ Authentication

❑ Access Control

❑ Data Integrity

❑ Confidentiality

We'll begin by taking a look at Authentication.

Authentication

Authentication establishes who the user is. This allows the servlets to make decisions about who is allowed to access what information. There are four forms of authentication supported in the 2.2 servlet specification, which can be found at http://java.sun.com/products/servlet/index.html. The four forms are

❑ HTTP basic authentication

❑ HTTP digest authentication

❑ Form-based authentication

❑ SSL client authentication

Let's run through these types of authentication in order.

HTTP Basic Authentication

HTTP basic authentication is the simplest form of authentication that a servlet might employ. The server asks the browser for a username and password, which the user has to supply. From that point onwards, each request that the browser makes includes the username and password, BASE64-encoded.

There are two problems with basic authentication. The first is that it's ugly. Few people like the dialog box that the browser pops up, which typically looks like this:

Most designers and users would prefer something a little more consistent with the design of the site that caused the authentication request.

The second problem with basic authentication is its weak security. Because the username and password are BASE64-encoded and sent with every request, it's easy to intercept and read the request, and running a simple BASE64-decode on it will give the user's name and password. This can be solved by only allowing users to access the restricted pages through SSL, which prevents anyone from eavesdropping on the exchange. Alternatively, **HTTP digest authentication** can be used.

HTTP Digest Authentication

Digest authentication uses message digests to exchange information proving that the user knows their password without actually sending the password itself. Here's how the protocol works:

1. The server creates a **nonce**, a random value that is unique. One example of a good nonce would be the client IP address, followed by a timestamp, and then a random chunk of data created by the server. This might look something like: `"127.0.0.1: 958579743033: upAlDVQnsTs="`.

2. The server sends that nonce to the client.

3. The client then hashes the nonce along with its username and password.

4. The client sends its hash back to the server.

5. The server then computes its own hash with the username, password and the nonce, all of which it already knows.

6. The server compares the hash it computed with the one the client sent. If they match, the client is given access to the protected resource. If not, access is denied.

By having a timestamp and a random value, the server ensures that a replay attack cannot succeed. That is, no one can snoop a session's packets and then reuse the same hash value later, because the nonce will have changed. This is quite different from basic HTTP authentication, where someone snooping the transaction can easily pose as the user at a later date, because the password is sent in the clear.

Unfortunately, not all browsers and servers support digest authentication. Most commonly, they support only basic and form based.

Form-Based Authentication

Form-based authentication tackles the ugliness problem of basic authentication. Designers and users typically don't like the way the pop-up dialog box works, and most would prefer something more attractive and consistent with the web site being accessed. Form-based authentication allows a standard HTML page to be used to request the username and password, without displaying one of those gray dialog boxes. A designer must create such a page that includes a form with the action `j_security_check`, and two fields: `j_username` and `j_password`. These fields specify to the servlet engine that it is to process this information as a login, and the names are required by the servlet specification. Here's an example:

```
<HTML>
<HEAD>
  <TITLE>Log in</TITLE>
</HEAD>
<BODY>
  <FORM METHOD="POST" ACTION="j_security_check">
    Username: <INPUT TYPE="TEXT" NAME="j_username"><BR>
    Password: <INPUT TYPE="PASSWORD" NAME="j_password"><BR>
    <INPUT TYPE="SUBMIT" VALUE="Submit">
  </FORM>
</BODY>
</HTML>
```

When a user requests a resource that has been protected, the server checks to see if they're authenticated. If not, the server stores the URL they were requesting and forwards them to the authentication form page. The user fills out the form and submits the request back to the server. If the username and password grant access to the original URL, then the client is redirected to it. Otherwise, access is denied and an error page is displayed.

Form-based authentication is not as secure as digest authentication, as the password is sent in the clear from the client to the server. Also, after the password is sent, a cookie is typically passed back-and-forth between client and server to indicate that the client is already authenticated. This cookie could potentially be intercepted on the wire and used to masquerade as a legitimate user. The best solution to this problem is to SSL the connection between server and client to prevent anyone from snooping the password (or cookie) as it is sent.

HTTPS Client Authentication (SSL)

The strongest form of authentication in standard use is **HTTPS client authentication**. HTTPS is simply HTTP over SSL. HTTPS authentication is quite different from the three other methods of authentication we've described up until now. While the others require only a username and password, HTTPS Authentication requires the client to have a private key and a corresponding certificate in order to be authenticated. This adds considerable security.

Essentially, the server only allows in clients that have a certificate that has been authorized to access the given resource. This is somewhat more difficult to implement than a username/password combination, as most users do not have a certificate for their browser. In order to ensure that each of your users has a certificate, you will need to either send them to a CA such as Verisign or become your own CA so that you can issue browser certificates.

Configuration of HTTPS client authentication is highly server-dependent. Many do not even support HTTPS authentication. However, most J2EE (Java 2 Enterprise Edition) servlet containers will support it. Consult your server documentation for configuration information.

Note that client authentication is not required to use SSL, and SSL on its own can be used to hide usernames and passwords when using basic or form-based authentication.

Access Control

The servlet security model is **role-based**. This means that access to resources is granted to roles, which users are then assigned to. To check whether a user has access to a given resource, the server checks what roles are allowed and then checks whether the user is in any of those roles.

For instance, if you had a banking application, you might define a role of customer that would have access to certain basic functions. Then you could add a second role, that of banker, that would have access to administrative functions, like viewing all accounts or correcting account balances. You would then map users to those roles based on who they were.

The server handles mapping users to roles with server-specific tools. Vendors have their own way of telling the server which users are in what roles. Some use the underlying security mechanism of the operating system, while others store users and roles in a database or in the filesystem.

There are two ways to specify what roles have access to which resources – **declarative** and **programmatic**.

Declarative Security

In the deployment descriptor for a web application, the deployer can specify whether a resource is protected, and what roles can access it. The main advantage to using declarative restrictions is that they are very easy to change and require no coding.

The deployment descriptor defines a web application's configuration. It includes such things as initialization parameters, URL-to-servlet mappings and security information. The deployment descriptor is a file, web.xml, which is located in the WEB-INF directory of the web application. As you would expect due to its name, it's in XML format.

You can add security-constraint elements to the descriptor to prevent unauthorized users from accessing certain resources. The security-constraint element contains a web-resource-collection that names each of the protected resources and an auth-constraint element that names the roles allowed to access those resources. Users are authenticated through one of the methods mentioned above (basic, form-based, etc.), and then mapped to roles, which can be compared against those specified in the deployment descriptor.

Here is an example of a section of the deployment descriptor specifying what roles can access a specific resource:

```
<security-constraint>
  <web-resource-collection>
    <web-resource-name>Admin Area</web-resource-name>
    <url-pattern>/admin/*</url-pattern>
  </web-resource-collection>
  <auth-constraint>
    <role-name>administrators</role-name>
  </auth-constraint>
</security-constraint>
```

This restricts anyone not in the administrators role from accessing any servlets in the /admin/ directory, relative to the web root.

Defining users, their passwords and roles is different for each server. In Tomcat 3.2, for example, there is a file in the conf directory, tomcat-users.xml, that defines these three things. Here is the format:

```
<tomcat-users>
  <user name="user1" password="password1" roles="role1,role2" />
  <user name="user2" password="password2" roles="role1" />
</tomcat-users>
```

These declarative restrictions apply equally to JSPs and servlets. JSPs are really only servlets that are compiled from JSP source code, so the same security model applies.

Programmatic Security

In certain applications, declarative security is not specific enough. For example, imagine that you want a servlet that displays an employee's information, and you want to be sure that only the manager for a specific employee can view that information. You'd want to be able to check the identity of the user before displaying the information, and then determine whether or not that specific user had access to that specific record.

There are three methods in `javax.servlet.http.HttpServletRequest` that provide a developer with the ability to programmatically define behavior based on the user making the request:

❑   `String getRemoteUser()`

   `getRemoteUser()` returns a `String` of the username that was used to log in to the web site, using one of the four authentication methods listed at the beginning of this chapter. It will return `null` if the user is not logged in.

❑   `boolean isUserInRole(String role)`

   `isUserInRole()` returns a `boolean`, indicating whether or not the user accessing the servlet is in a given role.

❑   `Principal getUserPrincipal()`

   `getUserPrincipal()` returns a `java.security.Principal` object representing the user that is logged in. It will return `null` if the user is not logged in.

The user's identity is established by using one of the authentication mechanisms we discussed earlier, like Form-based or SSL Client authentication. Once the user has established their identity, we can programmatically make decisions based on it.

Example

We will now create a simple servlet (`UserExampleServlet`) that will programmatically change behavior based on the identity of the user. If it's Bob, we'll send him a special message. Anyone else will receive a simple "`Hello`", followed by their username if they are logged in.

```java
import javax.servlet.*;
import javax.servlet.http.*;

/**
 *   UserServletExample.java
 *
 *   Simple Servlet Example using the getRemoteUser() method.
 */

public class UserServletExample extends HttpServlet {

  public void doGet (HttpServletRequest req, HttpServletResponse res)
         throws ServletException, java.io.IOException {

    // Start printing out the HTML page

    res.setContentType("text/html");
    java.io.PrintWriter out = res.getWriter();
    out.println("<HTML>");
    out.println("<HEAD><TITLE>User Example</TITLE></HEAD>");
    out.println("<BODY>");

    // Get the username from the request.
    // This will be null

    String username = req.getRemoteUser();
    if (username == null) {

      // User is not logged in.
```

```
                  out.println("Hello. You are not logged in.");
              } else if ("Bob".equals(username)) {
                  out.println("Hello, Bob. Nice to see you again.");
              } else {
                  out.println("Hello, "+username+".");
              }

              // Finish the HTML page

              out.println("</BODY>");
              out.println("</HTML>");
              out.close();
          }
      }
```

In order to actually see this example in action, you'll need to have a user that is logged in. This can be done by protecting the web resource in the deployment descriptor as mentioned in the previous section on declarative security, like so:

```xml
<security-constraint>
  <web-resource-collection>
    <web-resource-name>UserServletExample</web-resource-name>
      <url-pattern>/admin/*</url-pattern>
  </web-resource-collection>
  <auth-constraint>
    <role-name>users</role-name>
  </auth-constraint>
</security-constraint>
```

Then you'll need to add users to the `users` group. You'll have to check your web server's documentation for how to do this, as it's different for each server. In Tomcat, you need to edit the file `tomcat-users.xml` in the `conf` directory. Here's an example of a declaration that will work for the previous example:

```xml
<tomcat-users>
  <user name="user1" password="password" roles="users" />
  <user name="Bob" password="Bob" roles="users" />
</tomcat-users>
```

Data Integrity

The next major component of servlet security is ensuring **data integrity**; that none of the information being transmitted has been changed in any way. SSL handles this automatically, adding a checksum to each chunk of data sent across the wire. If anything changes on the way, the server or browser is notified.

There isn't really anything you can do in your servlets to handle data integrity – it's a servlet container issue. If you need this level of security, configure your web server to use SSL for all connections. This is a vendor-specific configuration issue, but should be relatively easy to accomplish. We will discuss it more fully in our chapter on SSL later in the book.

Confidentiality

Confidentiality is what most people think of when they consider web security. Encrypting the connection between browser and web server ensures confidentiality. As with data integrity, SSL is almost always the way to go about handling this. See Chapter 9 on SSL for more information on SSL itself.

Servlet engines are all different in the way SSL is configured. Tomcat 3.2 includes SSL support, though you will need to download Sun's Secure Socket Extension (the JSSE). See your server's documentation for information on how to configure SSL. In Chapter 11, we will be using Tomcat with SSL and providing detailed steps to enable SSL.

The `ServletRequest` class contains a method, `isSecure()`, for programmatically determining whether a connection has taken place over SSL. `isSecure()` returns a `Boolean` value of `true` if the request came in over a secure connection. The definition of secure is left up to the servlet container programmer.

Now that we've covered servlets, let's take a look at Enterprise JavaBeans.

Enterprise JavaBeans

Enterprise JavaBeans are a distributed component model. They are part of Sun's J2EE specification, and are detailed at http://java.sun.com/products/ejb/index.html. As with servlets, we're not going to investigate the use of EJB itself in detail, but rather the EJB security model. Anyone reading this section should already have an understanding of how EJB itself works and what problems it solves.

EJB Architecture Roles

Various EJB Architecture Roles handle EJB development and deployment. These roles should not be confused with security roles that control access. Rather, they define who does what when developing and deploying EJBs. The roles are:

- ❑ **Bean Provider**
- ❑ **Application Assembler**
- ❑ **Deployer**
- ❑ **EJB Service Provider**
- ❑ **EJB Container Provider**
- ❑ **System Administrator**

We'll discuss each of these in turn:

Bean Provider

The Bean Provider writes the individual Enterprise JavaBeans. These are typically either business entities or systems encapsulated as entity or session beans. The Bean Provider also creates the deployment descriptor, which is an XML file that indicates to the EJB Container how the bean should be handled.

Application Assembler

The Application Assembler creates a full application from individual beans. They may also create JSPs and servlets that utilize those beans. The Assembler will probably need to edit the deployment descriptors to fit the application.

Deployer

The Deployer actually deploys the application into a running EJB Server. They manages setting up the interaction between the application architecture as envisioned by the Assembler, and the actual environment in which the application runs.

EJB Service Provider and EJB Container Provider

The EJB Service Provider and the Container Provider work together to write the EJB Server itself. We're not concerned with either of these roles in this chapter, as we will simply be assuming that the EJB Server and Container work according to spec.

System Administrator

The system administrator takes care of the computer systems that run the EJB Server and related services. They are responsible for administrating the operating systems and the network relating to the server.

The EJB Security Model

The EJB 1.1 security model is quite similar in concept to the servlet security model we described in the last section. It is role-based, restricting access to beans and their methods based on a client's role. Permissions can be defined programmatically in the bean itself, but it is better to define them in the deployment descriptor. Then permissions can be easily granted and denied without needing to change the underlying code.

The Application Assembler must define roles for the application in the deployment descriptor. These roles are defined using security-role elements, each with a role-name element inside it. A description element can optionally be added to provide more information to anyone reading the deployment descriptor.

Defining Roles

Let's say we are writing an online banking application. We might define three roles: banker, customer, and admin. Here's what our security role definitions might look like in our deployment descriptor:

```
<assembly-descriptor>
  <security-role>
    <description>
      This role includes employees of the bank who will
      be allowed to view and edit bank accounts.
    </description>
    <role-name>banker</role-name>
  </security-role>
```

```
<security-role>
   <description>
      This role includes all customers of the bank who
      have an account. The role is allowed to view its balance
      and edit personal information.
   </description>
   <role-name>customer</role-name>
</security-role>

<security-role>
   <description>
      This role is for administrators of the application.
   </description>
   <role-name>admin</role-name>
</security-role>

</assembly-descriptor>
```

Method Permissions

You can limit access to beans and their methods based on roles directly in the deployment descriptor. To do that, each role must be listed in the deployment descriptor, with the beans and methods that the role will be allowed to use. An asterisk (*) can be used as a wildcard to specify all permissions.

Method permissions are defined using method-permission elements, again in the deployment descriptor. Each method-permission element contains a `role-name` element and one or more EJBs and their methods, as defined by the `ejb-name` and `method-name` elements. Here is a sample of the method-permissions section of the deployment descriptor, defining the beans and methods that each role can access:

```
<method-permission>
   <role-name>customer</role-name>
   <method>
      <ejb-name>CustomerOperations</ejb-name>
      <method-name>*</method-name>
   </method>
   <method>
      <ejb-name>Account</ejb-name>
      <method-name>findByName</method-name>
   </method>
   <method>
      <ejb-name>Account</ejb-name>
      <method-name>updatePersonalInfo</method-name>
   </method>
   <method>
      <ejb-name>Account</ejb-name>
      <method-name>getBalance</method-name>
   </method>
</method-permission>

<method-permission>
   <role-name>banker</role-name>
```

```
  <method>
    <ejb-name>BankerOperations</ejb-name>
    <method-name>*</method-name>
  </method>
  <method>
    <ejb-name>Account</ejb-name>
    <method-name>*</method-name>
  </method>
</method-permission>

<method-permission>
  <role-name>admin</role-name>
  <method>
    <ejb-name>AdminOperations</ejb-name>
    <method-name>*</method-name>
  </method>
  <method>
    <ejb-name>Account</ejb-name>
    <method-name>*</method-name>
  </method>
</method-permission>
```

Mapping Roles to Principals

Once the Application Assembler has defined the roles and what permissions each will have, it's up to the Deployer to decide how principals will map to those roles. How to do this is specific to the EJB server and operating system you are using. Some EJB servers will utilize the underlying authentication system in the operating system they are running on, while others may use some sort of Public Key Infrastructure (PKI). Check the documentation for your particular EJB server.

Principal Delegation

When one EJB calls another EJB, the principal of the caller is normally propagated. Because of this, each role must have permission to all the beans and methods that might be called within a single call. For instance, imagine a client in the customer role calls a method in the `CustomerOperations` bean. That bean might then call the `viewBalance()` method of the `Account` bean. If you wish this call to be allowed, you will need to grant the customer role permission to call `Account.viewBalance()`.

Some EJB servers will allow you to configure this behavior. You may have a bean that requires special permission and should be allowed to call other beans that its caller would not be allowed to call. This is similar to the `doPrivileged()` method in `java.security.AccessController`. See Chapter 7 for more information on privileged code. Configuring principal delegation behavior is specific to each EJB server. Consult your EJB server documentation for instructions.

Programmatic Security

Normally the Application Assembler and the Deployer configure security for an EJB server. Occasionally, it is necessary for the Bean Provider to access some security information programmatically.

EJB provides two methods for checking security credentials inside a bean, both in the `javax.ejb.EJBContext`. They are:

```
Principal getCallerPrincipal()
boolean isCallerInRole(String roleName)
```

getCallerPrincipal()

getCallerPrincipal() returns a Principal object corresponding to the identity of the caller. This allows us to use the identity of the caller inside the code of the bean.

Imagine, for instance, that you want your customers to be able to view their own balance, but nobody else's. You could get the principal of the caller, and use that to fetch the account and the balance within. Here's an excerpt:

```
public class CustomerOperationsBean implements SessionBean {

   EJBContext mEjbContext;
   AccountHome mAccountHome;

   /**
    *  Returns the balance in a customer's account.
    */

   public long getMyBalance() {

     // Get the caller principal

     Principal callerPrincipal = mEjbContext.getCallerPrincipal();

     // Get the caller's name

     String callerName = callerPrincipal.getName();

     // Get the account for the caller

     Account account = mAccountHome.findByName(callerName);

     return account.getBalance();
   }

   // Insert other methods here

}
```

isCallerInRole()

isCallerInRole() takes a String argument representing a role, and returns true if the caller is in that role, false otherwise. Since the EJB security model already allows you to configure method permissions in the deployment descriptor, isCallerInRole() should not be used simply to check for the caller's role at the beginning of a method to determine whether the method should be executed or not. Rather, it should only be used when simple permissions are not enough. For instance, imagine that you have a limit to the number of times a certain method should be called by a single role, or a transaction size limit based on role.

In our banking application, we want to only allow bankers to add up to $1000 to an account at a time. An admin on the other hand should be allowed to make any change they like. Here's what that code might look like:

```
public class AccountBean {

   EJBContext mEJBContext;
   long mBalance;

   public void addToBalance(long amount) {
     if (amount > 1000) {

       // Need to check the role.

       if (!mEJBContext.isCallerInRole("admin")) {
         throw new SecurityException(...);
       }
     }
     mBalance += amount;
   }

   // Rest of methods go here

}
```

Note that we already declared in the deployment descriptor that only the banker and the admin could call this method in the Account bean, so we don't need to check that the caller is in the banker group.

The security-role-ref element

If you, as the Bean Provider, use a security role in your code, as we use admin in the code excerpted above, you must declare that role in the deployment descriptor. That way the Application Assembler and the Deployer will be alerted that there is a dependency on a particular role inside that bean.

Use a security-role-ref element inside the enterprise-beans section to declare those roles. The security-role-ref requires a role-name element containing the role, and optionally can include a description element. Here is a sample:

```
<enterprise-beans>
  <entity>
    <ejb-name>Account</ejb-name>
    ...
    <security-role-ref>
      <description>
        This security role will have no limit
        on the size of transactions.
      </description>
      <role-name>admin</role-name>
    </security-role-ref>
    ...
  </entity>
  ...
</enterprise-beans>
...
```

When programming an EJB application, the same security considerations that you would follow in a normal application still apply. The EJB security model just provides an easy way to control who can call which beans and methods, and automatically establishes the identity of the caller. Depending on the EJB vendor you have chosen and the requirements of your project, that may be enough. If not, all the standard Java security programming techniques can be applied to EJB.

JAAS

JAAS stands for **Java Authentication and Authorization Service**. Java's default security model grants permissions based on **where** code comes from. JAAS, on the other hand, grants permissions based on **who** is executing the code. This is probably a more familiar security model to most programmers, as it is similar to the UNIX and Windows NT security models. It is also quite similar to the servlet and EJB security specifications that we've just described. In fact, BEA's WebLogic EJB Server uses JAAS to implement security.

JAAS uses **PAM** for authentication. PAM stands for Pluggable Authentication Modules. It allows an authentication mechanism to be dropped into your environment and used to authenticate users running Java code. For instance, the default authentication mechanism in the reference implementation of JAAS is username-password. When a user runs some code that requires privileges, the application requests a username and a password and uses that to authenticate the user against the host operating system. If authentication succeeds, then extra permissions are granted.

Different modules can be plugged in, allowing the user to be authenticated against most PAM-capable mechanisms, including Kerberos and various PKI implementations.

JAAS will be integrated into J2EE, Java 2 Enterprise Edition. It will also be added to the core Java APIs with the release of JDK 1.4.

> **For the moment however, to make use of JAAS, you'll have to download JAAS from http://java.sun.com/products/jaas/. To run the examples ensure JAAS is installed by placing the `jaas.jar` file is placed in your `jre/lib/ext` folder inside your JDK.**

When running applications that use JAAS, we've found it to be somewhat sensitive to Java installations. If it doesn't work for you, make sure you've got `jaas.jar` installed in your correct `lib/ext` folder, and that you do not have multiple JVMs installed. We also recommend upgrading to the latest JVM, which was v1.3.0_02 at the time of writing.

JAAS Classes

JAAS defines the following packages:

- `javax.security.auth`
- `javax.security.auth.callback`
- `javax.security.auth.login`
- `javax.security.auth.spi`

In those packages are a number of classes and interfaces that are used to establish authentication and authorization. The most important ones are:

- `javax.security.auth.Subject`
- `javax.security.auth.spi.LoginModule`
- `javax.security.auth.login.LoginContext`
- `javax.security.auth.login.Configuration`
- `javax.security.auth.callback.Callback`
- `javax.security.auth.callback.CallbackHandler`

We're going to go over each of those classes and interfaces, and then present a short example of writing a JAAS module. We're going to talk mostly about authentication at first, with a discussion of authorization to follow. Authentication is verifying an identity, while authorization is allowing access to resources based on that identity. For instance, Authentication would allow a server to determine that your username is jsmith. Authorization would determine whether jsmith should be allowed to view the credit card database.

Authentication is started within the LoginContext class. JAAS then uses that LoginContext and a Configuration to create a LoginModule, which then authenticates a subject using CallbackHandlers and Callbacks. If all is successful, JAAS adds the subject to the current context, allowing anyone to check the currently valid subject. Now let's take a look at those classes and interfaces and we'll explain in more detail how this all works.

Subject

The Subject class represents a single entity using the system. A subject can possess one or more identities for different resources, each represented by an instance of java.security.Principal. The method getPrincipal() returns a Set of those principals. A single entity (a person or a company, for instance) typically has just one subject. On the other hand, they may be viewed as different principals on different systems. For instance, you might have one login for your corporate intranet and a different one for the source control system. That's one subject (you) and two principals (one for each of the applications).

Subjects also contain a list of **credentials**, objects such as passwords and certificates. There are public and private credentials, which are classified as such by how sensitive their information is. A password or a private key, for instance, is a private credential, while a public key or a user name is a public credential. Credentials can be accessed via Subject.getPublicCredentials() and Subject.getPrivateCredentials(). Credentials are just objects, and don't inherit from a superclass or implement an interface. This allows already existing classes like PublicKey and Certificate to be used as credentials.

Subjects represent **who** is running the currently executing code. Access to certain resources can be granted based on which subject is currently active. The active subject can be fetched with the static method Subject.getSubject(). JAAS itself, in coordination with a LoginModule, is responsible for assigning the active subject.

LoginModule

LoginModule is an interface that must be implemented in order to provide authentication. There must be an implementation of LoginModule for each type of authentication that you need to support. A couple examples are username-password authentication and RSA authentication.

Multiple login modules can be used at a time, and JAAS will attempt to log in via each of them. JAAS can be configured to allow or deny logins based on which of those various attempts succeed. For instance, you might have a case where you tried to log in via RSA or username-password, and if either one succeeds, you want to allow the user to continue.

LoginModule defines five methods: initialize(), login(), commit(), abort(), and logout(). These methods are called by JAAS to implement a two-phase commit for authentication when using multiple authentication methods. First initialize() is called, and then login(). If login() succeeds, then commit() is called. If login() fails, abort() is called. After commit() is called, JAAS will add the subject to the current context.

initialize(Subject subject, CallbackHandler handler, Map sharedState, Map options)

This method sets up the `LoginModule` to be used to attempt a login. The `LoginModule` should set its state with the objects passed in, and be ready for the `login()` method to be called.

login()

This method checks the credentials of the subject passed in earlier. Exactly how this is done is implementation-dependent. A database could be consulted, a password file could be read in, or any number of various methods of verification could be used.

commit()

If the necessary logins were successful, JAAS will call `commit()` on each login module. This should add the necessary principals and credentials to the subject if the login was successful. The login module should also clean up its state during the commit.

abort()

If the overall login failed, that is, the necessary login modules failed to log the subject in, then the `abort()` method is called and the login module should clean up its state.

logout()

This method logs out a subject. It could also remove the appropriate principals and credentials from the subject.

LoginContext

The login context is used to actually log in. The code performing the authentication instantiates a `LoginContext`, which then uses a `Configuration` to determine which login modules to use to authenticate a subject. The code attempting to authenticate then calls `login()` on the `LoginContext`.

Configuration

`Configuration` is an abstract class that defines how a `LoginContext` and `LoginModules` should be used. Sun provides an implementation of `Configuration` that is used by default in JAAS.

The main use of a configuration is to determine which login modules need to be called and how their success or failure determines the ultimate success or failure of the entire login process. There are called flags, and there are four possibilities for a login module: `Required`, `Requisite`, `Sufficient`, and `Optional`.

- **Required** – The login module must succeed for the entire login to succeed. Even if it fails, however, the other login modules are queried.

- **Requisite** – The login module must succeed for the entire login to succeed. If it fails, the login process is short-circuited and no more login modules are called.

- **Sufficient** – If this module succeeds and no required or requisite modules fail, the entire login succeeds.

- **Optional** – This modules' success doesn't impact on the remainder of the login process. If no sufficient, requisite, or required modules fail, the login succeeds, regardless of whether an optional module succeeds.

Callback

The `Callback` interface contains no methods. It is simply there to tag classes that can be used to provide information from code attempting a login to the login module. Sun provides a number of `Callback` implementation such as `PasswordCallback` and `NameCallback` that have methods and data that can be used to pass usernames and passwords to the login module. You can use any of the callbacks provided in JAAS or you can create your own if you have extra data that needs to be passed to a login module like a digital signature.

CallbackHandler

The `CallbackHandler` interface defines one method: `handle(Callback[] callbacks)`. This method iterates through the callbacks provided and adds the requested information to each one. For instance, if the `callbacks` array contains a `NameCallback` and a `PasswordCallback`, then the callback handler might pop up a dialog box for the user to enter each one and then set the data on each of those callbacks.

Authentication Example

We're going to write a simple example of authenticating a user. We'll use password-based authentication, but it could be swapped out for any other sort of authentication you might wish to use.

We need to create a callback handler (the `UsernamePasswordCallbackHandler` class) that handles username and password callbacks. We need to implement the `CallbackHandler` interface, and in the `handle()` method fill in the data for both a `NameCallback` and a `PasswordCallback`. The name and password will be set in the constructor for our callback handler and stored as instance variables.

The `handle()` method takes an array of `Callbacks`. We need to go through the array and fill out any `NameCallbacks` and `PasswordCallbacks` with the information we have. If we get a callback that we can't handle, we throw an `UnsupportedCallbackException`.

```java
import java.io.*;
import java.security.*;
import javax.security.auth.*;
import javax.security.auth.callback.*;

/**
 *  CallbackHandler that handles usernames and passwords.
 */

public class UsernamePasswordCallbackHandler
implements CallbackHandler {

  private String mUsername;
  private char[] mPassword;

  /**
   *  We need a stateful handler to return the username and password.
   */
  public UsernamePasswordCallbackHandler(String username, char[] password) {
    mUsername = username;
    mPassword = password;
  }
```

```
/**
 *  Handle each callback. We support only NameCallbacks
 *  and PasswordCallbacks.
 */

public void handle(Callback[] callbacks)
throws UnsupportedCallbackException {

  // Step through the callbacks

  for(int i=0;i<callbacks.length;i++) {
    Callback callback = callbacks[i];

    // Handle the callback based on its type.

    if (callback instanceof NameCallback) {
      NameCallback nameCallback = (NameCallback)callback;
      nameCallback.setName(mUsername);
    } else if (callback instanceof PasswordCallback) {
      PasswordCallback passwordCallback =
        (PasswordCallback)callback;
      passwordCallback.setPassword(mPassword);
    } else {
      throw new UnsupportedCallbackException
        (callback, "Unsupported Callback Type");
    }
  }
}
```

Now that we have our callback handler, we're going to write the login module that will use it. Before we can do that though, we need an implementation of the java.security.Principal interface. This is a very simple interface that really just has one method: getName(). Our class, PrincipalImpl, will just store a String for the name and return it when necessary:

```
import java.io.Serializable;
import java.security.Principal;

/**
 *  Implementation of the Principal interface.
 */

public class PrincipalImpl implements Principal, Serializable {

  private String mName;

  public PrincipalImpl(String name) {
    mName = name;
  }

  public boolean equals(java.lang.Object obj) {
    if (!(obj instanceof PrincipalImpl)) {
      return false;
    }
    PrincipalImpl other = (PrincipalImpl)obj;
    if (mName.equals(other.getName())) {
      return true;
    }
```

```
      return false;
    }

  public java.lang.String getName() {
    return mName;
  }

  public int hashCode() {
    return mName.hashCode();
  }

  public java.lang.String toString() {
    return getName();
  }
}
```

Now we're ready to write the login module. Login modules need to keep track of state, as JAAS uses a two-phase commit to log users in. We also need to keep track of the credentials that are being used, in case we need to store those credentials in the resulting subject.

Here is the start of our class, including instance variables that we'll be using to keep track of the state of a login attempt. This is `PasswordLoginModule.java`:

```
import javax.security.auth.*;
import javax.security.auth.spi.*;
import javax.security.auth.callback.*;
import javax.security.auth.login.*;
import java.io.*;
import java.security.*;
import java.util.*;

/**
 *  PasswordLoginModule.java
 *
 *  Login module that checks a username and password.
 */

public class PasswordLoginModule implements LoginModule {

  private Subject mSubject;
  private CallbackHandler mCallbackHandler;

  private boolean mLoginSucceeded = false;
  private boolean mCommitSucceeded = false;

  private String mUsername;
  private char[] mPassword;

  private Principal mPrincipal;
```

Next we'll define the `initialize()` method, which just sets up the state based on the arguments passed in. We'll also define a `clearPassword()` method for clearing out the char array that is the password.

```
/**
 *  Initialize this login module.
 */

public void initialize(Subject subject,CallbackHandler callbackHandler,
                       Map sharedState, Map options) {
  mSubject = subject;
  mCallbackHandler = callbackHandler;
  mLoginSucceeded = false;
  mCommitSucceeded = false;
  mUsername = null;
  clearPassword();
}

/**
 *  Clear out the password.
 */

private void clearPassword() {
  if (mPassword == null) {
    return;
  }
  for (int i=0;i<mPassword.length;i++) {
    mPassword[i] = ' ';
  }
  mPassword = null;
}
```

Now we'll write the actual login() method. Note that this doesn't fully log a user in, it just checks that their credentials are valid. The commit() method gets called when the subject gets added to the context.

```
/**
 *  Attempt to log a user in.
 *
 *  In this sample, we accept:
 *  username: "testuser"
 *  password: "sasquatch"
 */

public boolean login() throws LoginException {
  if (mCallbackHandler == null) {
    throw new LoginException("No CallbackHandler defined");
  }

  // create two callbacks: one for username, one for password.

  Callback[] callbacks = new Callback[2];
  callbacks[0] = new NameCallback("Username");
  callbacks[1] = new PasswordCallback("Password", false);

  try {
```

```
    // Call the callback handler to fill out information

    mCallbackHandler.handle(callbacks);
    mUsername = ((NameCallback)callbacks[0]).getName();
    char[] tempPassword =
      ((PasswordCallback)callbacks[1]).getPassword();
    mPassword = new char[tempPassword.length];
    System.arraycopy(tempPassword, 0,
      mPassword, 0, tempPassword.length);

    // Clear out the password in the callback

    ((PasswordCallback)callbacks[1]).clearPassword();
  } catch (IOException ioe) {
    throw new LoginException(ioe.toString());
  } catch (UnsupportedCallbackException uce) {
    throw new LoginException(uce.toString());
  }

  // Now we need to check for the validity of the username and password.
  // If we were using a database or a file, we would check against
  // that resource.

  if (
    "testuser".equals(mUsername) &&
    mPassword.length == 9 &&
    mPassword[0] == 's' &&
    mPassword[1] == 'a' &&
    mPassword[2] == 's' &&
    mPassword[3] == 'q' &&
    mPassword[4] == 'u' &&
    mPassword[5] == 'a' &&
    mPassword[6] == 't' &&
    mPassword[7] == 'c' &&
    mPassword[8] == 'h'
    ) {

    // username and password are correct.

    mLoginSucceeded = true;
    return true;
  } else {

    // Authentication failed. Clean up state and throw exception.

    mLoginSucceeded = false;
    mUsername = null;
    clearPassword();
    throw new FailedLoginException("Incorrect Password");
  }
}
```

Now we'll write the `commit()` method. This should actually add a principal to the subject if the `Login` was successful.

```
/**
 *  This is called if all logins succeeded.
 */

public boolean commit() throws LoginException {
  if (mLoginSucceeded == false) {
    return false;
  }

  // Login succeeded, so create a Principal and add it to the Subject.

  mPrincipal = new PrincipalImpl(mUsername);
  if (!(mSubject.getPrincipals().contains(mPrincipal))) {
    mSubject.getPrincipals().add(mPrincipal);
  }

  // If we wanted our Subject to contain our credentials,
  // now would be the time to add them. We don't need to
  // do that for this simple example however.

  // Clear out the username and password.

  mUsername = null;
  clearPassword();
  mCommitSucceeded = true;
  return true;
}
```

If something goes wrong during the login process, JAAS will call the `abort()` method, which should clean up the state.

```
/**
 *  Called if overall login failed.
 */

public boolean abort() throws LoginException {

  // If login failed, return false;

  if (mLoginSucceeded == false) {
    return false;
  } else if (mLoginSucceeded == true && mCommitSucceeded == false) {

    // Our login succeeded, but others failed.

    mLoginSucceeded = false;
    mUsername = null;
    clearPassword();
    mPrincipal = null;
  } else {

    // We committed, but someone else's failed.

    logout();
  }
  return true;
}
```

The last method we need to implement for a login module is `logout()`. This should remove the principal from the subject.

```
/**
 * Logout the user.
 */

public boolean logout() throws LoginException {

  // Need to remove the principal from the Subject.

  mSubject.getPrincipals().remove(mPrincipal);
  mLoginSucceeded = false;
  mCommitSucceeded = false;
  mUsername = null;
  clearPassword();
  mPrincipal = null;
  return true;
  }
}
```

Our JAAS module is complete. Now we need some code that will actually use it. We're going to write a very simple command-line application that will attempt to log in using a username and password passed in as arguments.

In order to use our login module, our application needs to create a `LoginContext` with our `UsernamePasswordCallbackHandler` instantiated with the proper values. The `LoginContext` also requires a name, which will be used by JAAS to determine how to configure the modules. We'll use the name `Sample`, which we'll define in our configuration shortly. Then we simply call `login()` on the context. This will throw a `FailedLoginException` if it fails. If it succeeds, we will get the `Subject` out of the context and display it.

Here's the `JAASSampleApp` class we need:

```
import javax.security.auth.*;
import javax.security.auth.login.*;
import java.security.*;

public class JAASSampleApp {

  public static void main(String[] args)
  throws Exception {
    if (args.length != 2) {
      System.err.println
        ("Usage: java JAASSampleApp username password");
      System.exit(1);
    }

    String username = args[0];
    char[] password = args[1].toCharArray();
    LoginContext loginContext = new LoginContext(
      "Sample", new UsernamePasswordCallbackHandler
        (username, password));
```

```
        loginContext.login();

        // Now we're logged in, so we can get the current subject.

        Subject subject = loginContext.getSubject();

        // Display the subject

        System.out.println(subject);
    }
}
```

In order to actually execute the example, we need that configuration we mentioned earlier. The configuration files for JAAS are quite simple: You specify a name, then the login modules, whether they are required or not and any options that you wish to pass to them. Here's our `jaas.config` file:

```
Sample {
    PasswordLoginModule required;
};
```

Running the Example

Next, place all the files we just defined into a working directory, such as `C:\JAASApp`. You should have the following files:

- ❏ `jaas.config`
- ❏ `JAASSampleApp.java`
- ❏ `PasswordLoginModule.java`
- ❏ `PrincipalImpl.java`
- ❏ `UsernamePasswordCallbackHandler.java`

Compile them with:

```
C:\> javac *.java.
```

We need to specify the location of the config file to the VM when we actually execute the application like so:

```
C:\> java -Djava.security.auth.login.config==jaas.config JAASSampleApp testuser
          sasquatch
```

The username and password are provided as arguments to the application.

If all is successful, you should see your authenticated subject displayed like so:

```
Subject:
        Principal: testuser
```

You can test failure with a different username or password, like so:

```
C:\> java -Djava.security.auth.login.config==jaas.config JAASSampleApp testuser
     bad_password
```

You should see the following exception thrown:

```
Exception in thread "main" javax.security.auth.login.FailedLoginException:
Incorrect Password
        at PasswordLoginModule.login(PasswordLoginModule.java:98)
        at java.lang.reflect.Method.invoke(Native Method)
        at javax.security.auth.login.LoginContext.invoke(LoginContext.java:595)
        at
javax.security.auth.login.LoginContext.access$000(LoginContext.java:125)
        at javax.security.auth.login.LoginContext$3.run(LoginContext.java:531)
        at java.security.AccessController.doPrivileged(Native Method)
        at
javax.security.auth.login.LoginContext.invokeModule(LoginContext.java:528)
        at javax.security.auth.login.LoginContext.login(LoginContext.java:449)
        at JAASSampleApp.main(JAASSampleApp.java:22)
```

You can catch a FailedLoginException in your application and allow the user to try logging in again with a different username and password. Depending on your requirements, you might want to log failures, or limit the user to three tries at logging in before denying them the ability to try again.

So far, we've mainly focused on the authentication aspect of JAAS. That is, the ability to determine who the user is. Now we want to talk about authorization, allowing or denying access to resources based on the authenticated subject.

Authorization

There are two types of authorization when using JAAS: declarative and programmatic. Just like in the servlet and EJB security models, we can define static configurations that allow and disallow access to resources, or we can write code that uses more sophisticated logic to determine how to dole out our resources based on who is running the code.

Declarative Authorization

JAAS adds a new configuration directive to the policy file that defines permissions. We talked about the codebase and the signedby directive in Chapter 7, but now we're going to describe the Principal directive. This directive allows you to specify who must be running some code in order to have a certain permission. Here's a sample entry that you might use in a policy file:

```
grant  Principal PrincipalImpl "testuser" {
    permission java.io.FilePermission "c:\test\test.txt", "read,write";
};
```

Declarative authorization is seldom actually used. Programmatic authorization is much more common, and typically more useful. If you're still interested in more information on declarative authorization, take a look at the sample code that Sun includes with the JAAS documentation download.

Programmatic Authorization

As we mentioned in the sections on servlets and EJBs, it can be valuable to determine who is running the current code. For instance, you might want to allow access to an account based on who has been authenticated.

You can get the current subject by calling the static method getSubject() in the Subject class. This method requires an instance of java.security.AccessControlContext, which can be retrieved by using the method getContext() in java.security.AccessController. Here's what the code would look like:

```
AccessControlContext context = AccessController.getContext();
Subject subject = Subject.getSubject(context);
```

The retrieved subject can then be checked for principals to see what action should be performed. Let's create a new class, JAASAuthorizationExample. We'll have one method, getSecretText(), that will return a certain secret phrase, squeamish ossifrage, if the authenticated subject contains a PrincipalImpl with the name testuser. Otherwise it will return a different phrase: secret word.

In order to run code as a specific subject, we need to use the Subject.doAs() method, which takes a subject and a java.security.PrivilegedAction, and runs the action as the subject. You may remember PrivilegedAction from Chapter 7. PrivilegedAction has one method, run(), which returns an Object. In our run() method, we'll get the secret word.

Let's start taking a look at JAASAuthorizationExample.java, specifically the getSecretText() method, which will examine the subject the code is being run by, and return different text based on that subject:

```
import java.security.*;
import java.util.*;
import javax.security.auth.*;
import javax.security.auth.login.*;

public class JAASAuthorizationExample {

  private static final String GENERIC_SECRET_TEXT = "secret word";
  private static final String TEST_USER_SECRET_TEXT = "squeamish ossifrage";

  /**
   *  We return a different string based on the user.
   */

  public static String getSecretText() {

    AccessControlContext context = AccessController.getContext();
    Subject subject = Subject.getSubject(context);

    if (subject == null) {
      return GENERIC_SECRET_TEXT;
    }

    // Get all the principals that are
    // instances of our PrincipalImpl class.
```

```
      Set principals = subject.getPrincipals();
      Iterator iterator = principals.iterator();
      while (iterator.hasNext()) {
        PrincipalImpl principal = (PrincipalImpl)iterator.next();
        if (principal.getName().equals("testuser")) {
          return TEST_USER_SECRET_TEXT;
        }
      }
      return GENERIC_SECRET_TEXT;
   }
```

Next we'll write a `main()` method, which will do the login and call a `PrivilegedAction`, `ExampleAction`, which we will define in a moment. Our `main()` method is quite similar to the one we wrote for the last example, `JAASSampleApp`. The difference is that at the end, we're going to call `Subject.doAs()` to perform an action that uses authorization.

```
   /**
    * Try to log a user in and then run ExampleAction.
    */
   public static void main(String[] args) {
     if (args.length != 2) {
       System.err.println
       ("Usage: java JAASSampleApp username password");
       System.exit(1);
     }

     LoginContext loginContext = null;

     String username = args[0];
     char[] password = args[1].toCharArray();

     try {
       loginContext = new LoginContext(
         "Sample", new UsernamePasswordCallbackHandler
         (username, password));
       loginContext.login();
       System.out.println("\nLogin succeeded");
     } catch (LoginException le) {
       System.out.println("\nLogin failed");
     }

     // Now we're logged in, so we can get the current subject.

     Subject subject = loginContext.getSubject();

     // Perform the example action as the authenticated subject.

     subject.doAs(subject, new ExampleAction());
   }
}
```

Now let's look at ExampleAction, which is an implementation of PrivilegedAction, as we mentioned earlier. All we want to do is call getSecretText() and print it. We'll make ExampleAction an inner class of JAASAuthorizationExample.

```
class ExampleAction implements PrivilegedAction {

  public ExampleAction() {
  }

  public Object run() {
    System.out.println("Secret text: "
                        + JAASAuthorizationExample.getSecretText());
    return null;
  }
}
```

Compile JAASAuthorizationExample.java and you're ready to run it with the following command:

```
C:\> java -Djava.security.auth.login.config==jaas.config JAASAuthorizationExample
          testuser sasquatch
```

Your login should succeed, and you will see the secret phrase, squeamish ossifrage. You can test what happens if the login fails by changing the username or the password. You should get the phrase secret word instead.

Summary

In this chapter we've gone over some of the security models that have been layered over the top of the core Java security model. We've covered servlets, Enterprise JavaBeans, and JAAS. The security models of each provide services that assist in the writing of code for those specific applications. While these security models aren't yet used very commonly in the real world, it seems likely that as they gain acceptance, and as JAAS is now incorporated into the core JDK, we will see them more often.

The servlet 2.2 spec contains some useful methods for handling security directly in the servlets as well as in the servlet container and web server. Normal application security programming principles still apply, however. You may very well need to encrypt data in the database, and tighten the operating system security on your application servers. See Chapter 11 for more information on securing an entire web-based application.

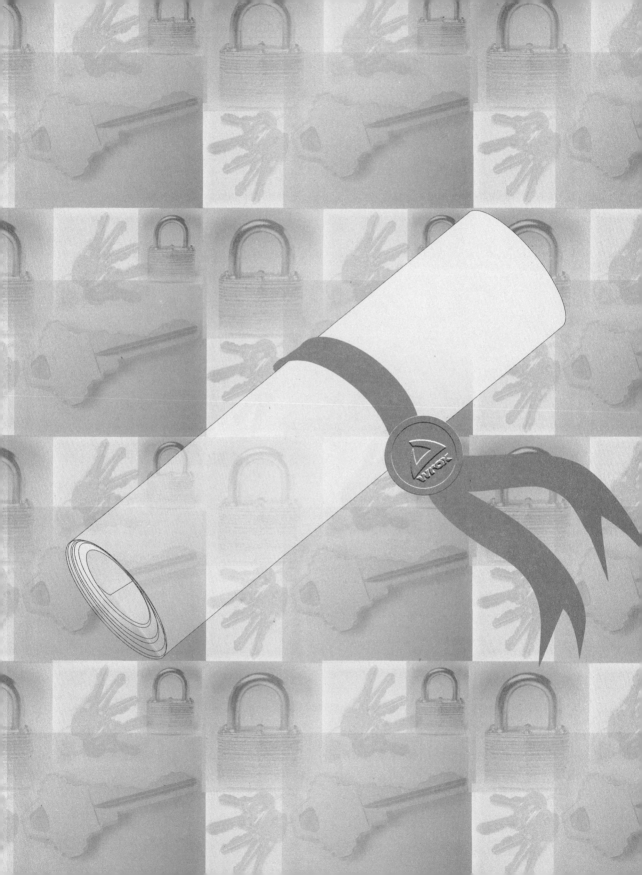

SSL

Java is a network-centric language. It has support for TCP/IP built into the `java.net` package, and applets were designed to work over the Web. Unfortunately, network communications in Java are unencrypted by default, and there is no support directly in the Java language or the core APIs for encrypting that network traffic.

The Web was in the same position when it was created: all traffic sent over HTTP was unencrypted, so you could never be certain that no one was eavesdropping on your communications. Netscape Communications saw an opportunity for e-commerce on the Web, but realized that unsecured communications would pose a real problem. They created **SSL** (**Secure Sockets Layer**) to solve that problem.

Java can support SSL with the addition of some libraries, such as Sun's **Java Secure Sockets Extension** (**JSSE**), which we'll be utilizing in this chapter. With these libraries, it's fairly easy to encrypt network traffic, securing it from eavesdroppers using packet sniffers.

To see how we can use SSL and JSSE in our applications we're going to be looking at:

❑　SSL basics7

❑　How to use SSL within Java applications

❑　Advanced SSL topics like client authentication and using RMI over SSL

❑　Some limitations of SSL within application development

> *Sun's JSSE, which we've used in this chapter, is available for download from http://java.sun.com/products/jsse; and remember all the code in the chapter is available from http://www.wrox.com.*

SSL Basics

SSL (Secure Sockets Layer) is a protocol for encrypting TCP/IP traffic that also incorporates authentication and data integrity. The newest version of SSL is sometimes referred to as **Transport Layer Security** (**TLS**) (the specification for which can be found at www.ietf.org/rfc/rfc2246.txt) and TLS v1.0 is equivalent to SSL v3.1.

SSL runs on top of TCP/IP and can be applied to almost any sort of connection-oriented communication. It is most commonly used to secure HTTP. When HTTP is secured in this fashion, it is referred to as **HTTPS**. Most browsers now support HTTPS connections, allowing secure communication with a web server supporting SSL.

SSL is based on session-key encryption, which we discussed in Chapter 5. It adds a number of extra features, including authentication based on X.509 certificates and integrity checking with message authentication codes.

SSL is an extension of sockets, which allow a client and a server to establish a stream of communication with each other. They begin with a **handshake**, which allows identities to be established and keys to be exchanged. Below is a handshake using RSA for key exchange and RC4 for the session key.

The SSL Handshake

Let's have a closer look at an SSL handshake as illustrated here. During the handshake, the client and server create a shared session key and can verify each other's identity. To do this they exchange a number of messages – within the handshake there are some messages that are optional and these are shown in parentheses.

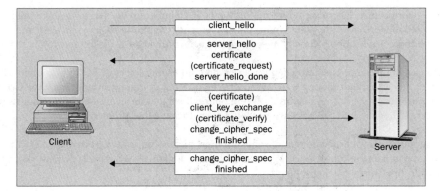

Step 1

The exchange begins when the client sends a `client_hello` message, which contains:

- ❏ The SSL versions supported by the client
- ❏ 32 bytes of random data that the client creates
- ❏ A session ID that it makes up
- ❏ A list of supported ciphers
- ❏ A list of supported compression methods

Step 2

The server responds with a `server_hello`, containing:

- ❑ The SSL version the server selects from the client's list
- ❑ 32 bytes of random data that the server creates
- ❑ The session ID
- ❑ The ciphers chosen from the client's list (in this case RSA and RC4)
- ❑ The compression method selected (typically no compression is used)

Next the server typically sends its certificate, which is an X.509 certificate signed by a certificate authority. In addition to information about the owner of the server, the certificate contains the server's public key, so it will now be possible for the client to send encrypted messages to the server using this public key. Only the owner of the private key corresponding to this certificate can decrypt these messages.

Following the certificate, the server can request a certificate of the client, but this is not normally required for HTTPS. The client is said to be **anonymous**, while the server's identity is known through its certificate signed by a CA.

Finally, the server sends the `server_hello_done` message to indicate that it has completed its communication and is waiting for a response from the client.

Step 3

The client checks the server's certificate and the various parameters it just sent. If a client certificate was requested, the client responds with a certificate message, which contains its X.509 certificate.

Next the client sends the `client_key_exchange`, which is 48 bytes of random data that the client and server will each use to construct a session key. The random bytes are created from the random data that the client and server exchanged earlier. These random bytes are RSA-encrypted with the server's public key, extracted from the certificate it sent to the client.

Following this a `certificate_verify` message is sent if the client provided a certificate. The client hashes all the messages that have been sent so far, and signs them with its private key. The server will then be able to verify that the client actually possesses the key corresponding to its certificate. This step is not required if the server has not requested client verification.

The client then computes a key for encryption using RC4, and a key for the message authentication code (MAC) that will be used to verify data integrity. These keys are generated using the secret random number that the client and server have exchanged up to this point. The client then sends a `change_cipher_spec` message, which indicates that future communication will be handled with these ciphers and parameters, but does not need to tell the server the keys, as the server will compute them independently, using that same random data that was previously exchanged.

Finally the client sends a finished message, encrypted with the session key and including a MAC for integrity.

Step 4

The server responds with its own `change_cipher_spec` message, which indicates to the client that it too will encrypt all future communication with the same parameters as the client. It can compute the same keys that the client has, as it earlier received the random data that the client used to create its keys.

To finish the handshake, the server sends its own finished message, encrypted with the agreed-upon specs and keys. Up until now, all encryption has been performed with asymmetric encryption.

The rest of the communication between client and server will now be encrypted using symmetric encryption. Java SSL libraries like the JSSE handle this transparently. Except for the creation of the socket, no change needs to be made to the code that handles the communication. It just uses an `InputStream` and an `OutputStream`, just like a standard socket, and the securing of the communication is taken care of.

A number of different algorithms are specified by SSL. Let's go over some of the possibilities, as they have some security implications depending on your application.

Key Exchange

Communication in SSL is encrypted between client and server with a session key. In order to establish that session key, client and server must agree on a shared key without sending any secret data in the clear that could be eavesdropped on by an attacker. There are five different key exchange algorithms that can be used:

❑ **RSA** – RSA is the standard method for SSL key exchange, and by far the most commonly supported in browsers and servers. In RSA key exchange, the client encrypts a number of random bytes with the server's public RSA key and they both use this shared secret to create an identical session key.

❑ **Fixed Diffie-Hellman** – Since RSA has until recently been restricted to the United States, the Diffie-Hellman key exchange algorithm is used in certain implementations. Fixed Diffie-Hellman requires that the server have a certificate with its DH public key, signed by a CA. The client then sends its public DH key, either as a certificate if client authentication is required, or in a `client_key_exchange` message if it is not. Then using Diffie-Hellman, client and server can agree on a shared session key. Note that because the server's DH key came inside a certificate, the client can be sure of the identity of the server.

❑ **Ephemeral Diffie-Hellman** – This protocol also uses Diffie-Hellman, but in a slightly different way. In this case, the server and client generate DH keys on the fly, and send the public keys each to the other. The public keys are signed by the owner's private RSA or DSS key, and certificates are used to authenticate the public keys used to verify those signatures. This is a bit more secure than Fixed Diffie-Hellman, as the keys are only used once, and regenerated for the next client or server.

❑ **Anonymous Diffie-Hellman** – Both client and server send the other a Diffie-Hellman public key. No authentication is done, and each uses the other's public key to generate a shared session key. This protocol should *not* be used, as it is vulnerable to man-in-the-middle attacks. Nonetheless, it is supported by the SSL protocol and is what takes place when a server does not have a certificate.

❑ **Fortezza** – Fortezza is a proprietary encryption scheme that SSL can support. We will not discuss it here, as it is not typically used in Java SSL implementations.

Ciphers

SSL supports a number of different ciphers for actually encrypting the traffic sent between client and server. Again, not all SSL implementations support all algorithms. Also, key strength is often restricted in export versions of various SSL libraries. For sensitive data, you should use symmetric ciphers of 128 bits or more – RC4 at 128-bit strength is the most commonly used strong cipher. The ciphers and strengths supported by SSL are as follows:

- ❑   RC4 – 128-bit or 40-bit keys
- ❑   TripleDES – 168-bit keys, with 112 bits of effective strength
- ❑   IDEA – 128-bit keys
- ❑   Fortezza – 80-bit keys
- ❑   DES – 56-bit keys
- ❑   DES40 – 40-bit keys
- ❑   RC2 – 40-bit keys

MAC

SSL supports MD5 and SHA-1 for creating message authentication codes. MACs guarantee the integrity of messages. They're used in SSL to ensure that no one has altered data in transit.

Now we know what SSL is, let's discuss where we may want to apply it.

Uses for SSL

As we mentioned before, the most common use for SSL is in encrypting communication between a web browser and a web server. At this time, almost all e-commerce transactions on the web take place over SSL. Almost any network traffic can be encrypted with SSL, including POP, IMAP, telnet, and FTP.

It's a good idea to use SSL any time you're sending information that is even marginally sensitive. POP and IMAP are great examples because your e-mail password is normally sent in the clear each time you read your mail. By using an SSL connection, you retain the secrecy of your password.

Another scenario in which SSL can be useful is network communication with an application server. Using an SSL the connection prevents eavesdropping and message modification. By enabling client and server authentication, it can be made much more difficult for an unauthorized user to log in to your application server. They would need to steal the client's private key in order to get in, rather than simply their password.

> *The biggest drawback to using SSL is performance. Because every byte must be encrypted or decrypted, it takes significantly more horsepower to communicate. As computers become faster, this is becoming less of an issue, but it's important to be aware of when you're determining your hardware needs. There are SSL accelerator cards that are available to decrease the load on the processor, but they are quite expensive. In our experience, we've found the performance liabilities of SSL to be overwhelmed by the additional security that it provides.*

RMI can be encrypted with SSL, as can JDBC connections. These can be a bit difficult to implement though, so we'll discuss RMI over SSL in the *Advanced SSL Topics* section later, while we'll look at providing secure connections to data sources in the next chapter.

Using SSL in Java

At this point, you should have a good idea what SSL is about in general, and when it can be useful. Now we're going to write some simple Java applications that use SSL.

So in this section we're going to:

❑ Discuss the JSSE

❑ Develop a simple JSSE using client and HTTPS server example

❑ Code an SSL socket example without using HTTPS

Let's start by taking a look at the JSSE.

JSSE (Java Secure Sockets Extension)

The JSSE is two things:

❑ An API for using SSL in Java

❑ A reference implementation of that API

As we said previously, to use the examples in this section, you'll need a copy of the JSSE (it can be downloaded from http://java.sun.com/products/jsse).

The JSSE is a non-commercial reference implementation, but the license states that it can be used for commercial purposes and freely redistributed with commercial applications. Why do they then call it non-commercial? We're not entirely sure, but would hazard a guess that it has to do with the fact that they licensed libraries from RSA, who until recently had a patent on the RSA algorithm used in most SSL implementations. In order to avoid the appearance of competing with RSA, Sun may have agreed to refer to the JSSE as non-commercial.

The JSSE is a reasonable SSL implementation. It is not fully optimized, but performs fairly well and is good enough for most uses. If you have an extremely high-traffic situation that requires a Java SSL implementation, you may need something that performs better, like Phaos' SSLava or RSA's SSL-J. Such implementations are, however, unlikely to be cheap.

For our examples, we're going to use Sun's JSSE. In order to compile and run them, you'll need to download and install the JSSE.

Installing the JSSE

Once you've downloaded the JSSE, you should untar or unzip it, which will create a directory containing a number of files. We're interested in the files in the `lib/` directory – `jcert.jar`, `jnet.jar`, and `jsse.jar` – as they are the JARs necessary to use the examples we're about to describe.

You will need to install all three of them as trusted extensions:

❑ On UNIX, place them in `$JAVA_HOME/jre/lib/ext/`

❑ On Windows, you will need to copy them into two places:
First, into `$JAVA_HOME\jre\lib\ext\` (probably `C:\jdk1.3\jre\lib\ext\`);
then you need to copy them into `$JRE_HOME\lib\ext\` (probably `C:\Program Files\JavaSoft\JRE\1.3\lib\ext\`)

Next the JSSE needs to be added as a security provider to your `java.security` file(s):

- ❑ On UNIX, there is one copy in `$JAVA_HOME/jre/lib/security/`
- ❑ On Windows, there are two copies:

  One in `$JAVA_HOME\jre\lib\security\`, and one in `$JRE_HOME\lib\security\`

Add the following line to the `java.security` file(s):

```
security.provider.x=com.sun.net.ssl.internal.ssl.Provider
```

where x should be the next number in the sequence of currently installed security providers. For instance, a security provider list could look like the following:

```
security.provider.1=sun.security.provider.Sun
security.provider.2=com.sun.rsajca.Provider
security.provider.3=com.sun.net.ssl.internal.ssl.Provider
```

This should now mean that the JSSE has been properly installed; however this doesn't necessarily mean life will be trouble free.

Troubleshooting SSL Problems

The JSSE doesn't provide the most obvious error messages, so here is a list of common exceptions and what the problem might be.

Problem	Explanation and possible solutions
Compile-time error, a package does not exist (for example, `package javax.net.ssl does not exist`)	The JSSE classes are not accessible by the compiler. Check that the three `.jar` files, `jcert.jar`, `jnet.jar`, and `jsse.jar` are all in the `lib/ext` directory under your Java installation. Check to make sure there are no extra Java installations on your machine. If there are, either remove them, or add the JARs to their `lib/ext` directories as well.
Compiles, but get the following exception when run: `Exception in thread "main" java.lang.NoClassDefFoundError: javax/net/ssl/SSLServerSocketFactory`	The JSSE classes are not accessible by the run-time JVM. Check that the three `.jar` files, `jcert.jar`, `jnet.jar`, and `jsse.jar` are all in the `lib/ext` directory under your Java installation. Check to make sure there are no extra Java installations on your machine. If there are, either remove them, or add the JARs to their `lib/ext` directories as well.

Table continued on following page

Problem	Explanation and possible solutions

Compiles, but get one of the following errors when run:
 	
`Exception in thread "main" java.net.SocketException: no SSL Server Sockets`
 	
or
 	
`SSL implementation not available`
	Two possibilities:
	
	The first is that the provider is not registered properly. Check your `java.security` files and make sure that you have created an entry for `com.sun.net.ssl.internal.ssl.Provider`. Then make sure there are no extra `java.security` files on your hard drive that are being used by your runtime to configure you providers. If there are, make sure to add the providers to them as well.
	
	Secondly there may be a problem with your `keystore`. Make sure that you are providing the proper file and password for your `keystore`. Check with `keytool` that you can read an entry for the `keystore` that you expect.

Compiles, but get the following exception when run:
 	
`javax.net.ssl.SSLException: untrusted server cert chain`
 	
or
 	
`javax.net.ssl.SSLException: untrusted client cert chain`
	There is a problem with the certificate being received from the remote server or client. Check that your trust store contains the certificate of the remote machine or the CA that signed it and that the certificate has not expired.
	
	Also, be sure that both machines are using the latest version of the JSSE.

Now we've installed JSSE, and have covered a few of the common problems that occur when attempting to establish an SSL connection, let's do some coding.

A Simple HTTPS Client and Server

Our first illustration of using SSL is to write a simple HTTPS (HTTP over SSL) client. From there we'll create a server-side program that will deliver HTML pages over SSL using the same HTTPS protocol. We'll then rewrite our client to be able to attach to it, as well as connecting to it with Netscape or Internet Explorer.

The HTTPS Client

Writing a simple client that uses the JSSE to fetch a web page over SSL is actually quite easy to do, as the JSSE includes support for HTTPS.

Incidentally, most web servers use port 8443 for HTTPS, though this isn't required.

We need to register HTTPS support with the system, and then, when we fetch a URL that begins with https://, the VM will automatically invoke the JSSE. Let's take a look at the code, which is in `HTTPSClient.java`:

```
import java.io.*;
import java.net.*;

/**
 *  HTTPSClient
 *
 *  This class fetches an HTTPS url to illustrate
 *  the use of HTTPS on the client. It requests
 *  a URL and prints its content to standard out.
 */

public class HTTPSClient {

  public static void main (String[] args) throws Exception {

    /** Begin by setting the URL handler so that it
     *  will find the HTTPS classes.
     *  This could also be done by setting the property
     *  at runtime with:
     *
     *  java -Djava.protocol.handler.pkgs=com.sun.net.ssl.internal.www.protocol
     */

    System.setProperty("java.protocol.handler.pkgs",
                        "com.sun.net.ssl.internal.www.protocol");

    URL url = new URL("https://www.verisign.com/");
    BufferedReader in = new BufferedReader(
                new InputStreamReader(url.openStream()));

    String line;
    while ((line = in.readLine()) != null) {
      System.out.println(line);
    }
    in.close();
  }
}
```

Running this example should display the content of the URL https://www.verisign.com. If it fails, go over the installation instructions for the JSSE, make sure the JARs are installed, and that your `java.security` files correctly list `com.sun.net.ssl.internal.ssl.Provider`.

Note that in order to request an HTTPS URL, we had to set a system property to register HTTPS support. Instead of doing this programmatically, it's possible to register HTTPS at startup by passing a property to the VM like so (all on one line):

```
java -Djava.protocol.handler.pkgs=com.sun.net.ssl.internal.www.protocol
       HTTPSClient
```

If we do this, we don't need to set that property in the code at all. This might be handy if you're switching SSL providers. You could set the class name in a startup script and not need to recompile your application.

The HTTPS Server

In addition to handling HTTPS client requests, the JSSE can be used to create SSL server sockets that are a drop-in replacement for regular sockets in Java. SSL sockets are created through the use of a socket factory, `javax.net.ssl.SSLServerSocketFactory`. By calling the static method `getDefault()` on that class, we acquire an instance of `SSLServerSocketFactory` that generates SSL sockets. You can call `createServerSocket()` with the port number and a server socket will be created.

That server socket extends `java.net.ServerSocket`, so it is used just like a regular server socket.

Calling `accept()` on the server socket causes it to wait for an incoming connection. Once a connection comes in, `getInputStream()` and `getOutputStream()` can be called, respectively returning an input stream and an output stream for the network connection that was just made.

We're going to write a simplified HTTPS server (`HTTPSServer.java`) that can serve up a simple page to clients.

Note that it is by no means complete. All we'll do is wait for a connection and display the request coming in, and then return a short message to the client.

```
import java.io.*;
import java.net.*;
import javax.net.ssl.*;

public class HTTPSServer {

  public static void main(String[] args) throws IOException {

    // First we need a SocketFactory that will create
    // SSL server sockets.

    SSLServerSocketFactory ssf =
      (SSLServerSocketFactory)SSLServerSocketFactory.getDefault();
    ServerSocket ss = ssf.createServerSocket(8080);

    // Keep on accepting connections forever

    while (true) {
      try {
        Socket s = ss.accept();

        // Get the input and output streams. These will be
        // encrypted transparently.

        OutputStream out = s.getOutputStream();
        BufferedReader in = new BufferedReader(
          new InputStreamReader(s.getInputStream()));

        // Read through the input from the client,
        // and display it to the screen.
```

```
           String line = null;
           while (((line = in.readLine())!= null)
             && (!("".equals(line)))) {
             System.out.println(line);
           }
           System.out.println("");

           // Construct a response

           StringBuffer buffer = new StringBuffer();
           buffer.append("<HTML>\n");
           buffer.append(
             "<HEAD><TITLE>HTTPS Server</TITLE></HEAD>\n");
           buffer.append("<BODY>\n");
           buffer.append("<H1>Success!</H1>\n");
           buffer.append("</BODY>\n");
           buffer.append("</HTML>\n");

           // HTTP requires a content-length.

           String string = buffer.toString();
           byte[] data = string.getBytes();
           out.write("HTTP/1.0 200 OK\n".getBytes());
           out.write(new String(
             "Content-Length: "+data.length+"\n").getBytes());
           out.write("Content-Type: text/html\n\n".getBytes());
           out.write(data);
           out.flush();

           // Close the streams and socket.

           out.close();
           in.close();
           s.close();
         } catch (Exception e) {
           e.printStackTrace();
         }
       }
     }
   }
}
```

You'll notice that there's nothing terribly complicated in the above code that's related to SSL. The trickiest stuff happens after we've gotten the input and output streams from the sockets.

Running the Example

In order to run the above code, you need to provide a certificate and private key to the SSL server. We want to use an RSA certificate, since that's what most browsers support. Storing and dealing with certificates and keys is probably the most difficult aspect of using SSL in Java.

We'll create a certificate and private key with `keytool` – to do this execute the following command from the directory in which you'll be running the `HTTPSServer`:

```
C:\> keytool -genkey -v -keyalg RSA -keystore .keystore
```

This will create a file called .keystore, that contains a certificate and private key. Before creating it, keytool will ask you for a password. Since you're creating the keystore from scratch, this will be a brand-new password set for this keystore.

As this is just an example, we'll use the password "sasquatch". Then keytool will ask a few questions about the certificate. The name that you specify should be the machine name for the certificate, *not* your first and last name.

> *We've already encountered this question and answer routine in Chapter 6, so from here we're just going to highlight any particular nuances of the methodology and will show the X.500 name generated.*

```
C:\> keytool -genkey -v -keyalg RSA -keystore .keystore
Enter keystore password: sasquatch
What is your first and last name?
  [Unknown]: localhost

and so on until:

Is <CN=localhost, OU=Dev, O=ISNetworks, L=Seattle, ST=Washington, C=US> correct?

  [no]: yes

Generating 1024 bit RSA key pair and self-signed certificate (MD5WithRSA)
        for: CN=localhost, OU=Dev, O=ISNetworks, L=Seattle, ST=Washington, C=US
Enter key password for <mykey>
        (RETURN if same as keystore password):
[Saving .keystore]
```

In order to actually run the application, we need to indicate to the SSL engine the keystore containing our certificate, as well as the password for accessing it. There are two ways to do this: **programmatically** and **declaratively**. We're going to opt for the second manner of configuration for this example, specifying the keystore and password on the command line. Later in this chapter we'll show you how you can open a keystore programmatically.

We need to set two system properties:

- ❏ javax.net.ssl.keyStore
- ❏ javax.net.ssl.keyStorePassword.

Here's how to run HTTPSServer:

```
java -Djavax.net.ssl.keyStore=.keystore -Djavax.net.ssl.keyStorePassword=sasquatch
    HTTPSServer
```

If you're running a CPU monitor you'll notice your CPU usage shoot up to 100% while the SSL libraries initialize. This is due mostly to the use of SecureRandom, which we've mentioned before. Once the CPU usage drops down, the server is ready to accept connections. On our test machine, a 266 MHz Pentium II, it takes about 10 seconds for the server to start.

We can test the server against a browser. Try opening up Netscape or Internet Explorer and going to https://localhost:8080 (note the https in the URL, rather than http):

Since we have created the certificate ourselves and self-signed it, neither IE nor Netscape will recognize us as a CA. The connection can still be allowed, but the user will be notified of the problem and asked if they wish to proceed. Here's what the user sees under Netscape:

Then they will have to click through a series of dialog boxes asking whether or not the browser should trust the server in question. As annoying as this may be, it is a good idea on the browser vendor's part to do this, as it prevents a number of possible man-in-the-middle attacks.

Eventually the user will reach the page:

The process is similar under IE. The user sees this window:

The IE process is a little easier, since the user only has to deal with one dialog box as opposed to four under Netscape, but in both cases the user would probably be made a bit uneasy.

In order to get rid of these warnings, you need to get your certificate signed by a CA like Verisign. This is a fairly easy procedure, but it does cost some money (from US$125-900). You can export a certificate request with the -certreq option in keytool. The resulting request is then given to your CA, who will sign it and return it as an actual certificate.

For most cases involving browsers as clients, however, we recommend using an existing web server with support for SSL, rather than writing your own. Apache with mod_ssl is fast (and free!), and has been tested quite thoroughly. It was also written outside the US, and so is not subject to US export restrictions. More details can be found at www.modssl.org.

Declaring the Password on the Command Line

You'll notice in the example that we passed the VM our keystore password on the command-line. This is not ideal, as it is now possible for anyone with an account on that machine to discover our keystore password by viewing a list of the currently running processes. In a case like this, it's imperative that the keystore itself be protected by the underlying operating system.

Also, we were using the default keystore that Sun provides, the JKS. This does *not* include encryption, so whether someone knows the password or not, it is possible to extract keys from the keystore if they have read access to it. Again, the best thing to do is set file permissions so that no one can read the keystore file.

Another approach is to use the JCEKS keystore, which is part of Sun's JCE. This keystore uses password-based encryption to store the keys, adding a level of protection even if someone is able to access the file. To use the JCEKS keystore, you need to:

- ❑ When running keytool, pass it the option: -storetype JCEKS

- ❑ Add the option -Djavax.net.ssl.keyStoreType=JCEKS to the invocation of the server

We still have that password problem though, even if the keystore is encrypted. We could put the password in the code itself, but that just moves the problem from the keystore into the `.java` or `.class` file. Now if someone has read access to either of those they'll be able to extract the password and read the keystore file. You could prompt the user for a password, and use that to open the keystore. That way, the password is never on the disk anywhere to be read. This has a serious disadvantage though: it now requires user interaction to start the program, preventing it from being automated, which you might want in a web server.

There's yet another problem with relying on password protection in the keystore: the way the JSSE APIs currently work, the password needs to be a `String` that is placed in the system properties. As we discussed in the last chapter, it's generally frowned upon to use a `String` to store passwords, as they are immutable and can't be cleared. There is a way around using `String` to pass the keystore password, but it requires using some `com.sun` classes in Sun's JSSE, which breaks compatibility with other JSSE implementations.

If your application requires a password-encrypted keystore, you don't mind user interaction at start-up, and you're afraid of someone snooping the memory of your program while it's running, then you probably want to check out how Sun loads the keystore in the examples that come with the JSSE. They use two `com.sun.net.ssl` classes (`SSLContext` and `KeyManagerFactory`) to open a keystore and create SSL sockets using that keystore. Here's an example:

```
SSLContext context;
KeyManagerFactory keyManagerFactory;
KeyStore keystore;
char[] password = "sasquatch".toCharArray();

context = SSLContext.getInstance("TLS");
keyManagerFactory = KeyManagerFactory.getInstance("SunX509");
keystore = KeyStore.getInstance("JKS");

keystore.load(new FileInputStream(".keystore"), password);
keyManagerFactory.init(ks, password);
context.init(keyManagerFactory.getKeyManagers(), null, null);

SSLServerSocketFactory serverSocketFactory = context.getServerSocketFactory();
// serverSocketFactory can now be used to create server sockets.
```

Most applications though, won't require this level of security. Chances are, no one can read the memory of your running process. And even if they can, clearing the password doesn't prevent them from reading your private key, which is also stored in RAM. In general, it will suffice to protect the private key from being read with the native operating system file permissions. You'll still need to use a password, but knowing it won't give anyone access to the file.

As always, you need to balance your security with your requirements. If your keystore is vulnerable to other users or applications reading it, you need to encrypt it – there's no getting around it. That will then require you to get a password from a user every time the application is started. If this causes problems, you may want to look into setting up a separate box to run the application on – one that no one else will have access to!

Attaching to the HTTPSServer with the HTTPSClient

Let's change the HTTPS client to attach to a URL specified on the command line. That way we can run our client against our server, all over SSL. Here's the new version of HTTPSClient:

```java
import java.io.*;
import java.net.*;

/**
 *   HTTPSClient
 *
 *   This class fetches an HTTPS url to illustrate
 *   the use of HTTPS on the client. It requests
 *   a URL and prints its content to standard out.
 *
 *   If an argument is passed, it will use it as the URL
 *   to connect to. Example:
 *
 *   java HTTPSClient https://www.verisign.com
 *
 */

public class HTTPSClient {

  public static void main (String[] args) throws Exception {

    /**  Begin by setting the URL handler so that it
     *   will find the HTTPS classes.
     *  This could also be done by setting the property
     *  at runtime with:
     *
     *  java -Djava.protocol.handler.pkgs=com.sun.net.ssl.internal.www.protocol
     */

    System.setProperty("java.protocol.handler.pkgs",
                    "com.sun.net.ssl.internal.www.protocol");

    // Here's the default URL

    String urlString = "https://www.verisign.com/";

    // If an argument has been passed, use it
    // as the url to attach to.

    if (args.length > 0) {
      urlString = args[0];
    }

    URL url = new URL(urlString);
    BufferedReader in = new BufferedReader(
      new InputStreamReader(url.openStream()));

    String line;
    while ((line = in.readLine()) != null) {
      System.out.println(line);
    }
    in.close();
  }
}
```

When an SSL client attaches to an SSL server, the server typically sends its certificate to the client to verify so that the client knows that the server is the one it intended to talk to. The client then validates that certificate, and ascertains that it trusts the CA that signed the certificate. Our server's certificate is self-signed, so we need to tell our client that we can be trusted as a CA. We do this by setting the trustStore System property (javax.net.ssl.trustStore). Note that the truststore doesn't require a password. Here's how we'll run our new client (all on one line):

```
C:\> java -Djavax.net.ssl.trustStore=.keystore HTTPSClient
        https://localhost:8080/
```

You will, of course, need to have the server currently running in order to run the client against it. But provided you do, you should see the output from our server like so:

```
<HTML>
  <HEAD><TITLE>HTTPS Server</TITLE></HEAD>
  <BODY>
    <H1>Success!</H1>
  </BODY>
</HTML>
```

CACERTS

Normally the client and the server have distinct keystores, and the client would have no access to the private key of the server. In fact, if the trustStore property isn't set, it defaults to $JRE_HOME/lib/security/cacerts, with a password of changeit.

Using the command:

```
C:\> keytool -list -keystore cacerts
```

will display the contents of the cacerts file. As shipped in JDK 1.3 you will see the following output:

```
thawtepersonalfreemailca, Fri Feb 12 12:12:16 PST 1999, trustedCertEntry,
Certificate fingerprint (MD5): 1E:74:C3:86:3C:0C:35:C5:3E:C2:7F:EF:3C:AA:3C:D9
thawtepersonalbasicca, Fri Feb 12 12:11:01 PST 1999, trustedCertEntry,
Certificate fingerprint (MD5): E6:0B:D2:C9:CA:2D:88:DB:1A:71:0E:4B:78:EB:02:41
verisignclass3ca, Mon Jun 29 10:05:51 PDT 1998, trustedCertEntry,
Certificate fingerprint (MD5): 78:2A:02:DF:DB:2E:14:D5:A7:5F:0A:DF:B6:8E:9C:5D
thawtepersonalpremiumca, Fri Feb 12 12:13:21 PST 1999, trustedCertEntry,
Certificate fingerprint (MD5): 3A:B2:DE:22:9A:20:93:49:F9:ED:C8:D2:8A:E7:68:0D
thawteserverca, Fri Feb 12 12:14:33 PST 1999, trustedCertEntry,
Certificate fingerprint (MD5): C5:70:C4:A2:ED:53:78:0C:C8:10:53:81:64:CB:D0:1D
verisignclass4ca, Mon Jun 29 10:06:57 PDT 1998, trustedCertEntry,
Certificate fingerprint (MD5): 1B:D1:AD:17:8B:7F:22:13:24:F5:26:E2:5D:4E:B9:10
verisignserverca, Mon Jun 29 10:07:34 PDT 1998, trustedCertEntry,
Certificate fingerprint (MD5): 74:7B:82:03:43:F0:00:9E:6B:B3:EC:47:BF:85:A5:93
verisignclass1ca, Mon Jun 29 10:06:17 PDT 1998, trustedCertEntry,
Certificate fingerprint (MD5): 51:86:E8:1F:BC:B1:C3:71:B5:18:10:DB:5F:DC:F6:20
thawtepremiumserverca, Fri Feb 12 12:15:26 PST 1999, trustedCertEntry,
Certificate fingerprint (MD5): 06:9F:69:79:16:66:90:02:1B:8C:8C:A2:C3:07:6F:3A
verisignclass2ca, Mon Jun 29 10:06:39 PDT 1998, trustedCertEntry,
Certificate fingerprint (MD5): EC:40:7D:2B:76:52:67:05:2C:EA:F2:3A:4F:65:F0:D8
```

These are certificates that the JVM trusts by default. Each entry as listed includes:

❑ The name of the certificate

❑ The date it was created

❑ Its classification as a trustedCertEntry

❑ The fingerprint of the certificate – an MD5 hash of the bytes of the certificate

The certificates are all issued, effectively, by Verisign (since Thawte is a subsidiary of Verisign).

Entries can be added to cacerts with keytool, using the -import option. For example a certificate file named myCert.cer could be imported into your cacerts file with the following command:

```
C:\> keytool -import -alias myCert -file myCert.cer -keystore cacerts
```

After executing the command you will be prompted for the password, which by default is changeit, and when asked if you want to trust this new certificate, say yes.

> *You should also change the password on the cacerts file with the -storepasswd option, and modify the file permissions to ensure that no one will alter this file, as it would be possible to mount a man-in-the-middle attack if cacerts were compromised.*

SSL Socket Example

Now let's write an example of using SSL sockets directly, without using HTTPS. Here we'll be making use of javax.net.ssl.SSLSockets, which are a subclass of java.net.Socket, allowing it to be dropped in as a replacement in many cases.

We're going to write a simple one-way talk application, similar to the one that we did in Chapter 5 using Diffie-Hellman, but this time we'll use SSL. If you look back at the source to that application (KeyAgreementServer.java and KeyAgreementClient.java) you'll see that a lot of work was needed in setting up the encryption – public keys were exchanged, session keys created, and CipherStreams established.

By using SSL, we simplify that immensely. We just need to use SSLSockets instead of Sockets and the underlying SSLSocket implementation will take care of encryption for us. Additionally, the client will automatically authenticate the server based on the CA that signed its certificate.

SSL Socket Server

The code for the SSL socket server (SSLSocketServer.java) is as follows:

```
import java.io.*;
import java.net.*;
import javax.net.ssl.*;

/**
 *   SSLSocketServer
 *
```

```
 *   This is a demonstration of using SSL over simple
 *   socket communication.
 *
 *   The server opens a server socket on port 8080 using SSL,
 *   and waits for a connection. Once a connection is made,
 *   it displays everything sent to the server.
 */

public class SSLSocketServer {

  private static final int PORT = 8080;

  public static void main (String[] args) throws Exception {

    // First we need a SocketFactory that will create
    // SSL server sockets.

    SSLServerSocketFactory ssf =
      (SSLServerSocketFactory)SSLServerSocketFactory.getDefault();
    ServerSocket ss = ssf.createServerSocket(PORT);

    // Wait for a connection

    Socket s = ss.accept();

    // Get the input stream. These will be
    // encrypted transparently.

    BufferedReader in = new BufferedReader(
      new InputStreamReader(s.getInputStream()));

    // Read through the input from the client,
    // and display it to the screen.

    String line = null;
    while (((line = in.readLine())!= null)) {
      System.out.println(line);
    }
    in.close();
    s.close();
  }
}
```

This is almost identical to how this program would be written if it were using plain sockets rather than SSL sockets. The only difference is in the following lines:

```
SSLServerSocketFactory ssf =
      (SSLServerSocketFactory)SSLServerSocketFactory.getDefault();
ServerSocket ss = ssf.createServerSocket(PORT);
```

If we were using regular sockets, we would perform the following instead:

```
ServerSocket ss = new ServerSocket(PORT);
```

SSL Socket Client

Our client application is very similar to the server. We open an SSL socket, and instead of reading from it, we write to it. Here's `SSLSocketClient.java`:

```java
import java.io.*;
import java.net.*;
import javax.net.ssl.*;

/**
 *  SSLSocketClient
 *
 *  This is a demonstration of using SSL over simple
 *  socket communication.
 *
 *  The client opens a connection to localhost:8080 using SSL,
 *  and then sends each character typed to the other end,
 *  encrypted through SSL.
 */

public class SSLSocketClient {

    private static final String HOST = "localhost";
    private static final int PORT = 8080;

    public static void main(String[] args) throws Exception {

        // First we need a SocketFactory that will create
        // SSL  sockets.

        SSLSocketFactory sf =
            (SSLSocketFactory)SSLSocketFactory.getDefault();
        Socket s = sf.createSocket(HOST,PORT);

        // Get the input and output streams. These will be
        // encrypted transparently.

        OutputStream out = s.getOutputStream();
        out.write("\nConnection established.\n\n".getBytes());
        out.flush();

        System.out.print("\nConnection established.\n\n");

        // Now send everything the user types

        int theCharacter=0;
        theCharacter = System.in.read();
        while (theCharacter != '~') // The '~' is an escape character to exit
        {
            out.write(theCharacter);
            out.flush();
            theCharacter = System.in.read();
        }

        out.close();
        s.close();
    }
}
```

As you can see, the code for dealing with the SSL sockets is quite simple.

Running the Example

As before, however, starting the VM requires extra arguments for the keystore and the truststore. Assuming you want to use the same keystore as in the previous example, you can start the server with the following (all on one line):

```
C:\> java -Djavax.net.ssl.keyStore=.keystore
          -Djavax.net.ssl.keyStorePassword=sasquatch SSLSocketServer
```

Give it about 10 seconds to initialize `SecureRandom`, and after that fire up the client by using:

```
C:\> java -Djavax.net.ssl.trustStore=.keystore SSLSocketClient
```

The client will also take some time to start (between 5 and 45 seconds), due to its initialization of `SecureRandom`, but it will eventually connect to the server and allow you to type messages into the client and have them display on the server, encrypting the communication between them.

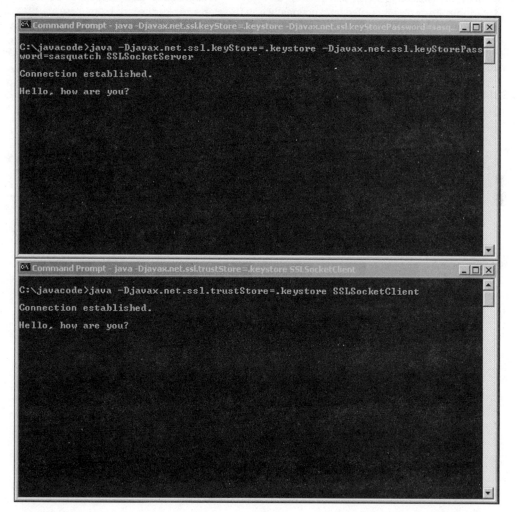

If you have time, inclination, and the software you may find it interesting to try running the example on two different machines and using a packet sniffer to examine the data passed between them.

Protecting the Password

As we saw previously, Sun's JSSE provides an additional way to open a keystore that keeps the password more private. Unfortunately, doing this requires using classes in the com.sun.net.ssl package. It's not clear at this point if other vendors will have access to these same classes, or if they will be restricted to the classes in the javax package.

There are three classes that we'll be examining in com.sun.net.ssl:

❑   KeyManagerFactory

❑   TrustManagerFactory

❑   SSLContext

They allow the creation of secure sockets using a keystore for the certificate and private key. To do this, a KeyManagerFactory is created (and optionally a TrustManagerFactory). From these an SSLContext is created, which can then be used to create an SSLSocketFactory or an SSLServerSocketFactory.

To illustrate this we'll rewrite SSLSocketClient and SSLSocketServer to use the com.sun classes to open a keystore, rather than passing in the keystore information on the command line.

SunSSLSocketClient Class

Our reworked socket client (SunSSLSocketClient) looks like this:

```
import java.io.*;
import java.net.*;
import java.security.*;

import javax.net.ssl.SSLSocketFactory;

import com.sun.net.ssl.SSLContext;
import com.sun.net.ssl.TrustManagerFactory;
import com.sun.net.ssl.TrustManager;

/**
 *    SunSSLSocketClient
 *
 *    This is a demonstration of using SSL over simple
 *    socket communication.
 *
 *    The client opens a connection to localhost:8080 using SSL,
 *    and then sends each character typed to the other end,
 *    encrypted through SSL.
 *
 *    This example uses the com.sun.net.ssl classes to avoid
 *    having to pass keystore information on the command-line.
 */

public class SunSSLSocketClient {

  private static final String HOST = "localhost";
  private static final int PORT = 8080;

  public static void main(String[] args) throws Exception {
```

First we need to load a keystore:

```
char[] passphrase = "sasquatch".toCharArray();
KeyStore keystore = KeyStore.getInstance("JKS");
keystore.load(new FileInputStream(".keystore"), passphrase);
```

Next we initialize a `TrustManagerFactory` with the keystore:

```
TrustManagerFactory tmf = TrustManagerFactory.getInstance("SunX509");
tmf.init(keystore);
```

Now that we have our `TrustManagerFactory`, we can create an `SSLContext` with `TrustManagers` we get from that `TrustManagerFactory`:

```
SSLContext context = SSLContext.getInstance("TLS");
TrustManager[] trustManagers = tmf.getTrustManagers();

context.init(null, trustManagers, null);
```

We can get an `SSLSocketFactory` from the context that we just initialized:

```
SSLSocketFactory sf = context.getSocketFactory();
```

Now we create a socket and get the input and output streams, which will be transparently encrypted:

```
Socket s = sf.createSocket(HOST,PORT);
OutputStream out = s.getOutputStream();
out.write("\nConnection established.\n\n".getBytes());
System.out.print("\nConnection established.\n\n");
```

The connection is established, so all we need to do is loop over the input from the keyboard and send it across the wire through the output stream. We'll stop when we get a tilde (~) character.

```
int theCharacter=0;
theCharacter = System.in.read();
while (theCharacter != '~') // The '~' is an escape character to exit
{
  out.write(theCharacter);
  out.flush();
  theCharacter = System.in.read();
}

out.close();
s.close();
  }
}
```

SunSSLSocketServer Class

The server side of this application (`SunSSLSocketServer`) is very similar to the client, except that we'll be using a server socket and calling `accept()` on it, rather than making a connection directly ourselves.

```
import java.io.*;
import java.net.*;
import java.security.*;

import javax.net.ssl.*;

import com.sun.net.ssl.*;

/**
 * SunSSLSocketServer
 *
 * This is a demonstration of using SSL over simple
 * socket communication.
 *
 * The server opens a server socket on port 8080 using SSL,
 * and waits for a connection. Once a connection is made,
 * it displays everything sent to the server.
 *
 * This example uses the com.sun.net.ssl classes to open
 * a keystore for use by the SSLSockets.
 */

public class SunSSLSocketServer {

  private static final int PORT = 8080;

  public static void main (String[] args) throws Exception {

    // First we need to load a keystore

    char[] passphrase = "sasquatch".toCharArray();
    KeyStore keystore = KeyStore.getInstance("JKS");
    keystore.load(new FileInputStream(".keystore"), passphrase);

    // Now we initialize a KeyManagerFactory with the KeyStore

    KeyManagerFactory kmf = KeyManagerFactory.getInstance("SunX509");
    kmf.init(keystore, passphrase);

    // Now we create an SSLContext and initialize it with
    // KeyManagers from the KeyManagerFactory

    SSLContext context = SSLContext.getInstance("TLS");
    KeyManager[] keyManagers = kmf.getKeyManagers();

    context.init(keyManagers, null, null);
```

Here's where we get an SSL *server* socket factory, rather than just a regular SSL socket factory:

```
    SSLServerSocketFactory ssf = context.getServerSocketFactory();
    ServerSocket ss = ssf.createServerSocket(PORT);

    // Wait for a connection

    Socket s = ss.accept();

    // Get the input stream. These will be
    // encrypted transparently.

    BufferedReader in = new BufferedReader(
      new InputStreamReader(s.getInputStream()));

    // Read through the input from the client,
    // and display it to the screen.

    String line = null;
    while (((line = in.readLine()) != null)) {
      System.out.println(line);
```

```
    }
    in.close();
    s.close();
  }
}
```

The KeyManager uses a keystore to get the private key and certificate to be used for the SSLServerSockets, while the TrustManager uses a keystore to determine whether or not the certificate can be trusted.

> *Typically in SSL, the client validates the server, but not vice-versa, so the server needs a KeyManager and the client needs a TrustManager.*

Running the code will give a familiar result:

```
C:\javacode>java SunSSLSocketServer
Connection established.
Hello, how are you?
```

```
C:\javacode>java SunSSLSocketClient
Connection established.
Hello, how are you?
```

Advanced SSL Topics

To complete our look at SSL let's take a look at a variety of more complex areas of application such as:

- ❑ Certificate-based client authentication
- ❑ Controlling client access to resources
- ❑ Making **Remote Method Invocation** (**RMI**) calls over SSL
- ❑ Using SSL to secure applet-server communication

So how can we authenticate our client using certificates?

Client Authentication

When SSL is used to encrypt connections to web servers, the client typically authenticates the web server, while the server allows any client to connect. There are times, however, when it might be important to check the identity of the client connecting in order to determine if they have permission to access a certain resource.

> *The reason client authentication is less common than server authentication is because each client to be authenticated must have a certificate issued by a CA such as Verisign. There is a high maintenance cost associated with client authentication, but for certain sensitive applications, it's worth it.*

We're going to alter our web server, from the simple example we created at the start of the chapter, so that it requires client authentication. The first thing we need to do to accomplish this is call `setNeedClientAuth(true)` on the `SSLServerSocket`. This will require the client to present a certificate when it connects to the server, and the server to accept the CA that signed that certificate.

Here's our updated `HTTPSServer.java`:

```
import java.io.*;
import java.net.*;
import javax.net.ssl.*;
```

```
/**
 *   HTTPSServer
 *
 *   A very simple HTTPS Server, using the JSSE.
 *   It returns a success message over HTTPS.
 *
 *   This version has been altered to require client authentication.
 *
 *   In order to run this example, you will need to set the
 *   following System properties on the command-line:
 *
 *   javax.net.ssl.keyStore
 *   javax.net.ssl.keyStorePassword
 *   javax.net.ssl.trustStore
 *
```

```
 *   Here's an example (enter all on one line):
 *
 *   java -Djavax.net.ssl.keyStore=.keystore
 *     -Djavax.net.ssl.keyStorePassword=password
 *     -Djavax.net.ssl.trustStore=.truststore
 *   HTTPSServer
 *
 */

public class HTTPSServer {

  public static void main(String[] args) throws IOException {

    // First we need a SocketFactory that will create
    // SSL server sockets.

    SSLServerSocketFactory ssf =
      (SSLServerSocketFactory)SSLServerSocketFactory.getDefault();
    SSLServerSocket ss = (SSLServerSocket)ssf.createServerSocket(8080);

    // Require client authentication
    ss.setNeedClientAuth(true);

    // Keep on accepting connections forever

    while (true) {
      try {
        Socket s = ss.accept();

        // Get the input and output streams. These will be
        // encrypted transparently.

        OutputStream out = s.getOutputStream();
        BufferedReader in = new BufferedReader(
          new InputStreamReader(s.getInputStream()));

        // Read through the input from the client,
        // and display it to the screen.

        String line = null;
        while (((line = in.readLine())!= null) &&
          (!("".equals(line)))) {
          System.out.println(line);
        }
        System.out.println("");

        // Construct a response

        StringBuffer buffer = new StringBuffer();
        buffer.append("<HTML>\n");
        buffer.append(
          "<HEAD><TITLE>HTTPS Server</TITLE></HEAD>\n");
        buffer.append("<BODY>\n");
        buffer.append("<H1>Success!</H1>\n");
        buffer.append("</BODY>\n");
        buffer.append("</HTML>\n");
```

```
                // HTTP requires a content-length.

                String string = buffer.toString();
                byte[] data = string.getBytes();
                out.write("HTTP/1.0 200 OK\n".getBytes());
                out.write(new String(
                   "Content-Length: "+data.length+"\n").getBytes());
                out.write("Content-Type: text/html\n\n".getBytes());
                out.write(data);
                out.flush();

                // Close the streams and socket.

                out.close();
                in.close();
                s.close();
            } catch (Exception e) {
                e.printStackTrace();
            }
          }
        }
      }
```

We need to cast the `ServerSocket` returned by the `SSLServerSocketFactory` to an `SSLServerSocket` so we can call the `setNeedClientAuth()` method on it.

We'll run it against our `HTTPSClient` class from the earlier example. We don't need to make any modifications to that class, but we will need to specify a keystore when running it, so that it can extract a key and certificate to use to authenticate against the server.

Generating Keystores

When the client and the server authenticate each other, they must share a CA in common in both cases. The client must trust the CA that signed the server's certificate, and the server must trust the CA that signed the client's certificate.

So in essence, we need 4 key stores in order to run this example: two private key and certificate key stores and two certificate trust stores. Client and server will each need a keystore and a truststore.

The four keystores needed, will be, unsurprisingly, named:

❑   clientKeyStore

❑   serverKeyStore

❑   clientTrustStore

❑   serverTrustStore

The client keystore is generated using the following (note, a server keystore was created with a similar command earlier this chapter):

```
C:\> keytool -genkey -v -keyalg RSA -keystore clientKeyStore
```

A password, and some information for the client, like the common name, the organization, and the location will again need to be specified. Once that's done, the server's keystore can be generated:

```
C:\> keytool -genkey -v -keyalg RSA -keystore serverKeyStore
```

Here, specify `localhost` as the name for the certificate.

Now we need to create the client's trust store, which should contain the certificate of the server. We can do this by exporting the server's certificate to a file and then importing it into a new key store:

```
C:\> keytool -export -v -file server.cer -keystore serverKeyStore
C:\> keytool -import -v -alias serverCert -file server.cer
             -keystore clientTrustStore
```

A password will be needed for the truststore, and then it will ask whether the certificate should be trusted – answer `yes`.

Next we will create a truststore for the server with the client's certificate:

```
C:\> keytool -export -v -file client.cer -keystore clientKeyStore
C:\> keytool -import -v -alias clientCert -file client.cer
             -keystore serverTrustStore
```

Again, you'll want to trust the certificate being imported.

Now that the key stores and truststores have been created, we can try out the server and client. We need to pass four arguments to each one:

❑   The keystore

❑   The keystore password

❑   The truststore

❑   The truststore password

We're going to set these on the command line, but they could also be specified in the code, with `System.setProperty()`.

Running the Application

To start the server, enter the following as usual all on one line. Be sure to replace `password` with the password you chose for your server keystore. Note that the keystore requires a password but the trust store does not. This is because a trust store contains only certificates, and not private keys, and so is not considered sensitive information.

```
C:\> java -Djavax.net.ssl.keyStore=serverKeyStore
          -Djavax.net.ssl.keyStorePassword=password
          -Djavax.net.ssl.trustStore=serverTrustStore HTTPSServer
```

Once the server has completely started up (usually takes about 10 seconds), the client can be started:

```
C:\> java -Djavax.net.ssl.keyStore=clientKeyStore
         -Djavax.net.ssl.keyStorePassword=password
         -Djavax.net.ssl.trustStore=clientTrustStore HTTPSClient
                                     https://localhost:8080
```

You should see the following message on the client:

```
<HTML>
<HEAD><TITLE>HTTPS Server</TITLE></HEAD>
<BODY>
<H1>Success!</H1>
</BODY>
</HTML>
```

This indicates that the client authentication was successful. If you see an exception there are three areas for initial checking:

❑   The SSL troubleshooting tips provided at the start of the chapter

❑   The command-line arguments being used to start the client and server

❑   That the keystores and truststores have been created exactly as described

Browser Authentication

It is possible to authenticate a browser attaching to the web server, provided it has a client certificate. Such client certificates can be purchased from Verisign or one could be downloaded for free from Thawte. They are often referred to as e-mail certificates, because they can be used for signing S/MIME e-mail (see Appendix A).

In order to present a browser certificate, the certificate must be signed by one of the CAs that the server trusts. These are defined by the trust store in the JSSE, which by default is the `cacerts` file in `$JRE_HOME/lib/security`.

If you have a client certificate signed by a certificate authority in your `cacerts` file, it's possible to set up your `HTTPSServer` to accept authentication from your browser. If you want to try it out, start the server without specifying a `trustStore` entry and it will default to `cacerts` for its trusted certificates:

```
C:\> java -Djavax.net.ssl.keyStore=serverKeyStore
         -Djavax.net.ssl.keyStorePassword=password HTTPSServer
```

Then you should be able to attach to it with a browser by going to the following URL: https://localhost:8080.

You should see the following dialog box, provided that you have a client certificate that is signed by a CA that the server accepts:

You can then select a certificate to present to the server and continue. If you connect using Internet Explorer, you'll see a slightly different dialog, with the same essential functionality:

In this case, I happen to have two certificates with the common name Jess Garms, so I have to view each certificate to differentiate between them.

An Aside – Using Thawte E-Mail Certificates to Authenticate Internet Explorer Users

There is a bug in either the JSSE, or in Internet Explorer, that surfaces when a Thawte Freemail certificate is used to authenticate to a server using the JSSE. The Freemail certificate is signed by a certificate chain, with the root Thawte certificate validating an intermediate certificate, which, in turn, validates the user's certificate. IE fails to detect this chain and refuses to allow the user to use their Thawte certificate to authenticate. So, to use a certificate chain with the JSSE and IE, you will need to trust the certificate that was used to sign the certificate you wish to accept – this is a relatively straightforward procedure that we walk through in Chapter 11.

Flexible Client Authentication

Our example performed client authentication based on whether or not a client's certificate was signed by a certain CA. In a large system, you might have your own CA, and be able to devote a particular signing certificate to a single purpose, like access to a particular machine or resource. Often though, you don't want to create your own certificates, you just want to be able to grant access based on some information in the certificate, such as the e-mail address.

To do this, the server needs to examine the certificate that the client is presenting. Once we have a reference to the SSLSocket, we can get the SSLSession by calling getSession() on it. SSLSession has a method getPeerCertificateChain(), which returns an array of Certificate objects, the first of which is the client's certificate.

Once we have the client's Certificate, we can extract the principal it vouches for with getSubjectDN(). We can then call getName() on the Principal object. We can examine the string that's returned and determine whether or not the client should be allowed to perform a given action.

It is possible to create a certificate that has any SubjectDN you desire, but not with any CA signature. Because of that, it's important to limit the certificates your server accepts. Check your cacerts file or specify a trustStore on the command line.

Typically you should only accept one CA for authentication based on the name in a client certificate. Since it's not possible to create an arbitrary certificate signed by a specific CA, this should thwart any attempts to hack in by creating a fake certificate.

Authenticating via Certificate's Common Name (CN)

To illustrate this approach we'll modify the HTTPSServer class to handle programmable authentication. We'll start by creating an interface, SSLAuthenticator, with one method, checkPermission(). If that method fails, it will throw an exception, which we will define as an AuthenticationException:

```
/**
 *  AuthenticationException
 *
 *  Exception to throw if SSL Authentication fails.
 */

public class AuthenticationException extends Exception {

  public AuthenticationException() {
    super();
  }

  public AuthenticationException(String info) {
    super(info);
  }
}
```

Here's SSLAuthenticator.java:

```
/**
 *  SSLAuthenticator
 *
 *  Defines an interface for determining if a client
 *  in an SSL session should be allowed
 *  to connect.
 */

public interface SSLAuthenticator {

  public void checkPermission() throws AuthenticationException;
}
```

Now we'll create an implementation of `SSLAuthenticator` that checks if the subject's CN is `Hamlet`. If it is, it allows the connection. If not, it will display an error. We'll ensure that the correct certificate is being used by only allowing certificates issued by a certain CA.

In order to get the subject's `CommonName`, we need to go through several steps:

❑ Get the peer certificate chain from the `SSLSession`

❑ Get the client `Certificate` from that chain – it will be the first one

❑ Get the `java.security.Principal` from that certificate

❑ Get the name from the `Principal` object (this will look something like `CN=Hamlet`, `OU=Dev`, `O=ISNetworks`, `L=Seattle`, `ST=WA`, `C=US`)

❑ Make sure that the CN is `Hamlet`

If any one of the above steps fails, we need to throw an `AuthenticationException`.

The HamletAuthenticator Class

So our implementation of `SSLAuthenticator` for checking the certificate CN is `Hamlet` (`HamletAuthenticator.java`) is as follows:

```
import javax.net.ssl.*;
import javax.security.cert.*;

/**
 *   HamletAuthenticator
 *
 *   This class is an implementation of the SSLAuthenticator
 *   interface, and provides a mechanism for checking that the
 *   certificate used in SSLAuthentication is for an entity
 *   with the Common Name of Hamlet.
 *
 *   Note that in the setup of the SSL Server, care should be taken
 *   to only allow specific CAs that will check the identity of an
 *   entity before granting a certificate with the Common Name of
 *   Hamlet.
 */

public class HamletAuthenticator implements SSLAuthenticator {

  private SSLSession mSession;

  public HamletAuthenticator (SSLSession session) {
    mSession = session;
  }

  public void checkPermission() throws AuthenticationException {
    X509Certificate[] certChain = null;
    try {

      // Get the cert chain
```

```
                certChain = mSession.getPeerCertificateChain();
            } catch (SSLPeerUnverifiedException spue) {

                // There isn't one!

                throw new AuthenticationException("Peer unverified");
            }

            // Get the client's certificate

            X509Certificate clientCert = certChain[0];

            // Get the Principal corresponding to the client

            java.security.Principal client = clientCert.getSubjectDN();

            // Get the name of the client

            String name = client.getName();

            // The name should start with "CN=Hamlet,". If not,
            // the user should not be allowed in.

            if (name.indexOf("CN=Hamlet,")!=0) {
               throw new AuthenticationException("Peer is not Hamlet");
            }

            //System.out.println("Client name: " + name);

        }
    }
}
```

A Modified SSL Server

Now we need to modify our SSL Server to use the `HamletAuthenticator` to check whether a client should be allowed access. If the client is allowed, we'll display a welcome message. If not, we'll display `Failure`.

If a user doesn't have a certificate though, or their CA doesn't match the web server's, they won't even get far enough to see the failure HTML page. Instead, the socket will be closed during the SSL Handshake.

Our `HTTPSAuthServer` class will look very similar to the `HTTPSServer` class developed in the *Client Authentication* section so we'll only highlight the three areas of code that are changed:

```
import java.io.*;
import java.net.*;
import javax.net.ssl.*;

/**
 *   HTTPSAuthServer
 *
 *   A very simple HTTPS Server, using the JSSE.
 *   It returns a success message over HTTPS.
 *
```

```
 *    This version has been altered to require client authentication,
 *    through the use of a programmable Authenticator.
 *
 *    In order to run this example, you will need to set the
 *    following System properties on the command-line:
 *
 *    javax.net.ssl.keyStore
 *    javax.net.ssl.keyStorePassword
 *    javax.net.ssl.trustStore
 *
 *    Here's an example (enter all on one line):
 *
 *    java -Djavax.net.ssl.keyStore=.keystore
 *      -Djavax.net.ssl.keyStorePassword=password
 *      -Djavax.net.ssl.trustStore=.truststore HTTPSServer
 *
 */

public class HTTPSAuthServer {

    public static void main(String[] args) throws IOException {


        // Keep on accepting connections forever

    while (true) {
        try {
            Socket s = ss.accept();
            boolean allowed = false;

            SSLSession session = ((SSLSocket)s).getSession();

            // Check the client's authentication with
            // the HamletAuthenticator.
            // If we wanted to use a different Authenticator,
            // we could just
            // replace this line.

            SSLAuthenticator authenticator =
              new HamletAuthenticator(session);
            try {
              authenticator.checkPermission();
              allowed = true;
            } catch (AuthenticationException ae) {
              allowed = false;
              System.out.println("Client denied access: "+ae);
            }

            // Construct a response

            StringBuffer buffer = new StringBuffer();

            buffer.append("<HTML>\n");
            buffer.append(
              "<HEAD><TITLE>HTTPS Server</TITLE></HEAD>\n");
            buffer.append("<BODY>\n");
            if (allowed) {
              buffer.append(
                "<H1>Success!</H1>\nWelcome, Hamlet.\n");
            } else {
              buffer.append(
                "<H1>Failure!</H1>\nYou are not Hamlet.\n");
            }
            buffer.append("</BODY>\n");
            buffer.append("</HTML>\n");
```

Running the Example

In order to run the example, we need a client certificate, and the server needs to know the corresponding CA for that certificate.

We'll create a certificate for our client with the name of Hamlet, *but first we must remove the files* clientKeyStore *and the* serverTrustStore *created in the last example.*

Once that's been done, generate the certificate and private key for the client, and then create the serverTrustStore, which will contain the client's certificate:

```
C:\> keytool -genkey -v -keyalg RSA -keystore clientKeyStore
```

You will need to specify Hamlet as your first and last name, like so:

```
What is your first and last name?
  [Unknown]:  Hamlet
```

That way when the server checks the name on the certificate, it will return Hamlet.

Now we need to create the file serverTrustStore that will contain the client's certificate:

```
C:\> keytool -export -v -file client.cer -keystore clientKeyStore
C:\> keytool -import -v -alias clientCert -file client.cer
             -keystore serverTrustStore
```

Answer yes when asked if the certificate should be trusted.

Now we can start the server. We need to pass the same arguments we've been using throughout this chapter to set the keystore and the truststore:

```
C:\> java -Djavax.net.ssl.keyStore=serverKeyStore
          -Djavax.net.ssl.keyStorePassword=password
          -Djavax.net.ssl.trustStore=serverTrustStore HTTPSAuthServer
```

To run the client, enter the following:

```
C:\> java -Djavax.net.ssl.keyStore=clientKeyStore
          -Djavax.net.ssl.keyStorePassword=password
          -Djavax.net.ssl.trustStore=clientTrustStore HTTPSClient
          https://localhost:8080
```

If everything was successful, you should see the following appear on the client:

```
<HTML>
<HEAD><TITLE>HTTPS Server</TITLE></HEAD>
<BODY>
<H1>Success!</H1>
Welcome, Hamlet.
</BODY>
</HTML>
```

If you attempt to use a different client certificate, the authentication should fail. You can try it with a browser if you like. Just go to https://localhost:8080. The connection should be closed by the server when the browser cannot authenticate itself as Hamlet, signed by the CA the server is expecting.

Options

In addition to authenticating based on the certificate, requirements for the connection, like a specific algorithm or cryptographic strength, can be added. `SSLSession.getCipherSuite()` will return a `String` with the algorithms and strengths specified. The possible `String` values include (from the JSSE API documentation for `getCipherSuite()`) are:

- ❏ **SSL_RSA_WITH_RC4_128_MD5** – a non-exportable SSL v3 cipher suite supporting 128 bit RC4 encryption keys and full RSA key sizes

- ❏ **SSL_DHE_DSS_WITH_3DES_EDE_CBC_SHA** – a non-exportable SSL v3 cipher suite supporting 168 bit TripleDES encryption keys (the effective strength of this cipher is only 112 bits)

- ❏ **SSL_CK_RC4_128_EXPORT40_WITH_MD5** – an exportable SSL v2 cipher suite using weakened RC4 encryption and limited RSA key sizes

- ❏ **SSL_DH_anon_EXPORT_WITH_DES40_CBC_SHA** – an exportable SSL v3 cipher suite using weakened DES encryption, and which doesn't support authentication of servers

- ❏ **SSL_RSA_WITH_NULL_MD5** – an exportable SSL version 3 cipher suite using *no encryption* and full RSA key sizes

The cipher suites will vary depending on the client and server. The `String` representing the cipher suite indicates what the key exchange algorithm is, as well as the encryption algorithm and the message authentication algorithm.

In the first cipher suite (`SSL_RSA_WITH_RC4_128_MD5`), RSA is used to exchange keys and authenticate the server, and 128-bit RC4 is used for encryption. MD5 is used for a message authentication code (MAC). If you check the connection between client and server, you may find that the cipher suite reported is `SSL_RSA_WITH_RC4_128_SHA`, which is nearly identical to the first cipher suite in the list, but it uses SHA rather than MD5 for its MAC.

In most cases, you probably want to check that the cipher suite is either `SSL_RSA_WITH_RC4_128_SHA` or `SSL_RSA_WITH_RC4_128_MD5`, ensuring that the strongest SSL ciphers are being used.

RMI over SSL

Remote Method Invocation (**RMI**) enables an object in one Java virtual machine to invoke methods on an object in a different virtual machine. By default, RMI messages are sent over TCP/IP in clear text. If anyone were to eavesdrop on the communication between client and server, they could read the information that was being sent. Also, client authentication is not cryptographically secure in RMI, so it may be possible for an attacker to masquerade as a legitimate client, and alter the state of some objects.

By making RMI calls over SSL, it's possible to encrypt the data being sent over the wire, and authenticate the client and server. We'll need to write our own custom socket factory that RMI can then use. Those sockets will then be encrypted, transparently to the RMI mechanism itself.

This section of the book assumes you're familiar with RMI.

A Simple Unencrypted RMI Application

Before we write an encrypted RMI application, we should start with an unencrypted one. We'll create a very simple RMI app that serves up the current time.

We'll start by creating our remote interface, `TimeServer`. It will extend `java.rmi.Remote`, as all RMI interfaces must. It will have a single method, `getTime()`. Here's `TimeServer.java`:

```
import java.rmi.*;
import java.util.*;

public interface TimeServer extends Remote {

  public Date getTime() throws RemoteException;

}
```

Next, we will write an implementation of that interface that is a remote object. Remote objects need to extend `UnicastRemoteObject` and implement a remote interface that defines the methods a client can call. We've already defined the interface, `TimeServer`. This is `TimeServerImpl.java`:

```
import java.rmi.*;
import java.rmi.server.*;
import java.util.*;

public class TimeServerImpl extends UnicastRemoteObject implements TimeServer {

    public TimeServerImpl() throws RemoteException {
      super();
    }

    public Date getTime() {
      Date theTime = new Date();
      System.out.println("Time requested: "+theTime);
      return theTime;
    }

    public static void main (String[] args) {

      if (System.getSecurityManager() == null) {
        System.setSecurityManager(new RMISecurityManager());
      }

      try {

        TimeServerImpl self = new TimeServerImpl();

        Naming.rebind("//localhost/TimeServer", self);
        System.out.println("TimeServer bound in registry");

      } catch (Exception e) {
        System.out.println("Error binding to the registry:");
        e.printStackTrace();
      }
    }
}
```

`TimeServerImpl` is quite simple. All it does is define an implementation of the `getTime()` method, and provide a `main()` method that can be called to start the application. The `main()` method creates an instance of `TimeServerImpl` and binds it to the local RMI registry.

Now we will write a client that will call the remote server and print out the time it receives. This is `TimeClient.java`:

```java
import java.rmi.*;

public class TimeClient {

  private static String host = "localhost";

  public static void main (String[] args) {

    // If we received any arguments, then the first one
    // is the host to connect to.

    if (args.length != 0) {
      host = args[0];
    }
    if (System.getSecurityManager()==null) {
      System.setSecurityManager(new RMISecurityManager());
    }
    try {
      TimeServer remoteTimeServer =
        (TimeServer)Naming.lookup("//"+host+"/TimeServer");
      System.out.println(remoteTimeServer.getTime());
    } catch (Exception e) {
      e.printStackTrace();
    }
  }
}
```

Finally, we need to create a policy file that will allow us to connect on ports greater than 1024. Here is `rmi.policy`:

```
// Permissions for RMI.
// Change "localhost" for remote connections. It should be
// the name of the RMI Server.

grant codeBase "file:." {
  permission java.net.SocketPermission "localhost:1024-", "connect";
};
```

> *Note* `localhost` *in* `rmi.policy` *should be changed to the host name of the machine upon which you will be running the RMI server, if it is not the same machine as your client.*

Running the Example

Once you have all the source files in one directory, compile them all, then run `rmic` on `TimeServerImpl` to create the stubs. We'll use the `-v1.2` option because we won't be running this against a 1.1 VM:

```
C:\> rmic -v1.2 TimeServerImpl
```

This will create the file `TimeServerImpl_stub.class`.

To execute the code the first task is to start the `rmiregistry` with the command `rmiregistry`, run from the directory containing your class files.

Next, start `TimeServer` with:

```
C:\> java -Djava.security.policy=rmi.policy TimeServerImpl
```

This should yield the output:

```
TimeServer bound in registry
```

Now we need to copy some files over to the client. This is not necessary if you're running the client and server on the same machine, but if you want to run them separately, copy the following files:

- ❑   `TimeServer.class`
- ❑   `TimeClient.class`
- ❑   `TimeServerImpl_stub.class`
- ❑   `rmi.policy`

To run the client, execute the following:

```
C:\> java -Djava.security.policy=rmi.policy TimeClient <hostname>
```

where `<hostname>` is the hostname of the server. If you're running on a single machine, you can omit the hostname and `TimeClient` will use `localhost`.

You should see a message like the following on both the client and the server when `TimeClient` executes:

```
Wed Mar 7 14:48:39 PDT 2001
```

Adding SSL to the RMI Example

Now we're going to modify our simple RMI example by encrypting the RMI communication using SSL.

You'll need the JSSE installed on both client and server as described previously.

In order to run RMI over SSL, we need to write two custom socket factories, one for the client and one for the server. These are fairly simple classes, as almost all of the work is already done for us by the JSSE. We just need to implement `RMIClientSocketFactory` which has one method – `createSocket()`, and `RMIServerSocketFactory` which has one method – `createServerSocket()`.

In both cases, we need to return the appropriate kind of SSL secured socket:

- ❑   An `SSLSocket` for the `RMIClientSocketFactory`
- ❑   An `SSLServerSocket` for the `RMIServerSocketFactory`

The socket factories should also handle authentication, if necessary. Typically, this is done automatically through the `javax.net.ssl.TrustStore` System property, but you may wish to programmatically check whether a client or server is authorized as well.

Let's start with the client socket factory (RMISSLClientSocketFactory.java) – this should implement RMIClientSocketFactory:

```
import java.io.*;
import java.net.*;
import java.rmi.server.*;
import javax.net.ssl.*;

public class RMISSLClientSocketFactory
implements RMIClientSocketFactory, Serializable {

    public Socket createSocket(String host, int port)
  throws IOException
  {
      SSLSocketFactory sf = (SSLSocketFactory)SSLSocketFactory.getDefault();
      SSLSocket socket = (SSLSocket)sf.createSocket(host, port);
      return socket;
  }
}
```

The server socket factory (RMISSLServerSocketFactory.java) is almost identical, except that we implement RMIServerSocketFactory:

```
import java.io.*;
import java.net.*;
import java.rmi.server.*;
import javax.net.ssl.*;

public class RMISSLServerSocketFactory
implements RMIServerSocketFactory, Serializable {

    public ServerSocket createServerSocket(int port)
  throws IOException
  {
      SSLServerSocketFactory ssf = (SSLServerSocketFactory)
        SSLServerSocketFactory.getDefault();
    SSLServerSocket serverSocket =
      (SSLServerSocket)ssf.createServerSocket(port);
    serverSocket.setNeedClientAuth(true);
    return serverSocket;
  }
}
```

Note that by calling setNeedClientAuth(true) on the server socket, we are enabling client authentication. If you do not want clients to be authenticated, simply remove this line. The server, however, is always authenticated.

Finally, we need to modify our server so that it uses the new socket factories. We replace the call to super() in the constructor with one that includes the socket factories, and make sure to bind an instance of TimeServerImplSSL in the RMI registry. Here's the code for TimeServerImplSSL.java:

```
import java.rmi.*;
import java.rmi.server.*;
import java.util.*;

public class TimeServerSSLImpl extends UnicastRemoteObject implements TimeServer {
```

```
    public TimeServerSSLImpl() throws RemoteException {
      super(0, new RMISSLClientSocketFactory(),
        new RMISSLServerSocketFactory());
    }

    public Date getTime() {
      Date theTime = new Date();
      System.out.println("Time requested: "+theTime);
      return theTime;
    }

    public static void main (String[] args) {

      if (System.getSecurityManager() == null) {
        System.setSecurityManager(new RMISecurityManager());
      }

      try {

        TimeServerSSLImpl self = new TimeServerSSLImpl();

        Naming.rebind("//localhost/TimeServer", self);
        System.out.println("TimeServer bound in registry");

      } catch (Exception e) {
        System.out.println("Error binding to the registry:");
        e.printStackTrace();
      }
    }
  }
```

The client will automatically use whatever socket factory the server provides, so we don't need to make any alterations to the client code.

Running the Example

The first task is to compile all of the relevant classes:

- ❑ TimeServer.java
- ❑ TimeClient.java
- ❑ TimeServerSSLImpl.java
- ❑ RMISSLClientSocketFactory.java
- ❑ RMISSLServerSocketFactory.java

Then, run the RMI compiler on TimeServerSSLImpl:

```
C:\> rmic -v1.2 TimeServerSSLImpl
```

Now we're going to use the same keystores and truststores as earlier in the chapter (which will need to be set up if not already present).

Now, for the server, the following files need to be in a single directory (for example, `c:\rmi_server`):

- ❏ `TimeServer.class`
- ❏ `TimeServerSSLImpl.class`
- ❏ `TimeServerSSLImpl_stub.class`
- ❏ `RMISSLServerSocketFactory.class`
- ❏ `RMISSLClientSocketFactory.class`
- ❏ `rmi.policy`
- ❏ `serverKeyStore`
- ❏ `serverTrustStore`

While in the client directory (for example, `c:\rmi_client`), the following files are required:

- ❏ `TimeClient.class`
- ❏ `TimeServer.class`
- ❏ `TimeServerSSLImpl_stub.class`
- ❏ `RMISSLClientSocketFactory.class`
- ❏ `rmi.policy`
- ❏ `clientKeyStore`
- ❏ `clientTrustStore`

Then to run the example the first task is to execute `rmiregistry` in the server directory.

Then, in that same directory, we will execute the server code, `TimeServerSSLImpl`. This requires some arguments to be passed to the server, including the policy file to be used, the key store, the truststore, and the keystore password:

```
C:\> java -Djava.security.policy=rmi.policy
         -Djavax.net.ssl.keyStore=serverKeyStore
         -Djavax.net.ssl.keyStorePassword=password
         -Djavax.net.ssl.trustStore=serverTrustStore TimeServerSSLImpl
```

This may take up to 30 seconds to start, as it needs to initialize a `SecureRandom` object. Once you see the message `TimeServer bound in registry`, the server is running.

Next we need to start the client. In the client directory, execute the following command, replacing `localhost` if necessary with the name of the machine running the server:

```
C:\> java -Djava.security.policy=rmi.policy
         -Djavax.net.ssl.keyStore=clientKeyStore
         -Djavax.net.ssl.keyStorePassword=password
         -Djavax.net.ssl.trustStore=clientTrustStore TimeClient localhost
```

Again, it may take some time for the client to initialize, but eventually you will receive the time from the server, which was transmitted over SSL.

Programmatic Authentication

It can be a little tricky to do programmatic authentication using RMI over SSL. Due to encapsulation, the SSL information is not easily available to your RMI objects, unlike in our `HTTPSAuthServer` earlier in this chapter.

You could write a subclass of `SSLServerSocket` that performed some authentication, but this has some limitations. You cannot control access to particular methods of an RMI object in this fashion, because the socket doesn't know about methods, it only sees a connection. The RMI object, on the other hand, doesn't know about the socket, and so cannot know who called it, only that it has been called.

Probably the best way to handle SSL authentication with RMI is with careful configuration of your truststore. Make sure that it contains only the certificates that you wish to be authorized before starting your server. This should take care of most authentication needs.

If you need something more advanced, like checking permission on a specific method by certificate, you'll need to do something considerably more complicated. One option is to use Enterprise JavaBeans. Another is to create your own version of `rmic`, which could add an argument to every method call that would include a token for security checks. It is beyond the scope of this book to provide such an implementation.

Secure RMI

Sun is working on a secure RMI specification. Secure RMI handles authentication and encryption automatically, but an implementation is not yet available. It appears likely that it will be part of JDK 1.4, which should be released around the end of 2001.

Applets and SSL

Another common use for SSL is to protect communication between an applet and a server. By default, applet communication is limited to the server that the applet originated from, but SSL can be used to protect that communication.

The two major browsers, Netscape and Internet Explorer, both support HTTPS and extend that HTTPS support to applets. They do not provide a complete SSL library allowing socket connections, but it is possible to communicate with a server by sending HTTPS requests. This works both with the internal browser VMs and the Java Plug-in.

Here's some code for sending a GET request over HTTPS that could be used in an applet:

```
URL url = new URL("https://myserver/aServlet");
InputStream is = url.openStream();
```

The `InputStream` that results is automatically encrypted and this is transparent to the applet.

If you want to do a POST request, you'll need to use the `URLConnection` class as in the following example:

```
URL url = new URL("https://myserver/aServlet");
URLConnection connection = url.openConnection();
connection.setDoOutput(true);
connection.setUseCaches(false);
connection.setAllowUserInteraction(false);
connection.setRequestProperty("content-type","application/x-www-form-urlencoded");
```

```
OutputStream os = connection.getOutputStream();
out.write("arg1=test".getBytes());
out.close();

InputStream is = connection.getInputStream();
```

This code sends a value of `test` for the parameter `arg1`. Again, the input and output streams will be encrypted as the data is sent over the wire.

It's not possible to carry out SSL secured socket communication from an applet. It would require installing the JSSE on the client and using the Java Plug-in. It's probably better to create a servlet that will accept data from the applet, and have the servlet make the necessary socket calls.

Limitations of SSL

SSL is one of the most valuable tools available for securing Java applications. Nevertheless, it's not a panacea. It has a number of serious limitations that you need to be aware of when analyzing your application's security.

First of all, SSL is a network communication protocol only. It can't be used to store data in files or in memory. It will only secure your network communication.

Secondly, just because you've applied SSL to some of your network communications, that doesn't mean that your entire application is secure. There may be some unsecured network connections being made, or perhaps the application is running on an unsecured box. It's important to not be lulled into thinking that just because you're using SSL your application is completely safe.

Lastly, not all clients support SSL. It's quite common to decide to use SSL on your server and then discover that your clients can't communicate with your server because they are applets, are using Java 1.1, or for any number of additional reasons. WAP applications, for example, are often unable to take advantage of SSL due to the computational requirements.

Nonetheless, SSL (when properly used) can add a great deal of security to your applications.

Summary

SSL can be used for any TCP/IP communication that takes place over an untrusted network. Perhaps one of the best uses for SSL other than HTTPS is encrypting communication with a database. Other uses include encrypting communication with a mail server by using SSL for the POP or IMAP connection.

In this chapter we've presented the most common ways of using SSL in Java, and some of the more exotic ones, like client authentication and RMI over SSL. In the next chapter, we'll use SSL to create a proxy that automatically encrypts JDBC connections to a database.

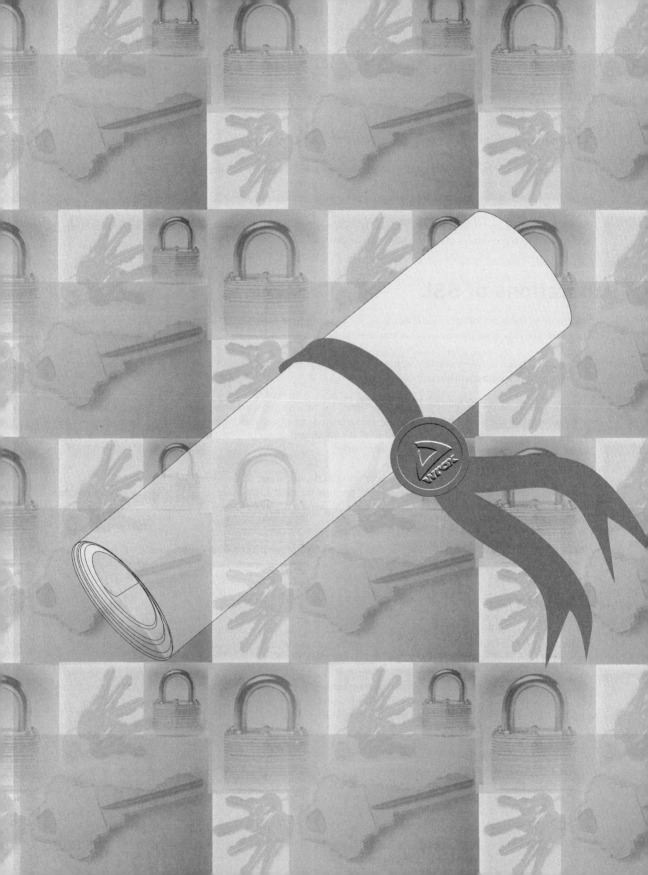

10

Securing a Database

In this chapter, we will deal with an important aspect of securing a Java application that is often neglected by the developer – securing the connection to a database. There are two obvious points of attack against your database. The most obvious and most vulnerable point of attack is the connection between your client and the port on which the database is listening. Most databases will have clients for connecting remotely to the database. Some of those can encrypt the transmission of the request, some cannot.

If your database is securely behind a firewall and you aren't afraid of snoops between your database and its clients, encryption might not be necessary. However, if your application server and database communicate over the Internet and are not part of a **VPN** (**Virtual Private Network**), this can be extremely dangerous. Information such as your username and password as well as any important data will be included in those packets, and unless the connection is secured, you are vulnerable.

The second point of vulnerability is the data in the database itself. In a well-secured network, this is generally less of a weakness, but we will address it here for situations where a database is accessible to users who should be able to view some data but not all.

We're going to deal with these topics in order, so the chapter breaks down into the following major sections:

- ❑ Securing client-database communication
- ❑ Securing data in the database
- ❑ A sample e-commerce type application

Because this is a Java book, we assume that the application being built is utilizing JDBC to connect the application layer to the data store and over the course of the chapter, we will construct an RMI-based JDBC driver that provides secure connections to any JDBC-enabled data source over an SSL connection.

> To run the code in this chapter you will need a database, a JDBC driver, and the
> JSSE. For the SSL tunneling, two networked machines are required, and for the
> secure JDBC driver the Xerces XML parser is needed. SSL and the JSSE were
> covered in Chapter 9, while Appendix B describes how to set up the MySQL database
> and JDBC driver used in this example. The source code for the chapter is available
> from http://www.wrox.com and the package names refer to the code download.

Due to the nature and likely areas of application of security type code your attention is drawn to the
disclaimer in the preliminary pages of this publication, specifically:

*The author and publisher have made every effort in the preparation of this book to ensure the accuracy
of the information. However, the information contained in this book is sold without warranty, either
express or implied. Neither the authors, Wrox Press nor its dealers or distributors will be held liable
for any damages caused or alleged to be caused either directly or indirectly by this book.*

Let's start by looking at approaches for securing database connections.

Securing the JDBC Driver Transmission

This is not a JDBC book so we won't be providing an exhaustive explanation of how to write a JDBC
application, but, in brief, JDBC provides a set of standard interfaces in the java.sql package that the
driver-developer must implement to allow database access from within a Java application. It is the JDBC
driver manufacturer's responsibility to translate the database protocol to the high-level JDBC APIs. The
driver provides implementation classes of interfaces such as Connection and ResultSet (to name but
two) that provide a means of connecting to the database and scrolling through the result of a SQL
query, respectively.

The user need not know about the implementation of the JDBC API, just the API itself. In fact, the
JDBC API allows the developer to seamlessly load alternative implementations dynamically by the use
of a factory class called the DriverManager. By simply changing the arguments passed to the
getConnection() method, you can change what driver implementation you are using as well as the
database you are accessing. For more details about JDBC, including availability of drivers and details
about the latest specifications, see http://java.sun.com/products/jdbc/.

In this chapter we're going to be presenting two different ways of securing the JDBC driver transmission
over SSL:

- ❑ The first method involves running a daemon on the client machine, which acts like the
  database, but in fact just forwards all traffic via SSL to a peer on the server, which in turn
  forwards it to the database. For this process, we will create the TunnelServer class. This
  approach has the advantage of simplicity and performance. There is not a great deal of
  overhead beyond the cost of encrypting the connection. Unfortunately, it does not provide
  much in the way of authentication. You can ensure that client is connecting via a certificate
  that is signed by a trusted CA, but, because the client machine is running a daemon process, it
  is very difficult to prevent other users on the same machine from using the local server. In a
  multi-user environment like Unix, this is a particularly significant problem.

❑ The second method involves writing a full JDBC driver that serves as a proxy to the driver for the database. Because there is no extra daemon running on the client side, this method is a bit more secure, but much more complex.

Let's begin by looking at our first approach – **SSL-tunneling**.

The Tunnel Server

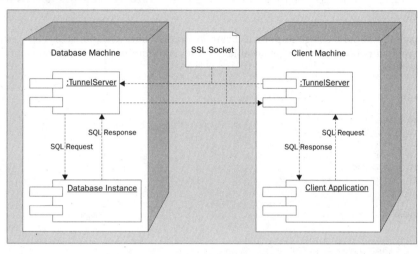

The diagram above shows that basic high-level view of TunnelServer. There are two instances of the tunnel server running – one on the client machine and one on the server. On both sides, the tunnel server reads data in from the client and writes it to the server. The only differences between the instances on the client and server machines are:

❑ On the *client*, the tunnel server reads unencrypted data from the JDBC client and writes it to the database server machine over SSL. It also reads the response over SSL and returns it unencrypted to client.

❑ On the *database server*, the tunnel server reads the encrypted data from its peer on the client machine and sends it unencrypted to the database over localhost. It also reads the response from the database and sends it to the client machine over SSL.

In essence, the client-side instance of the tunnel server is pretending to be the database to the client and the database-side instance of the tunnel server is pretending to be the client to the database. Thus, for the client, the tunnel server is a proxy to the real data store on the database machine.

This practice of **SSL-tunneling** allows us to encrypt all the remote transmission (and returns) with minimal code and minimal overhead. It relies on the fact that connections to localhost cannot be snooped so only the actual on-the-wire connection needs to be encrypted.

Before we describe the code that implements the tunnel server, please note that the example has been written to run on two networked machines:

❑ The database machine runs the database and JDBC driver discussed in Appendix B, and the server-side tunnel server

❑ The client machine runs the client-side tunnel server and a client application

Implementing the Tunnel Server

The code for this operation is surprisingly simple. In fact, the bulk of the code is for handling command-line parameters and asking for passwords. We need to consider two classes, `TunnelServer` and `TunnelThread`. Note the classes are built for the package that can be downloaded from the Wrox web site.

The TunnelServer Class

Remember that you will need the JSSE libraries installed according to the instructions provided in the last chapter.

First we have the initial package imports to bring in the SSL libraries and classes for certificate handling. Then we create a number of instance variables for the configuration of each instance of `TunnelServer`:

```java
package com.isnetworks.crypto.net;

import java.io.*;
import java.net.*;
import java.security.*;
import java.security.cert.*;
import javax.net.*;
import javax.net.ssl.*;

/**
 * TunnelServer.java
 */

public class TunnelServer {

    /**
     * The port on which to attach locally
     */

    private int mTunnelPort;

    /**
     * The server to which to connect
     */

    private String mDestServer;

    /**
     * The port of the remote server
     */

    private int mAppPort;

    /**
     * Whether to continue listening or not
     */

    private boolean mListening = true;

    /**
     * Whether the service is running as a proxy for the
     * client (mRemote == false) or the server (mRemote == false)
     */

    private boolean mRemote;
```

Our constructor sets the configuration values and calls `waitForConnections()`:

```
/**
 * Creates new TunnelServer
 * @param server the remote server to which to connect
 * @param appPort the port on which the target application us running
 * @param tunnelPort the port on which the SSL connection is to be made
 * @param remote true if this is the remote TunnelServer instance
 */

public TunnelServer(String server, int appPort, int tunnelPort, boolean remote)
{
    super();
    mDestServer = server;
    mAppPort = appPort;
    mTunnelPort = tunnelPort;
    mRemote = remote;
    waitForConnections();
}
```

The real work of this class happens here. The `waitForConnections()` method gets a `ServerSocket`, either SSL or normal depending on the mode, and then blocks waiting for connections from a client. When a client connects, this method connects to its destination and creates a couple of new instances of `TunnelThread`, one to do the forwarding from the client to the server and one to do the server to the client:

```
/**
 * Wait for incoming connections
 */

private void waitForConnections() {
    ServerSocket serverSocket;    // The waiting serverSocket
    Socket srcSocket;             // The incoming client Socket
    Socket destSocket;            // The destination server Socket
    TunnelThread fromClient;
    TunnelThread toClient;
    serverSocket = getServerSocket();

    while (mListening) {
      try {
        logMessage("Waiting for connections.");
        srcSocket = serverSocket.accept();

        // if this is a local server, make sure it is from localhost

        if (!mRemote && isRemote(srcSocket)) {
          throw new Exception("Illegal access from IP outside localhost");
        }

        logMessage("Connection accepted from " + srcSocket.getInetAddress()
                + ".");
        destSocket = connect();
        logMessage("Connected to remote server at "
                + destSocket.getInetAddress() + ".");
        fromClient = getTunnelThread ("fromClient");
        toClient = getTunnelThread("toClient");

        // Provide the TunnelThreads with peer InputStreams and
        // OutputStreams to read from and write to
```

```
        fromClient.setInputStream(srcSocket.getInputStream());
        fromClient.setOutputStream(destSocket.getOutputStream());
        toClient.setInputStream(destSocket.getInputStream());
        toClient.setOutputStream(srcSocket.getOutputStream());
        fromClient.start();
        toClient.start();
      } catch (Exception e) {
        handleException(e);
      }
    }
  }
}
```

The isRemote() method is used for a security reasons. You don't want clients from outside the machine to be able to connect to this service if you are running in local mode because then the data that is being encrypted between the two instances of TunnelServer would be transmitted to the local instance in the clear. So we check the InetAddress and disallow all non-local connections.

```
/** Is the connector from localhost or not?
 * @param clientSocket the socket to check for remote/local
 * @return true if the socket is from a remote machine
 * @throws java.net.UnknownHostException The host to check was not found
 */

public boolean isRemote(Socket clientSocket) throws UnknownHostException {

  // Make sure that the address is coming from the loopback
  // address 127.0.0.1

  InetAddress localhost = InetAddress.getByName("127.0.0.1");
  System.out.println("Connection from: " + clientSocket.getInetAddress());
  System.out.println("Localhost: " + localhost);
  if (localhost.equals(clientSocket.getInetAddress())) {
    System.out.println("The connection is local");
    return false;
  } else {
    System.out.println("The connection is remote");
    return true;
  }
}
```

At this point, the main thread of execution creates the ServerSocket. If the process is remote, the server socket is over SSL; if the process is local, it should be in the clear. Note that we call setNeedClientAuth(true) on each SSLServerSocket. This ensures that TunnelServer does not accept connections from clients without a certificate or with a certificate with an unknown issuer.

```
/**
 * Create the ServerSocket
 * @returns a custom ServerSocket for SSL connections
 */

protected ServerSocket getServerSocket() {
  try {
    if (mRemote) {
      SSLServerSocketFactory factory =
```

```
                       (SSLServerSocketFactory)SSLServerSocketFactory.getDefault();
            SSLServerSocket serverSocket =
                       (SSLServerSocket)factory.createServerSocket(mTunnelPort);
            serverSocket.setNeedClientAuth(true);
            return serverSocket;
        }else {
            return
                ServerSocketFactory.getDefault().createServerSocket(mAppPort);
        }
    }catch (Exception e) {
        handleException(e);
        mListening = false;    // Stop the server
        return null;
    }
}
```

Of course, once a connection comes in, we are going to have to connect to our delegate. If the process is running on the remote machine, then we want to do a plain socket connection. If the process is local, we create an SSL connection to the `TunnelServer` on the server side.

```
/**
 * Connect to the delegate through SSL or clear
 * @returns a socket to the peer or application
 */

private Socket connect() throws UnknownHostException, IOException {

    if (mRemote) {

        // Make normal connection

        Socket socket = new Socket(mDestServer, mAppPort);
        return socket;

    } else {

        // Make SSL connection

        SSLSocketFactory factory =
                        (SSLSocketFactory)SSLSocketFactory.getDefault();
        return factory.createSocket(mDestServer, mTunnelPort);
    }
}

/**
 * Handle a fatal exception
 * @param e the nasty exception
 */

private void handleException (Throwable e) {
    System.err.println("A fatal error has occured.");
    e.printStackTrace();
    System.exit(1);
}
```

```
/**
 * Return a thread, this could be pooled for better performance
 * @param name the name of the thread (for debugging, etc.)
 */

private TunnelThread getTunnelThread(String name) {
  TunnelThread thread = new TunnelThread(name);
  return thread;
}

/**
 * Log a message - currently logs to stdout, but could print to a log file
 * @param message The message to log
 */

private void logMessage(String message) {
  System.out.println(message);
}
```

All the `main` method needs to do is figure out, based on the arguments, where it is running and create an instance of `TunnelServer` with the correct parameters.

```
/**
 * Main entry point.
 * @param args Command line arguments
 */

public static void main (String [] args) {

  if (args.length < 4 || !(args[3].equals("local") ||
  args[3].equals("remote"))) {
    usage();
  }

  String destServer = args[0];
  int appPort = Integer.parseInt(args[1]);
  int tunnelPort = Integer.parseInt(args[2]);
  String mode = args[3];

  //Intialize the SecureRandom system to prevent delay from
  // occurring on first connection

  new SecureRandom().nextBytes(new byte[1]);
  System.out.println("Initialized Random Number generator.");

  TunnelServer server;
  if (mode.equals("local")) {
    server = new TunnelServer(destServer, appPort, tunnelPort, false);
  } else {
    server = new TunnelServer(destServer, appPort, tunnelPort, true);
  }

}
```

```
        private static void usage() {
            System.err.println("usage: java com.isnetworks.crypto.net.TunnelServer "
                            + " dest_server app_port tunnel_port [local | remote]");
            System.exit(1);
        }
    }
```

The TunnelThread Class

Instances of `TunnelThread` are what do the forwarding of requests and responses. Every incoming byte is immediately forwarded to its peer. This is not tremendously efficient, but flushing the `OutputStream` is the only way we can be certain the bytes are all sent without writing a complicated buffering system with timeouts.

```java
package com.isnetworks.crypto.net;

import java.io.*;

/*
 * TunnelThread.java
 *
 * Handles the actual SSL tunelling between client and server
 */

public class TunnelThread extends Thread {

  // The source of incoming bytes

  private InputStream mIn;

  // The stream to write outgoing bytes

  private OutputStream mOut;

  /**
   * Creates new TunnelThread
   * @param name a name for this thread
   */

  public TunnelThread(String name) {
    super(name);
    setDaemon(true);
  }

  /**
   * Default constructor - create a tunnel thread with a default name
   */

  public TunnelThread() {
    super();
    setDaemon(true);
  }

  /**
   * Set the source of the bytes
   * @param in the source InputStream
   */

  public void setInputStream(InputStream in) {
    mIn = in;
  }
```

```
/**
 * Set the destination stream
 * @param out the destination OuputStream
 */

public void setOutputStream(OutputStream out) {
  mOut = out;
}
```

The following code is the actual byte forwarding process. The code is extremely simple. Note that IOExceptions are caught without any message. Any interrupted connection will throw an IOException and there really isn't anything we can do about them, aside from perhaps logging.

```
/**
 * Read from the InputStream and write to the OutputStream until EOF or
 * exception
 */

public void run() {
  log("Starting tunnel");
  try {
    int i;
    while ((i = mIn.read()) != -1) {
      mOut.write(i);
      mOut.flush();
    }

    mIn.close();
    mOut.close();
  } catch (IOException e) {

      // We can't really do anything with this. Most likely, the
      // connection has been disconnected. So just exit.

  }

  log("Tunneling complete");

}

/**
 * Log a message - currently this only writes to standard out,
 * but it should probably log to a non-blocking output stream
 * @param msg The message to log
 */

public void log(String msg) {
  System.out.println(getName() + ": " + msg);
}
}
```

Running the Tunnel Server with JDBC

In order to use the tunnel server, we need to perform several steps:

❏   Generate keystores with key pairs and certificates for client and server

❏   Start the tunnel server on the server side (on the database machine)

❏   Start the tunnel server on the client side (the client machine)

❏   Run a test application on the client machine

One of the hardest parts of running this application is, like other SSL applications, specifying that all the correct command-line parameters are set up – for the purpose of simplicity there is little error handling in the application so wrong configuration parameters can lead to the example just hanging. This whole example runs using the MySQL database and JDBC driver discussed in Appendix B, which also contains some troubleshooting details.

Let's run through each of these in turn.

Generate Keystores

First we'll create keystores for the client and server. The client and server need to trust each other, so we'll create a keystore for each of them and then place copies of the generated certificates into the others' keystores. The keystores can be generated with the following commands:

```
C:\> keytool -genkey -keyalg RSA -keystore serverKeyStore
C:\> keytool -genkey -keyalg RSA -keystore clientKeyStore
```

You'll need to specify a password and enter information for each certificate. When asked the name for the certificate, enter the name of the machine you'll be running the program on.

Next we want to export the certificates so that they can be imported into the opposite keystore, establishing trust. Export can be achieved with the following commands:

```
C:\> keytool -export -keystore serverKeyStore -file server.cer
C:\> keytool -export -keystore clientKeyStore -file client.cer
```

This will generate files containing the certificates, which we can import with:

```
C:\> keytool -import -file client.cer -alias client -keystore serverKeyStore
C:\> keytool -import -file server.cer -alias server -keystore clientKeyStore
```

When asked if the certificates should be trusted, enter **yes**.

Start the Tunnel Server on the Server

The tunnel server needs to be run on the database machine. Copy the server keystore and the tunnel server classes to the database machine. The server can then be started with the following command (all on one line):

```
C:\> java -Djavax.net.ssl.keyStore=serverKeyStore
          -Djavax.net.ssl.keyStorePassword=password
          -Djavax.net.ssl.trustStore=serverKeyStore
          com.isnetworks.crypto.net.TunnelServer localhost 3306 6543 remote
```

Note that you'll need to insert the appropriate keystore password. Let's consider the last command in detail (noting it's using the download code package structure):

❑   The first argument is the machine that the database is running on, `localhost` in this case

❑   The second argument is the port the database is running on – since we're using MySQL, we're running on port 3306

❑   The third argument in the port we wish to listen for connections on – we'll use 6543

❑   The last argument, `remote`, indicates the mode for the tunnel server – we'll be accepting connections remotely and calling locally

The server will take a few moments to start up. Once it's started, you should see the following message:

```
Initialized Random Number generator.
Waiting for connections.
```

Now we're ready to start the client.

Start the Tunnel Server on the Client

Copy the client keystore and the tunnel server classes to the client. The client can then be started with (again all on one line):

```
C:\> java -Djavax.net.ssl.keyStore=clientKeyStore
          -Djavax.net.ssl.keyStorePassword=password
          -Djavax.net.ssl.trustStore=clientKeyStore
          com.isnetworks.crypto.net.TunnelServer database_machine 3306 6543
          local
```

Again the appropriate password is required. Looking at the last command:

❑ The first argument specifies the name of the machine that's running the database, database_machine (which will need to be amended as appropriate)

❑ The second is the port that we will be running on locally, pretending to be the database – since we're using MySQL, this will be 3306

❑ The third argument is the port we wish to connect to, 6543

❑ The last argument, local, is the mode the tunnel server will be placed into – it will accept connections locally and connect over SSL to the database machine

Once you run the client, you will see output identical to the server above. Now you're ready to connect to the database.

Run a Test Application on the Client Machine

We're going to run a very simple JDBC application that will simply connect to the database and read the contents of a single table. We're taking this example from Appendix B, but you could use any JDBC-compliant test code you like, however.

Here's JDBCTest.java:

```java
import java.sql.*;

public class JDBCTest {

  private static final String DRIVER_NAME="org.gjt.mm.mysql.Driver";
  private static final String DB_URL="jdbc:mysql://localhost/projava";
  private static final String USERNAME="projava";
  private static final String PASSWORD="sasquatch";

  private static final String QUERY="SELECT * FROM credit_card";

  public static void main(String[] args) throws Exception {
    Class.forName(DRIVER_NAME);
    Connection conn = DriverManager.getConnection(DB_URL, USERNAME,
```

```
                                                            PASSWORD);
    Statement stmt = conn.createStatement();
    ResultSet rslt = stmt.executeQuery(QUERY);
    rslt.next();
    rslt.close();
    stmt.close();
    conn.close();
    System.out.println("Success! Connected to database.");
  }
}
```

Notice that it connects to localhost for the database. This is required, as that's where our tunnel-server client is running.

To run the test, make sure your JDBC driver is in the classpath, and run the test with the following command:

C:\> java JDBCTest

The connection will now take place over SSL and should respond with the following message:

Success! Connected to database.

So, on the client side you should have a couple of console screens that look like this:

Our second approach for securing the database connection is to build a full implementation of a driver, accessible through the DriverManager.

The JDBC Driver

Our JDBC driver will provide the encryption and authentication features necessary for many applications. Because we assume that all vendors' drivers implement the correct interfaces, we can delegate all our calls to whichever dynamically bound driver we choose at run-time. In fact, other than some complexity in the crypto code, the implementation of our classes will not be particularly difficult. Instead of providing a "real" driver implementation, the secure driver will be providing **proxies** to JDBC driver classes doing the real work. Like any other JDBC driver, the secure driver will only require a few unique arguments passed to `DriverManager`. The rest of the JDBC calls will not have to change.

The **proxy design pattern** is very important in distributed computing. It provides a level of abstraction that enables the developer to add additional services, such as encryption or "remoteness" to an existing implementation without altering the interfaces or changing the original code.

> *There is an important point that should be mentioned here. The encryption of the JDBC wire protocol that this driver provides is only of value if your database client (such as the application server) is on a separate machine from the database. Most JDBC drivers connect to the database over the network and so it is crucial that the server side of the secure driver runs on the same machine as the database. That way, even if the driver is connecting via a TCP connection, it will do so via loopback. Loopback connections do not actually cross over the network but are handled within machine, so there is no danger of snooping. It is due to this loopback mechanism that we are able to use virtually any JDBC driver as our delegate.*

Now that we have decided that the data needs to be encrypted, how do we do it? Due to all the features it offers, we are going to use SSL for the connection. This way it will be extremely easy for us to add authentication later on.

> **We'll be using this JDBC driver in the application we build in Chapter 11. Since the code for this driver is rather lengthy, and in some places repetitive, in this section we're concentrating on the more interesting aspects of the implementation. Of course, the complete code is available at http://www.wrox.com.**

Client-Server Communication

Our application will contain client and server components. The server will handle all the configuration, managing connections to the database, and delegation of the JDBC calls. The client will simply delegate all the connections to the server. In order to do this we have to choose a network transport for communication between client and server. We have the option to use raw sockets, RMI, or CORBA. Because RMI gives us so much, like the automatic marshaling and unmarshaling of Java objects, and the ability to install custom sockets, we will use RMI over the lower-level socket API. Support for SSL in CORBA is not available in the current JDK and it doesn't support the serialization of arbitrary objects, so again, RMI is the obvious choice.

RMI has one requirement that is going to make our job a little more difficult. The `rmic` compiler requires all methods that need to be remotely accessible throw a `java.rmi.RemoteException`. The architects of RMI created this requirement with the intention of requiring developers to anticipate problems that arise from the vagaries of remote computing such as dropped connections and network outages. When you are making a method call across the network or across the web, any number of additional problems can arise that will not when the object you are calling is local.

In order to fulfill this requirement, we are going to have to add one more layer to the remote call. We will create a series of thin `Serializable` proxies that will take responsibility for handling those exceptions. We don't want to simply catch the exceptions, but rather re-throw an exception that is compatible with the JDBC interfaces we are implementing. We are lucky that JDBC is already a remote-aware protocol and, in anticipation of network problems, requires that each method throws a `java.sql.SQLException`.

Our methods will throw `RemoteSQLException`, which is a subclass of `SQLException`, which our driver will provide. This enables us to specifically catch RMI-related exceptions if we want to. The diagram below shows a basic class structure for our implementation of `java.sql.Connection`:

As you can see from the diagram, the client is unaware that it has a reference to a proxy. All it knows (or cares about) is that has a `java.sql.Connection` object.

As in our application server examples, we are going to take advantage of RMI's custom socket capabilities and use SSL sockets for the communication. Later we will take advantage of the same mechanism to provide authentication services to the JDBC data sources.

Implementation

The implementation for most of these classes is fairly simple, particularly if we delegate the common operations to an abstract super class. To further simplify the system we are going to use a single `remote` class that is capable of passing any method call using the Java reflection API instead of creating an RMI proxy class for each JDBC interface. Overleaf is a diagram of the architecture:

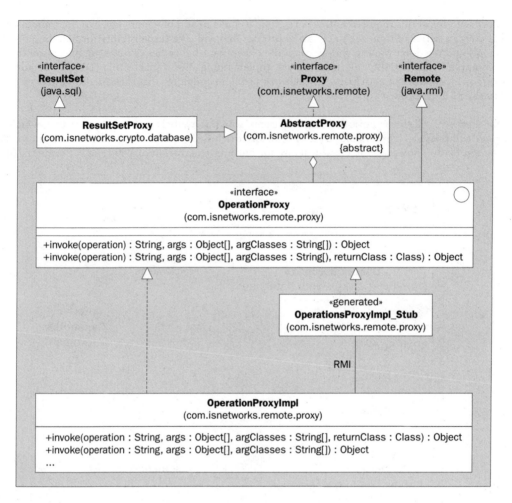

The SecureDriver Class

The SecureDriver class implements java.sql.Driver. Since it is the main entry point for our driver, it is a little more complicated than the rest of the proxy classes. It has to handle URL parsing and RMI bootstrapping among other things. Since it is the main entry point, it will be the first class we walk through.

```
package com.isnetworks.crypto.database;

import java.sql.*;
import java.net.MalformedURLException;
import java.rmi.*;
import java.util.*;
import com.isnetworks.utility.Debug;

/**
 *SecureDriver.java
 */
```

```
public class SecureDriver implements Driver{

  /**
   * SecureDriver major version
   */

  private static final int MAJOR_VERSION = 0;

  /**
   * SecureDriver minor version
   */

  private static final int MINOR_VERSION = 1;
```

This static block is called when the driver's class is loaded. This is a requirement of all drivers in the JDBC spec.

```
  /**
   * Register an instance of the driver when the class loads
   */

  static {
    try {
      new SecureDriver();
    } catch(SQLException e) {
      System.err.println("SecureDriver failed to register");
      e.printStackTrace();
    }
  }

  /**
   * Constructor. Register self with the JDBC DriverManager
   */

  public SecureDriver() throws SQLException {
    DriverManager.registerDriver(this);
  }
```

The acceptsURL() method checks whether the URL provided is indeed for this driver. Our implementation just checks that the URL starts with **jdbc:secureDriver:**. More sophisticated implementations might actually parse the entire URL to see if it complies with our driver's requirements.

```
  /**
   * Check if a URL is accepted by this driver
   * @param url The URL to test
   * @return true if the driver will accept the url
   * @exception java.sql.SQLException - a database error occured
   */

  public boolean acceptsURL(String url) throws SQLException {
    if (url.startsWith("jdbc:secureDriver:")){
      return true;
    }else{
      return false;
    }
  }
```

The `connect()` method is the method called by `DriverManager` to get the connection from the driver. The method is responsible for parsing the URL, then connecting to the RMI server process, which is where the actual JDBC connections reside.

To connect to the back-end RMI process, first we bootstrap the connection to the naming service with `Naming.lookup()`. This returns the remote stub for `SecureConnectionServer`. After we have retrieved the stub, we call `getConnection()` and return that connection. In the end, this call delegates to the `SecureConnectionServerImpl` instance which is running on the server side. We will look at the implementation for this class shortly.

```
/**
 * Return a connection
 * @param url JDBC connection URL
 * @param props Connection properties
 * @return a connection to the server
 * @exception java.sql.SQLException - Indicates a database or
 * network failure
 */

public Connection connect(String url, Properties props)
                          throws SQLException {

    System.out.println("SecureConnectionServerMain.connect(): " + props);
    SecureConnectionServer server = null;

    parseURL(url, props);

    String host = props.getProperty("host", "localhost");
    String port = props.getProperty("port", "1099");
    String hostPortAndName = "rmi:// " + host + ":" + port
                           + "/SecureDriver";
    System.out.println("Trying to connect to: " + hostPortAndName);
    try{
        if ( System.getSecurityManager() == null ) {
          System.setSecurityManager( new java.rmi.RMISecurityManager() );
        }
        System.out.println( "Security manager set to " +
                                        System.getSecurityManager() );
        server = (SecureConnectionServer)Naming.lookup(hostPortAndName);
    }catch (MalformedURLException e){
        throw new RemoteSQLException("The URL was malformed. Stacktrace:\n"
                            + Debug.getStackTraceAsString(e));
    }catch(NotBoundException e){
        throw new RemoteSQLException("The SecureDriver was not bound "
                            + "to the RMIRegistry. StackTrace: \n "
                            + Debug.getStackTraceAsString(e));
    }catch (AccessException e){
        throw new RemoteSQLException("AccessException: "
                            + Debug.getStackTraceAsString(e));
    }catch (RemoteException e){
        throw new RemoteSQLException("RemoteException: "
                            + Debug.getStackTraceAsString(e));
    }

    Connection conn = null;
    try{
        conn = server.getConnection(props);
    }catch(RemoteException e){
        throw new RemoteSQLException("RemoteException: "
                                + Debug.getStackTraceAsString(e.detail));
    }
    return conn;
}
```

The parseURL() method, which was called from connect() handles tokenizing the URL string and putting the values back in the Properties object. This properties object is where the connect() method fetches all its relevant information: username and password, host, port, etc.

```java
/**
 * Parse the URL and combine it with the properties object
 */
private Properties parseURL(String url, Properties props){

  // Parser States:
  // 0 Hasn't parsed
  // 1 Parsed protocol
  // 2 Parsed sub-protocol
  // 3 Parsed host

  // Add in parse props here

  StringTokenizer tokenizer = new StringTokenizer(url, ":" );
  String value = null;
  String property = null;
  int state = 0;

  while (tokenizer.hasMoreElements()){
    value = tokenizer.nextToken();
    if (state == 0){
      property = "protocol";
      state = 1;
    }else if (state == 1){
      property = "subprotocol";
      state = 2;
    }else if (state == 2){

      // If the value contains a '/' then it does not include the port

      int slashIndex = value.indexOf('/', 2);
      if (slashIndex==-1){

      // The port was specified

      property="host";
      state = 3;
    }else{

      // The port was not specified

      String host = value.substring(0, slashIndex);
      props.setProperty("host", host);
      value = value.substring(slashIndex+1);
      property="datasource";
      }
    }else if (state == 3){

      // Port and datasource

      int slashIndex = value.indexOf('/');
      String port = value.substring(0, slashIndex);
      props.setProperty("port", port);
      value = value.substring(slashIndex+1);
      property = "datasource";
      }
    props.setProperty(property, value);
  }
  return props;
}
```

You may be asking yourself at this point why there isn't any crypto in this code. The reason is that the client doesn't really need any knowledge of crypto at this level. This will all be handled by the custom RMI sockets and the SSL library that we are going to be setting up shortly. Before we do that, lets look at the server-side process without SSL.

The SecureConnectionServerMain Class

The following code sets up and registers the RMI object that will respond to the JDBC requests, eventually over SSL.

```
/**
 * SecureConnectionServerMain.java
 */

package com.isnetworks.crypto.database.server;

import java.io.*;
import java.rmi.*;
import com.isnetworks.util.*;
import com.isnetworks.crypto.database.*;
import com.isnetworks.crypto.rmi.*;
public class SecureConnectionServerMain {

    private static final String DEFAULT_BIND_NAME= "SecureDriver";
    private static XMLProperties mProps;
```

The main entry point of the application, shown below, does not do much. All it needs to do is parse a command-line argument, which points it to a configuration file, and delegate the reading of that configuration file to the XMLProperties object. The XMLProperties object is similar to a java.util.Properties object except that because XML provides a hierarchical structure (which suits an application like this one nicely) we need a different Properties object to parse it. For more information on XML and Java, go to http://java.sun.com/xml/.

Once the properties object is read, it is passed to the DataSourceManager, in this case an implementation of SimpleDataSourceManager, which is then passed to the main RMI object, an instance of SecureConnectionServerImpl for remote access. The DataSourceManager's only task is to provide Connections to clients on request from the Driver.

Here we finally have the few lines of code that provide encryption and client authentication. The RMISSLClientSocketFactory and RMISSLServerSocketFactory are factory classes that create the encrypted sockets as described in the last chapter.

```
/**
 * Entry point. Start up the server process and export the remote
 * objects
 */

public static void main( String [] args ){

  String bindName = null;

  // Add argument parsing function
```

```
if (args.length < 1){
  usage();
  System.exit(1);
}

String fileName = args[0];

// Parse the xml config file

DatasourceManager manager = null;
try{
  mProps = new XMLProperties();
  mProps.load(new FileInputStream(args[0]));

  // Send the root node of the datasources to the datasource pool

  XMLProperties dataSources =
      (XMLProperties)mProps.getProperty("dataSources").iterator().next();

  manager = new SimpleDatasourceManager(dataSources);

  // Pull the server name and bind

  bindName = (String)mProps.getProperty("id").iterator().next();
  if (bindName == null){
    bindName = DEFAULT_BIND_NAME;
  }

}catch(Exception e) {
  e.printStackTrace();
  System.exit(1);
}

try{
  System.out.println("Registering SecureDriver as "
                    + bindName + ".");

  // Create the SecureConnectionServerImpl with the DataSourceManager
  // and an anonymous port and SocketFactories. See
  // java.rmi.server.UnicastRemoteObject details.

  SecureConnectionServerImpl connectionServer = new
    SecureConnectionServerImpl( manager, 0,
                              new RMISSLClientSocketFactory(),
                              new RMISSLServerSocketFactory() );
  if ( System.getSecurityManager() == null ) {
    System.setSecurityManager( new java.rmi.RMISecurityManager() );
  }
  Naming.rebind(bindName, connectionServer);
  System.out.println(bindName + " registered.");
}catch(Exception e){
  e.printStackTrace();
  System.exit(1);
}

// SSL-RMI bug work-around
```

```
      while (true) {
        try{
          Thread.sleep( Long.MAX_VALUE );
        }
        catch( InterruptedException e ){
        }
      }
    }
    private static void usage(){
      System.err.println("usage: java com.isnetworks.crypto.database.server."
                            + "SecureConnectionServerMain config_file");
    }
  }
```

In this section of code there's a work-around for a bug in RMI over SSL (found in the JSSE v.1.0.2 and earlier). The JVM will shut down your application if you have no other threads running after binding your instance via RMI over SSL; thus a thread is created that does nothing but sleep.

The SimpleDatasourceManager Class

We will skip going into detail of the `SimpleDatasourceManager` class. Suffice to say, this class manages the mapping of different datasource names to their connections as well as checking username and password, if it is necessary.

The SecureConnectionServerImpl Class

The `SecureConnectionServerImpl`, on the other hand, bears some examination, even though it is a simple class. It is the implementation class of the RMI exported object, so it extends `UnicastRemoteObject` and implements our remote interface.

```java
package com.isnetworks.crypto.database.server;

import java.rmi.*;
import java.rmi.server.*;
import java.util.Properties;
import java.sql.*;
import com.isnetworks.remote.proxy.*;
import com.isnetworks.crypto.database.*;

/**
 * SecureConnectionServerImpl.java
 *
 * Implementation of SecureConnectionServer.
 */

public class SecureConnectionServerImpl extends UnicastRemoteObject
  implements SecureConnectionServer{

  /**
   * The manager responsible for different datasources
   */

  private DatasourceManager mDatasourceManager;
```

```
    public SecureConnectionServerImpl(DatasourceManager datasourceManager )
            throws RemoteException{
    mDatasourceManager = datasourceManager;
    }

    public SecureConnectionServerImpl( DatasourceManager datasourceManager,
                                       int port,
                                       RMIClientSocketFactory clientFactory,
                                       RMIServerSocketFactory serverFactory )
                                       throws RemoteException{
        super( port, clientFactory, serverFactory );
        mDatasourceManager = datasourceManager;
    }
```

Here, for the first time, we see the use of the OperationProxyImpl class. This server-side delegate handles all the RMI for all the various JDBC stubs. When a request for a connection comes in, a real JDBC connection is created (or retrieved from a pool) and passed to the OperationProxyImpl. The OperationProxyImpl is passed to the ConnectionProxy, which is then returned.

We return the proxy class, which is just a stripped-down implementation of Connection that delegates to the OperationProxy. This in turn sends the message via RMI to the OperationProxyImpl class, which executes the same method on its delegate, in this case, the real JDBC connection. This is quite complicated so a diagram describing this has been provided overleaf, just after the code.

```
    /**
     * Look up the correct datasource, delegate a security check, then
     * delegate the creation of the connection
     */

    public Connection getConnection(Properties props)
                                    throws RemoteException, SQLException{
      System.out.println("Getting connection with args: " + props);
      String dataSource = props.getProperty("datasource");
      String username = props.getProperty("user");
      String password = props.getProperty("password");
      if (dataSource == null){
          throw new SQLException("No datasource was a specified.");
      }

      // Assuming everything works, return a ConnectionProxy wrapping a real
      // connection

      Connection conn = getConnection(dataSource, username, password);
      OperationProxy impl =  new OperationProxyImpl(conn);
      ConnectionProxy proxy = new ConnectionProxy();
      proxy.setOperationProxy( impl );
      return proxy;
    }

    /**
     * Return a REAL database connection
     */

    protected Connection getConnection(String dataSource, String username,
                                       String password)
                                       throws SQLException {
      return mDatasourceManager.getConnection(dataSource, username, password);
    }
}
```

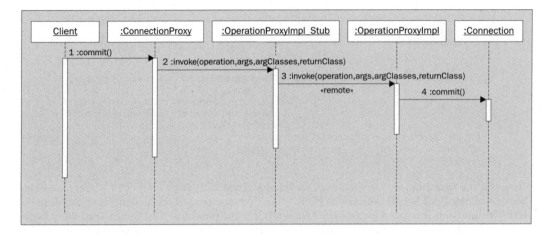

The ConnectionProxy Class

Some code will not be shown in its entirety, but here is the implementation of the various JDBC interfaces such as Connection, Statement, and ResultSet, mainly because each method looks the same. Like in the diagram above, these classes all delegate to the OperationProxy_Stub and OperationProxy_Impl to do the network access and delegation to the real JDBC driver. Here is a taste of the code from the ConnectionProxy class. The ellipses in the code indicate that the code has been truncated for this chapter. Note the invoke() method call. This is a call to the superclass, AbstractProxy, which has the actual logic for forwarding the request on to the delegate.

```java
public class ConnectionProxy extends AbstractProxy implements Connection {

    ...

    private static final Class[] PREPARE_CALL_2 =
      {java.lang.String.class, int.class, int.class};

    ...

    public java.sql.CallableStatement prepareCall(java.lang.String param0, int
                                                  param1, int param2)
                                                  throws SQLException {
      Object args[] = new Object[ 3 ];
      args[ 0 ] = param0;
      args[ 1 ] = new Integer( param1 );
      args[ 2 ] = new Integer( param2 );

      try {
        return (java.sql.CallableStatement)invoke("prepareCall", args,
                                                  PREPARE_CALL_2,
                  com.isnetworks.crypto.database.CallableStatementProxy.class);
      }catch(InvocationTargetException e){
            throw (SQLException)e.getTargetException();
      }catch(RemoteException e){
            throw new RemoteSQLException(Debug.getStackTraceAsString(e));
      }
    }
}
```

```
    public void commit() throws SQLException {
      try {
        invoke( "commit", null, null, null );
      }catch(InvocationTargetException e){
            throw (SQLException)e.getTargetException();
      }catch(RemoteException e){
            throw new RemoteSQLException(Debug.getStackTraceAsString(e));
      }
    }
}
```

The AbstractProxy Class

AbstractProxy is a convenience implementation of the Proxy class that wraps up a lot of the common functionality. The invoke() method arguments are the operation, the arguments to the operation, the classes of those arguments, and the class that will be returned.

```
package com.isnetworks.remote.proxy;

import java.lang.reflect.*;
import java.net.*;
import java.rmi.*;
import java.rmi.server.*;
import com.isnetworks.remote.*;
import com.isnetworks.util.Debug;

/**
 * AbstractProxy.java
 */

public abstract class AbstractProxy implements com.isnetworks.remote.Proxy{

    protected OperationProxy mDelegate;

    /**
    * Invoke the operation on the delegate returning any values from the
    * call to the delegate.
    * @param operation the name of the method to invoke
    * @param args the arguments to pass in to the method
    * @param argClasses the classes of the operations so the the method can
    * be found through introspection
    * @param returnClass the class of the return value. Necessary for
    * operations which need to wrap return values with a Serializable Proxy
    * class.
    */

    public Object invoke(String operation, Object [] args,
                         Class [] argClasses, Class returnClass )
                         throws RemoteException, InvocationTargetException{
      Object returnValue = null;
```

```
    try{
      returnValue = mDelegate.invoke(operation, args,
                                 getNamesForClasses(argClasses),
                                 returnClass);
    }catch(InstantiationException e){
        throw new RemoteException("AbstractProxy.invoke() failed with" +
                                 "the following nested exception.", e);
    }catch(NoSuchMethodException e){
        throw new RemoteException("AbstractProxy.invoke() failed with" +
                                 "the following nested exception.", e);
    }catch(IllegalAccessException e){
        throw new RemoteException("AbstractProxy.invoke() failed with" +
                                 "the following nested exception.", e);
    }catch (ClassNotFoundException e){
        throw new RemoteException("AbstractProxy.invoke() failed with" +
                                 "the following nested exception.", e);
    }
    return returnValue;
  }

  public OperationProxy getOperationProxy(){
    return mDelegate;
  }

  public void setOperationProxy(OperationProxy ops) throws RemoteException{
    mDelegate = ops;
  }
```

A note about the getNamesForClasses() method: It may seem strange that the subclasses pass in Class objects to the invoke() method, given that they are immediately changed into a String, and then back into a Class. The reason for this is that at the moment the 1.2 VM prevents successful serialization of a primitive Class. This is a workaround. At some point, the conversion to strings will not be necessary.

```
  public String [] getNamesForClasses(Class [] cls){
    String [] classNames = null;
    if (cls != null){
      classNames = new String[cls.length];
      for (int x=0; x<cls.length; x++){
        classNames[x] = cls[x].getName();
      }
    }else{
      classNames = new String[0];
    }
    return classNames;
  }
}
```

Implementation Summary

All the preceding code (and that available in the download) amounts to a fairly complete implementation of a JDBC driver. You will notice that certain methods in the driver throw UnsupportedOperationExceptions. These methods, like ResultSet.getBinaryStream(), will not function as the driver is currently written. That is because the method returns an instance of InputStream which is not Serializable, or part of the JDBC API. In order to enable these functions, you would have to write a Serializable InputStreamProxy that would delegate method calls to a real InputStream.

In the end, the example above is a rather complex solution to what should be a simple problem. It does demonstrate some very important techniques for securing a database or any other resource, particularly pre-existing legacy resources. The proxy pattern enables programmers to tunnel any service over SSL without changing a line of client code. That being said, if your database vendor provides a JDBC driver with encryption and authentication, by all means, use it.

Using the Secure JDBC Driver

As pointed out the section here has attempted to highlight the crucial and interesting bits of the secure JDBC driver code – if you wish to make use of the code we recommend you download it from http://www.wrox.com. The code download will contain pre-build Jars (SecureDriver.jar and SecureDriverClient.jar) that will allow you to use the driver as if it were a normal JDBC driver, with the addition of some extra configuration.

There are several steps that we must take to configure the driver. They are:

❏ Generate the keys and certificates to allow authentication between the client and server

❏ Edit the SecureDriver_config.xml file

❏ Create policy files for the server and client

Note that the configuration details here are picked up again when working through the application in Chapter 11.

Let's get started.

Generating Keys and Certificates

We need to create two keystores: one for the server and one for the client. We'll start by creating each of them with keytool:

```
C:\> keytool -genkey -keyalg RSA -keystore databaseKeyStore
C:\> keytool -genkey -keyalg RSA -keystore databaseClientKeyStore
```

You'll need to choose passwords for each keystore. For this demo, we'll use database for the database keystore and databaseClient for the database client keystore. Just leave the passwords on the keys the same as the passwords on the keystores.

When asked for the name on the certificate, give the domain name of the machine that it will be running on. "localhost" will work if you want to try running both client and server on the same machine. Note that this isn't useful in a production environment, but you may just wish to try it out.

Now that we've generated the keys and certificates, we need to allow the client and server to trust each other. We'll export their certificates and import each into the other's keystore. To export:

```
C:\> keytool -export -keystore databaseKeyStore -file database.cer
C:\> keytool -export -keystore databaseClientKeyStore
              -file databaseClient.cer
```

This will create two files, each containing a certificate. Now we want to import them into the appropriate keystore:

```
C:\> keytool -import -file database.cer alias databaseClient
             -keystore databaseClientKeyStore
C:\> keytool -import -file databaseClient.cer alias database
             -keystore databaseKeyStore
```

You'll need to enter the passwords for each keystore. When asked if you wish to trust these certificates, enter **yes**.

Edit SecureDriver_config.xml

`SecureDriver_config.xml` defines our JDBC connection directly to the database from the secure driver. Our configuration will define connecting to a MySQL database. Here is `SecureDriver_config.xml`:

```xml
<?xml version="1.0"?>
<!DOCTYPE connectionServer SYSTEM "SecureDriver_config.dtd">
<connectionServer id="SecureDriver" keystore="trusted" authclient="true">

    <dataSources>
      <dataSource id="dataSource1" loginRequired="false">
        <driver>
          org.gjt.mm.mysql.Driver
        </driver>
        <url>
          jdbc:mysql://localhost/projava
        </url>
        <username>
          projava
        </username>
        <password>
          sasquatch
        </password>
        <login>
          <username>
            username
          </username>
          <password>
            password
          </password>
        </login>
      </dataSource>
    </dataSources>

    <!-- Additional configuration info can be included here-->
    <include>
      /path/to/config
    </include>

</connectionServer>
```

You'll notice that two usernames and passwords are defined. The first, `projava` and `sasquatch`, are for logging in to the database. The second, `username` and `password` are the username and password that clients of the secure driver will have to use to log in.

> *If you prefer, you could have the usernames and passwords match, but typically you would want them to be different so that clients don't know the true username and password to log in to the database.*

Create Policy Files

RMI requires that code run with a security manager. Because of that, we need to define some policy files for our server and client that will allow them to talk on the network. If your application has special permissions that it requires, like reading or writing files, you should add those permissions to these policy files as well.

Let's start with the server policy file. We need three permissions:

- ❑ The ability to connect to the database
- ❑ The ability to talk to the RMI registry
- ❑ The ability to receive a connection from a remote client

Let's take a look at `SecureDriver.policy` to see how we can set these up:

```
grant {

    // Let the JDBC proxy connect to the database
    // SETUP: change the machine name to that of your database server
    // SETUP: change to your database's JDBC port number if using something
    // other than MySQL

    permission java.net.SocketPermission "localhost:3306", "connect,resolve";

    // Allow a connection to the RMI registry
    // SETUP: change from localhost if running the registry elsewhere

    permission java.net.SocketPermission "localhost:1099", "connect,resolve";

    // Allow receiving connections over RMI
    // SETUP: change from localhost if running the Bank elsewhere

    permission java.net.SocketPermission "localhost:1024-", "listen,resolve";
};
```

The policy file for the client is similar: it must have two permissions:

- ❑ The ability to connect to the secure driver server
- ❑ The ability to connect to the RMI registry

Here's `SecureDriverClient.policy` where we'll set these two permissions:

```
grant {

    // Let the JDBC proxy connect to the database
    // SETUP: change the machine name to that of your database server

    permission java.net.SocketPermission "192.168.1.101:1024-", "connect,resolve";
    permission java.net.SocketPermission "localhost:1099", "connect,resolve";

};
```

The first IP address needs to be the IP address of the machine running the secure driver server. Unfortunately, it *must* be the IP address. `localhost` will not work, and neither will `127.0.0.1`.

Once the policy files are created, we're ready to actually try connecting to the database.

Running the Example

The first thing we need to do is start up the database. Again we're going to assume a MySQL database set up identically to the one in Appendix B.

Both our client and server require the JSSE installed in `lib/ext` and configured in `java.security` as described in Chapter 9.

Next we want to start up our driver. Begin by running the RMI registry on the machine that will be running the driver itself, with the following command:

```
C:\> rmiregistry -J-classpath -JSecureDriver.jar
```

You'll need to run this command from the directory containing the `SecureDriver.jar` file.

Once the RMI registry is started, you can start the secure driver itself. This requires a great number of command-line parameters to be passed to it, including the keystore that we'll be using and the classpath. It also requires the following files be in the directory that you're running the command from:

- ❏ `databaseKeyStore`
- ❏ `mysql_comp.jar`
- ❏ `SecureDriver.policy`
- ❏ `SecureDriver.jar`
- ❏ `SecureDriver_config.dtd`
- ❏ `SecureDriver_config.xml`
- ❏ `xerces.jar`

If you've downloaded the code from the book, you can find all of this in the `chapter10` directory under `test`, apart from `xerces.jar`. You can download that file from http://xml.apache.org/xerces-j/index.html as part of the latest binary download (v1.3.1 at time of writing).

Here is the command to run (all on one line):

```
C:\> java -Djava.security.policy=SecureDriver.policy
           -Djavax.net.ssl.trustStore=databaseKeyStore
           -Djavax.net.ssl.keyStore=databaseKeyStore
           -Djavax.net.ssl.keyStorePassword=database
           -cp mysql_comp.jar;SecureDriver.jar;xerces.jar
            com.isnetworks.crypto.database.server.SecureConnectionServerMain
            SecureDriver_config.xml
```

The driver will have to initialize the SSL libraries, which will take up to 30 seconds. After you've waited a while, we'll be ready to actually connect to the database through the secure driver.

Now we need a test of some sort. We're going to use an appropriately modified version of the simple JDBC test from earlier, but modify it to use our driver rather than connecting directly to MySQL.

```java
import java.sql.*;

// JDBCTest.java

public class JDBCTest {

  private static final String
            DRIVER_NAME="com.isnetworks.crypto.database.SecureDriver";
  private static final String
            DB_URL="jdbc:secureDriver://localhost/dataSource1";
  private static final String USERNAME="username";
  private static final String PASSWORD="password";

  private static final String QUERY="SELECT * FROM credit_card";

  public static void main(String[] args) throws Exception {
    Class.forName(DRIVER_NAME);
    Connection conn = DriverManager.getConnection(DB_URL, USERNAME,
                                                  PASSWORD);
    Statement stmt = conn.createStatement();
    ResultSet rslt = stmt.executeQuery(QUERY);
    rslt.next();
    rslt.close();
    stmt.close();
    conn.close();
    System.out.println("Success! Connected to database.");
  }
}
```

This is a very simple class. All it does is connect to the database, execute a very simple SQL query and display a message if it was successful. If an error occurs, it will throw an exception.

To run the class, you will need the following files in your working directory:

❑   databaseClientKeyStore

❑   SecureDriverClient.jar

❑   SecureClient.policy

Compile JDBCTest.java and you should be able to run it with the following (rather lengthy) command (again, all on one line):

```
C:\> java -Djava.security.policy=SecureClient.policy
          -Djavax.net.ssl.trustStore=databaseClientKeyStore
          -Djavax.net.ssl.keyStore=databaseClientKeyStore
          -Djavax.net.ssl.keyStorePassword=databaseClient
          -cp .;SecureDriverClient.jar JDBCTest
```

It will take a while to perform the SSL handshake (30 seconds or so) and then you should see the following message:

```
Success! Connected to database.
```

You can now use the secure driver client in place of any regular JDBC driver. Just keep in mind that you'll need to specify the policy file and keystore as listed above. Making a connection via SSL will take longer than making a normal database connection, so you would be wise to use some sort of connection pooling in your applications that use the secure driver.

Securing Data in the Database

In the last section we discussed securing the connection between a client and the database. Now we're going to see how we can secure the data in the database with encryption. You may wonder why this is necessary if the connection is encrypted. Isn't that protection enough? Not necessarily, as it turns out. If someone gets access to your database, they will be able to read all of the data you so carefully protected by encrypting the communications channel.

There are several ways to protect your data including: database permissions, read- or write-only databases, symmetric encryption, and asymmetric encryption:

❑   Database permissions should be set properly by your database administrator. Careful assignment of permissions goes a long way to ensuring database security. Many Oracle databases, for instance, are left with default usernames, passwords, and permissions. By setting the permissions properly, your database will have some protection against illegitimate requests.

❑   A read- or write-only database is a good solution if your database is well protected, access to it is highly controlled, and you don't often need access to the information. You may have a separate database for sensitive information that is behind a firewall and physically secured. A number of large online retailers use write-only databases to store credit card information sent to their web servers.

❑   Symmetric encryption can be useful when your database isn't completely safe, but your application is. Here your application could store a secret key that the database does not have. Breaking into the database yields no useful information. This is a good option for shared databases with secure clients. Using symmetric encryption does raise some difficult problems, however. You need to store the symmetric key in the application somehow, and ensure that if the application is deleted, the key is not also deleted unless that's desired. Also, if someone breaks into your application, they will then have access to the symmetric key, which can be used to decrypt the data that was so carefully encrypted.

❑ Asymmetric encryption solves this problem. You may fear your web servers getting attacked, and you may fear your database being read by unauthorized users. By using a public key to encrypt your data on the web server, your web server is prevented from ever reading the data back without the private key. That private key can be stored somewhere safe for when it is used, and the data in the database is then secure because the data is encrypted.

Encrypting data in the database is computationally expensive though, and it removes some of the value of using a database. If your data is encrypted, for example, you can no longer perform searches using standard SQL tools, as the data will look like line noise. There are times when this trade-off is well worth the price, however. If you're storing sensitive data like credit card numbers, you really need to encrypt them. In this chapter we'll present a simple example of encrypting credit card data in the database. In the next chapter, we'll expand on this example to create a very simple e-commerce server that uses this credit card storage mechanism as part of a larger system.

Sample Application – Encrypting Credit Cards

How you encrypt your data depends on how you need to use it. Let's imagine that we're running an e-commerce web site. Our server accepts credit card data submitted from browsers via SSL. The server then processes the credit card transaction and stores the credit card number in a database for future use, like returns, auditing, or repeat billing (for example, subscriptions). The web servers themselves, however, will never need access to that credit card information after the charge has been made. Because of that, we're going to use asymmetric encryption to encrypt that credit card data.

The server will possess a public key that it will use to encrypt the credit card. The corresponding private key will be given only to those who require access to the credit card data, like the finance department or customer service. That way, even if the web server is compromised, it will be impossible for a hacker to obtain the credit card data. This is a very important point: by storing only the public key on the server, there is no risk of a cracker stealing the private key from that machine. You will, however, have to be careful about where you store the private key.

In addition to preventing hackers from obtaining the data, you also will be protecting against rogue employees. If no one but the finance department possesses the private key, no one but the finance department can view the credit card data from the database. Here is a diagram of our simple architecture:

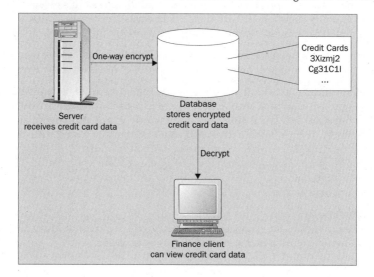

In order to accomplish this, we need to be sure to keep our private key private. It should never be transferred across the network unencrypted, and never stored on the server. Instead, the finance client should create the key pair and transfer the public key to the server. If another department needs the key, care will have to be taken in delivering it to them. Perhaps it could be carried over physically on floppy disk.

Our server will use that public key to encrypt the credit card data before storing it in the database. We're going to create a class, CreditCardFactory that will handle the encryption and storage. It, in turn, will delegate the database connectivity to another class, DatabaseOperations. The credit card factory will create two objects: a CreditCard, which is just a simple holder for credit card info, and CreditCardDBO, which will be a database object, used for holding the data that will be stored in the database. These credit card objects will be read-only to simplify database access. Here is a diagram of our classes so far:

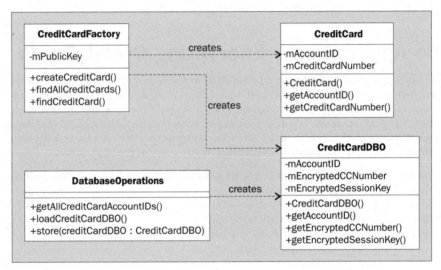

- ❑ CreditCard – This is a simple object for holding cleartext credit card data, specifically an account ID and a credit card number. It could be used to charge or refund money on the card. The account ID isn't correlated to the credit card directly at this object, but could in the future be used to connect customers with their credit cards. For this example, we've simplified things a bit and aren't handling expiration dates, the name on the credit card, etc.

  The CreditCard object, because it contains cleartext credit card data, should not be stored directly. We'll use the next object, CreditCardDBO, to perform the encryption.

- ❑ CreditCardDBO – This contains three fields – an account ID, an encrypted credit card number, and an encrypted session key. We're going to be using RSA with PKCS#1 padding to encrypt our data, as it is the most commonly used form of asymmetric encryption. Unfortunately, it is vulnerable to certain attacks if the data stored with it is in a regular format, as credit card numbers are. So, rather than encrypt the number directly with RSA, we'll create a 128-bit Blowfish session key and use that to encrypt our credit cards. Then we'll encrypt the session key with our public RSA key. This is a technique we described in Chapter 5 on asymmetric encryption.

- ❑ DatabaseOperations – This will handle all of our JDBC access. It will store CreditCardDBOs to the database, and retrieve existing ones. It knows nothing of encryption, but only handles storing and accessing CreditCardDBOs.

❑ CreditCardFactory – This is where the real work gets done. It handles encrypting and decrypting credit card data and delegating database access to a DatabaseOperations object. It is constructed with a public key, which it will use to encrypt all databases. CreditCardFactory also allows retrieval of existing credit card information, but only if the appropriate private key is passed in to the findCreditCard() method.

Setting Up the Database

The instructions for setting up the database for this example are in Appendix B. For the example we'll only make use of one table, credit_card, which will contain three fields: account_id, session_key, and cc_number.

Account_id is a number, and both session_key and cc_number will be strings. The two string fields will actually be BASE64-encoded binary data. By BASE64-encoding them into strings, we ensure that they can be stored in any database.

As in the appendix we'll be making use of a user with read/write access to that table. For this example, we'll be using a username of projava, and a password of sasquatch.

Configuration

In order to configure our database access and public key, we're going to use a Properties file, which corresponds to the Java class, java.util.Properties. In it, we'll specify a path to the public key, as well as the database URL, driver, username, and password. We're going to be storing the username and password in the clear. It would be nice to encrypt them, but then we'd need to provide a key to the application on startup to decrypt them. And that key would need to be stored unencrypted so that the application could access it. This is a problem that you'll run into time and time again when writing server applications that handle sensitive authorization information like passwords. Since this is a simple example, we're not going to bother ourselves with it unduly, but you should be aware of it. Typically the best solution is to use native operating system permissions to control who can read your configuration files and keys.

Here is our properties file, config.properties:

```
PublicKeyFilename:publicKey.cer
DBUsername:projava
DBPassword:sasquatch
DBUrl:jdbc:mysql://localhost/projava
DBDriver:org.gjt.mm.mysql.Driver
```

If you're using a different database, you need to change the DBUrl and DBDriver appropriately for your database.

We need to create a public key, which corresponds to the file publicKey.cer. This will actually be in the form of a certificate, so we can use keytool to generate our keys. Remember that this must be done on a secure machine, because we don't want the private key being compromised. It's probably best to do this on the machine that will later need to decrypt the credit card data. We'll create a keystore that will hold the private key, and then export the public key as a certificate:

```
C:\> keytool -genkey -keyalg RSA -keystore creditcardExample.ks
```

You can specify whatever password you wish. It should be different from the database password. Next we need to export the public key as a certificate:

```
C:\> keytool -export -file publicKey.cer -keystore creditcardExample.ks
```

Knowing how our properties and public key will be established will help us to write our classes, as we will have an idea of how the data we need to use will be passed in. Let's begin by writing our simple classes, CreditCard and CreditCardDBO.

The CreditCard Class

This is a very simple class for holding credit card data. There are two properties: an account ID, which is a number, and a credit card number, for which we'll use a string, as it not really a number, but just a sequence of digits. As mentioned before, credit cards will be read-only objects, so we need only provide a constructor and getter methods. No setters required. Here is CreditCard.java:

```java
package com.projavasecurity.ecommerce.creditcard;

/**
 * Creditcard.java
 */

public class CreditCard {

    private long mAccountID;
    private String mCreditCardNumber;

    /**
     *  Constructor is protected, as CreditCards should
     *  only be created from the CreditCardFactory.
     */

    protected CreditCard(long accountID, String creditCardNumber) {
        mAccountID = accountID;
        mCreditCardNumber = creditCardNumber;
    }

    public long getAccountID() {
        return mAccountID;
    }

    public String getCreditCardNumber() {
        return mCreditCardNumber;
    }
}
```

The CreditCardDBO Class

CreditCardDBO is very similar to the CreditCard object, except that it represents an encrypted credit cards as stored in the database, rather the credit card itself. In order to decrypt the information, one would need the private key corresponding to the public key that was used to encrypt the card.

There are three properties in CreditCardDBO: the account ID, the encrypted credit card number, and the encrypted session key used to encrypt the credit card number. The account ID will be a long, just as in the CreditCard object, and the key and the credit card number will both be byte arrays.

```
package com.projavasecurity.ecommerce.creditcard;

/**
 * CreditCardBO.java
 *
 * Read-only credit card object for holding information pulled directly from
 * the database.
 *
 */

public class CreditCardDBO {
  private long mAccountID;
  private byte[] mEncryptedSessionKey;
  private byte[] mEncryptedCCNumber;

  public CreditCardDBO(long accountID, byte[] encryptedSessionKey,
                       byte[] encryptedCCNumber) {
    mAccountID = accountID;
    mEncryptedSessionKey = (byte[])encryptedSessionKey.clone();
    mEncryptedCCNumber = (byte[])encryptedCCNumber.clone();
  }

  public long getAccountID() {
    return mAccountID;
  }

  public byte[] getEncryptedSessionKey() {
    return (byte[])mEncryptedSessionKey.clone();
  }

  public byte[] getEncryptedCCNumber() {
    return (byte[])mEncryptedCCNumber.clone();
  }
}
```

The DatabaseOperations Class

DatabaseOperations is somewhat complicated. It handles communication with the database, as its name implies. It has three methods: store(), loadCreditCard(), and getAllCreditCardAccountIDs(). When a DatabaseOperations object is instantiated, a Properties object is passed in that contains all the necessary information that will be required to open a connection to the database, like the username, password, driver, and location of the database. On construction, a connection will be opened to the database, and several PreparedStatements will be created, corresponding to the three operations that DatabaseOperations can perform. A PreparedStatement is a Java wrapper for a SQL statement that can be executed through JDBC.

Eventually we will be extending our small example to a more complete system. Because of that, we want to make sure that we have no threading issues during database reads and writes. We're going to synchronize our database access on the connection objects, thus ensuring that no two threads can execute SQL simultaneously. In a truly complete server implementation, you would want to do some sort of connection pooling so that multiple users could access the database simultaneously without being slowed down.

```
package com.projavasecurity.ecommerce;

import com.projavasecurity.ecommerce.creditcard.*;
```

We use Sun's built-in BASE64 classes. If you don't have access to these, we provide replacements in Appendix C.

```
import sun.misc.BASE64Encoder;
import sun.misc.BASE64Decoder;

import java.io.*;
import java.sql.*;
import java.util.*;

/**
 * DatabaseOperations.java
 * A class for performing database operations.
 */

public class DatabaseOperations {
```

We'll begin by defining our SQL statements for inserting and selecting credit cards from the database:

```
private final static String CREDIT_CARD_INSERT_SQL =
        "INSERT INTO credit_card (account_id, session_key, cc_number) "+
        "VALUES (?,?,?)";

private final static String CREDIT_CARD_SELECT_SQL =
        "SELECT session_key, cc_number FROM credit_card "+
        "WHERE account_id = ?";

private final static String CREDIT_CARD_SELECT_IDS_SQL =
        "SELECT account_id FROM credit_card";
```

Now our member variables, including our prepared statements and our BASE64-encoder and decoder:

```
private Connection mConnection;
private PreparedStatement mInsertCreditCard;
private PreparedStatement mSelectCreditCard;
private PreparedStatement mSelectCreditCardAccountIDs;
private BASE64Encoder mEncoder;
private BASE64Decoder mDecoder;
```

The constructor for DatabaseOperations takes a Properties object that contains our database configuration. We'll connect to the database on construction and create our prepared statements.

```
/**
 * Construct a DatabaseOperations object, based on the properties
 * passed in, which will include url, username, database, and JDBC driver
 * name.
 */

public DatabaseOperations(Properties properties) {

    // Load our connection and initialize objects.
```

```
      mEncoder = new BASE64Encoder();
      mDecoder = new BASE64Decoder();
      String driverName = properties.getProperty("DBDriver");
      String url = properties.getProperty("DBUrl");
      String username = properties.getProperty("DBUsername");
      String password = properties.getProperty("DBPassword");
      try {

        // Load the connection

        Class.forName(driverName);
        mConnection = DriverManager.getConnection(url, username, password);

        // Prepare the prepared statements.

        mInsertCreditCard = mConnection.prepareStatement
          (CREDIT_CARD_INSERT_SQL);
        mSelectCreditCard = mConnection.prepareStatement
          (CREDIT_CARD_SELECT_SQL);
        mSelectCreditCardAccountIDs = mConnection.prepareStatement(
          CREDIT_CARD_SELECT_IDS_SQL);
      } catch (Exception e) {
        e.printStackTrace();
      }
    }
```

Now we'll write a `store()` method, which actually stores a credit card DBO object in the database. We synchronize on the connection to prevent race conditions, and then insert a credit card using our `InsertCreditCard` prepared statement. All we really need to do is set three variables on the prepared statement: the account ID, the encrypted session key, and the encrypted credit card number.

```
    /**
     *  Store a CreditCardDBO object in the database.
     */

    public void store(CreditCardDBO creditCardDBO)
                      throws IOException {
      try {

        // Need to synchronize to prevent race conditions.

        synchronized(mConnection) {
          mInsertCreditCard.setLong (1,creditCardDBO.getAccountID());
          mInsertCreditCard.setString (2,mEncoder.encode
                              (creditCardDBO.getEncryptedSessionKey()));
          mInsertCreditCard.setString (3,mEncoder.encode
                              (creditCardDBO.getEncryptedCCNumber()));
          mInsertCreditCard.executeUpdate();
        }
      } catch (SQLException se) {
        se.printStackTrace();
        throw new IOException(se.getMessage());
      }
    }
```

Now we'll write a `loadCreditCardDBO()` method, which will load a credit card from the database. Again, we synchronize on the database connection to prevent race conditions.

```java
/**
 *  Creates a CreditCardDBO object with data from the database
 *  corresponding to the account id passed in.
 */

public CreditCardDBO loadCreditCardDBO(long accountID) throws IOException {
  CreditCardDBO creditCardDBO = null;
  try {

    // Need to synchronize to prevent race conditions.

    synchronized(mConnection) {
      mSelectCreditCard.setLong(1,accountID);
      ResultSet result = mSelectCreditCard.executeQuery();
      result.next();
      byte[] encryptedSessionKey =
                          mDecoder.decodeBuffer(result.getString(1));
      byte[] encryptedCCNumber =
                          mDecoder.decodeBuffer(result.getString(2));
      result.close();
      creditCardDBO = new CreditCardDBO (accountID, encryptedSessionKey,
                                    encryptedCCNumber);
    }
  } catch (SQLException se) {
    se.printStackTrace();
      throw new IOException(se.getMessage());
  }
  return creditCardDBO;
}
```

We'll define a method to get all the account IDs in the database. This will be used later when we display the credit cards. Again, note that we synchronize on the connection.

```java
/**
 *  Returns all the account ids in the database.
 *  Useful for displaying all credit cards.
 */

public long[] getAllCreditCardAccountIDs() throws IOException {
  Vector accountIDs = new Vector();
  try {
    synchronized(mConnection) {
      ResultSet result = mSelectCreditCardAccountIDs.executeQuery();
      while (result.next()) {
        accountIDs.add(new Long(result.getLong(1)));
      }
      result.close();
    }
  } catch (SQLException se) {
    se.printStackTrace();
      throw new IOException(se.getMessage());
  }
```

```
    // convert the vector to an array.

    long[] accountIDArray = new long[accountIDs.size()];
    for (int i=0; i<accountIDArray.length; i++) {
      Long accountIDLong = (Long)accountIDs.elementAt(i);
      accountIDArray[i] = accountIDLong.longValue();
    }
    return accountIDArray;
  }
}
```

The CreditCardFactory Class

This is where all the truly interesting work happens. Here we will encrypt and decrypt the credit cards. First, let's take a look at a sequence diagram illustrating how we want to create credit cards objects and store them in the database:

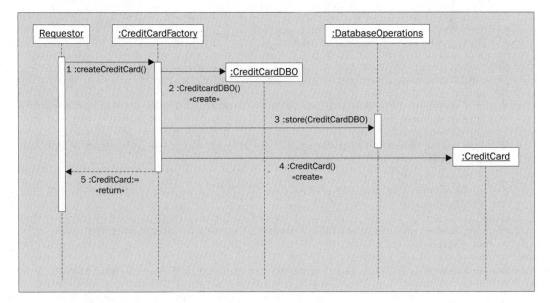

1. The requestor (in this case, a web server) makes a method call to `CreditCardFactory.createCreditCard()`.

2. `CreditCardFactory` then creates a session key, encrypts the credit card data, and then encrypts the session key and uses that data to create a `CreditCardDBO` object.

3. `CreditCardFactory` calls `DatabaseOperations.store()`, passing in the `CreditCardDBO` that was created. `DatabaseOperations` then stores that object's information in the database.

4. `CreditCardFactory` creates a `CreditCard` object.

5. `CreditCardFactory` then returns that `CreditCard` object to the caller.

In order to extract credit card information from the database, we will follow a different order of operations:

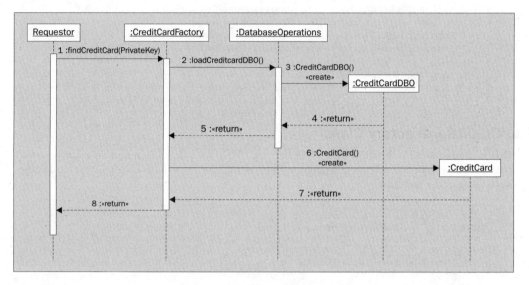

1. The requestor calls `CreditCardFactory.findCreditCard()` with the private key and also (not shown) an account ID.

2. `CreditCardFactory` calls `DatabaseOperations.loadCreditCardDBO()` with the account ID.

3. `DatabaseOperations` calls new `CreditCardDBO()` with information read from the database.

4. An instance of `CreditCardDBO` is created. The information contained within is encrypted.

5. `DatabaseOperations` returns that `CreditCardDBO` to `CreditCardFactory`.

6. `CreditCardFactory` decrypts the information in `CreditCardDBO` and calls a new `CreditCard()` with that information.

7. An instance of `CreditCard` is created, containing that decrypted information.

8. `CreditCardFactory` returns that instance of `CreditCard` for use by the requestor.

```
package com.projavasecurity.ecommerce.creditcard;

import com.projavasecurity.ecommerce.*;

import javax.crypto.*;
import javax.crypto.spec.*;
import java.security.*;
import java.io.*;
import java.util.*;
```

```
/**
 * CreditCardFactory.java
 * Creates or retrieves CreditCard objects
 */

public class CreditCardFactory {

   // Key to use to encrypt all new credit cards

   private PublicKey mPublicKey;

   // Handles all database calls

   private DatabaseOperations mDBOperations;
```

The CreditCardFactory constructor loads the public key to use for encrypting the credit cards. This is defined by a Properties object that's passed in.

```
/**
 *   Creates a new instance of CreditCardFactory
 *   using a Properties object to establish where the public
 *   key is, as well as what the database properties are.
 */
public CreditCardFactory (Properties properties) throws IOException {
   String certFilename = properties.getProperty("PublicKeyFilename");
   try {

      // Get the public key

      FileInputStream fis = new FileInputStream(certFilename);
      java.security.cert.CertificateFactory cf =
              java.security.cert.CertificateFactory.getInstance ("X.509");
      java.security.cert.Certificate cert = cf.generateCertificate(fis);
      fis.close();
      mPublicKey = cert.getPublicKey();
   } catch (Exception e) {
      e.printStackTrace();
        throw new IOException(e.getMessage());
   }

   // Create a new DatabaseOperations instance for
   // database calls.

   mDBOperations = new DatabaseOperations(properties);
}
```

createCreditCard() will actually credit a credit card, encrypt it, and store it in the database.

```
/**
 *   Create a credit card from an account id, a credit
 *   card number, and a public key.
 *
 *   Automatically encrypts the card and stores it in
 *   the database.
 */
```

```
    public CreditCard createCreditCard (long accountID, String
                                        creditCardNumber)
                           throws InvalidKeyException, IOException {

  CreditCardDBO creditCardDBO = null;
  byte[] encryptedSessionKey, encryptedCCNumber;
  try {
```

Now we're going to create a blowfish key for this card and encrypt the card number:

```
    KeyGenerator kg = KeyGenerator.getInstance ("Blowfish");
    kg.init(128);
    Key sessionKey = kg.generateKey();
```

Here's where the actual encryption takes place. First, the symmetric encryption:

```
    Cipher symmetricCipher =
                   Cipher.getInstance ("Blowfish/ECB/PKCS5Padding");
    symmetricCipher.init(Cipher.ENCRYPT_MODE, sessionKey);
    encryptedCCNumber = symmetricCipher.doFinal
                          (creditCardNumber.getBytes("UTF8"));
```

Now the asymmetric (public key encryption):

```
    // Use the public key to encrypt the session key.

    Cipher asymmetricCipher = Cipher.getInstance ("RSA/ECB/PKCS1Padding");
    asymmetricCipher.init(Cipher.ENCRYPT_MODE, mPublicKey);
    encryptedSessionKey =
                  asymmetricCipher.doFinal (sessionKey.getEncoded());
```

There are a lot of possible exceptions we could get, so we need to deal with them:

```
  } catch (NoSuchAlgorithmException nsae) {

    // We're in trouble. Missing RSA or Blowfish.

    nsae.printStackTrace();
    throw new RuntimeException("Missing Crypto algorithm");
  } catch (NoSuchPaddingException nspe) {

    // again, we're in trouble. Missing padding.

    nspe.printStackTrace();
    throw new RuntimeException("Missing Crypto algorithm");
  } catch (BadPaddingException bpe) {

    // Probably a bad key.

    bpe.printStackTrace();
    throw new InvalidKeyException("Missing Crypto algorithm");
  } catch (IllegalBlockSizeException ibse) {

    // Probably a bad key.

    ibse.printStackTrace();
    throw new InvalidKeyException("Could not encrypt");
  }
```

Now we've got our encrypted info, let's store it to the database:

```
    // Create a database object with the encrypted info.

    creditCardDBO = new CreditCardDBO (accountID, encryptedSessionKey,
                                       encryptedCCNumber);

    // Store the encrypted credit card in the database

    mDBOperations.store(creditCardDBO);
    CreditCard creditCard = new CreditCard(accountID, creditCardNumber);
    return creditCard;
}
```

Our `findCreditCard()` method will find and decrypt a credit card from the database, given an account ID and a private key:

```
/**
 * Given an account ID and a private key, load a credit card from the
 * database, decrypt it,and deliver it as a CreditCard object.
 * Requires the private key.
 */

public CreditCard findCreditCard (long accountID, PrivateKey privateKey)
                                  throws InvalidKeyException, IOException{
    String creditCardNumber = null;

    // Load the encrypted credit card info.

    CreditCardDBO creditCardDBO =
                          mDBOperations.loadCreditCardDBO(accountID);
    try {
```

Now we do the decryption, starting by decrypting the session key with the private key that was passed in:

```
    // Decrypt the encrypted session key.

    Cipher asymmetricCipher = Cipher.getInstance("RSA/ECB/PKCS1Padding");
    asymmetricCipher.init(Cipher.DECRYPT_MODE, privateKey);
    byte[] sessionKeyBytes = asymmetricCipher.doFinal
                                (creditCardDBO.getEncryptedSessionKey());
```

Now we have a session key to use to decrypt the credit card number:

```
    // Decrypt the credit card number with the session key.

    SecretKey symmetricKey =
                      new SecretKeySpec (sessionKeyBytes, "Blowfish");
    Cipher symmetricCipher =
                      Cipher.getInstance ("Blowfish/ECB/PKCS5Padding");
    symmetricCipher.init(Cipher.DECRYPT_MODE, symmetricKey);
    byte[] ccNumberBytes = symmetricCipher.doFinal
                              (creditCardDBO.getEncryptedCCNumber());

    creditCardNumber = new String(ccNumberBytes, "UTF8");
```

Just like encryption, we need to deal with a number of possible exceptions:

```
        } catch (NoSuchAlgorithmException nsae) {

            // Missing an algorithm.

            nsae.printStackTrace();
            throw new RuntimeException("Missing crypto algorithm");
        } catch (NoSuchPaddingException nspe) {

            // again, we're in trouble. Missing padding.

            nspe.printStackTrace();
            throw new RuntimeException("Missing Crypto algorithm");
        } catch (BadPaddingException bpe) {

            // This means the data is probably bad.

            bpe.printStackTrace();
            throw new InvalidKeyException("Could not decrypt");
        } catch (IllegalBlockSizeException ibse) {

            // Probably a bad key.

            ibse.printStackTrace();
            throw new InvalidKeyException("Could not decrypt");
        }

        CreditCard creditCard = new CreditCard (accountID, creditCardNumber);
        return creditCard;
    }
```

In order to display all the credit cards, we need a method to find all of them –
findAllCreditCards() is that method. We pass in a private key, which will be used to decrypt the credit cards:

```
    /**
     * Finds all credit cards and returns them as an Iterator.
     */

    public Iterator findAllCreditCards(PrivateKey privateKey)
                            throws InvalidKeyException, IOException {

        long[] accountIDs = mDBOperations.getAllCreditCardAccountIDs();
        Vector creditCards = new Vector();
        for (int i=0; i<accountIDs.length; i++) {
            creditCards.add(findCreditCard(accountIDs[i], privateKey));
        }
        return creditCards.iterator();
    }
}
```

Testing the Code

Now that we've created our framework, we need to write some code that actually creates credit card entries, as well as a client that can view those entries.

We'll begin with a simple creation example: some code that can be run from the command-line that creates a credit card based on a user-specified account ID and credit card number. This is actually very simple – we just have to create a `Properties` object from the file system before we create a `CreditCardFactory` object:

```
package com.projavasecurity.ecommerce;

import java.io.*;
import java.util.*;

import com.projavasecurity.ecommerce.creditcard.*;

/**
 *  CreateTest.java:
 *
 *  Creates credit cards and puts them in the database, encrypted.
 */

public class CreateTest {
  private static final String PROPERTIES_FILE = "config.properties";

  public static void main(String[] args) throws Exception {
    if (args.length != 2) {
      System.out.println
        ("Usage: java CreateTest ID CreditCardNumber");
      System.exit(1);
    }

    long id = Long.parseLong(args[0]);
    String ccNumber = args[1];

    // Load the database properties.

    Properties properties = new Properties();
    FileInputStream fis = new FileInputStream(PROPERTIES_FILE);
    properties.load(fis);
    fis.close();

    // Create the credit card

    CreditCardFactory factory = new CreditCardFactory(properties);
    CreditCard creditCard = factory.createCreditCard(id,ccNumber);
  }
}
```

In order to view credit cards, we need to have access to the private key. We'll use the keystore that we created earlier in this chapter, `creditcardExample.ks`. Our example will have the password set to `password`, but you should enter the password that you used to create the keystore.

```
package com.projavasecurity.ecommerce;

import com.projavasecurity.ecommerce.creditcard.*;
import java.io.*;
import java.security.*;
import java.util.*;

/**
 * ViewTest.java
 *
 * Displays all credit cards in the database, after decrypting them
 * with a private key.
 */

public class ViewTest {

    // Properties file for the database and public key information

    private static final String PROPERTIES_FILE = "config.properties";

    // Keystore that holds the private key
```

We need to define the location of the keystore. You should change this to an appropriate location for your machine.

```
    private static final String KEYSTORE = "creditcardExample.ks";
```

We're going to define the password statically in this class for brevity. In a real application, you should prompt the user for it, rather than storing it inside the application.

```
    // Password for the keystore

    private static final char[] PASSWORD = {'p','a','s','s','w','o','r','d'};

    /**
     * Attempts to display all credit cards in the database.
     */

    public static void main(String[] args) throws Exception {

        // Load the keystore to retrieve the private key.

        String ksType = KeyStore.getDefaultType();
        KeyStore ks = KeyStore.getInstance(ksType);
        FileInputStream fis = new FileInputStream(KEYSTORE);
        ks.load(fis,PASSWORD);
        fis.close();
        PrivateKey privateKey = (PrivateKey)ks.getKey("mykey",PASSWORD);

        // Load the database properties file.

        Properties properties = new Properties();
        fis = new FileInputStream(PROPERTIES_FILE);
        properties.load(fis);
        fis.close();
```

```
      // Create a credit card factory with the given properties.

      CreditCardFactory factory = new CreditCardFactory(properties);

      // Get all the credit cards.

      Iterator iterator = factory.findAllCreditCards(privateKey);

      // Display all credit cards.

      while(iterator.hasNext()) {
        CreditCard creditCard = (CreditCard)iterator.next();
        System.out.println("\nAccount ID: "+creditCard.getAccountID());
        System.out.println ("CC Number: "+creditCard.getCreditCardNumber());
      }
    }
  }
```

Compiling and Running the Example

In order to compile and run this application, you'll need a cryptographic provider that supports RSA and Blowfish. We recommend Bouncy Castle as discussed in Chapter 3 – ensure you have it properly installed, or the credit card encryption will not work.

Put all of the .java files into a single directory and issue the following command, after navigating to the directory:

```
C:\> javac -d . *.java
```

This will compile all of the .java files and place the class files in their appropriate subdirectory based on package.

You'll also need to have the public certificate that we created earlier (publicKey.cer) in this directory.

Next, make sure your JDBC driver is installed properly. For MySQL, you'll need the file mysql.jar on your CLASSPATH, along with ".".

Finally, the file config.properties should also be in the current directory. Make sure it contains the correct data for your setup, including your database driver, username, and password.

Now we can finally execute one of the sample programs and create a credit card entry. We'll create a credit card with the account ID of 1, and a credit card number of 1234 5678 9012 3456:

```
C:\> java com.projavasecurity.ecommerce.CreateTest 1 "1234 5678 9012 3456"
```

This may take a little while to run, as a SecureRandom has to be initialized in order to create a session key, and a connection needs to be established to the database. This could be greatly reduced in a server environment, where a long-running process could have already initialized SecureRandom, and could use some sort of connection pooling to the database.

You can create multiple credit card entries by running `CreateTest` as many times as you like. Here's a sample of what the database might look like after adding an entry:

```
mysql> projava=> select * from credit_card;
```

```
+--------------+-------------------------------------------------+---------------+
| account_id   |                 session_key                     |   cc_number   |
+--------------+-------------------------------------------------+---------------+
|      1       | CnyZHGtB/tZRRSntegw019b51AcgSUpMGasR18Y7n       | j6bzg4wKahwbX |
|              | UIqdPPFpjyF+IuYa158Vuf/aEVFN EC3Iz69KYJzP       | rWt1JN82owatp |
|              | 8uWcAIu1ZKYJzP8uWcAIu1Zg4gKsjKDi4KkD3Xwbc       | QF1fi         |
|              | nKHPM/QlAioFam5Neo09xaP/5zCw9dY+l/gz5g6bK       |               |
|              | IAEAqcZsH5oRF7K5LRZ3GI=                         |               |
+--------------+-------------------------------------------------+---------------+
(1 row)
```

In order to decrypt the info, we'll need the private key, which is stored in the keystore `creditcardExample.ks`. Typically this would be kept on a separate machine, so you should copy all the class files, the public key, and the `config` file over to that machine. Once there, you can execute the example with:

```
C:\> java com.projavasecurity.ecommerce.ViewTest
```

All of the credit card information will be displayed in clear text on that machine. This illustrates the application that the finance department might use for auditing or refunding mischarges.

Extending the Example

There are a number of alterations one could make to the example to make it both more secure and more useable in different settings. We aren't securing the private key very well in the viewer. It would be nice to store it encrypted, or perhaps even use a smart card. We are also storing a password directly in a class file, when we really should be requesting it from the user. We made these compromises to make the example more readable and to focus on the task at hand – encrypting sensitive data in the database.

To improve usability, you might want to store the public key used to encrypt the credit card data in an LDAP server so that it doesn't need to be stored on the local machine. This would be especially useful if multiple web servers were being used. Care must be taken that the public key in the LDAP server is not vulnerable to replacement, however.

In certain scenarios, it might be necessary to SSL the connection between the server and the database. It depends on whether or not your data is vulnerable to snooping between the database and the machines that will be connecting to it.

Summary

In this chapter we've discussed database security in Java. We've focused on two aspects: securing the connection to the database and securing the data within a database.

To achieve the former aim we highlighted two approaches. Our first section discussed SSL-tunneling, whereby a client application on a client machine works through a proxy to communicate with a database and that proxy communicates requests to, and receives responses from, a peer operating on the database machine with traffic going over SSL. Secondly we developed a secure JDBC driver, which serves as a proxy to the database driver.

To demonstrate how to secure data on a database we worked through a sample application that showed how to encrypt data going into a table.

In the next chapter we'll bring together much of the information we've covered in this book as we develop an application that is secured from front to back.

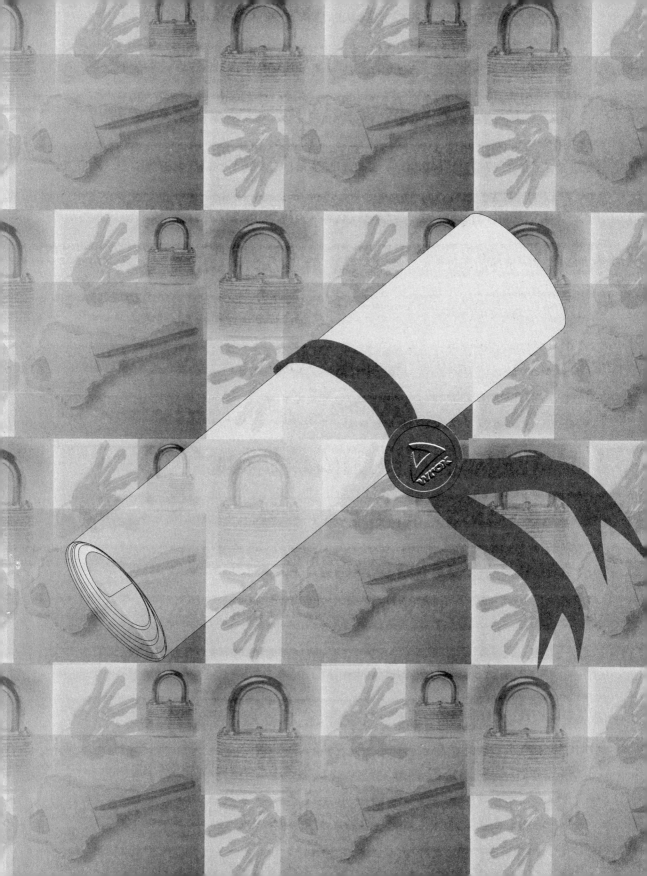

11

Securing a Large Application

We've examined a number of security technologies in this book so far, and in this chapter we're finally going to put them all together. We're going to write a sample application demonstrating the use of encryption, authentication, the Java security model, and SSL. We'll be basing the application on a MySQL database and using Tomcat as the web server. The application we'll be writing is artificial; it's meant to demonstrate many of the techniques that we've been describing in this book.

Your applications will likely not need all of the security features we'll be implementing in our application. For instance, if your network is behind a firewall, there is little need to encrypt your connection from the application server to the database. That being said, this application shows various security techniques, from which you should be able to pick and chose the components that you require.

Our route through the chapter will be to take each part of the application architecture in turn and see how we can secure the tier and communications between tiers. So we'll be looking at:

- ❑ Designing an online banking application with security in mind
- ❑ Setting up the keys and certificates for the application layers
- ❑ Configuring the database
- ❑ Building a database access tier
- ❑ Developing a web tier for customers
- ❑ Constructing a client application for approved users
- ❑ Looking at areas for improvements

> Again the reader is directed to http://www.wrox.com for downloads of the code and helpful batch and configuration files. This download contains all of the files needed to run the application on a single machine that is running MySQL and Tomcat 3.2.1 and has JSSE installed. There's also a ReadMe file to help you to get it up and running.

Note that we'll be building on the knowledge and coding carried out in previous chapters. Hence we'll be using the MySQL database alluded to in Chapter 10 (and discussed in Appendix B), the secure database driver developed in Chapter 10 and the JSSE highlighted in Chapter 9. Tomcat can be downloaded from http://jakarta.apache.org/tomcat/index.html. You'll also need a browser certificate, which we'll discuss later. The application download has been set up to be run on one machine, but, since correct configuration of parameters is a significant part of the development effort for such a system, we'll indicate settings for a multiple machine system as well throughout the chapter.

Let's start the ball rolling by taking an initial look at our application.

Sample Application – Online Banking

We're going to write a simple implementation of an online bank. Our bank will have three features:

- ❑ It will accept credit cards to open an account
- ❑ It will allow users to view only their own account balance, and not someone else's
- ❑ It will allow a certain user, the finance agent, to view all of the credit card data

The first two features will be accessed over the Web, while the third will require a custom client running on the user's workstation. Although this is not strictly required for security reasons, we want to demonstrate how you would secure a non-browser client.

Web Interface

The two web features are creating an account and viewing an existing account. Here's a diagram of the two functions, and what the user will see:

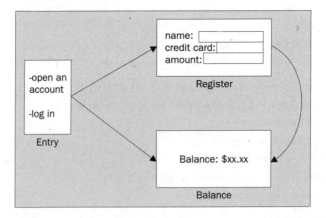

When a user first views the site, they will be presented with the entry page, and offered a choice of opening an account or logging in. If they choose to open an account, they will be asked to enter their name, credit card number, and amount. The account will then be opened, and they will be forwarded to a display of their balance. Later, they can return to the web site and view their balance by logging in.

Architecture

We know that this is a web-based application, and it's obvious we're going to need a database to keep track of accounts and credit cards. We're also going to break our application into a middle tier to handle access to the database. Though this isn't strictly necessary for this tiny application, it's a common technique in the real world to improve scalability and performance, and we want to illustrate some of the steps in securing a larger application.

Here's the network topology for our application:

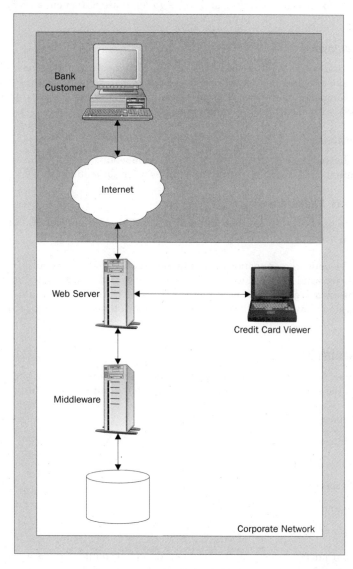

Now we need to investigate our architecture and determine where we are in the most danger from someone eavesdropping or attacking:

Network Connections

The architecture for our application obviously calls for several network connections. We'll briefly discuss the threats in each of these connections in turn (we'll see how this translates into a system of trust when we start implementing the application).

Customer to Web Server

This area is probably the most dangerous in our application. How do we make sure that the person accessing the account is who they claim to be, and that no one can listen in on their communication? SSL will enable us to encrypt the traffic, and we're going to use SSL client authentication to establish identity.

Web Server to Middleware

This communication is taking place via RMI over our imaginary corporate network. In an ideal scenario, we'd have a segmented network all to ourselves that we could trust no one could eavesdrop upon. For this example, however, we're going to assume that our network is untrusted. To deal with that, we'll use SSL with encryption and authentication to protect our data.

Middleware to Database

This is very similar to the web server to middleware connection. We'll use the same technique to protect our communication: RMI over SSL, using client and server authentication.

Credit Card Viewer to Middleware

Again, we want to use SSL with authentication to protect this communication, for the same reasons as our other internal network connections.

Many of the above network connections could be secured by alternate means. If we could trust the internal network, we wouldn't need to use SSL. One way to establish a trusted network would be to place it behind its own firewall, with no unauthorized access. Also, IPSec could be used between the machines. If you don't have control over your own network topology though, SSL provides the next best thing.

Application Security

We've decided how we're going to secure the network connections. Now we need to look at the possible vulnerabilities of the system itself. We'll look at each of our components in turn:

- ❑ The database
- ❑ The middleware
- ❑ The credit card client
- ❑ The web server
- ❑ The browser

Database

The database is our juiciest target. All the credit cards and account balances will be stored there, and we don't want anyone without authorization to have access.

The credit card numbers are probably the most sensitive data we're storing. To protect them, we'll encrypt them using a public key, as we did in our example in Chapter 10. This will keep the credit cards safe even if someone compromises the web server, as the web server will not store or have access to the private key needed to decrypt the card numbers.

The account balances need to be protected, but not quite to the same degree. Besides, our web application needs to be able to display those balances, so we really can't protect the balances in the same way that we can protect the credit card numbers. What we can do is use SSL authentication in our database driver to ensure that only the middleware client can read and write to the database.

We will be running our secure JDBC driver on the database box itself, as we did in Chapter 10.

Here's an illustration of how that will work in our application – our secure JDBC server runs on the database, and then we use our secure JDBC driver from the middleware to talk to the database through the secure JDBC server:

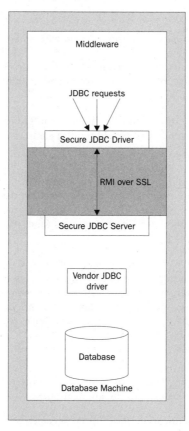

The secure JDBC driver and the secure JDBC server use SSL to communicate with each other, and certificate-based authentication to ensure that no unauthorized connections can be made or spoofed. The database itself should be configured to allow connections only from the machine it is running on, so that no one can go around the SSL-configured JDBC driver and make a connection directly to the database. It's important to use a database that can support this form of security.

Securing the database further is not really a Java problem. Instead, we need to make sure that the operating system that the database is running on top of is configured properly and has had all of the latest patches applied. Also, physical access should be restricted, and the database itself should be secured as much as possible by a DBA.

Middleware (Bank)

The middleware handles all of our application's communication with the database. We need to make sure that every access is authorized, and this will be accomplished using SSL authentication. We will only be allowing connections from the web server and the credit card client. All communications to and from the middleware will take place via RMI over SSL.

Again, we need to make sure that the box itself is as secure as possible. The system administrator needs to make sure that the operating system is up to date and that no unauthorized persons can log in to the machine.

In our example the middleware is the Bank component.

Credit Card Client

The credit card client is the one part of our application where credit cards can actually be decrypted and viewed. Because of that, we need to make sure that it is carefully protected. Again, this is not so much a Java issue, but rather a standard computer security issue. The keystore will be kept on the hard drive, meaning that a compromise of the credit card client machine could well mean a compromise for the credit card data stored in the application.

If we wanted further security on the credit card client, we might move the private key to a smart card, to ensure that it could never be copied. This would require some native code, however.

Web Server

Our web server will be reachable from the Internet. Because of that, it's likely to be the subject of external attacks. Again, we need to make sure that the machine itself is as secure as possible. It would be a good idea to block access to most ports with a firewall. No matter how secure our application is, it's not possible to protect it from the underlying operating system if someone changes the classes or the configuration on the machine itself.

From a programming perspective, we need to make sure that we never present any sensitive data without first properly authenticating the client. We're going to make sure that SSL authentication is required to access the web server, and then we will use the certificate that is presented to find the appropriate account information. The only way someone could view another customer's account information would be to steal the private key from his or her computer, or gain access to their computer directly and access the account from there.

Web Browser

We're not really going to have any control over the user's browser, but nonetheless it's good to understand how it relates to the security of the application.

Since we'll be using client authentication, most of our security is in the private key stored in the browser. Fortunately the browser protects the private key with password-based encryption, and without the decrypted private key, no one can impersonate someone else. This makes it pretty difficult, though not completely impossible, to view someone else's account balance. Certainly it's quite a bit more secure than having a password-protected account on the web site. We are giving up some usability, however, by adding this additional security. Your customers must use the same browser on the same machine to access the web site in the future. If this is too restrictive for your clients, you may wish to switch to something less secure but more convenient, like username/password-based authentication.

In order to use client authentication, the browsers will need to have a certificate. In a full application, you might generate them yourself when a user opens an account. For this example, we're going to allow either Thawte or Verisign certificates that must be previously established in order to use the application. You can get a free personal certificate from http://www.thawte.com/certs/personal/. You'll need to fill out some personal information (name, driver's license number, e-mail address), and they will issue you a certificate that you can use to authenticate to the web server.

In our application, we'll use the serial number of the certificate to differentiate accounts. Note that this is secure if you're generating your own certificates, but if you're relying on multiple CAs, you may want to make sure that no CA's serial numbers clash with any other CA's numbers.

Setting up the Keys

We're going to use SSL authentication for all network connections in our application. Because of this, there is a fairly complex system of trust that we must establish. Let's run down the list of each component and what other components it must trust:

Component	Trusted Component
Web Browser (IE or Netscape)	Web Server
Web Server (Tomcat)	Web Browser, Middleware
Middleware (Bank component)	Web Server, Credit Card Client, Database
Credit Card Client (CreditCardClient component)	Middleware
Database (MySQL)	Middleware

Notice that we don't simply allow each component to trust all other components. We don't want part of the application to be able to bypass the security checks of another. All database access goes first through the middleware component and then through the database component.

Note that if working on a multiple-machine system the appropriate trusted components will need to be transferred between machines. Incidentally, if using the download, much of this trust system has already been carried out.

Generate the Keys

We're going to use the default Java keystore to handle trust and authentication. We need to create private and public keys for each component, and then create truststores for each component that contain the appropriate public keys.

Web Browser

As we've mentioned, to get a private key and certificate for a browser requires a fairly in-depth process. There's no easy way to generate a key in Java and import it into the browser. For this example, we recommend that you get one from Thawte for free. The two major browsers will work fine for this application: either Netscape 4.x or higher or IE 4/5.

Credit Card Client, Middleware, and Database

We can use `keytool` to create the rest of the keys and certificates. Here are the commands we'll issue to generate the keystores:

```
C:\> keytool -genkey -keyalg RSA -keystore creditcardKeyStore
C:\> keytool -genkey -keyalg RSA -keystore bankKeyStore
C:\> keytool -genkey -keyalg RSA -keystore databaseKeyStore
```

> *When asked for the name for each certificate, give the fully qualified domain name of the machine it will be running on (such as* `bank.wrox.com` *or* `database.wrox.com`*). When clients connect via SSL, they will check that the name on the certificate matches the name of the machine.*
>
> *You can choose any password you like for each of the keystores. For the example, we'll use the name of the component:* `creditcard, theBank,` *and* `database`*.*

In a production environment, we would get our web server certificate from a trusted CA, such as Thawte or Verisign.

Export the Certificates

SSL authentication is based on certificates. In order to establish trust, we need to export all the certificates that need to be trusted. We'll create a file for each of the certificates by exporting them from their keystores:

```
C:\> keytool -export -keystore bankKeyStore -file bank.cer
C:\> keytool -export -keystore creditcardKeyStore -file creditcard.cer
C:\> keytool -export -keystore databaseKeyStore -file database.cer
```

Import the Certificates

Now we'll set up trust by creating trust stores. These are just keystores that contain only certificates. Here are the commands we'll use to create those trust stores enter each on a single line. When asked if the certificates should be trusted, answer yes. Remember that you'll have to send the database certificate and the bank certificate to the middleware and database machines respectively if they are different.

Middleware:

```
C:\> keytool -import -keystore bankTrustStore -alias database -file database.cer
C:\> keytool -import -keystore bankTrustStore -alias creditcard
          -file creditcard.cer
```

Database:

```
C:\> keytool -import -keystore databaseTrustStore -alias bank -file bank.cer
```

Credit Card:

```
C:\> keytool -import -keystore creditcardTrustStore -alias bank -file bank.cer
```

Web Server

Establishing trust for the web server is a little more complicated. Because we need to trust the web browser, we need to trust a number of certificates, not just the ones that we generate. Fortunately, Java comes with a list of commonly trusted Certificate Authorities that we can use. We also need to add our middleware component to the trust store. Also, due to the way Tomcat handles trust stores, we need to have both our key and our trusted certificates in one file.

The default trust store for Java is the file `$JAVA_HOME/jre/lib/security/cacerts`. Copy it to your working directory and rename it `jakartaKeyStore`. The default password for `cacerts` is `changeit`. You can change that password with the following:

```
C:\> keytool -storepasswd -keystore jakartaKeyStore
```

Then you can add the middleware component to the trust store:

```
C:\> keytool -import -keystore jakartaKeyStore -alias bank -file bank.cer
```

Finally, we need to create the key that our web server will use:

```
C:\> keytool -genkey -keyalg RSA -keystore jakartaKeyStore
```

And export that certificate and import it into the bank's trust store:

```
C:\> keytool -export -keystore jakartaKeyStore -file jakarta.cer
C:\> keytool -import -keystore bankTrustStore -alias jakarta -file jakarta.cer
```

Note that this keystore needs to be moved to the Tomcat root directory.

Certificate Recognition in Internet Explorer

As we mentioned in Chapter 9, there is a bug in Internet Explorer 5.x that prevents the Thawte Freemail certificates from being properly recognized in a certificate chain. For a Thawte Freemail certificate, for instance, the chain looks like this:

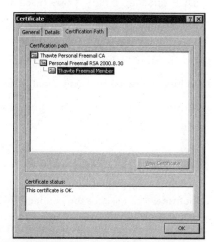

The Freemail certificate is signed by a certificate chain, with the root Thawte certificate validating an intermediate certificate, which in turn validates the user's certificate. As IE fails to detect this chain, if you wish to use such a certificate, you need to import the intermediate certificate into your Jakarta keystore. In order to do this, we need to first export the intermediate certificate from our IE certificate store. Open up IE and then select **Tools | Internet Options** from the menu and then the **Content** tab. Click on the **Certificates...** button to get a dialog similar to the following:

Click on the Intermediate Certification Authorities tab and select the Personal Freemail RSA 2000.8.30 certificate. You should see something like the following:

Click on the Export... button and follow the wizard for exporting that certificate, selecting the format DER encoded binary X.509 (.CER) as appropriate. Name the export file `thawte.cer`.

Now we need to import that certificate into the Jakarta keystore using:

```
C:\> keytool -import -keystore jakartaKeyStore -thawte2 bank -file thawte.cer
```

When you're asked if you should trust the certificate, say yes.

Now that our keys and trust stores are created, we can start working on the actual application. We're going to work from the bottom up, starting with the database and working our way to the web server.

The Database

We'll be using the database driver that we wrote in Chapter 10 to secure our database connections. But before we can secure the connections, we need to create the database itself. As mentioned previously, we'll use MySQL (http://www.mysql.com), because it is cross-platform and freely available for non-commercial use. In a real application, we would recommend a more-proven database, like Oracle.

The database construction is described in Appendix B, and here we'll just summarize the salient features.

The `projava` database created contains two tables:

❑ `accounts` – The account table will have the following fields: ID, customer name, balance, and certificate serial number. We'll use the serial number as a key to correlate one customer to one account. This probably isn't ideal, but we need to keep the application short enough to be written and described in one chapter. Ideally, you should probably store the entire certificate in a database and check it for validity. You might want to add an additional layer of password-based security to foil users who are surreptitiously using someone else's browser.

❑ `credit_card` – The `credit_card` table is identical to the one we used in Chapter 10 on securing data in a database.

Additionally, we'll have a user, `projava`, with the password `sasquatch`, that will have read and write access to those tables.

The Database Driver

The configuration for the database driver is again taken from Chapter 10 (see the *Running the Example* section related to the secure JDBC driver). We'll need the database driver and the Xerces XML parser available to run the example (Xerces can be downloaded from http://xml.apache.org/xerces-j/index.html – v1.3.1 was used when writing this code).

Of course we'll need to appropriately adjust some of the configuration-related files ,namely SecureDriver_config.xml and SecureDriver.policy.

Firstly our configuration file – SecureDriver_config.xml:

```xml
<?xml version="1.0"?>
<!DOCTYPE connectionServer SYSTEM "SecureDriver_config.dtd">
<connectionServer id="SecureDriver" keystore="trusted" authclient="true">

  <dataSources>
    <dataSource id="dataSource1" loginRequired="false">
      <driver>
        org.gjt.mm.mysql.Driver
      </driver>
      <url>
        jdbc:mysql://localhost/projava
      </url>
      <username>
        projava
      </username>
      <password>
        sasquatch
      </password>
      <login>
        <username>
          username
        </username>
        <password>
          password
        </password>
      </login>
    </dataSource>
  </dataSources>

  <!-- Additional configuration info can be included here-->
  <include>
    /path/to/config
  </include>

</connectionServer>
```

Let's highlight some points about this:

❑   The line jdbc:mysql://localhost/projava is the URL for the database itself. Remember that the secure driver is only useful if you're running it on the *same* machine that the database itself resides on.

❑   We've defined two sets of usernames and passwords – the first set are for logging into the database, while the second set are for users of the secure driver (we'll be setting those up for the middleware later).

Secondly, we need to create a policy file that enables the correct security for our application. Our database driver doesn't need to step outside the sandbox very much: it needs to be able to speak on the network to the database, the RMI registry, and the bank, our middleware. So, for SecureDriver.policy we have:

```
grant {

    // Let the JDBC proxy connect to the database
    // SETUP: change the machine name to that of your database server
    // SETUP: change to your database's JDBC port number if using something
    // other than MySQL

    permission java.net.SocketPermission "localhost:3306", "connect,resolve";

    // Allow a connection to the RMI registry
    // SETUP: change the IP address to your IP address

     permission java.net.SocketPermission "localhost:1099", "connect,resolve";

    // Allow the Bank to receive connections over RMI
    // SETUP: change to the machine running the bank

    permission java.net.SocketPermission "localhost:1024-", "listen,resolve";
};
```

You will need to change the machine names to match your environment. So, on a multiple machine system if the database was running on a machine called database, and the Bank component middleware was running on a machine called bank the last setting becomes:

```
    // Allow the Bank to receive connections over RMI
    // SETUP: change to the machine running the bank

    permission java.net.SocketPermission "bank:1024-", "listen,resolve";
```

So, on the database machine, you'll need to collect together all the files needed to run the driver in one folder. Thus the folder should contain the following files:

- ❑ SecureDriver.jar
- ❑ SecureDriver.policy
- ❑ SecureDriver_config.xml
- ❑ databaseKeyStore
- ❑ databaseTrustStore
- ❑ xerces.jar
- ❑ mysql_comp.jar

Remember we've just created the database keystore and truststore (databaseKeyStore and databaseTrustStore).

Before we start running the driver there are a couple of last points:

❑ Note the `mysql_comp.jar` may be named differently depending on the database driver that you are using

❑ Make sure the JSSE is installed (see Chapter 9 for more details if you haven't already installed it)

Running the JDBC Driver

You can start the database driver with the following commands:

```
C:\> rmiregistry -J-classpath -JSecureDriver.jar
```

The next command should be all on one line:

```
C:\> java -Djava.security.policy=SecureDriver.policy
          -Djavax.net.ssl.trustStore=databaseTrustStore
          -Djavax.net.ssl.keyStore=databaseKeyStore
          -Djavax.net.ssl.keyStorePassword=database
          -cp SecureDriver.jar;xerces.jar;mysql_comp.jar
           com.isnetworks.crypto.database.server.SecureConnectionServerMain
           SecureDriver_config.xml
```

> *Note that you must use the correct* keyStorePassword.

It is probably easiest to place these commands into two scripts and run those scripts (a number of helpful scripts are provided with the code download). While this won't do much on its own (just giving the screenshot shown), you can check the opening of a connection to the database through the database tools.

Now the database is up and running and ready to respond to requests from the middleware. Next we'll actually write that middleware – the `Bank` component.

The Middleware – The Bank

The bank implements the core functions of our application, which are:

❑ Create an account

❑ Retrieve an account

❑ Retrieve the encrypted credit cards

These functions are quite similar to the ones that we established in Chapter 10 for storing credit cards by themselves. In fact, we're going to take that basic design and extend it, matching credit cards to accounts, and adding RMI accessibility.

In this section we need to look at:

❑ Creating an interface for clients to use

❑ Building data objects to enable items to be stored in the database

❑ Creating an RMI object to connect the interface to the data objects

❑ Constructing a way of starting the middleware

❑ Configuring the middleware

> *Note the package structure is set up as per the code download.*

Let's start with the interface.

The Bank Interface

We need to create a `Bank` interface, which is what our clients will use. We will provide four methods: `register()`, `getAccount()`, `getCreditCardDBO()`, and `getAllCreditCardAccountIDs()`.

These are contained in the `Bank` class as described below:

```
package ecommerce_example;

import java.rmi.*;
import java.io.*;
import java.security.*;
import ecommerce_example.data.*;

/**
 * RMI interface that allows servlets and the credit card client to connect
 * over RMI to create and access account and credit card information
 */

public interface Bank extends Remote {

  /**
   * Register a new account given some basic user information
   */
```

```
        public Account register( RegistrationInformation info )
            throws RemoteException, IOException, InvalidKeyException;

    /**
      * Find the Account for a given client cert serial number
      */

    public Account getAccount( String certSerialNumber )
        throws RemoteException;

    /**
      * Fetch the encrypted credit card information for a given account id
      */

    public CreditCardDBO getCreditCardDBO( long accountID )
        throws RemoteException;

    /**
      * Get a list of all the account ids in the database
      */

    public long[] getAllCreditCardAccountIDs()
        throws RemoteException;
}
```

Data Objects

In the `Bank` interface, we used two classes that we haven't seen before:

- ❑ Account
- ❑ RegistrationInformation

These are both simple, read-only, serializable classes that hold information that we need to transfer between components.

`Account` contains an account ID, a balance, and a customer name. `RegistrationInformation` contains a name, a certificate serial number, a credit card number, and a balance. When a request comes in from a browser to open an account, our servlet will create an instance of `RegistrationInformation` to hold the information for that request. It then sends that `RegistrationInformation` to the middle-tier to actually create the account and charge the credit card.

Within this section we also need to look at some of the classes we encountered in Chapter 10 when we considered storing sensitive information in a database. Here we'll consider the `CreditCardDBO` class and the `DatabaseOperations` class.

Our first task is to look at the `account` class.

The Account Class

```
package ecommerce_example.data;

import ecommerce_example.*;
import java.io.*;

/**
  * Simple class to hold account information in the database, which is not
  * encrypted.  Each variable maps to a database field.
  */
```

```
public class Account implements Serializable {

  /**
    * Unique identifier - primary key in database
    */

  private long mAccountID;

  private float mBalance;

  private String mCustomerName;

  /**
    * Serial number for the browser's certificate
    */

  private String mCertificateSerialNumber;

  public Account( long accountID, float balance, String customerName, String
                   certSerialNumber ) {
    mAccountID = accountID;
    mBalance = balance;
    mCustomerName = customerName;
    mCertificateSerialNumber = certSerialNumber;
  }

  public long getAccountID() {
    return mAccountID;
  }

  public float getBalance() {
    return mBalance;
  }

  public String getCustomerName() {
    return mCustomerName;
  }

  public String getCertificateSerialNumber() {
    return mCertificateSerialNumber;
  }
}
```

The RegistrationInformation Class

```
package ecommerce_example.data;

import java.io.*;

/**
  * Class to wrap up all of the user-entered information on the
  * registration page
  */

public class RegistrationInformation implements Serializable {
  private String mName;

  private String mCertificateSerialNumber;
```

```
    private String mCreditCardNumber;

    private float mBalance;

    public RegistrationInformation( String name, String certSerialNumber, String
                                    creditCardNumber, float balance ) {
      mName = name;
      mCertificateSerialNumber = certSerialNumber;
      mCreditCardNumber = creditCardNumber;
      mBalance = balance;
    }

    public String getName() {
      return mName;
    }

    public String getCertificateSerialNumber() {
      return mCertificateSerialNumber;
    }

    public String getCreditCardNumber() {
      return mCreditCardNumber;
    }

    public float getBalance() {
      return mBalance;
    }
}
```

The CreditCardDBO Class

The CreditCardDBO class is unchanged from Chapter 10:

```
package ecommerce_example.data;

public class CreditCardDBO implements java.io.Serializable {

  private long mAccountID;
  private byte[] mEncryptedSessionKey;
  private byte[] mEncryptedCCNumber;

  public CreditCardDBO(long accountID, byte[] encryptedSessionKey,
                       byte[] encryptedCCNumber) {
    mAccountID = accountID;
    mEncryptedSessionKey = encryptedSessionKey;
    mEncryptedCCNumber = encryptedCCNumber;
  }

  public long getAccountID() {
    return mAccountID;
  }

  public byte[] getEncryptedSessionKey() {
    return mEncryptedSessionKey;
  }

  public byte[] getEncryptedCCNumber() {
    return mEncryptedCCNumber;
  }
}
```

The DatabaseOperations Class

We're counting on the JDBC driver to handle our database security, so we don't need to do anything special with it, just use it to create a `Connection` object.

We do need to add a couple of functions to `DatabaseOperations` for storing and loading an account, and getting the largest account ID number from the database. We need the largest account ID so we can generate the primary keys for the accounts, as we're going to number the accounts sequentially for this example. In a real application, we'd use a trigger in the database, but for clarity and ease-of-use, we're going to use this somewhat less robust approach.

The `DatabaseOperations` class (which uses the BASE64 encoder and decoder classes we cover in Appendix C) now has the following form:

```
package ecommerce_example.bank;

import ecommerce_example.data.*;
import com.isnetworks.base64.BASE64Encoder;
import com.isnetworks.base64.BASE64Decoder;

import java.io.*;
import java.sql.*;
import java.util.*;

/**
 *  Class for performing database operations.  Now uses the JDBC proxy
 * to encrypt the connection using RMI over SSL and deals with
 * credit cards and accounts separately
 */

public class DatabaseOperations {

  private final static String CREDIT_CARD_INSERT_SQL =
    "INSERT INTO credit_card (account_id, session_key, cc_number) "+
    "VALUES (?,?,?)";
```

We've added a few SQL statements, including the two below that handle accounts similarly to the way we handle credit cards.

```
  private final static String ACCOUNT_INSERT_SQL =
    "INSERT INTO account (account_id, balance, customer_name, cert_serial_number)"
                    + "VALUES (?,?,?,?)";

  private final static String ACCOUNT_SELECT_SQL =
                    "SELECT account_id, balance, customer_name FROM account "
                    + "WHERE cert_serial_number = ?";

  private final static String CREDIT_CARD_SELECT_SQL =
    "SELECT session_key, cc_number FROM credit_card "+
    "WHERE account_id = ?";

  private final static String CREDIT_CARD_SELECT_IDS_SQL =
    "SELECT account_id FROM credit_card";
```

In this application, we're going to create the account numbers ourselves. We need to get the largest account number on application startup, which we will then increment internally when accounts are added.

```java
private final static String ACCOUNT_SELECT_MAX_ID_SQL =
  "SELECT MAX( account_id ) FROM account";

private Connection mConnection;
private PreparedStatement mInsertCreditCard;
private PreparedStatement mInsertAccount;
private PreparedStatement mSelectAccount;
private PreparedStatement mSelectCreditCard;
private PreparedStatement mSelectCreditCardAccountIDs;
private PreparedStatement mSelectMaxAccountID;
private BASE64Encoder mEncoder;
private BASE64Decoder mDecoder;

/**
 *  Construct a DatabaseOperations object,
 *  based on the properties passed in which
 *  will include url, username, database, and
 *  JDBC driver name.
 */

public DatabaseOperations(Properties properties) {

  // Load our connection and initialize objects.

  mEncoder = new BASE64Encoder();
  mDecoder = new BASE64Decoder();

  String driverName = properties.getProperty("DBDriver");
  String url = properties.getProperty("DBUrl");
  String username = properties.getProperty("DBUsername");
  String password = properties.getProperty("DBPassword");
  try {

    // Load the connection

    Class.forName(driverName);
    mConnection = DriverManager.getConnection
      (url, username, password);

    // Prepare the PreparedStatements.

    mInsertCreditCard = mConnection.prepareStatement
      (CREDIT_CARD_INSERT_SQL);
    mInsertAccount = mConnection.prepareStatement
      (ACCOUNT_INSERT_SQL);
    mSelectAccount = mConnection.prepareStatement
      (ACCOUNT_SELECT_SQL);
    mSelectCreditCard = mConnection.prepareStatement
      (CREDIT_CARD_SELECT_SQL);
    mSelectCreditCardAccountIDs = mConnection.prepareStatement(
      CREDIT_CARD_SELECT_IDS_SQL);
    mSelectMaxAccountID = mConnection.prepareStatement(
      ACCOUNT_SELECT_MAX_ID_SQL);
  } catch (Exception e) {
    e.printStackTrace();
  }
}
```

```
/**
 *  Store a CreditCardDBO object in the database.
 */

  public void store(CreditCardDBO creditCardDBO)
    throws IOException {
  try {

    // Need to synchronize to prevent race conditions.

    synchronized(mConnection) {
      mInsertCreditCard.setLong
        (1,creditCardDBO.getAccountID());
      mInsertCreditCard.setString
        (2,mEncoder.encode
        (creditCardDBO.getEncryptedSessionKey()));
      mInsertCreditCard.setString
        (3,mEncoder.encode
        (creditCardDBO.getEncryptedCCNumber()));
      mInsertCreditCard.executeUpdate();
    }
  } catch (SQLException se) {
    se.printStackTrace();
    throw new IOException(se.getMessage());
  }
}


/**
 *  Store an Account object in the database.
 */

  public void store( Account account )
    throws IOException {
  try {

    // Need to synchronize to prevent race conditions.

    synchronized(mConnection) {
      mInsertAccount.setLong( 1, account.getAccountID() );
      mInsertAccount.setFloat( 2, account.getBalance() );
      mInsertAccount.setString( 3, account.getCustomerName() );
      mInsertAccount.setString( 4,
        account.getCertificateSerialNumber() );
      mInsertAccount.executeUpdate();
    }
  } catch (SQLException se) {
    se.printStackTrace();
    throw new IOException(se.getMessage());
  }
}

/**
 *  Creates a CreditCardDBO object with
 *  data from the database corresponding
 *  to the client certificate's serial number
 */

  public Account loadAccount( String certSerialNumber )
    throws IOException {

  Account account = null;
  try {
```

```
        // Need to synchronize to prevent race conditions.

        synchronized(mConnection) {
          mSelectAccount.setString( 1, certSerialNumber );
          ResultSet result = mSelectAccount.executeQuery();
          if ( result.next() ) {
            result.next();

            long accountID = result.getLong( 1 );
            float balance = result.getFloat( 2 );
            String name = result.getString( 3 );

            result.close();
            account = new Account( accountID,
              balance, name, certSerialNumber );
          }
        }
      } catch (SQLException se) {
        se.printStackTrace();
        throw new IOException(se.getMessage());
      }
      return account;
    }

  /**
   * Creates a CreditCardDBO object with
   * data from the database corresponding
   * to the account id passed in.
   */

    public CreditCardDBO loadCreditCardDBO(long accountID)
      throws IOException {

    CreditCardDBO creditCardDBO = null;
    try {

      // Need to synchronize to prevent race conditions.

      synchronized(mConnection) {
        mSelectCreditCard.setLong(1,accountID);
        ResultSet result = mSelectCreditCard.executeQuery();
        result.next();
        byte[] encryptedSessionKey = mDecoder.decodeBuffer
          (result.getString(1));
        byte[] encryptedCCNumber = mDecoder.decodeBuffer
          (result.getString(2));
        result.close();
        creditCardDBO = new CreditCardDBO (accountID,
                          encryptedSessionKey, encryptedCCNumber);
      }
    } catch (SQLException se) {
      se.printStackTrace();
      throw new IOException(se.getMessage());
    }
    return creditCardDBO;
  }
```

Our getMaxAccount() method returns the largest account number in the database. We'll use this on application startup only, and then store that account ID in memory. As accounts are added, we'll increment the in-memory counter, to avoid race conditions.

```
   public long getMaxAccountID() throws IOException {
     long accountID = 1;
     try {
       synchronized(mConnection) {
         ResultSet result = mSelectMaxAccountID.executeQuery();
         if ( result.next() ) {
           try {
             accountID = result.getLong( 1 ) + 1;
           }
           catch( Exception e ) {

             // If there's no accounts in the database,
             // use the default value
             // of 1 from above

           }
         }
         result.close();
       }
     }
     catch (SQLException se) {
       se.printStackTrace();
       throw new IOException(se.getMessage());
     }
     return accountID;
   }

   /**
    * Returns all the account ids in the database.
    * Useful for displaying all credit cards.
    */

   public long[] getAllCreditCardAccountIDs()
     throws IOException {

     Vector accountIDs = new Vector();
     try {
       synchronized(mConnection) {
         ResultSet result =
           mSelectCreditCardAccountIDs.executeQuery();
         while (result.next()) {
           accountIDs.add(new Long(result.getLong(1)));
         }
         result.close();
       }
     } catch (SQLException se) {
       se.printStackTrace();
       throw new IOException(se.getMessage());
     }

     // convert the vector to an array.

     long[] accountIDArray = new long[accountIDs.size()];
     for (int i=0; i<accountIDArray.length; i++) {
       Long accountIDLong = (Long)accountIDs.elementAt(i);
       accountIDArray[i] = accountIDLong.longValue();
     }
     return accountIDArray;
   }
 }
```

That concludes our work on data objects; now we need to look at putting things together.

Bank Implementation

Now that we've established the interface to the bank and how we can store items in the database, we need to actually hook those two things together. We'll do that by creating an RMI object, `BankImpl`. This is really quite similar to the `CreditCardFactory` object in Chapter 10, but we've added a few methods to support accounts, and made it extend `UnicastRemoteObject` so that we can use it over RMI.

Notice that the constructor calls `super()` with the RMI SSL socket factories that we defined in Chapter 9. This will enable RMI over SSL.

When you compile `BankImpl.java`, be sure to run `rmic` against it. This will generate the stubs for RMI.

The BankImpl Class

```
package ecommerce_example.bank;

import ecommerce_example.*;
import ecommerce_example.data.*;
```

We're using the SSL socket factories from Chapter 9, so we need to import them:

```
import com.isnetworks.crypto.rmi.*;
import javax.crypto.*;
import javax.crypto.spec.*;
import java.security.*;
import java.io.*;
import java.util.*;
import java.rmi.*;

public class BankImpl extends java.rmi.server.UnicastRemoteObject
  implements Bank {

  /**
    * Some garbage value to denote that the next account id is not yet known
    */
  private static final long UNKNOWN_ACCOUNT_ID = Long.MIN_VALUE;

  /**
    * The port that we'll open a server socket on to respond to incoming requests.
    */
  private static final int SERVER_SOCKET_PORT = 16547;

  /**
    * Maximum account ID in use
    */
  private long mMaxAccountID = UNKNOWN_ACCOUNT_ID;

  /**
    * Key to use to encrypt all new credit cards before going to the database
    */
  private PublicKey mPublicKey;

  /**
    * Handles all database calls
    */
  private DatabaseOperations mDBOperations;
```

Our constructor will load a certificate from the filesystem and create an instance of `DatabaseOperations` to handle our database operations. We need to start by calling `super()` in order to accept incoming connections.

```java
public BankImpl( Properties properties) throws IOException {
  super( SERVER_SOCKET_PORT, new RMISSLClientSocketFactory(),
    new RMISSLServerSocketFactory() );

  String certFilename = properties.getProperty("PublicKeyFilename");
  try {

    // Get the public key

    FileInputStream fis = new FileInputStream(certFilename);
    java.security.cert.CertificateFactory cf =
      java.security.cert.CertificateFactory.getInstance
      ("X.509");
    java.security.cert.Certificate cert =
      cf.generateCertificate(fis);
    fis.close();
    mPublicKey = cert.getPublicKey();
  } catch (Exception e) {
    e.printStackTrace();
    throw new IOException(e.getMessage());
  }

  // Create a new DatabaseOperations instance for
  // database calls.

  mDBOperations = new DatabaseOperations(properties);
}
```

Our `register()` method will create a credit card entry and an account entry in the database. We will encrypt the credit card entry before storing it. Our account and credit card information gets passed to us in an `Account` object.

```java
public Account register( RegistrationInformation registrationInfo )
    throws InvalidKeyException, IOException, RemoteException {

  Account account = null;
  CreditCardDBO creditCardDBO = null;
  byte[] encryptedSessionKey, encryptedCCNumber;

  try {

    // Create a blowfish key and encrypt the credit card number.

    KeyGenerator kg = KeyGenerator.getInstance( "Blowfish" );
    kg.init( 128 );
    Key sessionKey = kg.generateKey( );

    Cipher symmetricCipher =
      Cipher.getInstance( "Blowfish/ECB/PKCS5Padding" );
    symmetricCipher.init( Cipher.ENCRYPT_MODE, sessionKey );
    encryptedCCNumber = symmetricCipher.doFinal(
      registrationInfo.getCreditCardNumber().getBytes(
      "UTF8" ) );

    // Use the public key to encrypt the session key.
```

```
        Cipher asymmetricCipher = Cipher.getInstance(
          "RSA/ECB/PKCS1Padding" );
        asymmetricCipher.init( Cipher.ENCRYPT_MODE, mPublicKey );
        encryptedSessionKey = asymmetricCipher.doFinal(
          sessionKey.getEncoded() );

    // Need to catch a large number of possible exceptions:

    }
    catch( NoSuchAlgorithmException nsae ) {

        // We're in trouble. Missing RSA or Blowfish.

        nsae.printStackTrace();
        throw new RuntimeException( "Missing Crypto algorithm" );
    }
    catch( NoSuchPaddingException nspe ) {

        // again, we're in trouble. Missing padding.

        nspe.printStackTrace();
        throw new RuntimeException( "Missing Crypto algorithm" );
    }
    catch( BadPaddingException bpe ) {

        // Probably a bad key.

        bpe.printStackTrace();
        throw new InvalidKeyException( "Missing Crypto algorithm" );
    }
    catch(IllegalBlockSizeException ibse) {

        // Probably a bad key.

        ibse.printStackTrace();
        throw new InvalidKeyException( "Could not encrypt" );
    }

    long accountID = getNextAccountID();

    // Create a database object with the encrypted info.

    creditCardDBO = new CreditCardDBO(
      accountID, encryptedSessionKey, encryptedCCNumber );

    // Store the encrypted credit card in the database

    mDBOperations.store( creditCardDBO );
    account = new Account( accountID, registrationInfo.getBalance(),
      registrationInfo.getName(),
      registrationInfo.getCertificateSerialNumber() );
    mDBOperations.store( account );

    return account;
}
```

In order to create a new account, we need to have an account ID. The next method, getNextAccountID(), will return the next available ID in the database. We won't be going to the database every time, just if we don't already know what the next account number is. This method is synchronized to prevent race conditions.

```
private synchronized long getNextAccountID() throws IOException {
  if ( mMaxAccountID == UNKNOWN_ACCOUNT_ID ) {
    mMaxAccountID = mDBOperations.getMaxAccountID();
  }

  mMaxAccountID++;
  return mMaxAccountID;
}
```

Our Bank also needs the ability to look up an account by the client certificate serial number. We will return null if no account exists.

```
public Account getAccount( String certSerialNumber ) throws RemoteException {
  try {
    Account account = mDBOperations.loadAccount(
      certSerialNumber );
    return account;
  }
  catch( IOException e ) {
    throw new RemoteException( e.getMessage() );
  }
}
```

We also need a way to fetch all of the credit card IDs in the database:

```
public long[] getAllCreditCardAccountIDs() throws RemoteException {
  try {
    return mDBOperations.getAllCreditCardAccountIDs();
  }
  catch( IOException e ) {
    throw new RemoteException( e.getMessage() );
  }
}
```

Our next method, getCreditCardDBO() returns a credit card from an account ID. This credit card will be encrypted, and must be decrypted by the client:

```
public CreditCardDBO getCreditCardDBO( long accountID )
  throws RemoteException {
  try {
    return mDBOperations.loadCreditCardDBO( accountID );
  }
  catch( IOException e ) {
    throw new RemoteException( e.getMessage() );
  }
}
```

Now we need to create a way to actually start up the BankImpl object so it can respond to requests.

Starting the Bank

What we need to do is construct a `BankImpl` object with a `Properties` object that we read off the file system, and then call `Naming.rebind()` on it so that it becomes available for RMI clients. We will pass a command-line argument indicating the properties file to read.

The BankInit Class

```
package ecommerce_example.bank;

import java.rmi.*;
import java.rmi.registry.*;
import java.io.*;
import java.util.*;

/**
 * Start up BankImpl and bind it to the registry.  Takes a command line
 * argument of the properties file to be used
 */
public class BankInit {
  public static void main( String args[] ) throws Exception {

    if ( args.length != 1 ) {
      usage();
      System.exit( 1 );
    }

    Properties properties = new Properties();
    FileInputStream fis = new FileInputStream( args[ 0 ] );
    properties.load( fis );
    fis.close();

    BankImpl bank = new BankImpl( properties );

    if ( System.getSecurityManager() == null ) {
      System.setSecurityManager( new java.rmi.RMISecurityManager() );
    }
    Naming.rebind("ecommerce_example.Bank", bank);
```

The next chunk of code is a work-around for a bug in RMI over SSL. The JVM will shut down your application if you have no other threads running after binding your instance via RMI over SSL. This appears to be a bug in the JSSE v.1.0.2 and earlier. The work-around is simple: create a thread that does nothing but sleep:

```
    while (true) {
      try {
        Thread.sleep(Long.MAX_VALUE);
      } catch (InterruptedException e) {
        e.printStackTrace();
      }
    }
  }

  private static void usage() {
    System.out.println( "Usage: java\t-Djava.security.policy=BankInit.policy" );
    System.out.println( "\t\t-Djavax.net.ssl.trustStore=TRUST_STORE_FILE" );
    System.out.println( "\t\t-Djavax.net.ssl.keyStore=KEY_STORE_FILE" );
    System.out.println( "\t\t-Djavax.net.ssl.keyStorePassword=KEY_STORE_PASSWORD"
);
    System.out.println( "\t\tecommerce_example.BankInit PROPERTIES_FILE" );
  }
}
```

Having worked through the bulk of the code for the middleware we now need to set up some configuration files.

Configuration

As in the last component, the JSSE needs to be installed. We also need to define two files to start up the bank:

❑   `config.properties` – This defines the JDBC configuration and the location of the public key to use to encrypt the credit cards as accounts are created

❑   `BankInit.policy` – This is the `java.policy` file that we'll use to start up the Bank

Let's start with `config.properties`.

config.properties

```
PublicKeyFilename:creditcard.cer
DBUsername:projava
DBPassword:sasquatch
DBUrl:jdbc:secureDriver://databaseMachine/dataSource1
DBDriver:com.isnetworks.crypto.database.SecureDriver
```

You should change the machine name `databaseMachine` to be the name of whatever machine you are using for the database server (so in the case where the database and middleware are on different machines the `DBUrl` becomes `jdbc:secureDriver://database/dataSource1`).

You may also need to change the username and password as appropriate (to be consistent with the second set of usernames and passwords defined for users of the secure driver).

Our policy file is quite simple.

BankInit.policy

We just need to be able to connect to the local machine's RMI registry and to the database proxy. We're going to do a universal grant, and just make sure that the `classpath` is set correctly. If we already knew the location of our class files, we might grant these permissions to just those classes.

```
grant {

  // Allow connections to the JDBC proxy RMI object
  // SETUP: change to IP of the machine running the JDBC proxy

  permission java.net.SocketPermission "192.168.1.146:1024-",
    "connect,resolve";

  // Allow a connection to the local RMI registry to register

  permission java.net.SocketPermission "127.0.0.1:1099", "connect,resolve";

};
```

So, on a multiple machine installation the IP address `192.168.1.146` corresponds to that of the machine `database`, on which the database and secure driver are running.

Collecting the Files

Now we're ready to actually start up the middleware.

If you download the application, you should have the following available – `SecureDriverClient.jar`, `Bank.jar`, and a keystore, truststore, and certificate.

SecureDriverClient.jar

In case you're building this app from scratch, `SecureDriverClient.jar` should contain the following files:

- ❑ com/isnetworks/crypto/rmi/RMISSLClientSocketFactory.class
- ❑ com/isnetworks/crypto/rmi/RMISSLServerSocketFactory.class
- ❑ com/isnetworks/base64/BASE64Decoder$StringWrapper.class
- ❑ com/isnetworks/base64/BASE64Decoder.class
- ❑ com/isnetworks/base64/BASE64Encoder.class
- ❑ com/isnetworks/util/Debug.class
- ❑ com/isnetworks/util/NestedException.class
- ❑ com/isnetworks/util/XMLProperties$PropertyDocumentHandler.class
- ❑ com/isnetworks/util/XMLProperties.class
- ❑ com/isnetworks/crypto/database/ArrayProxy.class
- ❑ com/isnetworks/crypto/database/BlobProxy.class
- ❑ com/isnetworks/crypto/database/CallableStatementProxy.class
- ❑ com/isnetworks/crypto/database/ClassProcessor.class
- ❑ com/isnetworks/crypto/database/ClobProxy.class
- ❑ com/isnetworks/crypto/database/ConnectionProxy.class
- ❑ com/isnetworks/crypto/database/DatabaseMetaDataProxy.class
- ❑ com/isnetworks/crypto/database/PreparedStatementProxy.class
- ❑ com/isnetworks/crypto/database/RefProxy.class
- ❑ com/isnetworks/crypto/database/RemoteSQLException.class
- ❑ com/isnetworks/crypto/database/ResultSetMetaDataProxy.class
- ❑ com/isnetworks/crypto/database/ResultSetProxy.class
- ❑ com/isnetworks/crypto/database/SecureConnectionServer.class
- ❑ com/isnetworks/crypto/database/SecureDriver.class
- ❑ com/isnetworks/crypto/database/SQLDataProxy.class
- ❑ com/isnetworks/crypto/database/SQLInputProxy.class
- ❑ com/isnetworks/crypto/database/SQLOutputProxy.class
- ❑ com/isnetworks/crypto/database/StatementProxy.class
- ❑ com/isnetworks/crypto/database/StructProxy.class
- ❑ com/isnetworks/crypto/database/server/SecureConnectionServerImpl_Stub.class
- ❑ com/isnetworks/remote/Proxy.class
- ❑ com/isnetworks/remote/proxy/AbstractProxy.class
- ❑ com/isnetworks/remote/proxy/OperationProxy.class
- ❑ com/isnetworks/remote/proxy/OperationProxyImpl.class
- ❑ com/isnetworks/remote/proxy/OperationProxyImpl_Stub.class

Bank.jar

Bank.jar should contain:

- ❏ ecommerce_example/bank/BankImpl_Stub.class
- ❏ ecommerce_example/data/Account.class
- ❏ ecommerce_example/data/CreditCard.class
- ❏ ecommerce_example/data/CreditCardDBO.class
- ❏ ecommerce_example/data/RegistrationInformation.class
- ❏ ecommerce_example/bank/DatabaseOperations.class
- ❏ ecommerce_example/bank/BankImpl.class
- ❏ ecommerce_example/bank/BankInit.class
- ❏ ecommerce_example/Bank.class

Associated Data

Place the bank's keystore and truststore into the current working directory. You'll also need the file creditcard.cer that we generated with the keys earlier.

Now we're ready to start the Bank.

Running the Bank

Remember that when BankImpl.java, is compiled we need to run rmic against it to generate the stubs for RMI:

```
C:\> rmic ecommerce_example.bank.BankImpl
```

The bank itself requires two processes: the RMI registry and the bank itself. We can start the RMI registry with:

```
C:\> rmiregistry -J-classpath -JSecureDriverClient.jar
```

Note, if you're already running an RMI registry on the machine (for instance, you're using the same machine for the database and middleware), you don't need to start another instance of the RMI registry.

The bank itself can be started with the following, all on one line:

```
C:\> java -Djava.security.policy=BankInit.policy
        -Djavax.net.ssl.trustStore=bankTrustStore
        -Djavax.net.ssl.keyStore=bankKeyStore
        -Djavax.net.ssl.keyStorePassword=theBank
        -cp Bank.jar;SecureDriverClient.jar ecommerce_example.bank.BankInit
         config.properties
```

Again, please note the need to input the appropriate `keyStorePassword` into this command.

The `Bank` may take a few seconds to start up as the SSL engines are initialized.

This application has been left simple (without lots of error handling) so the crucial areas of code can be inspected easily. Executing the above gives no feedback (and hopefully no error messages) – the middleware merely waits to be used. However if the `mysqladmin` tool is used, a new sleeping connection should be apparent. If a `'Listen failed on port 16547'` message is received, try checking the password that is being used on the middleware side.

Now we're ready to move on to the web server

The Web Server

The web server has two main functions: registration and account viewing. In order to secure these functions, we need to set up SSL client authentication to establish the user's identity before allowing them to register or view their account. We're going to require SSL client authentification to identify users.

The client is authenticated based on who signed their certificate. In our case, we're going to allow anyone to connect to the web server who has a certificate signed by Verisign or Thawte (a free personal certificate can be obtained from http://www.thawte.com/certs/personal/). Then once the client is allowed in, we'll give that client access to an account based on what certificate they actually have.

The servlet 2.2 specification defines an attribute in the `ServletRequest` object that holds the client's certificate: `javax.servlet.request.X509Certificate`. The certificate can be easily accessed from inside a servlet with the following line of code:

```
X509Certificate clientCertificate = (X509Certificate)req.getAttribute
                ("javax.servlet.request.X509Certificate");
```

For this application, we're going to use Tomcat 3.2.1, which supports SSL directly. Other servlet engines could be used, like iPlanet from Sun and Netscape, or WebSphere from IBM.

Our route through this part of the chapter is to:

❑   Build the servlets and JSPs for the web tier

❑   Look at packaging the web application and deploying to Tomcat

❑   Run the application

We'll begin by looking at the design of this tier.

Servlets and JSPs

Here is a diagram of the flow of execution on the web server, with all servlets, JSP, and HTML. The user will enter at `index.html`:

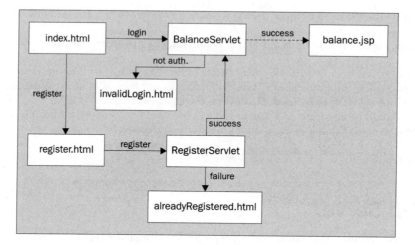

Let's go through each of the components. We'll begin with the HTML, then the servlets, and finally the JSP.

HTML

index.html presents the user with two options:

❑ Register – This will take the user to register.html where accounts can be created. It contains fields for name, credit card number, and opening balance. When the form is submitted, the client will send the data to the RegisterServlet.

❑ Login – This takes users to the BalanceServlet.

The files are quite straightforward:

index.html

```
<html>
  <head>
    <title>Bank Homepage</title>
  </head>

  <body>
    <a href="register.html">Register an account</a><p>
    <a href="balanceServlet">Log in</a>
  </body>
</html>
```

register.html

```
<html>
  <head>
    <title>Register an account</title>
  </head>

  <body>
    <form method="post" action="registerServlet">
      <table cellpadding="4">
```

```
            <tr>
              <td>Name:</td>
              <td><input name="Name" type="text" size="30"></td>
            </tr>
            <tr>
              <td>Credit card number:</td>
              <td><input name="CreditCard" type="text" size="16"></td>
            </tr>
            <tr>
              <td>Current balance:</td>
              <td><input name="Balance" type="text" size="8"></td>
            </tr>
            <tr>
              <td></td>
              <td><input type="Submit" value="Register">
            </tr>
          </table>
        </form>
    </body>
  </html>
```

Those are our main HTML pages. We also make use of two further HTML pages to handle error conditions, invalidLogin.html and alreadyRegistered.html. We're not going to include the contents of those files here. They merely need to contain a message indicating to the user that they were unable to login or create an account and why.

Let's move on to the servlets, which are the actual execution layer in the web server.

Servlets

We have two servlets: RegisterServlet and BalanceServlet. RegisterServlet handles creating accounts, and BalanceServlet loads account information and sends it to a JSP for display.

Both servlets are subclassed from AbstractEcommerceServlet, which will handle the functionality that the two servlets share, like accessing the Bank RMI object and fetching the certificate from the client. AbstractEcommerceServlet has a protected member variable, mBank, which holds a reference to the Bank itself. In the init() method, an RMI connection is established and placed in mBank.

Since we want this application to be configurable without requiring a recompile, we want the location of the bank server to be placed in a configuration file, web.xml (more on that later). The important thing is that once configured, we can pull that bank server name out of the servlet configuration by calling getServletConfig().getInitParameter("BankServerName").

Another method we're going to place in AbstractEcommerceServlet is getCertificate(). This will return the client certificate.

The last method we need to create is getRedirectURL(). Some web servers do not support standard redirects from an SSLed session. They change the protocol from https to http. To deal with this problem, we need to be able to construct an entire URL from the servlet engine including the "https" at the beginning.

Let's have a look at the code for these servlets.

AbstractEcommerceServlet

```
package ecommerce_example.servlet;

import ecommerce_example.*;
import javax.servlet.*;
import javax.servlet.http.*;
import javax.security.cert.*;
import java.util.*;

/**
 * Base class for the RegisterServlet and BalanceServlet.
 * Connects to the RMI bank object and gets certificate
 */

public abstract class AbstractEcommerceServlet extends HttpServlet {
  protected Bank mBank;

  /**
   * Connect to the RMI bank object on startup
   */

  public void init() throws ServletException {
    ServletConfig config = getServletConfig();
    String bankServerName = config.getInitParameter("BankServerName");
    try {
      if ( System.getSecurityManager() == null ) {
        System.setSecurityManager(
          new java.rmi.RMISecurityManager() );
      }
      mBank = (Bank)java.rmi.Naming.lookup( "//" +
        bankServerName + "/ecommerce_example.Bank" );
    }
    catch( Exception e ) {
      e.printStackTrace();
      throw new ServletException( e );
    }
  }

  /**
   * Grab the browser's certificate as an attribute and cast it correctly
   */
  protected X509Certificate getCertificate( HttpServletRequest request ) {
    return (X509Certificate)request.getAttribute(
      "javax.servlet.request.X509Certificate" );
  }

  /**
   * Jakarta doesn't like doing redirects as a non-standard HTTPS, so
   * build the full URL correctly
   */

  protected String getRedirectURL( HttpServletRequest request, String url ) {
    StringBuffer result = new StringBuffer( "https://" );
    result.append( request.getServerName() );
    result.append( ":" );
    result.append( request.getServerPort() );
    result.append( url );

    return result.toString();
  }
}
```

RegisterServlet

Since much of our work is already done by `AbstractEcommerceServlet`, we just need to implement `doGet()` and `doPost()`. We don't want to allow GETs to our registration servlet, as that might expose some credit card data or other sensitive information.

This is an important point, which we should look at in more detail. A GET puts the entire request, including all forms, in the URL when it requests a page. That means that if you're entering your username and password, the URL might look like:

http://sampleserver.com/register?username=jess_garms&password=sasquatch

Most web servers log all requests, so that entire URL will get stored in a log somewhere that you may not want. If you sent the same request using POST, the URL would be:

http://sampleserver.com/register

Only the servlet would see the underlying content. In addition, the content would not be logged to the standard web server log files.

Our `doGet()` method then, will just throw an exception, while `doPost()` will actually register an account. We'll get the user's certificate from our superclass, `AbstractEcommerceServlet`, and then get its serial number. We can then use that serial number to ask the bank if an account exists. If so, we send them to the already-registered page. If they don't have an account, we create an account and send them to the balance servlet so they can view their balance.

```
package ecommerce_example.servlet;

import ecommerce_example.data.*;
import java.io.*;
import javax.servlet.*;
import javax.servlet.http.*;
import javax.security.cert.*;
import java.math.*;

public class RegisterServlet extends AbstractEcommerceServlet {
```

As we mentioned, GET strings are cached and stored as part of the URL, so for security they should not be used for sensitive data.

```
protected void doGet( HttpServletRequest request,
  HttpServletResponse response )
  throws IOException {

  throw new IOException(
    "Connections not allowed over GET for security reasons" );
}
```

Our `post()` method does the real work of registering users.

```
protected void doPost( HttpServletRequest request,
  HttpServletResponse response )
  throws IOException {

  // Grab the browser cert's serial number

  X509Certificate cert = getCertificate( request );
  String serialNumber = cert.getSerialNumber().toString();
```

If the user is already registered, then we want to send them to a page indicating they've already registered:

```
try {
  if ( mBank.getAccount( serialNumber ) != null ) {
    response.sendRedirect(
      getRedirectURL( request,
      "/alreadyRegistered.html" ) );
    return;
  }
```

Otherwise, we can continue and register them:

```
    String name = request.getParameter( "Name" );
    String creditCard = request.getParameter( "CreditCard" );
    float balance = Float.parseFloat(
      request.getParameter( "Balance" ) );
    RegistrationInformation info = new RegistrationInformation(
      name, serialNumber, creditCard, balance );

    Account account = mBank.register( info );

    // Send to the balance page

    response.sendRedirect( getRedirectURL( request,
      "/balanceServlet" ) );
  }
  catch( java.rmi.RemoteException e ) {
    throw new IOException( e.getMessage() );
  }
  catch( java.security.InvalidKeyException e ) {
    throw new IOException( e.getMessage() );
  }
 }
}
```

BalanceServlet

`BalanceServlet` will get a user's balance from the bank and then forward the user to a JSP that will display the balance. Again, we use the client's certificate serial number to get a record from the bank, and then we place an account object into the request. Then the JSP will be able to display the necessary information from that account.

In this servlet, we can use either GET or POST, as no sensitive data is sent in the request.

```
package ecommerce_example.servlet;

import ecommerce_example.data.*;
import java.io.*;
import javax.servlet.*;
import javax.servlet.http.*;
import javax.security.cert.*;
import java.math.*;

/**
  * Gather the correct info to show a customer's balance and forward to
  * the JSP
  */

public class BalanceServlet extends AbstractEcommerceServlet {

  /**
    * Treat GETs and POSTs the same
    */
```

```
protected void doGet( HttpServletRequest request,
  HttpServletResponse response )
  throws IOException, ServletException {

  doPost( request, response );
}

protected void doPost( HttpServletRequest request,
  HttpServletResponse response )
  throws IOException, ServletException {

  // Get the cert's serial number

  X509Certificate cert = getCertificate( request );
  String serialNumber = cert.getSerialNumber().toString();

  try {
    Account account = mBank.getAccount( serialNumber );

    // Check if the user has already registered an account

    if ( account == null ) {
      response.sendRedirect(
        getRedirectURL( request, "/invalidLogin.html" ) );
      return;
    }

    // Forward to the JSP for display

    request.setAttribute( "Account", account );
    request.getRequestDispatcher( "/balance.jsp" ).forward(
      request, response );
  }
  catch( java.rmi.RemoteException e ) {
    e.printStackTrace();
    throw new IOException( e.getMessage() );
  }
}
}
```

We have only one JSP in this system: `balance.jsp`.

balance.JSP

This displays the balance of an account loaded by `BalanceServlet`. There will be an account object in the request that the JSP receives, so it will pull the account ID, the name, and the balance from that account and display each of them. We're going to use `java.text.DecimalFormat` to display the account balance so that it displays the appropriate number of decimal places.

```
<%@ page import="ecommerce_example.data.*, java.text.*" %>
<%
DecimalFormat decimalFormat = new DecimalFormat( "###,###,###.00" );
Account account = (Account)request.getAttribute( "Account" ); %>
<html>
  <head>
    <title>Account Balance</title>
  </head>
```

```
    <body>
      <table cellpadding="4">
        <tr>
          <td>Account id:</td>
          <td><%= account.getAccountID() %></td>
        </tr>
        <tr>
          <td>Customer name:</td>
          <td><%= account.getCustomerName() %></td>
        </tr>
        <tr>
          <td>Current balance:</td>
          <td>$<%= decimalFormat.format( account.getBalance() ) %></td>
        </tr>
      </table>
    </body>
  </html>
```

Packaging the Web Application

How you package your application will vary on different web servers. We're going to provide instructions for Tomcat 3.2.1. If you're using a different web server or servlet engine, you'll need to figure out how to package the app for your particular setup.

So in this section we will show how to:

1. Set the policy file for Tomcat

2. Create our web.xml config file

3. Jar up the servlets, HTML files, and config files, creating a Web Application Archive file (or WAR)

4. Copy the WAR file into the webapps directory of Tomcat

5. Delete the default web applications that ship with Tomcat and replace them with the bank application

6. Enable SSL in Tomcat

7. Add any additional necessary support files, like the keystores and trust stores

8. Edit the startup script to send additional information to RMI on startup

To start with we need to edit the Tomcat policy file.

Policy File for Tomcat

Tomcat 3.2 includes a policy file for use in secure installations. That file is called tomcat.policy, and is stored in Tomcat's conf directory. We're going to edit that policy file to allow our servlets to connect to an RMI server. Overleaf is our policy file:

```
// Additional permissions for tomcat.javac

grant codeBase "file:${java.home}/../lib/-" {
        permission java.security.AllPermission;
};

grant codeBase "file:${java.home}/-" {
        permission java.security.AllPermission;
};

// Tomcat gets all permissions

grant codeBase "file:${tomcat.home}/lib/-" {
        permission java.security.AllPermission;
};

grant codeBase "file:${tomcat.home}/classes/-" {
  permission java.security.AllPermission;
};

// Bankapp webapp policy

grant codeBase "file:${tomcat.home}/webapps/bankapp/-" {

  // Need permission to read the class files

  permission java.io.FilePermission "${tomcat.home}${/}webapps${/}bankapp${/}
                                      WEB-INF${/}classes", "read";
  permission java.io.FilePermission "${tomcat.home}${/}webapps${/}bankapp${/}
                                      WEB-INF${/}classes${/}-", "read";

  // allows servlets to connect to the RMI Bank object
  // SETUP: replace the IP and name with the machine the bank runs on

  permission java.net.SocketPermission "localhost:1024-", "connect,resolve";
  permission java.net.SocketPermission "192.168.1.146:1024-", "connect,resolve";

  // Permissions needed for standard webapps

  permission java.net.SocketPermission "localhost:1024-", "listen";
  permission java.util.PropertyPermission "*", "read";
};
```

You need to change the machine names and the IP addresses to correspond with your installation. So this file is currently configured for the application to run on a single machine with the IP corresponding to the machine itself. In a multiple-machine system this would need to change (the name and IP of the machine running the middleware named bank would have to be used).

If you're using a different web server, it will likely have different requirements for a policy file. You may need to experiment a bit to determine what permissions are necessary for a different web server. The only special permissions you should need to grant to the servlets and JSPs is the ability to talk on the network to the bank object.

Modifying web.xml

Next we need to modify the file `WEB-INF/web.xml`, which contains configuration information for the application. We need to tell Tomcat about the two servlets we have written: `RegisterServlet` and `BalanceServlet`. We need to provide the bank server name to each of the servlets and provide the URL that will execute the servlets.

This configuration is specific to Tomcat, but similar configuration will need to be done if you are using a different servlet engine. Consult your vendor's documentation for instructions on configuring servlets.

```xml
<?xml version="1.0" encoding="ISO-8859-1"?>

<!DOCTYPE web-app
  PUBLIC "-//Sun Microsystems, Inc.//DTD Web Application 2.2//EN"
  "http://java.sun.com/j2ee/dtds/web-app_2.2.dtd">

<web-app>
  <servlet>
    <servlet-name>
      register
    </servlet-name>
    <servlet-class>
      ecommerce_example.servlet.RegisterServlet
    </servlet-class>
  </servlet>
  <servlet>
    <servlet-name>
      balance
    </servlet-name>
    <servlet-class>
      ecommerce_example.servlet.BalanceServlet
    </servlet-class>
  </servlet>

  <servlet-mapping>
    <servlet-name>
      register
    </servlet-name>
    <url-pattern>
      /registerServlet/*
    </url-pattern>
  </servlet-mapping>
  <servlet-mapping>
    <servlet-name>
      balance
    </servlet-name>
    <url-pattern>
      /balanceServlet/*
    </url-pattern>
  </servlet-mapping>
</web-app>
```

Build the WAR file

Tomcat uses WAR (Web Application Archive) files for easily deploying web applications. These are just JAR files with a special structure. We need to place our HTML files, our classes, and our `web.xml` file in specific locations in a JAR file and then we'll be able to easily deploy it in Tomcat.

Start by creating a directory, such as c:\bankApp, to hold our files. Now we need to create a number of subdirectories and copy our files into them so that Tomcat can find them. Our HTML and JSP files should go in the root directory, and our classes and configuration should go into a new directory called WEB-INF. Here is a listing of the files and directories:

- ❑ /alreadyRegistered.html
- ❑ /balance.jsp
- ❑ /index.html
- ❑ /invalidLogin.html
- ❑ /register.html
- ❑ /WEB-INF/
- ❑ /WEB-INF/classes/
- ❑ /WEB-INF/classes/com/
- ❑ /WEB-INF/classes/com/isnetworks/
- ❑ /WEB-INF/classes/com/isnetworks/crypto/
- ❑ /WEB-INF/classes/com/isnetworks/crypto/rmi/
- ❑ /WEB-INF/classes/com/isnetworks/crypto/rmi/RMISSLClientSocketFactory.class
- ❑ /WEB-INF/classes/ecommerce_example/
- ❑ /WEB-INF/classes/ecommerce_example/bank/
- ❑ /WEB-INF/classes/ecommerce_example/bank/BankImpl_Stub.class
- ❑ /WEB-INF/classes/ecommerce_example/Bank.class
- ❑ /WEB-INF/classes/ecommerce_example/data/
- ❑ /WEB-INF/classes/ecommerce_example/data/Account.class
- ❑ /WEB-INF/classes/ecommerce_example/data/CreditCard.class
- ❑ /WEB-INF/classes/ecommerce_example/data/CreditCardDBO.class
- ❑ /WEB-INF/classes/ecommerce_example/data/RegistrationInformation.class
- ❑ /WEB-INF/classes/ecommerce_example/servlet/
- ❑ /WEB-INF/classes/ecommerce_example/servlet/AbstractEcommerceServlet.class
- ❑ /WEB-INF/classes/ecommerce_example/servlet/BalanceServlet.class
- ❑ /WEB-INF/classes/ecommerce_example/servlet/RegisterServlet.class
- ❑ /WEB-INF/web.xml

Now we can create our WAR file by jarring up the contents of our bankApp directory. To do that navigate into that directory and execute the following command, which will create our WAR file:

```
C:\> jar cvf BankApp.war *
```

Copy the WAR File into Tomcat

Tomcat stores its web applications in the directory $TOMCAT_HOME/webapps/. We need to copy our BankApp.war file into that directory.

Delete other Webapps and Add the BankApp

One of the more common mistakes people make when setting up servers is to leave some or all of the default configuration in place. Security holes have been found in a number of sample applications that ship with servers. To avoid this potential problem, we're going to delete the other applications in Tomcat.

Next we're going to delete the other webapps, which are in $TOMCAT_HOME/webapps. Simply delete the directories admin, examples, and test, as well as any .war files in that directory, including ROOT.war. Leave BankApp.war, however, as we're going to be using that.

Finally, we need to remove the configuration information for those apps that no longer exist. Open up the file $TOMCAT_HOME/conf/server.xml and remove the following lines:

```
<Context path="/examples"
         docBase="webapps/examples"
         crossContext="false"
         debug="0"
         reloadable="true" >
</Context>

<Context path="/admin"
         docBase="webapps/admin"
         crossContext="true"
         debug="0"
         reloadable="true"
         trusted="false" >
</Context>
```

Now we're going to add a Context entry for our application, by adding the following lines in place of those others:

```
<Context path="/"
         docBase="webapps/bankapp"
         crossContext="false"
         debug="0"
         reloadable="true"
         trusted="false" >
</Context>
```

This lets Tomcat know that our application should be called for all requests to the root directory of the web server.

Enable SSL

To set up SSL in Tomcat, we need to edit the server.xml file and add the following entry, which will enable SSL on part 8443 and turn on client authentification:

```
<Connector className="org.apache.tomcat.service.PoolTcpConnector">
   <Parameter name="handler"
              value="org.apache.tomcat.service.http.HttpConnectionHandler"/>
   <Parameter name="port" value="8443"/>
   <Parameter name="socketFactory" value="org.apache.tomcat.net.SSLSocketFactory"/>
   <Parameter name="keystore" value="../jakartaKeyStore" />
   <Parameter name="keypass" value="jakarta"/>
   <Parameter name="clientAuth" value="true"/>
</Connector>
```

You'll need to change the keystore location to the location on your machine where you stored the jakartaKeyStore file. We're also turning on client authentication in this code, as it is required by our application. Tomcat uses the keystore as a standard keystore for SSL as well as a trust store.

Note the appropriate password needs to be set for the keystore we created earlier – here we've shown it changed to jakarta.

Now you can start Tomcat and you should be able to connect to the web server using SSL on port 8443. Since client authentication is turned on, you will need to have a certificate installed in your web browser as mentioned earlier in the chapter.

Enable Policy Support

To enable Tomcat's handling of a policy file open server.xml and look for the following lines:

```
<!-- Uncomment out if you have JDK1.2 and want to use policy
<ContextInterceptor
    className="org.apache.tomcat.context.PolicyInterceptor" />
-->
```

Remove the comments, changing those lines to:

```
<ContextInterceptor
    className="org.apache.tomcat.context.PolicyInterceptor" />
```

Add Support File

Next we need the keystore (jakartaKeyStore) in the application root directory (for us, c:>\jakarta).

Edit Web Server Startup Scripts

Now we need to edit the startup script for the web server. We need to add the keystore and truststore to the VM so that our RMI calls will use them for talking to the middleware (the bank). There are two different startup files, one for Windows and one for UNIX. We'll walk through editing each.

Windows

In the directory $TOMCAT_HOME\bin, we need to edit the file tomcat.bat. Look for the following lines:

```
:startSecure
echo Starting Tomcat with a SecurityManager
%_SECSTARTJAVA% %TOMCAT_OPTS% -Djava.security.manager
-Djava.security.policy=="%TOMCAT_HOME%/conf/tomcat.policy"
-Dtomcat.home="%TOMCAT_HOME%" org.apache.tomcat.startup.Tomcat %3 %4 %5 %6 %7 %8
%9
goto cleanup
```

These are the lines that get executed when we start Tomcat with a security manager. We want to add a keystore, the keystore password, and a trust store to our arguments. Change the line starting with %_SECSTARTJAVA% to the following, noting the need to set keyStorePassword, (all on one line):

```
%_SECSTARTJAVA% %TOMCAT_OPTS% -Djavax.net.ssl.keyStore=../jakartaKeyStore
-Djavax.net.ssl.keyStorePassword=jakarta
-Djavax.net.ssl.trustStore=../jakartaKeyStore -Djava.security.manager
-Djava.security.policy=="%TOMCAT_HOME%/conf/tomcat.policy"
-Dtomcat.home="%TOMCAT_HOME%" org.apache.tomcat.startup.Tomcat %3 %4 %5 %6 %7 %8 %9
```

There is another entry under :runSecure. That entry should be changed to match the one we just created.

UNIX

We need to edit the file $TOMCAT_HOME/bin/tomcat.sh. The command that starts the server appears twice, so we'll have to change it twice. Look for this line:

```
    $JAVACMD $TOMCAT_OPTS -Djava.security.manager
-Djava.security.policy==${TOMCAT_HOME}/conf/tomcat.policy -
Dtomcat.home=${TOMCAT_HOME}  org.apache.tomcat.startup.Tomcat "$@" &
```

Change it by adding three -D options for the keystore, the keystore password and the trust store, like so:

```
    $JAVACMD $TOMCAT_OPTS -Djavax.net.ssl.keyStore=../jakartaKeyStore -
Djavax.net.ssl.keyStorePassword=jakarta -
Djavax.net.ssl.trustStore=../jakartaKeyStore -Djava.security.manager -
Djava.security.policy==${TOMCAT_HOME}/conf/tomcat.policy -
Dtomcat.home=${TOMCAT_HOME}  org.apache.tomcat.startup.Tomcat "$@" &
```

Then do the same for the second entry, again note the keyStorePassword setting.

Start the Application

Okay, now we're finally ready to actually execute the application. This needs to be done in a specific order:

1. Start the RMI registry on the database server

2. Start the database driver

3. Start the RMI registry on the bank

4. Start the bank

5. Start the web server

We've detailed how to start all the applications except the web server. You start it just like Tomcat normally, except that we need to pass a -security option.

For Windows:

```
C:\jakarta\bin>startup.bat -security
```

UNIX:

```
C:\> startup.sh -security
```

You should allow up to 30 seconds between starting each of the tiers, as initializing the SSL libraries can take a little while.

Once your application is started, you can open an account by sending a web browser to the web server. If it's running on a machine named bankWebServer, your URL will be https://bankWebServer:8443. You may see some warnings about the certificate that the server is presenting. This is due to the fact that you generated your own certificates earlier. In a production application, you would have a CA sign your web server's certificate to remove those warnings.

When you connect to the web server, you should be asked to select a certificate to use to authenticate your identity. You'll see a dialog box similar to one of the following:

Netscape

Internet Explorer

Click OK or Continue, and if your certificate was signed by a valid authority, you should see the index page, which will allow you to register an account or log in. Note that the authentication was performed using SSL authentication on the web browser.

At this point, you should create an account by registering. The account will be matched to your certificate, so in the future you'll only be able to view it using the same browser. Registration will present the following page:

Registration will then create an account and credit card record in the database. The account record's primary key is the serial number of the certificate used to open the account. The credit card record will be encrypted with a public key, the public key of the credit card client. The web server and bank server are unable to decrypt the credit card, as only the credit card client has the correct private key.

Once you've created an account, you will see your balance. When you return to the site at a later date, you will be able to log in using SSL client authentication and view the balance for that same account.

Credit Card Client

This is the last component in our application. It allows a user to view all of the credit cards in the database, decrypting them with the private key. It's based on the client we wrote in Chapter 10, with a couple of minor modifications.

In this application, rather than set the keystore password on the command line, we're going to ask the user for it. We can't do this without a GUI, as Java doesn't allow us to intercept keystrokes as they are typed on the command line so the password would be visible when the client was run.

Instead, we'll create a Swing component, JPasswordField, that will take care of this for us. Here's what it will look like:

And here's the code:

```
/**
 *  Create a Swing password dialog box and
 *  return the password entered.
 */

private static char[] getPassword() {
```

```
    // dialog is final so that an inner class can access it.

    final JDialog dialog = new JDialog((JFrame)null, "Password", true);

    JLabel passwordLabel = new JLabel("Enter Password:");
    JPasswordField passwordField = new JPasswordField(10);

    dialog.getContentPane().setLayout(new BorderLayout(5, 5));
    dialog.getContentPane().add(passwordLabel, BorderLayout.WEST);
    dialog.getContentPane().add(passwordField, BorderLayout.CENTER);

    // Once someone enters a password, we are done.

    passwordField.addActionListener(new ActionListener() {
      public void actionPerformed(ActionEvent e) {
        dialog.dispose();
          }
    });

    dialog.pack();

    // This next call blocks until someone enters a password.

    dialog.setVisible(true);

    char[] password = passwordField.getPassword();
    return password;
  }
```

The other modification we've made to the client is adding support for RMI, so we can talk to the bank object. This is done via the `CreditCardClient` class:

```
package ecommerce_example.client;

import ecommerce_example.data.*;
import ecommerce_example.*;
import java.io.*;
import java.security.*;
import java.util.*;
import java.rmi.*;
import javax.crypto.*;
import javax.crypto.spec.*;
import javax.swing.*;
import javax.swing.border.*;
import java.awt.*;
import java.awt.event.*;

/**
 * Displays all credit cards in the database,
 * after decrypting them with a private key.
 */

public class CreditCardClient {
```

Our first method is `decryptCreditCardDBO()`. Given an encrypted credit card and a private key, this method will decrypt it and return it as a regular `CreditCard`. This is nearly identical to Chapter 10's `ViewTest`.

```
private static CreditCard decryptCreditCardDBO(
  CreditCardDBO ccdbo, PrivateKey privateKey )
  throws UnsupportedEncodingException, InvalidKeyException {

  String creditCardNumber = null;
  try {

    // Decrypt the encrypted session key.

    Cipher asymmetricCipher = Cipher.getInstance(
      "RSA/ECB/PKCS1Padding" );
    asymmetricCipher.init( Cipher.DECRYPT_MODE, privateKey );
    byte[] sessionKeyBytes = asymmetricCipher.doFinal(
      ccdbo.getEncryptedSessionKey() );

    // Decrypt the credit card number with the session key.

    SecretKey symmetricKey = new SecretKeySpec(
      sessionKeyBytes, "Blowfish" );
    Cipher symmetricCipher = Cipher.getInstance(
      "Blowfish/ECB/PKCS5Padding" );
    symmetricCipher.init( Cipher.DECRYPT_MODE, symmetricKey );
    byte[] ccNumberBytes = symmetricCipher.doFinal(
      ccdbo.getEncryptedCCNumber() );

    creditCardNumber = new String( ccNumberBytes, "UTF8" );

  // Need to catch a large number of possible exceptions:

  }
  catch (NoSuchAlgorithmException nsae) {

    // Missing an algorithm.

    nsae.printStackTrace();
    throw new RuntimeException("Missing crypto algorithm");
  }
  catch (NoSuchPaddingException nspe) {

    // again, we're in trouble. Missing padding.

    nspe.printStackTrace();
    throw new RuntimeException("Missing Crypto algorithm");
  }
  catch (BadPaddingException bpe) {

    // This means the data is probably bad.

    bpe.printStackTrace();
    throw new InvalidKeyException("Could not decrypt");
  }
  catch (IllegalBlockSizeException ibse) {
```

```
      // Probably a bad key.

      ibse.printStackTrace();
      throw new InvalidKeyException("Could not decrypt");
   }

   CreditCard creditCard = new CreditCard(
      ccdbo.getAccountID(), creditCardNumber );
   return creditCard;
}
```

Our `main()` method displays all the credit cards in the database. The first command-line parameter is the filename of the keystore containing the private key. The user will be prompted for the password.

```
public static void main( String[] args ) throws Exception {

   if ( args.length != 1 ) {
      usage();
      System.exit( 1 );
   }

   // Load the keystore to retrieve the private key.

   String ksType = KeyStore.getDefaultType();
   KeyStore ks = KeyStore.getInstance( ksType );
   FileInputStream fis = new FileInputStream( args[ 0 ] );

   char[] password = getPassword();
   ks.load( fis, password );
   fis.close();

   // Pull the default key from the keystore, which will have the alias "mykey".

   PrivateKey privateKey = (PrivateKey)ks.getKey( "mykey", password );

   // In order for our SSL sockets to use the keystore, we need
   // the password set.

   System.setProperty("javax.net.ssl.keyStorePassword",
      new String(password));

   System.out.println("\nGetting the credit cards...\n");

   Bank bank = (Bank)Naming.lookup( "ecommerce_example.Bank" );

   // Get all the credit card account ids

   long ids[] = bank.getAllCreditCardAccountIDs();

   // Decrypt all credit cards, then display them

   for( int i = 0; i < ids.length; i++ ) {
      CreditCardDBO ccdbo = bank.getCreditCardDBO( ids[ i ] );
      CreditCard creditCard = decryptCreditCardDBO( ccdbo, privateKey );
      System.out.println( "\nAccount ID: " + creditCard.getAccountID() );
      System.out.println( "CC Number: " +
         creditCard.getCreditCardNumber() );
   }

   // Need to manually exit, as the awt event thread would run forever.

   System.exit(0);
}
```

Finally, we have the code for displaying the Swing password dialog box and getting a password from the user.

```
private static char[] getPassword() {

    // dialog is final so that an inner class can access it.

    final JDialog dialog = new JDialog((JFrame)null, "Password", true);

    JLabel passwordLabel = new JLabel("Enter Password:");
    JPasswordField passwordField = new JPasswordField(10);

    dialog.getContentPane().setLayout(new BorderLayout(5, 5));
    dialog.getContentPane().add(passwordLabel, BorderLayout.WEST);
    dialog.getContentPane().add(passwordField, BorderLayout.CENTER);

    // Once someone enters a password, we are done.

    passwordField.addActionListener(new ActionListener() {
      public void actionPerformed(ActionEvent e) {
        dialog.dispose();
            }
    });

    dialog.pack();

    // This next call blocks until someone enters a password.

    dialog.setVisible(true);

    char[] password = passwordField.getPassword();
    return password;
}
```

```
private static void usage() {
    System.out.println(
      "Usage: java\t-Djava.security.policy=CreditCardClient.policy" );
    System.out.println(
      "\t\t-Djavax.net.ssl.trustStore=TRUST_STORE_FILE" );
    System.out.println( "\t\t-Djavax.net.ssl.keyStore=KEY_STORE_FILE" );
    System.out.println(
      "\t\t-Djavax.net.ssl.keyStorePassword=KEY_STORE_PASSWORD" );
    System.out.println( "\t\tecommerce_example.client.CreditCardClient" );
    System.out.println( "\t\tPRIVATE_KEY_KEYSTORE_FILE" );
  }
}
```

Credit Card Client Policy File

As in the other components, we need a policy file for the credit card client. We need permission to talk on the network to the bank server. This requires two permission entries in our policy file, one for the network connection and one to resolve the hostname.

Here's CreditCardClient.policy:

```
grant {

    // Permission to connect to the RMI server.
    // SETUP: Replace the IP address with the bank's IP.

    permission java.net.SocketPermission "127.0.0.1:1024-",
        "connect,resolve";

    // SETUP: Replace the name with the name of the bank server.

    permission java.net.SocketPermission "localhost", "resolve";
};
```

You should edit the policy file for your environment by changing the IP address and the hostname above. So in a multiple machine installation the first permission will need the IP address changed to 192.168.0.151; the IP of bank, which was running the middleware.

Packaging the Credit Card Client

You should create a JAR file, CreditCardClient.jar, with the following files in it:

- ❑ ecommerce_example/Bank.class
- ❑ ecommerce_example/bank/BankImpl_Stub.class
- ❑ ecommerce_example/client/CreditCardClient.class
- ❑ ecommerce_example/client/CreditCardClient$1.class
- ❑ ecommerce_example/data/RegistrationInformation.class
- ❑ ecommerce_example/data/Account.class
- ❑ ecommerce_example/data/CreditCard.class
- ❑ ecommerce_example/data/CreditCardDBO.class
- ❑ com/isnetworks/crypto/rmi/RMISSLClientSocketFactory.class

Create a directory for the credit card client, and place the following files in it:

- ❑ CreditCardClient.jar
- ❑ CreditCard.policy
- ❑ creditcardKeyStore
- ❑ creditcardTrustStore

Running the Credit Card Client

Make sure that the database driver and the bank object are running, and you can start the credit card client with the following command (as with all of the code in this chapter, you must have a JCE and the JSSE installed):

```
C:\> java -Djava.security.policy=CreditCardClient.policy
          -Djavax.net.ssl.trustStore=creditcardTrustStore
          -Djavax.net.ssl.keyStore=creditcardKeyStore -cp CreditCardClient.jar
           ecommerce_example.client.CreditCardClient creditcardKeyStore
```

The password dialog box will come up, and you'll need to enter your keystore password. The default example password we chose earlier in the chapter was `creditcard`. Once you enter your password, the application will connect to the bank server and should return the credit card numbers, like so:

```
Account ID: 1
CC Number: 1234 5678 9012 3456

Account ID: 2
CC Number: 8801 2208 0826 4432

Account ID: 3
CC Number: 5843 9548 0958 4098
```

Possible Modifications

In this chapter, we've presented an outline for an application that has security as one of its design goals. In creating the application, we made certain choices about how secure we needed to be, by doing things like using SSL for all network connections and encrypting the credit cards in the database. We made these choices based on a business scenario that we invented.

If you have different requirements, you might change a number of the particulars in our application design. Let's go over a few of the modifications that you might make:

Logging

Logging could definitely be improved. We could add logging to the bank and to the database, as well as improve logging on the web server by saving the certificate that was used for each request.

Using SSL

Using SSL slows down our application. You can watch the processor get pegged when each component starts up and the SSL libraries are loaded and initialized. It would be nice if we could have gotten by without it, and sometimes that's possible. If we were on a secure private network for instance, we might have felt comfortable leaving the RMI connections in the clear. These include the communication between the middleware and the database, and between the web server and the middleware.

Securing the network is not a job for Java. Instead it requires a good network administrator and the judicious use of firewalls and routers.

Note that if you are sending sensitive data between the web browser and web server, you're still going to need to use SSL for that particular connection if it takes place over the Internet.

Web Browser Authentication

SSL web browser client authentication can be confusing for some customers. Certificate management isn't yet as straightforward as we would like it to be. Most online services, including banks, simply use username-password authentication, and they consider it sufficient.

If you do decide to use username-password authentication in place of SSL client authentification, the important thing to remember is not to store passwords in the clear on the server. The best solution is to hash them with a salt and store the salt and resulting hash. There are examples in Chapter 6 of hashing passwords and using them for authentication later.

If you need to be able to retrieve the original password for use in the future, you should encrypt it in the database, rather than hash it.

The Database

If you're not storing sensitive data like credit card numbers or passwords, you may not need to encrypt any of the data in the database. Alternatively, you may be storing more sensitive information, like electronic medical records, and may need to encrypt *more* information than we did.

Also, if you no longer need sensitive information you've been storing, it should be deleted. For instance, a user's credit card is not really necessary after they've had an account open for six months or so. It should be deleted, so that if someone were to compromise the database, the number of compromised cards would be reduced.

Encrypting SSL keys

Our SSL keys were weakly protected with the standard JDK keystore implementation. You may find that you want to protect those keys with a stronger keystore, like the one that comes with Sun's JCE, JCEKS. There are additional keystores available as well, from alternative providers like Bouncy Castle (http://www.bouncycastle.org). Additionally, you could use Smart Cards to store your keys, or a hardware-based key storage device.

Summary

Good application security involves balancing security with usability. It's important for your applications to be secure, but if users are frustrated by it, they may not be users for long.

In our application, SSL encryption is fairly unobtrusive, and shouldn't affect the user experience adversely. Indeed, savvy users would expect that their bank would use SSL to protect their account information on the wire.

On the other hand, depending on your application, SSL authentication may not be ideal, as we mentioned. It adds a great deal of security, at the expense of possible customer problems. You'll have to decide if it's worth it for you.

No application is completely secure, but you can guard against the most probable attacks. The key is to focus on your most valuable resources and make security as transparent for the users as possible.

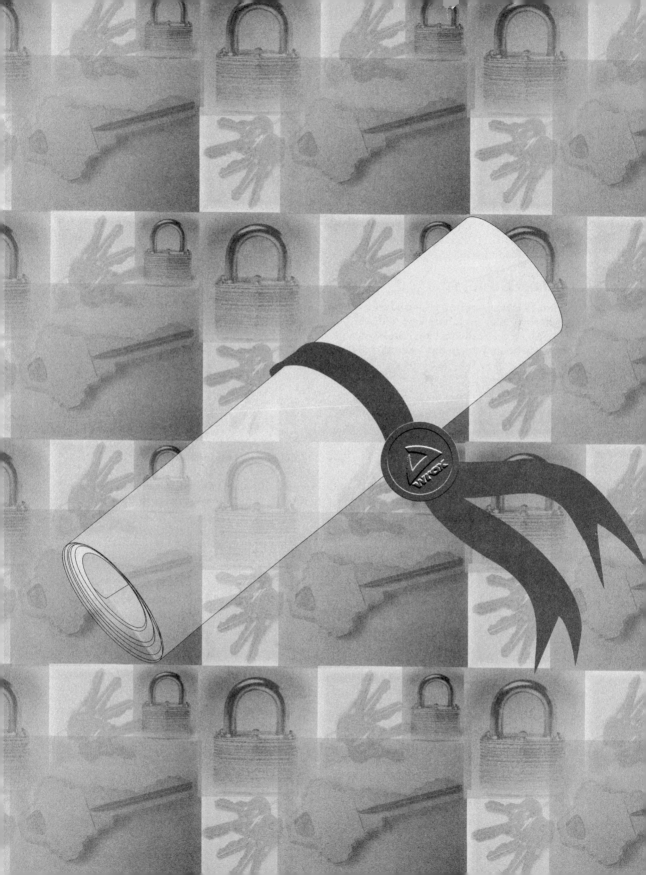

Implementing Your Own Provider

In this chapter we're going to implement our own cryptographic service provider, using Sun's Java Cryptography Architecture (JCA) and Java Cryptography Extension (JCE). As we discussed in Chapter 3, a cryptographic service provider adds support to Java for one or more cryptographic algorithms, like RSA digital signatures or DES encryption. As we already know, there are a number of providers out there already, like Bouncy Castle's or RSA's, but there are a couple of reasons you might want to write your own:

❑ You need an algorithm that isn't currently available in most JCEs, like Elliptic Curve or 256-bit Rijndael

❑ You need to be able to modify and/or redistribute the provider, and you can't find one that has the right license and cost

❑ You just want to learn how to do it

We're writing our provider in this chapter for the third reason. There are other providers out there that have support for the algorithms we're going to use, but it's interesting to see exactly how they work by investigating them in detail.

Our provider will implement the RSA algorithm for a cipher and a signature. This is one of the algorithms that Sun does not provide in its JCE, although the 1.3 version of the JDK does provide RSA *signature* support. It is likely that Sun will support RSA ciphers in future versions of the JCE, and perhaps even the JDK itself, now that export restrictions in the United States are eased.

This is a pretty heavy-duty chapter, as we'll be discussing the mechanism of the RSA algorithm as well as showing detailed code, so this is how we'll break the topic down by looking at:

❑   The requirements for developing a cryptographic provider

❑   A further look at the architecture of the JCE

❑   The mathematics behind the RSA algorithm

❑   Java support for RSA

❑   Implementing RSA encryption

❑   Implementing RSA signatures

❑   Some limitations of the approach we've taken

So, let's look at what we'll need when we want to develop a provider.

Provider Requirements

In order to write and run your provider, you will need an implementation of the JCE itself, specifically three packages: `javax.crypto`, `javax.crypto.interfaces`, and `javax.crypto.spec`. In order to get these classes, you could use Sun's JCE v1.2.0, or a clean-room implementation of the JCE framework such as Bouncy Castle (http://www.bouncycastle.org), or Virtual Unlimited (http://www.virtualunlimited.com). If you're outside the United States, you'll probably be unable to download Sun's JCE 1.2.0, and will need to use one of the other providers. You don't technically need an entire provider, just those classes for the JCE framework itself.

Sun's JCE 1.2.1 adds an interesting requirement to a cryptographic provider: they must be approved by Sun and digitally signed. As we've mentioned previously, this is a bad idea, and should be avoided, although we consider the subject further below. By requiring that all providers be signed, Sun is limiting the choice of cryptographic services. Instead, it is better to use one of the clean-room implementations, which will not require Sun's approval. Sun has added this signing requirement to their JCE in order to be able to export it. Unfortunately, the signing requirement makes the JCE unusable in most situations. For instance, there are no readily available RSA encryption providers that function with Sun's JCE 1.2.1. Sun's JCE also places restrictions on what algorithms and key strengths can be used.

Install the JARs for the JCE that you wish to use in `$JAVA_HOME/jre/lib/ext`. This will allow the classes that we are writing to see the `javax.crypto` classes.

Getting Your Provider Signed

Our provider won't work with Sun's JCE 1.2.1 due to the fact that Sun requires all encryption providers be signed by Sun. Sun provides a procedure for getting your provider signed in the downloadable JCE documentation (http://java.sun.com/products/jce). The instructions are in the file `doc/guide/HowToImplAProvider.html`.

We attempted to get our provider signed while writing this book and unfortunately had little success. Our experience indicates that, if you find yourself in a situation requiring a signed provider, you should allow plenty of time for the process. Our experience is that at least four to six months may be required, as you'll need to deal with Sun and the U.S. Bureau of Export Control. Other cryptographic providers don't appear to be keen on this route since, at the time of writing, we are unaware of any other signed providers; even RSA Security's provider will not work with Sun's JCE 1.2.1.

Sun may be forcing provider signing with JDK 1.4. If this is the case, then alternative cryptographic providers will likely change their package naming structure to something that doesn't conflict with Sun's. Perhaps `xjava.crypto` will become the new standard for alternative providers.

How the JCE Works

The JCE presents an interface to the world for using cryptographic algorithms. Behind the scenes, it allows many different possible implementations of those algorithms, from different providers. You could have, for instance, a pure-Java provider for most of your algorithms and a native driver for a smart-card or **Hardware Security Manager** (**HSM**) for specific algorithms.

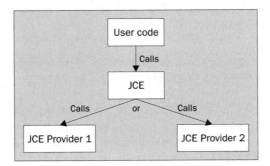

The user code need not be aware of the existence of any of the providers, just the `javax.crypto` classes. The JCE then delegates all requests for cryptographic functions to those provider classes. This requires configuration of the VM. This can be done by modifying the `java.security` file, by passing in parameters to the VM on startup or by adding providers programmatically in your code.

The `javax.crypto` classes, then, provide a framework for those cryptographic functions. By extending the abstract classes called **Service Provider Interfaces** (**SPI**), vendors can create implementations of various algorithms. We will provide an implementation of the RSA algorithm by extending `javax.crypto.CipherSpi` and `java.security.SignatureSpi`. These abstract classes provide a framework for cipher and signature operations. If we implement each method, then any classes that use the JCA or the JCE can use our underlying implementation.

Here is a diagram showing the relation of the `Signature` and `SignatureSPI` classes to a provider's implementation of a digital signature algorithm:

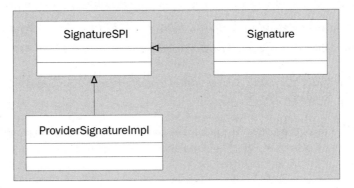

`SignatureSPI` and `Signature` are both abstract classes, with `Signature` subclassing `SignatureSPI`. Our provider must extend `SignatureSPI` in a new, concrete class that will perform the actual cryptographic functions.

The cipher architecture is similar but not identical:

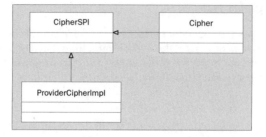

There is an abstract class, `CipherSPI`, that we must subclass in our implementation. The `Cipher` class contains a reference to an instance of `CipherSPI`, which will be our provider's implementation.

Before we start implementing our provider, we need to discuss the cryptography involved.

The RSA Algorithm

RSA is an acronym for the three men who invented the RSA cryptosystem in 1977: Ron Rivest, Adi Shamir, and Leonard Adleman. It was the first public-key encryption algorithm, and is widely considered the best to date. RSA is used in various cryptographic protocols such as SSL and S/MIME. It is an asymmetric cipher, utilizing two different keys, the public and the private, to perform encryption and decryption. It can also be used as a signature algorithm.

RSA is based on arithmetic with very large positive integers. Fortunately for us, Java provides us with an easy way to handle arbitrarily large integers, the class `java.math.BigInteger`. All information that will be transformed with RSA must be in the form of a number. We'll discuss the best way for transforming generic data to numbers a bit later. For now, we'll just investigate the mathematics behind RSA.

If you wish to learn more about RSA, the following resources are all recommended, and have provided the basis for the background information presented here:

❑ RSA Laboratories' PKCS#1 documentation (http://www.rsalabs.com/pkcs/pkcs-1/)

❑ Bruce Schneier's *Applied Cryptography, ISBN 0-471117-09-9, John Wiley and Sons*

❑ William Stallings's *Cryptography and Network Security, ISBN 0-13869-017-0, Prentice Hall*

> *Just for the record, RSA likes its PKCS documentation to be referred to as* 'RSA Security Inc. Public-Key Cryptography Standards (PKCS) ''.

RSA keys are each a set of two values. The public key contains a modulus, n, and a public exponent, e. The corresponding private key has that same modulus plus a private exponent, d.

n, e, and d are all large, non-negative integers, and have some interesting properties, which we will get to a bit later. Keys are often written like this:

> **RSA Public and Private keys: Public key = {n,e} Private key = {n,d}**

Encryption and decryption are very similar. If M is the message to be encrypted, then the ciphertext C can be created with a simple formula: $C = M^e \bmod n$. Decryption is nearly identical, but uses the private exponent: $M = C^d \bmod n$. Since taking the modulus of a number is a one-way transformation, it is very difficult to undo encryption without knowing the private key.

> **RSA Encryption and Decryption:**
>
> **Encryption: $C = M^e \bmod n$**
>
> **Decryption: $M = C^d \bmod n$.**
>
> **M is the message and C is the corresponding ciphertext.**

We'll go over an example of encryption and decryption shortly, but first we need to show how to generate the numbers used by our keys.

Generating Key Pairs

In order to use the RSA algorithm, however, we must have a key pair that fulfils certain mathematical requirements. Here's how to do it:

1. Generate two prime number, p and q.

2. Multiply p by q to get n, the modulus.

3. Multiply (p-1) by (q-1) to get ϕ(n).

4. Pick a number, e, less than ϕ(n) and relatively prime to ϕ(n) (that is, they have no factors in common besides 1).

5. Calculate a number, $d = e^{-1} \bmod \phi$(n). That is, calculate a number, d, that satisfies the formula $de = 1 \bmod \phi$(n).

6. The public key is {n,e} and the private key is {n,d}.

> **RSA Key Generation:**
>
> **p and q are prime numbers**
> **n = pq**
> **ϕ(n) = (p-1)(q-1)**
> **e is relatively prime to ϕ(n)**
> **$de = 1 \bmod \phi$(n), $d = e^{-1} \bmod \phi$(n)**
>
> **Public key = {n,e}**
> **Private key = {n,d}**

Simple RSA Encryption Example

Let's go through an example of creating a key pair and then encrypting and decrypting some information.

1. Select two prime numbers, p and q. p = 7 and q = 13.

2. n = p * q = 7 * 13 = 91.

3. $\phi(n) = (p-1)(q-1) = 6*12 = 72$.

4. Select e, less than ϕ (n) and relatively prime to it. We'll choose e = 5.

5. $d = e^{-1} \mod \phi (n) = 29$.

6. Public key = {n,e} = {91,5}. Private key = {n,d} = {91,29}.

Now we have our public and private keys, so let's try to encrypt and decrypt some data, using the formula for RSA that we mentioned earlier. As we mentioned, all operations are performed on numbers, so let's pick a number less than n that we will use for the message, 42:

M = 42
$C = M^e \mod n = 42^5 \mod 91 = 130691232 \mod 91 = 35$.
C = 35

So with the public key {91,5} 42 is encrypted to 35. Let's try decrypting 35:

C = 35
$M = C^d \mod n = 35^{29} \mod 91 = 5.9975...x10^{44} \mod 91 = 42$

An encrypted message of 35 then, is decrypted to 42, our original message. It's interesting to note that e and d could be interchanged. They function equivalently: what one encrypts, the other decrypts, and vice-versa.

The strength of RSA is based on the difficulty of factoring n. So far, that has proven to be computationally infeasible for a large enough n (1024 bits or greater). It seems unlikely that factoring numbers of this size will be possible with traditional computing techniques. Quantum computing, however, suggests that factoring might become easy with large-scale quantum computers. At present though, quantum computers of that size are purely theoretical.

There's no need to worry about the vulnerability of RSA to factoring, unless you need to encrypt data for a very long time, say, greater than 20 years. If you need to keep data secret that long, you could use large keys (2048 bits or greater), or use a different cryptosystem, like elliptic curve. Elliptic curve cryptography is outside the scope of this book, but if you're interested in learning more about it, you can take a look at the FAQ (http://cryptoman.com/elliptic.htm).

RSA in Java

Java 2 has some minor built-in support for RSA. The package `java.security.interfaces` contains three interfaces that define RSA keys: `RSAPublicKey`, `RSAPrivateKey`, and `RSAPrivateCrtKey`. JDK 1.3 adds one more, `RSAKey`, a superinterface to all three. JDK 1.2 has no other support for RSA built in. JDK 1.3, on the other hand, comes with a provider written by RSA Security that provides RSA key generation, and digital signatures using the RSA algorithm.

Our provider will allow for key generation, encryption, decryption, and signing and verification of signatures. However, we will not be including support for ASN.1 encoding or decoding of RSA public and private keys. If you need that feature, we recommend JDK 1.3, which includes exactly that. Our provider can be combined with the provider in JDK 1.3, adding encryption and decryption to the already existent key generation, signature algorithms, and key encoding and decoding functions.

We will be using the class `java.math.BigInteger` for most of our operations. We will need to be able to convert from byte arrays to `BigInteger`s and back. We can construct a positive `BigInteger` from an arbitrary byte array with a `BigInteger` constructor: `new BigInteger(1,byteArray)`. Converting from a `BigInteger` to a byte array is a little trickier, as we will need to get back precisely what we put into it. `BigInteger` is signed, so we get a leading zero if we convert a positive number into a byte array. To get around this, we'll write a convenience method for converting `BigInteger`s to byte arrays that will return a byte array of a requested size from a `BigInteger`. If information would be lost from doing this – that is, the number is too big to fit in the requested size, an exception will be thrown.

We're going to hold off a bit on actually writing this utility method, until we know a little bit more about our overall architecture.

RSA Encryption Implementation

RSA Labs' PKCS #1 documentation (http://www.rsalabs.com/pkcs/pkcs-1/) describes, in detail, how to use the RSA algorithm. At the time of this writing, version 2.0 was the latest finished spec, and 2.1 was in draft. v2.0 defines encryption with two types of padding: OAEP (which stands for Optimal Asymmetric Encryption Padding) and PKCS1 (Public Key Cryptography Standard 1). We'll discuss those padding types in detail when we get to implementation. PKCS#1 also defines some cryptographic primitives, and utility methods for performing encryption and decryption. Their architecture is fairly simple and procedural. Let's go over the steps for encryption and decryption:

Encryption

Starting with a message M in the form of a byte array and a public key:

- ❑ Pad M using PKCS1 padding or OAEP padding, creating EM.
- ❑ Convert EM to an integer, m.
- ❑ Perform RSA encryption on m using the public key: $m^e \bmod n$, resulting in c.
- ❑ Convert c, a large number, to C, a byte array.
- ❑ Output C.

Decryption

Starting with an encrypted message C and a private key:

- ❑ Convert C to a large number, c.
- ❑ Perform RSA decryption on c using the private key: $m^d \bmod n$, resulting in m.
- ❑ Convert m to EM, a byte array.
- ❑ Un-pad EM using the method used for encryption, either PKCS1 or OAEP, producing M.
- ❑ Output M.

We need to define several distinct ideas in our provider:

- **Keys** – an implementation of RSA keys, both public and private. We will extend the classes in `java.security.interfaces`, `RSAPublicKey`, `RSAPrivateKey`, and `RSAPrivateCrtKey`.

- **Primitives** – the RSA algorithm operations, encryption and decryption, as well as simple conversion operations. We will write two utility classes, `RSA` and `Util`.

- **Paddings** – OAEP and PKCS#1 padding. We will write a padding interface, `Padding`, and two implementations, `OAEPPadding` and `PKCS1Padding`.

- **Cipher** – extension of `javax.crypto.CipherSpi`, invokes the padding and primitives to perform encryption or decryption.

Below is a diagram of the architecture we will be using to implement our cipher:

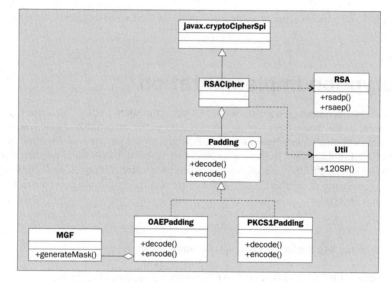

The key implementation and the key generator are not detailed, as they are called as interfaces from within all the objects above.

Let's now work through the different topics we've just mentioned.

Keys

Let's begin by creating implementations for our RSA keys. In the package `java.security.interfaces`, there are three interfaces that we need to implement: `RSAPublicKey`, `RSAPrivateKey`, and `RSAPrivateCrtKey`. The public and private keys we've discussed a bit, but we haven't mentioned a CRT key. CRT stands for **Chinese Remainder Theorem**, which is a way of speeding up RSA calculations using private keys if more information is available. CRT keys have some extra information gleaned from the original numbers p and q used to compute n and d. We're not going to go into the details of the mathematics of the Chinese Remainder Theorem, but if you're interested it's described in a number of cryptography books, including *Applied Cryptography* by Bruce Schneier, *ISBN 0-471117-09-9, John Wiley and Sons*. We'll take a brief look at each of these keys in order before taking a look at key generation itself.

RSAPublicKey

First we'll write our implementation of a public key, RSAPublicKeyImpl. It's a very straightforward class, containing two instance variables for e, the public exponent and n, the modulus. The constructor is protected, insuring that it can only be called from within its package.

There is one feature in our keys that we won't be implementing: key encoding. Our getEncoded() method should return an X.509-encoded representation of our public key. This would require a rather substantial amount of work, and doesn't really help us understand how a provider works in Java. So we're going to drop the feature and return NULL for our encoding. The getFormat() method should return the type of encoding our key uses. As we don't encode, we'll return the string "NONE".

Fortunately for us, JDK 1.3 includes implementations of RSA keys and encodings, which can be used with the rest of our provider. You don't need to do anything special to use the JDK 1.3 keys, as they are used by default.

```java
package com.isnetworks.crypto.rsa;

import java.math.BigInteger;
import java.security.*;
import java.security.interfaces.*;

// RSAPublicKeyImpl.java

public class RSAPublicKeyImpl implements RSAPublicKey {

  // The modulus, n

  private BigInteger mModulus;

  // The public exponent, e

  private BigInteger mPublicExponent;

  protected RSAPublicKeyImpl (BigInteger modulus, BigInteger publicExponent) {
    mModulus = modulus;
    mPublicExponent = publicExponent;
  }

  public BigInteger getModulus() {
    return mModulus;
  }

  public BigInteger getPublicExponent() {
    return mPublicExponent;
  }

  public String getAlgorithm() {
    return "RSA";
  }

  public String getFormat() {
    return "NONE";
  }

  public byte[] getEncoded() {
    return NULL;
  }
}
```

RSAPrivateKey

The implementation of a private key is nearly identical, except that rather than store the public exponent e, we store the private one, d. Again, we do not support encodings.

```java
package com.isnetworks.crypto.rsa;

import java.math.BigInteger;
import java.security.*;
import java.security.interfaces.*;

// RSAPrivateKeyImpl.java

public class RSAPrivateKeyImpl implements RSAPrivateKey {

  // The modulus

  private BigInteger mModulus;  // n

  // The private exponent

  private BigInteger mPrivateExponent;  // d

  protected RSAPrivateKeyImpl (BigInteger modulus, BigInteger privateExponent) {
    mModulus = modulus;
    mPrivateExponent = privateExponent;
  }

  public BigInteger getModulus() {
    return mModulus;
  }

  public BigInteger getPrivateExponent() {
    return mPrivateExponent;
  }

  public String getAlgorithm() {
    return "RSA";
  }

  public String getFormat() {
    return "NONE";
  }

  public byte[] getEncoded() {
    return NULL;
  }
}
```

RSAPrivateCrtKey

As we mentioned earlier, a CRT private key contains the same information as a regular private key, with some additional information that allows computation to be speeded up.

When generating an RSA private key, the original prime numbers p and q can be used to compute three extra variables: the prime exponent P, dP; the prime exponent Q, dQ; and the CRT coefficient, qInv.

```
dP = d mod (p-1)
dQ = d mod (q-1)
qInv = q⁻¹ mod p
```

If we have dP, dQ, and qInv available to us when performing decryption, the process is much faster. We'll go over the algorithm changes when we get to our encryption implementation.

Our CRT private key class will extend our RSAPrivateKeyImpl class, as all of its properties are duplicated.

```java
package com.isnetworks.crypto.rsa;

import java.math.BigInteger;
import java.security.*;
import java.security.interfaces.*;

// RSAPrivateCrtKeyImpl.java

public class RSAPrivateCrtKeyImpl extends RSAPrivateKeyImpl {

  private BigInteger mPublicExponent;  // e
  private BigInteger mPrimeP;          // p
  private BigInteger mPrimeQ;          // q
  private BigInteger mPrimeExponentP;  // d mod (p-1), dP
  private BigInteger mPrimeExponentQ;  // d mod (q-1), dQ
  private BigInteger mCrtCoefficient;  // (q^-1) mod p, qInv

  /**
   *  Constructor
   *
   *  Given n, d, e, p, and q, compute dP, dQ, and qInv.
   */
  protected RSAPrivateCrtKeyImpl (
    BigInteger modulus,
    BigInteger privateExponent,
    BigInteger publicExponent,
    BigInteger primeP,
    BigInteger primeQ) {

    super(modulus,privateExponent);

    mPublicExponent = publicExponent;
    mPrimeP = primeP;
    mPrimeQ = primeQ;

    mPrimeExponentP = super.getPrivateExponent().mod(
      mPrimeP.subtract(BigInteger.ONE));
    mPrimeExponentQ = super.getPrivateExponent().mod(
      mPrimeQ.subtract(BigInteger.ONE));
    mCrtCoefficient = mPrimeQ.modInverse(mPrimeP);
  }

  public BigInteger getPublicExponent() {
    return mPublicExponent;
  }
```

```
    public BigInteger getPrimeP() {
      return mPrimeP;
    }

    public BigInteger getPrimeQ() {
      return mPrimeQ;
    }

    public BigInteger getPrimeExponentP() {
      return mPrimeExponentP;
    }

    public BigInteger getPrimeExponentQ() {
      return mPrimeExponentQ;
    }

    public BigInteger getCrtCoefficient() {
      return mCrtCoefficient;
    }
  }
```

Key Generation

Now that we have implementations for all our interfaces, we need to actually create some keys. To do that, we will extend the abstract class java.security.KeyPairGeneratorSpi, which establishes the service provider interface for key pair generation. By extending that class, we allow KeyPairGenerator to use the services that we provide in a clean manner, without requiring users to reference any of our code directly.

Here are the steps we will use to generate a key pair:

1. Let k be the length of the keys requested. This will be the size of the modulus.

2. Calculate the length we want for p and q, each half the length of k.

3. Generate prime numbers p and q, given the size we determined.

4. Test that neither p-1 nor q-1 are relatively prime to the public exponent e. If they have any factors larger than 1 in common (that is, they are relatively prime), regenerate them.

5. Calculate n, the product of p and q. If the length of n is not equal to k, then regenerate p and q.

Note that we may need to create quite a number of p's and q's before we will have numbers that satisfy the requirements in steps 4 and 5.

Generating Primes

There is no known way to quickly generate large numbers that are guaranteed to be prime. Instead, BigInteger generates numbers that are *likely* to be prime, and then tests whether or not they are prime to a degree of certainty as specified by the call to BigInteger. The constructor looks like this:

```
BigInteger(int bitLength, int certainty, Random rnd)
```

The chance that the number is not prime is $1/2^{certainty}$. This allows us to achieve a very high level of confidence in the prime numbers by specifying a large certainty. We will use 85, giving us only a $1/2^{85}$ chance of a non-prime number. You can increase this value if you'd like to have even more confidence in your prime numbers, but be aware that it will increase the amount of time it takes to generate a key.

The Public Exponent

The public exponent is chosen, rather than generated. Certain values of e, in fact, can accelerate the encryption process because fewer exponentiations are required. 65537 fits the bill perfectly, as its binary representation is 10000000000000001, meaning that only 17 multiplications are required to exponentiate it. 65537 is also recommended by the X.509 spec for the value of e. We will, therefore, use 65537 as our chosen value of e.

Once e is chosen, computing the other values is straightforward, because `BigInteger` provides all the mathematical functions we need.

```
package com.isnetworks.crypto.rsa;

import java.security.*;
import java.math.BigInteger;

/**
 *   RSAKeyPairGenerator.java
 *
 *   Generates RSA keys of arbitrary size.
 */

public final class RSAKeyPairGenerator extends KeyPairGeneratorSpi {
```

We need to define some constants for our generator: our default e value, our certainty and the default strength of our keys. We've discussed why we chose 65537 for e. We'll use a certainty of 85, which provides us with a very high likelihood of generating a prime number, as the probability of primality is $1 - 1/2^{certainty}$. Finally we'll define our default key length to be 1024 bits:

```
private static final BigInteger E = BigInteger.valueOf(65537);

private static final int CERTAINTY = 85;

private static final int DEFAULT_STRENGTH = 1024;

private int mKeysize;
private SecureRandom mSecureRandom;
private BigInteger mPublicExponent;
private boolean mInitialized = false;
```

We'll create a default constructor:

```
public RSAKeyPairGenerator() {
    super();
}
```

Our `initialize()` method takes the key size and a random number generator:

```
public void initialize(int keysize, SecureRandom random) {
  mKeysize = keysize;
  mSecureRandom = random;
  mInitialized = true;
}
```

Now let's write the interesting part: the `generateKeyPair()` method. If we haven't been initialized, we call `initialize()` with our default values:

```
public KeyPair generateKeyPair() {
  if (!mInitialized) {
    initialize(DEFAULT_STRENGTH, new SecureRandom());
  }
```

p needs to be half the length of the key size, and q will need to be the remaining length of the desired key size:

```
int pSize = mKeysize/2;
int qSize = mKeysize - pSize;
```

We'll define the values we're going to use for our keys, and then we want to loop, generating p and q until n is the size we need.

```
BigInteger p,q,pMinus1,qMinus1,phi,n,d;
do {
```

We'll have another loop inside looping over p until p-1 is relatively prime to E, and will create a new value of p and p-1. We want that inner loop to continue until p-1 is relatively prime to E, which gives us the `while` condition:

```
do {
  p = new BigInteger(pSize, CERTAINTY, mSecureRandom);
  pMinus1 = p.subtract(BigInteger.ONE);
} while (!(pMinus1.gcd(E).equals(BigInteger.ONE)));
```

Now we'll generate q in the same way as p. It must be relatively prime to E, and well keep looping it until they're the right size:

```
do {
  q = new BigInteger(qSize, CERTAINTY, mSecureRandom);
  qMinus1 = q.subtract(BigInteger.ONE);
} while (!(qMinus1.gcd(E).equals(BigInteger.ONE)));
} while ((p.multiply(q)).bitLength() != mKeysize);
```

Now we can create our values. phi = (p-1)(q-1).

```
phi = pMinus1.multiply(qMinus1);
```

n = pq.

```
n = p.multiply(q);
```

$d = e^{-1}$ mod `phi`. We can call `modInverse()` on `E` with `phi` to achieve this result.

```
d = E.modInverse(phi);
```

Finally, we'll create the key pair from the numbers we've created and return it.

```
return new KeyPair(
  new RSAPublicKeyImpl(n,d),
  new RSAPrivateCrtKeyImpl(n,E,d,p,q)
);
}
}
```

Cryptographic Primitives

PKCS#1 defines two cryptographic primitives:

❑ RSA Encryption Primitive (RSAEP) for encryption

❑ RSA Decryption Primitive (RSADP) for decryption

They each take some data in the form of a large integer and a key, apply a cryptographic transformation, and output another large integer, the result of the transformation. We'll use Java's `BigInteger` class to implement the math. Most providers use `BigInteger` in the same way.

Neither RSAEP nor RSADP have any state that they need to keep track of between invocations. They simply provide a service, so we will place them in a class called RSA as static methods.

RSAEP is called with a public key {`n`, `e`} and a `BigInteger`, `m`. Here are the steps to perform encryption:

1. If $m < 0$ or $m > n-1$, the message cannot be encrypted. Throw an exception.

2. Let $c = m^e$ mod `n`.

3. Return `c`.

RSADP is similar, but we want to be able to accelerate it with the CRT if at all possible. CRT allows us to perform fewer mathematical operations when decrypting. If we have a CRT key, we will have the values {n, d, p, q, dP, dQ, qInv}. A simple private key will contain only the values {n, d}. We will also pass in c, the encrypted number in the form of a `BigInteger`:

1. If $c < 0$ or $c > n-1$, the message cannot be decrypted. Throw an exception.

2. If the private key is in the form {n, d}, let $m = c^d$ mod `n` and skip to step 7.

3. Let $m1 = c^{dP}$ mod `p`.

4. Let $m2 = c^{dQ}$ mod `q`.

5. Let $h = qInv(m1 - m2)$ mod `p`.

6. Let `m = m2 + hq`.

7. Return `m`.

If a problem occurs in either encryption or decryption, we want to throw an exception. The exception we'll throw is `javax.crypto.IllegalBlockSizeException`, which indicates that the data being encrypted or decrypted is too large or two small to be operated on with the given key.

```java
package com.isnetworks.crypto.rsa;

import java.math.*;
import java.security.*;
import java.security.interfaces.*;

import javax.crypto.*;

// RSA.java

public class RSA {
```

We'll start with our encryption step, `rsaep()`. This takes a public key and a `BigInteger` representing the message to encrypt. The first thing we need to do is pull the public exponent and the modulus out of the public key:

```java
public static BigInteger rsaep (RSAPublicKey publicKey, BigInteger m)
   throws IllegalBlockSizeException {

   BigInteger e = publicKey.getPublicExponent();
   BigInteger n = publicKey.getModulus();
```

Next we check if the modulus is in range. If not, we throw an exception:

```java
BigInteger nMinusOne = n.subtract(BigInteger.ONE);

// m > 0 and m < n-1

if (m.compareTo(BigInteger.ZERO) < 0) {
  throw new IllegalBlockSizeException("Ciphertext too small");
}
if (m.compareTo(nMinusOne) > 0) {
  throw new IllegalBlockSizeException("Ciphertext too large");
}
```

Finally, we can perform the actual encryption. Here it is – RSA encryption in all its glory:

```java
BigInteger c = m.modPow(e,n);
return c;
}
```

Now we'll write our decryption method, `rsadp()`. This takes a private key and the ciphertext as a big integer:

```java
public static BigInteger rsadp (RSAPrivateKey privateKey, BigInteger c) {
```

First we check if our private key is a CRT key. If not, we need to use the standard form of RSA decryption:

```
if (!(privateKey instanceof RSAPrivateCrtKey)) {

    // Can't use the Chinese Remainder Theorem

    BigInteger d = privateKey.getPrivateExponent();
    BigInteger n = privateKey.getModulus();
```

Here's the simple form of decryption:

```
    BigInteger m = c.modPow(d,n);
    return m;
}
```

If we get here, then we have a CRT key, so we can use the Chinese Remainder Theorem to speed up calculation. We'll begin by pulling all the necessary fields out of the private key, which we must cast to an RSAPrivateCrtKey in order to access:

```
RSAPrivateCrtKey privateCrtKey = (RSAPrivateCrtKey)privateKey;

BigInteger p = privateCrtKey.getPrimeP();
BigInteger q = privateCrtKey.getPrimeQ();
BigInteger dP = privateCrtKey.getPrimeExponentP();
BigInteger dQ = privateCrtKey.getPrimeExponentQ();
BigInteger qInv = privateCrtKey.getCrtCoefficient();
```

Now we'll perform our calculations. Even though this looks a lot harder than the simple form of RSA decryption, it can be performed much faster as it requires far fewer calculations under the covers, as it were.

```
BigInteger m1 = c.modPow(dP,p);
BigInteger m2 = c.modPow(dQ,q);

// Let h = qInv(m1 - m2) mod p

BigInteger h = m1.subtract(m2);
h = h.multiply(qInv);
h = h.mod(p);

// m = m2 + hq

BigInteger m = h.multiply(q);
m = m.add(m2);

return m;
    }
}
```

Encryption Padding

When using RSA for encryption, it is necessary that data be padded to protect against certain attacks, and to enable the original data to be reconstructed after encryption and decryption. PKCS#1 defines two types of padding:

❑ PKCS1v1_5

❑ OAEP

PKCS1v1_5 is the most commonly used form of padding, but is somewhat vulnerable to attack if used to encrypt information with strong regular patterns, like plaintext. It should only be used to encrypt random-looking data, like secret keys. OAEP is "plaintext-aware," according to PKCS#1, meaning that it can safely be used to encrypt anything, including regular text. If you are developing a new application and are free to choose your padding method, you should use OAEP. If you have to interact with pre-existing systems, however, you may be stuck with PKCS1v1_5.

We'll write a padding interface that will enable us to easily switch between padding types as necessary. The only methods Padding.java needs to declare are encode() and decode(). The encode() method will require the message to be encoded, as well as the size of the encoded block that should be returned. If the message is too large to be padded out to the size requested, encode() will throw a javax.crypto.IllegalBlockSizeException. The decode() method requires only the data to be decoded, and will throw a javax.crypto.BadPaddingException if the data cannot be properly decoded. We'll be discussing the details of padding shortly. For now, we'll just introduce the interface.

```java
package com.isnetworks.crypto;

import javax.crypto.*;

/**
 *  Padding.java
 *
 *  Interface to cover Padding requirements
 */

public interface Padding {

  /**
   *  Encodes the data.
   */

  public byte[] encode(byte[] message, int length)
    throws IllegalBlockSizeException;

  /**
   *  Decodes the data.
   */

  public byte[] decode(byte[] message) throws BadPaddingException;
}
```

PKCS1v1_5 Padding

PKCS1v1_5 padding is fairly simple. Two bytes and some random data are placed at the beginning of the block to fill it out to a specific size. Given a message M, in the form of a byte array, padding the message produces this block of data:

The 02 byte is a flag indicating that this is an encrypted block. PS stands for Padding String, and is an array of non-zero bytes. It should be at least 8 bytes long according to PKCS#1. When decoding, it is easy to parse through, removing the leading 02, non-zero octets, a zero, and then retrieve the message itself, M. By adding random data, PS, we make it much harder for an attacker to discern what the message might be.

The random padding string is especially important when encrypting a short message. Imagine if you were encrypting a DES key to send to someone using his or her public key. If you simply encrypt the key itself, there are 2^{56} possible messages you could have encrypted, because DES keys are 56 bits long. If an attacker knows this, he or she could create all possible DES keys and encrypt them using your associate's public key. Then once a matching message was found, the attacker would know the DES key. By inserting a large number of random bytes, the number of possible original messages becomes much larger. For instance, a DES key encrypted with a 1024-bit RSA key would have 117 bytes of random data added to it before encrypting. This causes the number of possible original messages to jump from 2^{56} to near 2^{1000}, making it unfeasible to attempt encrypting every possible message.

PKCS1Padding.java

Our implementation of PKCS1 padding will implement our Padding interface. We need to have a constructor that takes a SecureRandom object, so that we can specify the source of randomness for our padding string. Our encode operation will throw an IllegalBlockSizeException if the message is too long to be padded to the requested size. Our decode operation will throw a BadPaddingException if invalid padding is found while decoding.

```
package com.isnetworks.crypto.rsa;

import com.isnetworks.crypto.*;
import java.io.*;
import java.security.*;
import javax.crypto.*;

/**
 *   PKCS#1, v1.5
 *
 *   Encodes a message to a specific block size
 *
 */

public class PKCS1Padding implements Padding{

    private SecureRandom mRandom;
```

We'll have two constructors: one that takes an instance of SecureRandom and one that doesn't. We need a random number generator to create our padding bytes. The user may wish to swap out which random number generator is used:

```
public PKCS1Padding (SecureRandom random) {
  mRandom = random;
}

public PKCS1Padding() {
  this(new SecureRandom());
}
```

Our encode() method will take a byte array containing the message and the size of the encoded message to return:

```
public byte[] encode(byte[] M, int emLen)
  throws IllegalBlockSizeException {
```

The first thing we need to do is check the length of the message passed in. We need to add a byte to identify the block (0x02), at least eight bytes of padding and the padding separator (0x00). If our message isn't at least 10 bytes shorter than the length to be output, we won't be able to add the padding. We'll throw an exception because the message is too long:

```
if (M.length > emLen - 10) {
  throw new IllegalBlockSizeException("message too long");
}
```

To create the output, we're going to use a ByteArrayOutputStream. We'll start by generating the padding bytes. The padding bytes must be non-zero, so we will generate random numbers between 0 and 254 and add 1 to them:

```
ByteArrayOutputStream baos = new ByteArrayOutputStream();
byte[] PS = new byte[(emLen - M.length - 2)];

// Fill the padding string with random non-zero bytes

for (int i = 0; i < PS.length; i++) {
  PS[i] = (byte)(mRandom.nextInt(255)+1);
}
```

We'll write the identifier (0x02) to the output, then the padding string, then the separator (0x00), and finally the message:

```
try {
  baos.write((byte)0x02);
  baos.write(PS);
  baos.write((byte)0x00);
  baos.write(M);
} catch (IOException ioe) {

  // This should never happen

  ioe.printStackTrace();
}
```

The encoded message is the byte array stored in the `ByteArrayOutputStream`. We'll simply return that byte array:

```
    byte[] EM = baos.toByteArray();
    return EM;
}
```

Now let's write our `decode()` method, which will take an encoded message as a byte array and return it decoded.

```
    public byte[] decode(byte[] EM) throws BadPaddingException {
```

First we need to check the length. Our message should look like the following:

```
0x02 | PS (8 bytes or greater) | 0x00 | M
```

If our message isn't at least 10 bytes long (the identifier, the padding and the separator), then it's not a valid message. We'll throw an exception:

```
    if (EM.length < 10) {
       throw new BadPaddingException ("message too short");
    }
```

Now that we know it's long enough, we need to make sure it starts with `0x02`:

```
    if (EM[0] != (byte) 0x02) {
       throw new BadPaddingException
         ("message not formatted properly");
    }
```

Now we want to remove the padding, which is a stream of non-zero bytes. We'll look for the first zero byte, which is the separator. If we get to the end of the message and we can't find any zero bytes, the message must be invalid:

```
    int start = 0;
    while (EM[start] != (byte)0x00) {
      start++;
      if (start >= EM.length) {
        throw new BadPaddingException("bad padding");
      }
    }
    start++; // Ignore the first 00
```

We need to make sure we had at least 8 bytes of padding. If start is less than 10 (8 bytes of padding plus the identifier plus the separator), then we didn't have enough padding. We'll throw an exception:

```
    if (start < 10) {
       throw new BadPaddingException ("bad padding");
    }
```

If we get this far, the remainder of the array is the message. We need to copy out those remaining bytes into a new array and return that:

```
        byte[] M = new byte[EM.length - start];
        System.arraycopy(EM,start,M,0,M.length);
        return M;
    }
}
```

That's out PKCS#1 padding implementation. Now we're going to write OAEP padding.

OAEP

OAEP is quite a bit more complex than PKCS1v1_5. It uses random data to mask the plaintext, rather than simply to pad it. This masking is done by xoring (a bitwise exclusive or operation) the plaintext with the random data several times in slightly different ways.

OAEP uses a message digest and a **mask generation function (MGF)** to encode data. We've used message digests before, but mask generation functions are new. Essentially a mask generation function produces a mask from data provided to it in a deterministic fashion, similar to a message digest. The difference is that the resulting hash can be of variable length. The result looks random, but will always be the same if the same input is provided. OAEP defines MGF1 as its mask generation function. We'll examine it in detail shortly, but first we'll simply show using it to perform OAEP padding.

Here is a diagram of OAEP encoding, from RSA's documentation:

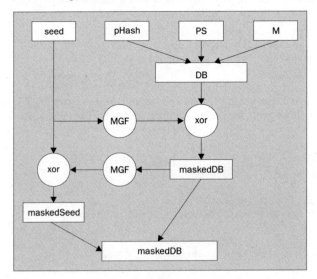

P: any algorithm parameters sent to the function. Algorithm parameters are typically not used for RSA, but they are here for compatibility with PKCS#1:

❑ pHash: a hash of P

❑ seed: a random octet string the same length as the hash function

❑ PS: a padding string of zeroes.

Encoding consists of the following steps:

1. Concatenate pHash, PS, a 01 byte and M to form the DataBlock, DB like so: DB = pHash||PS||01||M.

2. Run the Mask Generator Function (MGF) on the seed with a length of emLen - hLen. This will produce dbMask.

3. maskedDB = DB xor dbMask.

4. seedMask = MGF(maskedDB, hLen).

5. maskedSeed = seed xor seedMask.

6. EM will be the encoded message. EM = maskedSeed||maskedDB.

7. Return EM.

Where hLen is the length of the hash function and emLen is the length of the message.

Decoding is just encoding in reverse, with a couple small exceptions. Here are the steps, using similar variable names to the encoding operation:

1. Split EM into maskedSeed, the first hLen bytes, and maskedDB, the remaining bytes.

2. seedMask = MGF(maskedDB, hLen).

3. seed = maskedSeed xor seedMask.

4. dbMask = MGF(seed, emLen - hLen).

5. DB = maskedDB xor dbMask.

6. Split DB into pHashPrime, PS (all zeroes), a 01 byte, and M, the message as so: DB = pHashPrime||PS||01||M.

7. Check that pHash == pHashPrime. If not, an error occurred.

8. Return M.

OAEP requires a couple of utility functions to operate: a mask generation function and a method for converting big integers to byte arrays.

Mask Generation Function

MGF1 is a mask generation function defined in PKCS#1, v2.0. It's fairly simple in operation. Essentially it repeatedly hashes the data with an increasing counter, appending that hash as many times as it needs to in order to fill an array of the length requested. Here's MGF.java:

```
package com.isnetworks.crypto.rsa;

import java.security.*;

public class MGF {
```

We need to store two internal variables – the message digest we'll be using and the length of that message digest. MGF1 uses SHA-1 for hashing.

```
private MessageDigest mHasher;
private int mHLen;
```

Our constructor will get an instance of a message digest and set the length of the hash.

```
public MGF() {
  try {
    mHasher = MessageDigest.getInstance("SHA-1");
  } catch (NoSuchAlgorithmException nsae) {

    // This should never happen, as Sun
    // ships SHA-1 with the JDK.

    nsae.printStackTrace();
    throw new RuntimeException("No SHA-1 implementation found");
  }
  mHLen = mHasher.getDigestLength();
}
```

We have only one public method – generateMask(). It will generate a mask given a seed and a length. The seed is an array of bytes.

```
public byte[] generateMask(byte[] Z, int length) {
```

Start by computing the number of iterations we'll need to fill an array of the appropriate length. Each iteration will fill a number of bytes equal to the length of the hash.

```
int iterations = (int)Math.ceil((double)length / (double)mHLen);
```

Now we need to declare some variables to manage the mask generation. We're using the variable names from PKCS#1, so some of it doesn't follow Java capitalization and naming rules. These are as follows:

❑ hash is a temporary holding array for the result of a message digest operation.

❑ C is a byte array representing the counter that we're iterating over.

❑ T is a byte array holding our result.

```
byte[] hash,C;
byte[] T = new byte[iterations * mHLen];
mHasher.reset();
```

We'll loop over a counter for the number of iterations we need. From PKCS#1, the formula we will use in the loop to construct T is T = T || Hash(Z || C). As we mentioned C is an increasing counter 4 bytes in length. We will create C with a method intToBytes() that we will write later.

```
for (int counter = 0;counter < iterations; counter++) {
  C = intToBytes(counter);
  mHasher.update(Z);
  mHasher.update(C);
  hash = mHasher.digest();

  // Append to T.

  System.arraycopy(hash,0,T,counter * mHLen,mHLen);
}
```

We need to return a byte array with the length requested. T may be larger than we need, so we will create a new byte array of the appropriate length and copy the necessary bytes into it.

```
    byte[] bytesToReturn = new byte[length];
    System.arraycopy(T,0,bytesToReturn,0,length);
    return bytesToReturn;
}
```

Here is our convenience method for converting an int to a byte array of 4 bytes:

```
private static byte[] intToBytes(int i) {
  byte[] bytesToReturn = new byte[4];
  bytesToReturn[0] = (byte)(i >>> 24);
  bytesToReturn[1] = (byte)(i >>> 16);
  bytesToReturn[2] = (byte)(i >>> 8);
  bytesToReturn[3] = (byte)i;
  return bytesToReturn;
  }
}
```

We will use the MGF class within our OAEP encode and decode methods. Now let's take a look at how we're going to convert BigIntegers into byte arrays.

I2OSP – Integer to Octet String Primitive

Another utility we'll need is the ability to translate BigIntegers into byte arrays. There is a toByteArray() method in BigInteger, but it returns a signed version of the BigInteger, which could possibly have a leading zero. Also, there are times when we need a specific size array to be returned from a BigInteger, so we need to pad it with extra leading zeros. We'll create a utility method, I2OSP. This procedure comes directly from PKCS#1. We're going to create a class, Util, that will contain I2OSP() as a static method. That way if we need any other static utility methods, we can place them in Util.java as well.

```
package com.isnetworks.crypto.rsa;

import java.math.BigInteger;
import javax.crypto.*;

/**
 *  Utility class of static methods for use
 *  in RSA encryption and signature provider.
 */

public class Util {

  /**
   *  Convert a BigInteger into a byte array
   *  of length k.
   *
   *  @param  Input
   *  @param  length of desired array
   */
```

```
public static byte[] I2OSP(BigInteger c, int k)
    throws IllegalBlockSizeException {

  byte[] C = c.toByteArray();

  // remove the leading zero if necessary

  if (C[0] == 0) {
    byte[] temp = new byte[C.length - 1];
    System.arraycopy(C,1,temp,0,temp.length);
    C = temp;
  }

  if (C.length > k) {
    throw new IllegalBlockSizeException("Block too large");
  }

  if (C.length == k) {
    return C;
  }

  // C is not long enough

  byte[] result = new byte[k];
  System.arraycopy(C,0,result,k-C.length,C.length);
  return result;
  }
}
```

OAEP Encoding and Decoding

Now that we've defined some of the primitives we'll need to use, we need to actually implement OAEP encoding.

```
package com.isnetworks.crypto.rsa;

import java.io.*;
import java.security.*;
import java.util.*;
import javax.crypto.*;
import com.isnetworks.crypto.Padding;

// OAEPPadding.java

public class OAEPPadding implements Padding {
```

We need to store an internal message digest and the length of that message digest. We'll be using SHA-1. We also need an instance of `SecureRandom` for generating the seed and an instance of our mask generator. Finally, we'll store the encoded parameters, if they are passed in.

```
private MessageDigest mHasher;
private int mHLen;
private SecureRandom mRandom;
private MGF mMask;
private byte[] mPBytes;
```

Our first constructor will take an instance of `SecureRandom` so that the user can swap out how the seed is generated if desired. We will set our member variables during construction.

```
public OAEPPadding (SecureRandom random) {
  try {
    mHasher = MessageDigest.getInstance("SHA-1");
  } catch (NoSuchAlgorithmException nsae) {

    // Should never happen, as Sun ships
    // a SHA-1 implementation with the JDK.

    nsae.printStackTrace();
    throw new RuntimeException("No SHA-1 implementation found");
  }
  mHLen = mHasher.getDigestLength();
  mRandom = random;
  mMask = new MGF();
}
```

We'll also have a default constructor that will create a `SecureRandom` and call our previous constructor:

```
public OAEPPadding() {
  this(new SecureRandom());
}
```

This constructor is passing in a `java.security.AlgorithmParameters` object and an instance of `SecureRandom`. This object specifies any additional algorithm parameters that need to be used when encrypting and decrypting. These parameters are almost never used with RSA, however, so our provider ignores them. We support using them for padding, as it they're only used to create a hash for the mask. If in the future we decided to use the parameters in our provider for encryption, we wouldn't need to alter our padding.

```
public OAEPPadding(AlgorithmParameters P, SecureRandom random)
  throws InvalidAlgorithmParameterException {
  this(random);
  if (P != NULL) {
    try {
      mPBytes = P.getEncoded();
    } catch (IOException ioe) {
      throw new InvalidAlgorithmParameterException ("Bad AlgorithmParameters");
    }
  }
}
```

One last constructor, this one taking only an algorithm parameters object. We'll create a new instance of `SecureRandom` and call the previous constructor.

```
public OAEPPadding(AlgorithmParameters P)
  throws InvalidAlgorithmParameterException {

  this(P, new SecureRandom());
}
```

Now we'll write our `encode()` method. This takes a byte array of the message and the length of the output desired.

```
public byte[] encode(byte[] M, int length)
    throws IllegalBlockSizeException {
```

We need to use the encoded bytes of the algorithm parameters. If that value is NULL, we'll create a zero-length array instead.

```
if (mPBytes == NULL) {
    mPBytes = new byte[0];
}
```

Now we need to check that the message is small enough. PKCS#1 defines a formula for that, which we use in the code below:

```
if (M.length > (length - 2*mHLen -1)) {
    throw new IllegalBlockSizeException ("message too long");
}
```

We'll write our output to a `ByteArrayOutputStream`. Also, we need to create variables for our padding (PS), our encoded message (EM), and the hash of the parameters (pHash). The length of our padding string is defined by PKCS#1. It should be filled with all zero bytes.

```
ByteArrayOutputStream baos = new ByteArrayOutputStream();
byte[] PS = new byte[(length - M.length - 2*mHLen -1)];
byte[] EM;
mHasher.reset();
byte[] pHash = mHasher.digest(mPBytes);
```

Now we want to create DB, which is our data block. We write pHash, PS, a byte (0x01), and the message (M) to our `ByteArrayOutputStream` and get the resulting byte array:

```
// Create DB, the Data Block

try {
    baos.write(pHash);
    baos.write(PS);
    baos.write(0x01);
    baos.write(M);
} catch (IOException ioe) {

    // This will never happen

    ioe.printStackTrace();
}
byte[] DB = baos.toByteArray();
```

We'll generate the seed, which is just a random byte array equal in size to our hashing algorithm's output.

```
byte[] seed = new byte[mHLen];
mRandom.nextBytes(seed);
```

Our mask should be generated from that seed, and should be equal to the length minus the hash length. This value is taken from PKCS#1.

```
byte[] dbMask = mMask.generateMask(seed, length - mHLen);
```

Here, we'll xor DB and the mask. We'll then need a second mask generated from maskedDB, equal in length to the hash length. After this, we'll xor the seed and the seed mask to produce the masked seed.

```
byte[] maskedDB = xor(DB, dbMask);
byte[] seedMask = mMask.generateMask(maskedDB, mHLen);
byte[] maskedSeed = xor(seed, seedMask);
```

We'll write the masked seed and maskedDB to a byte array. This is our encoded message, which we can return.

```
baos.reset();
try {
  baos.write(maskedSeed);
  baos.write(maskedDB);
} catch (IOException ioe) {

  // This will never happen

  ioe.printStackTrace();
}
EM = baos.toByteArray();
return EM;
}
```

Now we'll write our decode() method. This takes in a byte array containing an encoded message, and will return a byte array containing the decoded message.

```
public byte[] decode(byte[] EM)
  throws BadPaddingException {
```

First we need to check the length. If the encoded message is less than twice the hash length + 1, the message is too short to be a properly OAEP-encoded message, so we'll thrown an exception.

```
if (EM.length < (2*mHLen + 1)) {
  throw new BadPaddingException("decoding error");
}
```

To decode, we need to be using the same algorithm parameters that were used to encode. As we mentioned, this will typically be NULL, so we'll turn it into a zero-length byte array.

```
if (mPBytes == NULL) {
  mPBytes = new byte[0];
}
```

We'll declare the variable to hold the decoded message. We then need to create the masked seed, which is the first chunk of our encoded message. Its length is equal to our hashing algorithm's output length.

```
byte[] M;
byte[] maskedSeed = new byte[mHLen];
System.arraycopy(EM,0,maskedSeed,0,mHLen);
```

Now we'll create `maskedDB`, which will be the remaining bytes in the encoded message. By running `maskedDB` through our mask generation function, we can derive the original seed mask.

```
byte[] maskedDB = new byte[EM.length - mHLen];
System.arraycopy(EM,mHLen,maskedDB,0,EM.length - mHLen);
byte[] seedMask = mMask.generateMask(maskedDB,mHLen);
```

The original seed is the masked seed `xored` with the seed mask as `xor` is symmetric. We can generate the `dbmask` by running the seed through the mask generator function. The length should be the length of the encoded message minus the hash length.

```
byte[] seed = xor(maskedSeed, seedMask);
byte[] dbMask = mMask.generateMask(seed, EM.length - mHLen);
```

We can regenerate our original `DB` variable by `xoring` the `maskeddb` with the `dbmask`. We need to create `pHash` just as we did in encoding, by hashing `mPBytes`.

```
byte[] DB = xor(maskedDB, dbMask);
mHasher.reset();
byte[] pHash = mHasher.digest(mPBytes);
```

We now have our original data in the form `pHashPrime||PS||01||M`. We can separate it out into its constituent parts. We'll start by pulling out `pHashPrime`.

```
byte[] pHashPrime = new byte[mHLen];
System.arraycopy(DB,0,pHashPrime,0,mHLen);
```

We need to check that the two hashes are equal. If not, there was a problem decoding.

```
if (!Arrays.equals(pHash,pHashPrime)) {
  throw new BadPaddingException("hashing error");
}
```

Now we want to strip off the padding. The padding is all zero bytes, followed by a `0x01` byte. We'll scan through, looking for that pattern. If we don't find it, there was a problem decoding.

```
int pos = mHLen;
while ( (DB[pos] != (byte)(0x01)) && (DB[pos] == (byte)(0x00)) ) {
  pos++;
  if (pos >= DB.length) {

    // no 0x01 found, and we're at the end

    throw new BadPaddingException("no message found");
  }
}
pos++;
```

Our original message is the remainder of our DB array. We can extract it and return it.

```
    M = new byte[DB.length - pos];
    System.arraycopy(DB,pos,M,0,DB.length - pos);
    return M;
}
```

Finally, we need to write our xor() method that will xor two byte arrays. We simply run through the arrays, xoring each byte. We need to start by determining which byte array is larger, so that we won't get accidentally walk off the end of the shorter array.

```
    private byte[] xor (byte[] firstArray, byte[] secondArray) {
    byte[] largerArray;
    byte[] smallerArray;
    if (firstArray.length > secondArray.length) {
      largerArray = firstArray;
      smallerArray = secondArray;
    } else {
      largerArray = secondArray;
      smallerArray = firstArray;
    }
```

Now we can create our result, which is the larger array xored with the smaller array.

```
    byte[] result = new byte[largerArray.length];
    System.arraycopy(largerArray,0,result,0,largerArray.length);
    for (int i=0;i<smallerArray.length;i++) {
      result[i] = (byte)(result[i] ^ smallerArray[i]);
    }
    return result;
  }
}
```

That takes care of our padding. We're ready to move on to writing the encryption components.

Cipher

Now that we've defined our keys, primitives, and padding, it's time to actually implement the cipher itself. We're going to extend the abstract class javax.crypto.CipherSpi, which is the service provider interface to the Cipher class. We could provide two classes, one for each padding type we support, but instead we're going to have one class that can dynamically choose a padding type when it is instantiated.

Since the CipherSpi class defines that data can be added a chunk at a time with the engineUpdate() method, we'll need some way of storing that data until we need it for encryption or decryption. We'll use a ByteArrayOutputStream, which we can then call toByteArray() on to retrieve the data in it entirety. Since we know that we'll be storing the data in that ByteArrayOutputStream, we can now write encrypt() and decrypt() methods. These aren't required by CipherSpi, but we can delegate calls to them as necessary, based on what calls get made to our Spi methods. We will define these methods based on the PKCS#1 documentation, which gives simple instructions on how to encrypt and decrypt.

Note that we call our cryptographic primitives `RSA.rsaep()` and `RSA.rsadp()`. We also use our `Padding` interface to call `encode()` and `decode()`. We will instantiate those padding objects in our `engineInit()` method, which comes from the `CipherSpi` class. Here are our `encrypt()` and `decrypt()` methods:

```
private byte[] encrypt() throws IllegalBlockSizeException {
```

Our data to be encrypted or decrypted is stored in `mBaos`, a `ByteArrayOutputStream` stored as a member variable. We'll create our message, `M`, from that byte array. We also need to know our key size.

```
byte[] M = mBaos.toByteArray();
int k = mKeysize;
```

We start by encoding the message. According to PKCS#1 documentation, the encoded message should be one byte shorter than the size of the key. We must convert our message into a `BigInteger` in order to encrypt it.

```
byte[] EM = mPadding.encode(M,k-1);
BigInteger m = new BigInteger(1, EM);
```

Encrypting will produce another `BigInteger`. We pass in our public key and the encoded message. Finally, we convert that `BigInteger` into a byte array, using our `I2OSP()` method, which we defined earlier in our `Util` class.

```
BigInteger c = RSA.rsaep((RSAPublicKey)mKey, m);
byte[] C = Util.I2OSP(c, k);
return C;
}
```

Now we can write our `decrypt()` method. This is quite similar to `encrypt()`, except for the order in which padding is dealt with.

```
private byte[] decrypt() throws BadPaddingException,
    IllegalBlockSizeException {
```

We'll define `C` as our ciphertext, to match the PKCS#1 documentation. Our ciphertext must be the same length as our key. If not, we throw an exception.

```
byte[] C = mBaos.toByteArray();
    int k = mKeysize;
    if (k != C.length) {
  throw new IllegalBlockSizeException("decryption error");
}
```

In order to perform decryption, we need to convert the ciphertext to a big integer. Then we can call `rsadp()` with our private key and the ciphertext.

```
BigInteger c = new BigInteger(1,C);
BigInteger m = RSA.rsadp((RSAPrivateKey)mKey,c);
```

We need to convert our big integer representation of the message into a byte array. The length must be one less than the key size. This byte array is the encoded message.

```
    byte[] EM = Util.I2OSP(m,k-1);
```

Now we'll decode that and return it.

```
    byte[] M = mPadding.decode(EM);
    return M;
}
```

Extending CipherSpi

CipherSpi defines a number of methods that we must implement. They are:

- ❑ engineSetMode() – sets the mode of the cipher. In our case, there is only one mode, ECB, for Electronic Code Book. RSA encryption supports only ECB mode.
- ❑ engineSetPadding() – sets the padding of the cipher. We support OAEP and PKCS1.
- ❑ engineGetBlockSize() – returns the block size of the cipher. For encrypting, this is the key size minus one byte. For decrypting, it is equal to the key size.
- ❑ engineGetOutputSize() – returns the size of the output of this cipher. This is the opposite of the input block size: for encrypting, it is equal to the key size. For decrypting, it is one byte less than the key size.
- ❑ engineGetIV() – gets the Initialization Vector for our cipher. As we support only ECB mode, no IV is used. This call returns NULL.
- ❑ engineGetParameters() – returns any parameters used by this cipher. This is typically NULL, but OAEP padding can support parameters, so if they have been specified, this call returns them.
- ❑ engineInit() – initializes the cipher. This sets the operating mode (encrypt or decrypt), the key, a source of randomness, and any algorithm parameters. There are multiple ways to call engineInit, some of which do not require all the parameters.
- ❑ engineUpdate() – adds more data to the data store to be encrypted or decrypted.
- ❑ engineDoFinal() – actually encrypts or decrypts the data, and returns the result. This call finishes off a single-part operation or a multi-part that was updated using engineUpdate().

JCE1.2.1 Methods

JCE 1.2.1 adds two extra methods: engineWrap() and engineUnwrap(). These methods allow you to encrypt one key with another and decrypt an encrypted key. We'll be supporting JCE 1.2, so we won't add these methods.

Let's write our cipher.

```
package com.isnetworks.crypto.rsa;

import com.isnetworks.crypto.Padding;
import java.io.*;
import java.math.BigInteger;
import java.security.*;
import java.security.interfaces.*;
import javax.crypto.*;

// RSACipher.java

public class RSACipher extends CipherSpi {
```

We'll define two constants for our padding types: PKCS#1 and OAEP.

```
private static final int PKCS1 = 1;
private static final int OAEP = 2;
```

We need to store several member variables including our padding type and our key. The padding type is defined as PKCS1 by default. Our class will also hold an instance of `Padding` to handle our padding operations:

```
private int mPaddingType = PKCS1;
private Key mKey;
private Padding mPadding;
```

There are two possible operating modes our cipher can be used in: encrypt or decrypt. These modes come from constants in the `Cipher` class: `Cipher.ENCRYPT_MODE` and `Cipher.DECRYPT_MODE`. We then need three more member variables: a byte array output stream to hold the data to be processed, an int holding our key size, and an instance of `AlgorithmParameters` to hold any parameters that are passed in.

```
private int mOperatingMode;
private ByteArrayOutputStream mBaos;
private int mKeysize;
private AlgorithmParameters mAlgorithmParameters;
```

We will have one constructor: the default one. We'll call `super()` and create a new byte array output stream to hold our data.

```
public RSACipher() {
    super();
    mBaos = new ByteArrayOutputStream();
}
```

Now we need to write two methods for setting the cipher options: one for setting the mode and one for setting the padding.

We support only one type of mode, ECB. If any other type is entered, we will throw an exception. This is the encryption mode, not the operating mode, which is either encryption or decryption.

```
protected void engineSetMode(String mode) throws NoSuchAlgorithmException {
    if (!mode.equalsIgnoreCase("ECB")) {
        throw new NoSuchAlgorithmException("RSA supports only ECB mode");
    }
}
```

Our padding can be set to one of two types: PKCS#1 or OAEP. We'll simply set the `mPaddingType` variable to the appropriate type or throw an exception if a different padding is requested.

```
protected void engineSetPadding(String padding)
throws NoSuchPaddingException {
    if(padding.equalsIgnoreCase("PKCS1") ||
    padding.equalsIgnoreCase("PKCS#1") ||
```

```
        padding.equalsIgnoreCase("PKCS1Padding")) {
            mPaddingType = PKCS1;
        } else if (padding.equalsIgnoreCase("OAEP") ||
                    padding.equalsIgnoreCase("OAEPPadding")) {
            mPaddingType = OAEP;
        } else {
            throw new NoSuchPaddingException
    ("Only PKCS1 and OAEP Padding supported");
        }
    }
```

We need to write some methods to get the options of this cipher: the block size, the output size, the initialization vector and the algorithm parameters.

The block size is one less than the key size if we're in encrypt mode, and equal to the key size if in decrypt mode.

```
    protected int engineGetBlockSize() {
        if (mOperatingMode == Cipher.ENCRYPT_MODE) {
            return mKeysize - 1;
        } else {
            return mKeysize;
        }
    }
```

Our output size is just the opposite: if in encrypt mode our output is equal to the key size. If in decrypt, it's the key size minus 1.

```
    protected int engineGetOutputSize(int inputLen) {
        if (mOperatingMode == Cipher.ENCRYPT_MODE) {
            return mKeysize;
        } else {
            return mKeysize -1;
        }
    }
```

Initialization vectors are not used in ECB mode, so if one is requested, we return NULL.

```
    protected byte[] engineGetIV() {
        return NULL;
    }
```

Our algorithm parameters are stored as a member variable. If they are requested, we simply return them.

```
    protected AlgorithmParameters engineGetParameters() {
        return mAlgorithmParameters;
    }
```

Now we need to write our engineInit() methods. There are quite a number of these, so we'll define one that performs most of the operations, and all our other engineInit() methods will call it.

Initialization resets all the values, resetting the cipher.

```
protected void engineInit(int opmode, Key key,
                          AlgorithmParameters params, SecureRandom random)
throws InvalidKeyException, InvalidAlgorithmParameterException {
```

We'll start by examining the key that was passed in. We'll also need to set the modulus length of the key. Public keys can be used for encrypting, and private keys for decrypting. If someone tries to use one for the wrong purpose, we'll throw an exception.

```
    int modulusLength = 0;
    if (key instanceof RSAPublicKey) {
if (!(opmode == Cipher.ENCRYPT_MODE)) {
    throw new InvalidKeyException
      ("Public Keys can only be used for encrypting");
}
        modulusLength = ((RSAPublicKey)key).getModulus().bitLength();
    } else if (key instanceof RSAPrivateKey) {
if (!(opmode == Cipher.DECRYPT_MODE)) {
    throw new InvalidKeyException
        ("Private Keys can only be used for decrypting");
}
        modulusLength = ((RSAPrivateKey)key).getModulus().bitLength();
    } else {
        throw new InvalidKeyException("Key must be an RSA Key");
    }
```

The key size is the size of the modulus in bytes. We'll add 7 to round up to the nearest byte.

```
    mKeysize = (modulusLength+7)/8;
```

If we're using OAEP padding, we may need to pass parameters to the padding object. Otherwise, we don't need the parameters to create our padding.

```
    if (mPaddingType == OAEP) {
        if (params == NULL) {
            mPadding = new OAEPPadding(random);
        } else {
            mPadding = new OAEPPadding(params, random);
        }
    } else {
        mPadding = new PKCS1Padding(random);
    }
```

Lastly, we set all our member variables and reset our byte array output stream.

```
    mAlgorithmParameters = params;
    mKey = key;
    mOperatingMode = opmode;
    mBaos.reset();
}
```

This `engineInit()` method doesn't have an `AlgorithmParameter` object, so we'll just call the previous constructor with a `NULL AlgorithmParameter`.

```
protected void engineInit(int opmode, Key key, SecureRandom random)
throws InvalidKeyException {
  try {
      engineInit(opmode, key, (AlgorithmParameters)NULL, random);
  } catch (InvalidAlgorithmParameterException iape) {

    // This should never happen, as the alg params are NULL

    iape.printStackTrace();
  }
}
```

Our last initialization method takes an `AlgorithmParameterSpec` object. We can't handle such an object, but we must have the method in order to compile. We'll throw an exception if it gets called.

```
protected void engineInit(int opmode, Key key,
java.security.spec.AlgorithmParameterSpec params, SecureRandom random)
    throws InvalidAlgorithmParameterException {
        throw new InvalidAlgorithmParameterException("This cipher does not accept
AlgorithmParameterSpec");
    }
```

Now we need to write our `engineUpdate()` methods. These two methods both should add data to our internal byte array output stream. We also need to return any encrypted or decrypted data. For RSA, though, we won't be supporting multiple blocks, so we don't need to return any data on an update.

The first method returns a byte array containing the result. As we have no result yet, we will always return `NULL` after updating our internal byte array output stream.

```
protected byte[] engineUpdate(byte[] input, int inputOffset, int inputLen) {
if (input != NULL) {
  mBaos.write(input, inputOffset, inputLen);
}
    return NULL;
}
```

Our second `engineUpdate()` method takes a byte array that should be used to store the output. It returns an int containing the number of bytes added to the output. As we have no output at this point, we'll always return 0. We'll call the other `engineUpdate()` method to actually update the internal data.

```
protected int engineUpdate(byte[] input, int inputOffset, int inputLen,
                           byte[] output, int outputOffset) {
    engineUpdate(input, inputOffset, inputLen);
    return 0;
}
```

Next we'll write our `engineDoFinal()` methods. These methods take input data and then perform encryption or decryption. We'll delegate the actual cryptography to our `encrypt()` and `decrypt()` methods. When we're done, we need to reset our internal byte array output stream so we're ready to perform new encryption.

Note that our cipher is not thread-safe. This is by design, as it improves performance. If you need thread safety for your ciphers, you will need to enclose their operation in a synchronized block. Most cipher implementations are not thread-safe.

```
protected byte[] engineDoFinal(byte[] input, int inputOffset, int inputLen)
    throws IllegalBlockSizeException, BadPaddingException {

engineUpdate(input, inputOffset, inputLen);

byte[] output;
```

Based on the operating mode, we'll call `encrypt()` or `decrypt()`.

```
if (mOperatingMode == Cipher.ENCRYPT_MODE) {
  output = encrypt();
} else {
  output = decrypt();
}
```

Finally, we reset our data buffer.

```
    mBaos.reset();
  return output;
}
```

We have a second `engineDoFinal()` method that takes a byte array from the caller to place the result into. We'll simply call our other `engineDoFinal()` method and place the result in that buffer.

```
protected int engineDoFinal(byte[] input, int inputOffset, int inputLen,
    byte[] output, int outputOffset)
    throws ShortBufferException, IllegalBlockSizeException, BadPaddingException {

byte[] buffer;
buffer = engineDoFinal(input, inputOffset, inputLen);
```

Now we need to copy our result into the byte array provided. If it's too short, we throw an exception.

```
if (output.length - outputOffset < buffer.length) {
  throw new ShortBufferException("Output longer than buffer");
}
System.arraycopy(buffer, 0, output, outputOffset, buffer.length);
return buffer.length;
}
```

Finally, we have our internal `encrypt()` and `decrypt()` methods. We've already gone over these in detail at the beginning of this section.

```
/**
 * Internal method for encrypting using padding.
 */
```

```
        private byte[] encrypt() throws IllegalBlockSizeException {
        byte[] M = mBaos.toByteArray();
            int k = mKeysize;
            byte[] EM = mPadding.encode(M,k-1);
            BigInteger m = new BigInteger(1, EM);
            BigInteger c = RSA.rsaep((RSAPublicKey)mKey, m);
            byte[] C = Util.I2OSP(c, k);
            return C;
        }

    /**
     *  Internal method for decrypting an padded message.
     */

        private byte[] decrypt() throws
        BadPaddingException, IllegalBlockSizeException {
        byte[] C = mBaos.toByteArray();
            int k = mKeysize;
            if (k != C.length) {
        throw new IllegalBlockSizeException("decryption error");
        }
        BigInteger c = new BigInteger(1,C);
        BigInteger m = RSA.rsadp((RSAPrivateKey)mKey,c);
        byte[] EM = Util.I2OSP(m,k-1);
        byte[] M = mPadding.decode(EM);
        return M;
        }
    }
```

The Provider

We've written the entire implementation for encrypting and decrypting, but we haven't actually hooked it into the JCE itself. To do that, we need to write a class that extends `java.security.Provider`, and connects the various algorithm names to our classes.

The `Provider` class represents a cryptographic service provider. It contains all of the algorithms that our provider supports and registers them with the VM so that they can be used. The VM than queries its providers when asked for a cryptographic algorithm, like RSA.

We need only implement a no argument constructor in our provider. This constructor will be called by the VM on initialization. The constructor then needs to call the constructor of its superclass with its name, version, and an information string. Then we need to associate each algorithm that we support with the class that implements it. Doing this may require extra privileges that the code calling us may not have. But provided that our code has permission, we'd like to be able to run. To that end, we need to create a privileged action, as mentioned in the *Privileged Code* section in Chapter 7.

We need to call `AccessController.doPrivileged()` with a new `PrivilegedAction` instance. We will define an anonymous inner class with one method, `run()`, which registers the two algorithms we support: an RSA cipher and an RSA key pair generator.

Here is `ISNetworksProvider.java`:

```
package com.isnetworks.crypto.jce;

import java.security.*;

/**
 *  ISNetworks cryptography provider
 *
 *  This provider supports RSA encryption, decryption,
 *  signatures, and key generation.
 */

public final class ISNetworksProvider extends java.security.Provider {

  private static final String NAME = "ISNetworks";

  private static final double VERSION = 1.0;

  private static final String INFO = "ISNetworks RSA Provider";

  public ISNetworksProvider() {
    super (NAME, VERSION, INFO);
```

We need to call `doPrivileged()` in order to register our algorithms, in case our caller doesn't have permission to register a provider, but we do.

```
    AccessController.doPrivileged(new java.security.PrivilegedAction() {
      public Object run() {

        put("Cipher.RSA","com.isnetworks.crypto.rsa.RSACipher");
        put("KeyPairGenerator.RSA",
            "com.isnetworks.crypto.rsa.RSAKeyPairGenerator");
        return NULL;


      }
    });
  }
}
```

There are a number of different services that a provider can define. We have created a `KeyPairGenerator` and a `Cipher` service, each supporting the RSA algorithm. They were defined as `"KeyPairGenerator.RSA"` and `"Cipher.RSA"`, respectively. When passing an algorithm to the provider's put () method, two strings get passed in. The first one is `"Service.Algorithm"`, like `"Cipher.RSA"`. The second is the class name as a string, like `"com.isnetworks.crypto.rsa.RSACipher"`.

Here are the services that a cryptographic service provider can define:

❑   Signature – Digital signatures. Extends `java.security.SignatureSpi`.

❑   MessageDigest – Message digests, like SHA-1 or MD5. Extends `java.security.MessageDigestSpi`.

❑   KeyPairGenerator – Generate key pairs for algorithms like RSA, DSA, or Diffie-Hellman. Extends `java.security.KeyPairGeneratorSpi`.

❑   SecureRandom – Random number generator. Extends `java.security.SecureRandomSpi`.

- ❑ KeyFactory – Create keys from encodings and vice-versa. Extends java.security.KeyFactorySpi.

- ❑ CertificateFactory – Create certificates from encodings. Extends java.security.cert.CertificateFactorySpi.

- ❑ KeyStore – Handle storage of keys. Extends java.security.KeyStoreSpi.

- ❑ AlgorithmParameterGenerator – Generate algorithm parameters for use by key generators. Extends java.security.AlgorithmParameterGeneratorSpi.

- ❑ AlgorithmParameters – Hold parameters for an algorithm. Extends java.security.AlgorithmParameterSpi.

- ❑ Cipher – Handle encryption and decryption. Extends javax.crypto.CipherSpi.

- ❑ KeyAgreement – Handle key agreements, like Diffie-Hellman. Extends javax.crypto.KeyAgreementSpi.

- ❑ KeyGenerator – Generate secret keys for algorithms like DES and Blowfish. Extends javax.crypto.KeyGeneratorSpi.

- ❑ MAC – Message Authentication Code. Extends javax.crypto.MacSpi.

- ❑ SecretKeyFactory – Convert encoded secret keys into keys. Extends javax.crypto.SecretKeyFactorySpi.

- ❑ ExemptionMechanism – Provides exemption mechanisms like key recovery, key weakening, key escrow. Extends javax.crypto.ExemptionMechanismSpi.

Putting It All Together

Now that we've written the necessary source code, we need to build our provider. Put all the source files in the same directory. You should have the following files:

- ❑ ISNetworksProvider.java
- ❑ MGF.java
- ❑ OAEPPadding.java
- ❑ Padding.java
- ❑ PKCS1Padding.java
- ❑ RSA.java
- ❑ RSACipher.java
- ❑ RSAKeyPairGenerator.java
- ❑ RSAPrivateCrtKeyImpl.java
- ❑ RSAPrivateKeyImpl.java
- ❑ RSAPublicKeyImpl.java
- ❑ Util.java

You can compile all of these from this directory with:

```
C:\> javac -d . *.java
```

This will place all of the class files into an appropriate subdirectory under the current directory. As mentioned before, you will need to have installed a JCE provider that has an implementation of the `javax.crypto.*` classes. For details on doing this, see Chapter 3 on the JCA/JCE.

If you downloaded the code and are compiling the encryption and signature classes, you may see a deprecation warning issued. You can safely ignore this warning.

Testing

Now we'll write a short class that will test our RSA ciphers and key generator, and make sure they're properly installed. We'll generate a key, encrypt a message, and then decrypt it. We'll just use standard Java and JCE classes, like `javax.crypto.Cipher` and `java.security.KeyPairGenerator`. The only catch is that we must register the provider at startup in order to be sure that our algorithms are available. In a regular distribution, the provider would be delivered as a JAR file that would be copied into the `lib/ext` directory. Then the provider would be registered in the `java.security` file.

```java
import java.security.*;
import javax.crypto.*;
import sun.misc.BASE64Encoder;

/**
 *  JCETest.java
 *
 *  Test class for our JCE provider of the RSA algorithm.
 *  Generates a key pair, then encrypts and decrypts a message.
 */

public class JCETest {

  public static void main(String[] args) throws Exception {

    String message = "This is a test";
    if (args.length != 0) {  // Args provided
      message = args[0];
    }
```

Here we'll create a BASE64 encoder for displaying binary data:

```java
    BASE64Encoder encoder = new BASE64Encoder();

    // Register the provider.

    Security.insertProviderAt(new
      com.isnetworks.crypto.jce.ISNetworksProvider(),1);
```

First we'll have to generate an RSA key pair:

```java
    KeyPairGenerator kpg =
      KeyPairGenerator.getInstance("RSA","ISNetworks");
    kpg.initialize(1024);
    System.out.println("Generating a key pair...");
    KeyPair keyPair = kpg.generateKeyPair();
```

```
        System.out.println("Done generating keys.\n");

        // Get the public and private keys.

        PublicKey publicKey =  keyPair.getPublic();
        PrivateKey privateKey = keyPair.getPrivate();

        // Create a byte array from the message.

        byte[] messageBytes = message.getBytes("UTF8");
```

Now we'll encrypt the message with the public key:

```
        Cipher cipher =
          Cipher.getInstance("RSA/ECB/OAEPPadding","ISNetworks");
        cipher.init(Cipher.ENCRYPT_MODE, publicKey);
        byte[] encryptedMessage = cipher.doFinal(messageBytes);

        System.out.println("Encrypted message:\n" +
          encoder.encode(encryptedMessage));
```

Here, we'll decrypt the encrypted data with the private key:

```
        cipher.init(Cipher.DECRYPT_MODE, privateKey);
        byte[] decryptedMessage = cipher.doFinal(encryptedMessage);
        String decryptedMessageString = new String(decryptedMessage,"UTF8");

        System.out.println("\nDecrypted message: " + decryptedMessageString);
```

We'll now check that the original and the newly decrypted messages are the same:

```
        if (decryptedMessageString.equals(message)) {
          System.out.println("\nTest succeeded.");
        } else {
          System.out.println("\nTest failed.");
        }
      }
    }
```

You can run the test with the following commands:

```
    C:\> javac JCETest.java
    C:\> java JCETest
```

You should see output similar to the following:

```
    Generating a key pair...
    Done generating keys.

    Encrypted message:
    B6ERQ725QLb1FdOZ7ThSvd1VEwHPLjOr1kKbUEwIFChwJkcZ+Fd4jdQQ7idJZ3Ru0oxToZ7cSGCG
    Wj2KSZQZMkCX9ST0vhj9FzKHZkDHGDRHZMtkPTvEQNFXh/eBcfcjBmGXi3L9+cTPTgd9rrBNom79
    u+rwly6WJCOz5agxDPc=

    Decrypted message: This is a test

    Test succeeded.
```

Generating the keys takes quite a bit of time(10 to 60 seconds), mostly due to the initialization of an instance of SecureRandom in the key generator itself.

Troubleshooting

If you can't compile the classes, then you need to make sure you have a JCE available. Refer to the section *Provider Requirements* at the beginning of this chapter and check that the JCE you've downloaded is on your classpath.

If you see the message, "Cannot set up certs for trusted CAs", then you probably have Sun's JCE 1.2.1 installed, which does not work with external providers unless they are signed by Sun. Remove Sun's JCE from your classpath or lib/ext and install one of the other JCE providers mentioned in the *Provider Requirements* section.

Now that you've hopefully got the RSA cipher functioning, we're going to add RSA signature support to our provider.

RSA Signatures

Since we've already created a number of RSA-handling classes for our cipher, creating an RSA signature implementation won't be too hard. Keys are finished, so we need only implement a few items:

- ❑ Padding
- ❑ Cryptographic signature primitives
- ❑ An implementation of java.security.SignatureSpi

Also, we'll need to add our signature classes to our provider.

To create a digital signature, one hashes the message that is to be signed and then encrypts that hash with a private key. That encrypted hash is the digital signature. To check that signature, one decrypts it with the corresponding public key, and then compares that with a hash of the message. If they match, the signature is valid.

This diagram shows signature generation:

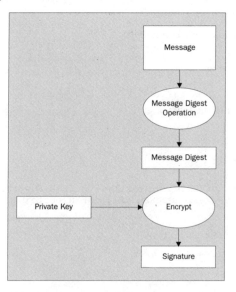

Signature verification is shown in the next diagram:

Padding

For our signatures, we're going to use PKCS1 signature padding. This is similar to PKCS1 padding for encryption, with two small changes. Here is what our block of data will look like after padding:

01	PS	00	T

The 01 is a flag to signify that this is signed data. PS is a Padding String of bytes, all of which have the value 255 (Hex FF). T is an ASN.1 DER encoding of a DigestInfo object, a hash of the message to be signed, along with an algorithm identifier, like so:

```
DigestInfo ::= SEQUENCE {
  digestAlgorithm AlgorithmIdentifier, digest OCTET STRING
}
```

ASN stands for **Abstract Syntax Notation**. It is a way of encoding binary data with tags to specify what it contains. We do not want to implement all of ASN.1 just to compute this one value, and fortunately for us, RSA's PKCS#1 documentation contains a shortcut: precomputed ASN.1 values for different hashing algorithms. We'll support MD5 and SHA-1. Here are the two possible encodings for T, where H is a hash of the message passed in:

```
MD5:   T = 30 20 30 0c 06 08 2a 86 48 86 f7 0d 02 05 05 00 04 10 || H
SHA-1: T = 30 21 30 1f 06 05 2b 0e 03 02 1a 05 00 04 14 || H
```

PKCS1SignaturePadding.java

We will implement our Padding interface, just as we did in our cipher implementation. PKCS 1 signature padding, however, has no decode function. We will throw a runtime exception if anyone tries to call decode().

We will have two internal static byte arrays, one for each of the possible ASN.1 encodings for T. The section of T reserved for the hash of the message will be filled with zeroes, which we will replace upon encoding.

```java
package com.isnetworks.crypto.rsa;

import com.isnetworks.crypto.*;

import java.io.*;
import java.security.*;

import javax.crypto.*;

/**
 *  Padding implementation for PKCS #1 signatures.
 */

public class PKCS1SignaturePadding implements Padding{
```

We need to store the length of the hash that our message digest function produces.

```java
private int mHLen;
```

We also need the default value of T for the chosen hash function.

```java
private byte[] mTDefault;
```

We'll have a pair of constants to allow us to refer to our two available hashing algorithms, SHA-1 and MD5.

```java
public static final int SHA1 = 1;
public static final int MD5 = 2;
```

We need two more constants, default digest info for each of the two algorithms. These are ASN.1 streams:

```java
private final static byte[] SHA1_DIGEST_INFO = {
    (byte)0x30, (byte)0x21, (byte)0x30, (byte)0x09, (byte)0x06,
    (byte)0x05, (byte)0x2b, (byte)0x0e, (byte)0x03, (byte)0x02,
    (byte)0x1a, (byte)0x05, (byte)0x00, (byte)0x04, (byte)0x14,
    (byte)0x00, (byte)0x00, (byte)0x00, (byte)0x00, (byte)0x00,
    (byte)0x00, (byte)0x00, (byte)0x00, (byte)0x00, (byte)0x00,
    (byte)0x00, (byte)0x00, (byte)0x00, (byte)0x00, (byte)0x00,
    (byte)0x00, (byte)0x00, (byte)0x00, (byte)0x00, (byte)0x00
};

private final static byte[] MD5_DIGEST_INFO = {
    (byte)0x30, (byte)0x20, (byte)0x30, (byte)0x0c, (byte)0x06,
    (byte)0x08, (byte)0x2a, (byte)0x86, (byte)0x48, (byte)0x86,
    (byte)0xf7, (byte)0x0d, (byte)0x02, (byte)0x05, (byte)0x05,
    (byte)0x00, (byte)0x04, (byte)0x10, (byte)0x00, (byte)0x00,
    (byte)0x00, (byte)0x00, (byte)0x00, (byte)0x00, (byte)0x00,
    (byte)0x00, (byte)0x00, (byte)0x00, (byte)0x00, (byte)0x00,
    (byte)0x00, (byte)0x00, (byte)0x00, (byte)0x00
};
```

One of our constructors will take a hash algorithm, either MD5 or SHA-1.

```
public PKCS1SignaturePadding(int hashAlgorithm) {
    String algorithmName = NULL;
```

We need to fill `mTDefault` with the appropriate byte array from one of our digest info arrays.

```
    if (hashAlgorithm == MD5) {
      algorithmName = "MD5";
      mTDefault = new byte[MD5_DIGEST_INFO.length];
      System.arraycopy(MD5_DIGEST_INFO,0,mTDefault,0,mTDefault.length);
      mHLen = 16;
    } else {
      algorithmName = "SHA";
      mTDefault = new byte[SHA1_DIGEST_INFO.length];
      System.arraycopy(SHA1_DIGEST_INFO,0,mTDefault,0,mTDefault.length);
      mHLen = 20;
    }
}
```

We'll have another constructor, this one with no arguments. It will simply call our other constructor with the default algorithm of SHA-1.

```
public PKCS1SignaturePadding() {
    this(SHA1);
}
```

Now we'll define our `encode()` method. It takes the hash to be encoded and the required length of the resulting padded block. The length needs to be at least 10 bytes longer than the default digest info, in order to store 8 bytes of padding and the two one-byte demarcations.

```
public byte[] encode(byte[] H, int emLen)
    throws IllegalBlockSizeException {
    if (emLen < mTDefault.length + 10) {
      throw new IllegalBlockSizeException("encoding too short");
    }
```

We'll create `T` from our default digest info. We also need to copy the hash after it.

```
    byte[] T = new byte[mTDefault.length];
    System.arraycopy(mTDefault,0,T,0,T.length);
    System.arraycopy(H,0,T,T.length - mHLen,mHLen);
```

Now we need to create our padding string. It should be the length of the message minus `T` and minus two more bytes for the demarcations. All the padding bytes are `0xFF`.

```
    byte[] PS = new byte[emLen - T.length - 2];
    for (int i = 0; i < PS.length; i++) {
      PS[i] = (byte)0xFF;
    }
```

Next we'll create the output block, which looks like this: 01 || PS || 00 || T. We'll use a byte array output stream to make this operation simple.

```
ByteArrayOutputStream baos = new ByteArrayOutputStream();
try {
  baos.write((byte)0x01);
  baos.write(PS);
  baos.write((byte)0x00);
  baos.write(T);
} catch (IOException ioe) {

  // This should never happen

  ioe.printStackTrace();
}
```

Finally, we want to return the byte array from the byte array output stream.

```
byte[] EM = baos.toByteArray();
return EM;
}
```

As we mentioned, we need to implement decode() in order to implement the Padding interface, but we do not actually support decoding a signature block. We'll throw an exception if this gets called.

```
public byte[] decode(byte[] H) {
  throw new RuntimeException("Decode not used in PKCS1 Signature Padding");
}
}
```

Cryptographic Primitives

There are two cryptographic primitives used in RSA signing: RSASP1, the **RSA Signing Primitive** and RSAVP1, the **RSA Verification Primitive**. These perform the actual mathematical operations used when signing and verifying with RSA.

RSASP1

We will pass in a private key in the form of {d, n} or {p, q, dP, dQ, qInv} for a CRT key, along with the message m, in the form of a large integer. RSASP1 will compute s, a signature representative, also a large integer. Note that this is mathematically identical to RSA decryption.

1. If the private key is in the form {d, n}, compute $s = m^d \bmod n$. Return s.

2. Otherwise, use the Chinese Remainder Theorem. Let $s1 = m^{dP} \bmod p$.

3. $s2 = m^{dQ} \bmod q$.

4. $h = qInv(s1 - s2) \bmod p$.

5. $s = s2 + hq$.

6. Return s.

RSAVP1

Pass in a public key in the form {e, n}, along with the signature representative, s, a large integer. Compute m, the message, also a large integer. This is mathematically identical to RSA encryption.

1. $m = s^e$ mod n.

2. Return m.

We will place both RSASP1 and RSAVP1 in the RSA class we defined earlier, as static methods. They will go in alongside `rsaep()` and `rsadp()`, as `rsasp1()` and `rsavp1()`.

```java
package com.isnetworks.crypto.rsa;

import java.math.*;
import java.security.*;
import java.security.interfaces.*;

import javax.crypto.*;

// RSA.java

public class RSA {

  /**
   *  Encrypt a BigInteger with an RSA public key.
   */

  public static BigInteger rsaep (RSAPublicKey publicKey, BigInteger m)
    throws IllegalBlockSizeException {

    BigInteger e = publicKey.getPublicExponent();
    BigInteger n = publicKey.getModulus();

    // Check if m is in range

    BigInteger nMinusOne = n.subtract(BigInteger.ONE);

    // m > 0 and m < n-1

    if (m.compareTo(BigInteger.ZERO) < 0) {
      throw new IllegalBlockSizeException("Ciphertext too small");
    }
    if (m.compareTo(nMinusOne) > 0) {
      throw new IllegalBlockSizeException("Ciphertext too large");
    }

    // Here it is: RSA encryption in all its glory:

    BigInteger c = m.modPow(e,n);

    return c;
  }
```

```
/**
 *  Decrypt a BigInteger with an RSA private key.
 */

public static BigInteger rsadp (RSAPrivateKey privateKey, BigInteger c) {

    if (!(privateKey instanceof RSAPrivateCrtKey)) {

        // Can't use the Chinese Remainder Theorem

        BigInteger d = privateKey.getPrivateExponent();
        BigInteger n = privateKey.getModulus();

        // RSA decrypt

        BigInteger m = c.modPow(d,n);

        return m;
    }

    // Use Chinese Remainder Theorem to speed up calculation

    RSAPrivateCrtKey privateCrtKey = (RSAPrivateCrtKey)privateKey;

    BigInteger p = privateCrtKey.getPrimeP();
    BigInteger q = privateCrtKey.getPrimeQ();
    BigInteger dP = privateCrtKey.getPrimeExponentP();
    BigInteger dQ = privateCrtKey.getPrimeExponentQ();
    BigInteger qInv = privateCrtKey.getCrtCoefficient();

    BigInteger m1 = c.modPow(dP,p);
    BigInteger m2 = c.modPow(dQ,q);

    // Let h = qInv(m1 - m2) mod p

    BigInteger h = m1.subtract(m2);
    h = h.multiply(qInv);
    h = h.mod(p);

    // m = m2 + hq

    BigInteger m = h.multiply(q);
    m = m.add(m2);

    return m;
}
```

Here's our `rsasp1()` method. It is nearly identical to our `rsadp()` method.

```
public static BigInteger rsasp1 (RSAPrivateKey privateKey, BigInteger m)
    throws IllegalBlockSizeException {

    BigInteger n = privateKey.getModulus();

    // Check if m is in range

    BigInteger nMinusOne = n.subtract(BigInteger.ONE);

    // m > 0 and m < n-1
```

```
      if (m.compareTo(BigInteger.ZERO) < 0) {
        throw new IllegalBlockSizeException("message too small");
      }
      if (m.compareTo(nMinusOne) > 0) {
        throw new IllegalBlockSizeException("message too large");
      }

      if (!(privateKey instanceof RSAPrivateCrtKey)) {
        BigInteger d = privateKey.getPrivateExponent();
        BigInteger s = m.modPow(d,n);
        return s;
      }

      // Use the Chinese Remainder Theorem for efficiency

      RSAPrivateCrtKey K = (RSAPrivateCrtKey)privateKey;
      BigInteger p = K.getPrimeP();
      BigInteger q = K.getPrimeQ();
      BigInteger dP = K.getPrimeExponentP();
      BigInteger dQ = K.getPrimeExponentQ();
      BigInteger qInv = K.getCrtCoefficient();

      BigInteger s1 = m.modPow(dP, p);
      BigInteger s2 = m.modPow(dQ, q);

      // h = qInv(s1 - s2) mod p

      BigInteger h = s1.subtract(s2);
      h = h.multiply(qInv);
      h = h.mod(p);

      // s = s2 + hq

      BigInteger s = h.multiply(q);
      s = s.add(s2);

      return s;
    }
```

rsavp1() is for signature verification. It is mathematically identical to RSA encryption.

```
    public static BigInteger rsavp1(RSAPublicKey publicKey, BigInteger s)
      throws IllegalBlockSizeException {
      BigInteger n = publicKey.getModulus();

      // Check if m is in range

      BigInteger nMinusOne = n.subtract(BigInteger.ONE);

      // s > 0 and s < n-1

      if (s.compareTo(BigInteger.ZERO) < 0) {
        throw new IllegalBlockSizeException("message too small");
      }
      if (s.compareTo(nMinusOne) > 0) {
        throw new IllegalBlockSizeException("message too large");
      }
      BigInteger e = publicKey.getPublicExponent();

      BigInteger m = s.modPow(e,n);

      return m;
    }
  }
```

Extend SignatureSpi

Just as we did for our cipher, we need to extend an abstract class, this time `java.security.SignatureSpi`. Here are the methods that we need to implement:

- ❑ `engineInitSign()` – Initialize for signing.

- ❑ `engineInitVerify()` – Initialize for verifying a signature.

- ❑ `engineSetParameter()` – Initialize with the specified parameters. RSA signatures take no parameters, so this will merely throw an exception. There are two forms of this method, one which takes a string and an object and the other which takes an `AlgorithmParameterSpec`. The first method has been deprecated, but we must implement it in order to compile our class.

- ❑ `engineGetParameter()` – Return the parameters. We use no parameters, so we will return NULL. This method has also been deprecated, but again, we will need to provide an implementation or we will be unable to compile.

- ❑ `engineUpdate()` – Pass some bytes to the engine for signing or verifying. They are appended to any data that's already been passed in.

- ❑ `engineSign()` – Actually sign the bytes that have been sent. Resets the engine, and returns the signature.

- ❑ `engineVerify()` – Verifies the signature on the bytes that have been sent. Resets the engine and returns a Boolean.

Ultimately, all of our operations take place on a hash of the message. Because of this, there's no need for us to actually store the data itself; we only need to store the resulting hash. Internally, every time we receive more bytes to update the message with, we will simply pass those bytes directly on to the message digest object we have.

There are two message digest types that we are going to support: MD5 and SHA-1. Because of this, we're going to write one signature class that's abstract, and two subclasses that will support one algorithm each. All of the work will take place in our superclass, and the subclasses will only define the padding and the message digest that is to be used.

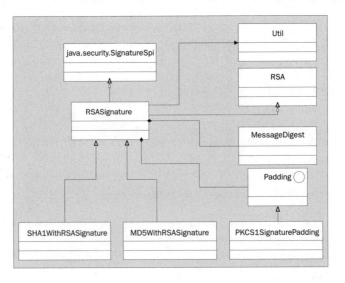

Now let's take a look at our `RSASignature` class.

```
package com.isnetworks.crypto.rsa;

import com.isnetworks.crypto.Padding;
import java.math.BigInteger;
import java.security.spec.*;
import java.security.interfaces.*;
import java.security.*;
import java.util.*;

// RSASignature.java

public abstract class RSASignature extends SignatureSpi {
```

We have two constants to define the operating mode: sign or verify:

```
private final static int SIGN_MODE = 1;
private final static int VERIFY_MODE = 2;
```

We need an internal message digest for digesting the data to be signed.

```
private MessageDigest mHasher;
```

We also need to store our padding. Currently there's only one possible implementation – PKCS#1. We store our operating mode in a member variable. It's either sign or verify:

```
private Padding mPadding;
private int mOperatingMode;
```

We have two more member variables: one for the key to use for signing or verifying and another for holding the status of initialization, and one constructor – the default one:

```
private Key mKey;
private boolean mInitialized = false;
public RSASignature() {
  super();
}
```

We want to be able to set the message digest and the padding from our subclasses, so we'll create mutator methods for those options.

```
protected void setMessageDigest(MessageDigest hasher) {
  mHasher = hasher;
}

protected void setPadding(Padding padding) {
  mPadding = padding;
}
```

Now we start getting into the meat of our signature implementation. We have two `engineInitSign()` methods. The first will set our mode, reset our message digest, and set the initialization status. The second will call the first, but we need to accept an instance of `SecureRandom` to match the API. We don't actually use any random numbers in PKCS#1 RSA signing, so we can simply ignore the random number generator.

```
protected void engineInitSign(PrivateKey privateKey) throws InvalidKeyException
{
    if (!(privateKey instanceof RSAPrivateKey)) {
      throw new InvalidKeyException("Key must be an RSAPrivateKey");
    }
    mOperatingMode = SIGN_MODE;
    mHasher.reset();
    mKey = privateKey;
    mInitialized = true;
}

protected void engineInitSign(PrivateKey privateKey, SecureRandom random)
    throws InvalidKeyException {

    // We use no random in PKCS1 signing.

    this.engineInitSign(privateKey);
}
```

We have only one `engineInitVerify()`. We'll set the operating mode, reset the message digest, set the key, and set the initialization status.

```
protected void engineInitVerify(PublicKey publicKey) throws InvalidKeyException
{
    if (!(publicKey instanceof RSAPublicKey)) {
      throw new InvalidKeyException("Key must be an RSAPublicKey");
    }
    mOperatingMode = VERIFY_MODE;
    mHasher.reset();
    mKey = publicKey;
    mInitialized = true;
}
```

We need to implement various ways of setting and getting the algorithm parameters. We don't support algorithm parameters, so we'll throw an exception if someone tries to set them and return NULL if someone wants to retrieve them.

```
protected void engineSetParameter(AlgorithmParameterSpec params)
    throws InvalidAlgorithmParameterException {

    throw new InvalidAlgorithmParameterException("RSASignature does not accept
algorithm parameters");
    }

    protected void engineSetParameter(String param, Object value) throws
InvalidParameterException {
    throw new InvalidParameterException("RSASignature does not accept algorithm
parameters");
    }

    protected Object engineGetParameter(String param) {
    return NULL;
    }
```

Now we need to write our two `engineUpdate()` methods. The difference between them is whether we should read in an entire byte array or just one byte. If someone passes in a single byte, we'll wrap it in a byte array and call the other method. This is not particularly efficient, but if we need to change what we do with an update, we've kept it in one method.

```
   protected void engineUpdate(byte[] b, int off, int len) throws
SignatureException {
      if (!mInitialized) {
         throw new SignatureException("Signature not initialized");
      }

      // We don't need to keep the message, just the message digest.

      mHasher.update(b, off, len);
   }

   protected void engineUpdate(byte b) throws SignatureException {
      byte[] byteArray = new byte[1];
      byteArray[0] = b;
      engineUpdate(byteArray,0,1);
   }
```

Next we'll write our signing routine. This returns a byte array containing the signature. We start by checking the operating mode and the initialization status.

```
   protected byte[] engineSign() throws SignatureException {
      if (!mInitialized) {
         throw new SignatureException("Signature not initialized");
      }
      if (mOperatingMode != SIGN_MODE) {
         throw new SignatureException("Signature not in signing mode");
      }
```

We need to get the size of the key in bytes, which we'll be using shortly.

```
      int k = (((RSAPrivateKey)mKey).getModulus().bitLength()+7)/8;
```

We can extract the hash from our message digest object, as we've received all the data we're going to sign.

```
      byte[] hash = mHasher.digest();
```

Now we can perform the signing. We pad the hash into a block 1byte less than the key size. Then we construct a big integer from that padded block and pass it to our `rsasp1` primitive. Finally, we transform the resulting big integer into a byte array using a utility method and return the result.

```
      byte[] S = NULL;
      try {
         byte[] EM = mPadding.encode(hash, k-1);
         BigInteger m = new BigInteger(1, EM);
         BigInteger s = RSA.rsasp1((RSAPrivateKey)mKey, m);
         S = Util.I2OSP(s, k);
      } catch (javax.crypto.IllegalBlockSizeException ibse) {
         throw new SignatureException(ibse.getMessage());
      }
      return S;
   }
```

Our second `engineSign()` method is nearly the same as the previous. The only difference is that the result should be placed in a user-defined array. We'll call our previous method to do the work.

```
protected int engineSign(byte[] outbuf, int offset, int len)
    throws SignatureException {

    byte[] output = engineSign();
    if (output.length > len) {
        throw new SignatureException("buffer too small");
    }
    System.arraycopy(output,0,outbuf,offset,output.length);
    return output.length;
}
```

Now we get to our verify method. We return a `boolean`: `true` if the signature verifies and `false` if it doesn't. We will receive the signature to verify as a byte array. We'll begin by checking the operating mode and the initialization status.

```
protected boolean engineVerify(byte[] sigBytes) throws SignatureException {

    if (!mInitialized) {
        throw new SignatureException("Signature not initialized");
    }
    if (!(mOperatingMode == VERIFY_MODE)) {
        throw new SignatureException("Signature not in verify mode");
    }
```

As in our signing method, we'll need the key size in bytes.

```
    int k = (((RSAPublicKey)mKey).getModulus().bitLength()+7)/8;
```

Now we can perform the actual verification. We need to transform the signature bytes passed in into a big integer. We then use our `rsavp1` primitive to get back a big integer, which is the padded block created in signing.

```
    BigInteger s = new BigInteger(1, sigBytes);
    byte[] EM = NULL;
    byte[] EMPrime = NULL;
    try {
        BigInteger m = RSA.rsavp1((RSAPublicKey)mKey, s);
```

We can convert that padded block into a byte array like so:

```
    EM = Util.I2OSP(m, k-1);
```

Now we will create our own version of the encoded message, called `EMPrime`, by encoding the hash we create from our own data.

```
        byte[] hash = mHasher.digest();
        EMPrime = mPadding.encode(hash, k-1);
    } catch (javax.crypto.IllegalBlockSizeException ibse) {
        throw new SignatureException(ibse.getMessage());
    }
```

If EM and EMPrime are equal, the signature verifies. Otherwise, the data has been altered, or the signature itself was incorrect. We'll return the result of comparing EM and EMPrime.

```
      return Arrays.equals(EM, EMPrime);

   }
}
```

Subclassing RSASignature

The only things missing from our RSASignature class are appropriately set padding and a message digest. Our two subclasses need only set those two options in order to be fully useable. First, let's tackle MD5 hashing:

```
package com.isnetworks.crypto.rsa;

import com.isnetworks.crypto.Padding;
import java.security.*;

/**
 *  MD5WithRSASignature.java
 *
 *  Implementation of RSASignature using the MD5
 *  hashing algorithm.
 */

public class MD5WithRSASignature extends RSASignature {

  public MD5WithRSASignature() {
    super();

    // Now we need to set the padding and the message digest.

    Padding padding = new
      PKCS1SignaturePadding(PKCS1SignaturePadding.MD5);
    MessageDigest messageDigest = NULL;
    try {
      messageDigest = MessageDigest.getInstance("MD5");
    } catch (NoSuchAlgorithmException nsae) {

      // This should never happen as Sun provides MD5

      nsae.printStackTrace();
    }
    super.setMessageDigest(messageDigest);
    super.setPadding(padding);
  }
}
```

Next, SHA-1 hashing.

```
package com.isnetworks.crypto.rsa;

import com.isnetworks.crypto.Padding;
import java.security.*;

/**
 *  SHA1WithRSASignature.java
 *
```

```
 *   Implementation of RSASignature using the SHA-1
 *   hashing algorithm.
 */

public class SHA1WithRSASignature extends RSASignature {

  public SHA1WithRSASignature() {
    super();

    // Now we need to set the padding and the message digest.

    Padding padding = new
      PKCS1SignaturePadding(PKCS1SignaturePadding.SHA1);
    MessageDigest messageDigest = NULL;
    try {
      messageDigest = MessageDigest.getInstance("SHA1");
    } catch (NoSuchAlgorithmException nsae) {

      // This should never happen as Sun provides SHA1

      nsae.printStackTrace();
    }
    super.setMessageDigest(messageDigest);
    super.setPadding(padding);
  }
}
```

Modify the Provider

Now that all our classes have been written, we need to modify our original provider so that our signature algorithm can be used through the JCA. We just need to add two entries, one for each type of hashing that our signature can handle. Here is ISNetworksProvider.java, modified:

```
package com.isnetworks.crypto.jce;

import java.security.*;

/**
 *   ISNetworks cryptography provider
 *
 *   This provider supports RSA encryption, decryption,
 *   signatures, and key generation.
 */

public final class ISNetworksProvider extends java.security.Provider {

  private static final String NAME = "ISNetworks";

  private static final double VERSION = 1.0;

  private static final String INFO = "ISNetworks RSA Provider";

  public ISNetworksProvider() {
    super (NAME, VERSION, INFO);

    // Need to call doPrivileged, in case our caller
    // does not have permission to register a security
    // provider, but we do.

    AccessController.doPrivileged(new java.security.PrivilegedAction() {
      public Object run() {
```

```
            put("Cipher.RSA","com.isnetworks.crypto.rsa.RSACipher");

            put("KeyPairGenerator.RSA",
              "com.isnetworks.crypto.rsa.RSAKeyPairGenerator");

            put("Signature.MD5withRSA",
              "com.isnetworks.crypto.rsa.MD5WithRSASignature");
            put("Signature.SHA1withRSA",
              "com.isnetworks.crypto.rsa.SHA1WithRSASignature");

            return NULL;
        }
      });

    }
  }
```

Compile and Test

Compilation is exactly the same as it was before: in the directory with all the classes, run:

```
C:\> javac -d . *.java
```

You will receive a warning about deprecated classes. That's our extension of SignatureSpi, which requires implementation of two deprecated methods. It's safe to ignore this warning.

Next we want to run a quick test case, just to make sure our provider works. We'll create an RSA key pair, sign a test message, and then verify that signature. Here's SignatureTest.java, which does exactly that:

```
import java.security.*;

import sun.misc.BASE64Encoder;

/**
 *   Test class for our JCE provider of RSA signatures.
 *
 *   Generates a key pair, then signs a message and verifies
 *   the signature.
 */

public class SignatureTest {

  public static void main(String[] args) throws Exception {

    String message = "This is a test";
    if (args.length != 0) {  // Args provided
      message = args[0];
    }

    // Create a base-64 encoder for displaying binary data.

    BASE64Encoder encoder = new BASE64Encoder();

    // Register the provider.

    Security.insertProviderAt(new
      com.isnetworks.crypto.jce.ISNetworksProvider(),1);

    // First generate an RSA key pair.
```

```
    KeyPairGenerator kpg = KeyPairGenerator.getInstance("RSA","ISNetworks");
    kpg.initialize(1024);
    System.out.println("Generating a key pair...");
    KeyPair keyPair = kpg.generateKeyPair();
    System.out.println("Done generating keys.\n");

    // Get the public and private keys.

    PublicKey publicKey =  keyPair.getPublic();
    PrivateKey privateKey = keyPair.getPrivate();

    // Create a byte array from the message.

    byte[] messageBytes = message.getBytes("UTF8");

    // Get a Signature instance.

    Signature signer = Signature.getInstance("SHA1withRSA","ISNetworks");

    // Sign the message.
    signer.initSign(privateKey);
    signer.update(messageBytes);
    byte[] signatureBytes = signer.sign();

    System.out.println("\nThe signature: \n"
                       +encoder.encode(signatureBytes)+"\n");

    // To verify, we need to re-initialize the Signature instance,
    // with the public key instead of the private.

    signer.initVerify(publicKey);
    signer.update(messageBytes);
    boolean valid = signer.verify(signatureBytes);

    if (valid) {
      System.out.println("Signature is valid.");
    } else {
      System.out.println("Signature is invalid.");
    }
  }
}
```

You can compile and run this test with the following:

```
C:\> javac SignatureTest.java
C:\> java SignatureTest
```

You should see output similar to the following:

```
Generating a key pair...
Done generating keys.


The signature:
AfW+Nc8cHDfnOnJdawvO/Es+qpY9+8Qgo/SiYxoy9wZBzvlOcAyfefvJpN8YdXEmYFBwpC8LH8rT
AkVBrLdNgpJj1kbFVkKT29CcYdWPIQrwDi3mIjv2MPaFUxD/BG5B/+8mAdCBEZxKuFqQKc1QTj8G
+nuK0tDNZ91V2M0BuMY=

Signature is valid.
```

Our provider is complete. If you like, you can jar up the classes and place them in `$JAVA_HOME/jre/lib/ext` and they will be available for all applications.

Limitations and Further Implementation

The biggest limitation of our provider is the lack of support for encoding and decoding RSA keys. This could be added, but it requires an ASN.1 library, which as we mentioned isn't particularly easy to come by. Fortunately, Sun's JDK 1.3 includes support for RSA signatures, key generation, and encoding and decoding of keys. If you're using the `ISNetworks` provider on JDK 1.3, you really only need the cipher functionality. The cipher works perfectly well with Sun-generated keys. It's only necessary that they implement the RSA key interfaces in `java.security.interfaces`.

If you're generating RSA keys on JDK 1.3 and you want to be able to export them with proper encodings, be sure not to use the `ISNetworks` `KeyPairGenerator`. Instead, use the default generator that comes with the JDK. For example, rather than using the following line of Java code:

```
KeyPairGenerator kpg = KeyPairGenerator.getInstance("RSA", "ISNetworks");
```

use this:

```
KeyPairGenerator kpg = KeyPairGenerator.getInstance("RSA");
```

If you need key encodings in JDK 1.2, you could implement your own ASN.1 encodings and add them to the key implementations. Alternatively, you could use another provider, like Bouncy Castle.

Summary

We began the book by looking at the different areas that need to be considered when thinking about developing secure computer systems before focusing on the core theme of the book – developing secure Java-based applications. After a discussion on writing secure code, we moved into the field of cryptography within the framework of the Java programming language.

We discussed the Java Cryptography Architecture (JCA) and the Java Cryptography Extension (JCE) and showed how symmetric and asymmetric encryption can be performed within this. We expanded into the area of authentication, covering message digests, digital signatures, and digital certificates in the process.

We then looked at the Java 2 security model and applet security in particular before we moved on to discuss security issues pertaining to enterprise-application development with a look at additional security aspects of the Java platform associated with servlets, Enterprise JavaBeans (EJBs), and the Java Authentication and Authorization Service (JAAS). We also covered Secure Sockets Layer (SSL) communications.

In the last few chapters we've taken all of the earlier chapters on board to show how the concepts can be approached in a full-blown enterprise type application. This included securing the connections to the database, securing the data contained in the database, and how encryption and authentication could be incorporated into a full-blown enterprise application.

Finally, in this chapter we've discussed how to implement your own cryptographic service provider using the JCA and JCE framework. We've written a provider that supports RSA encryption and signatures, and also described in detail how RSA works and how to implement it in Java. We've also provided some test classes so that we could test out our provider to ensure that it worked in the way that we expected it to.

473

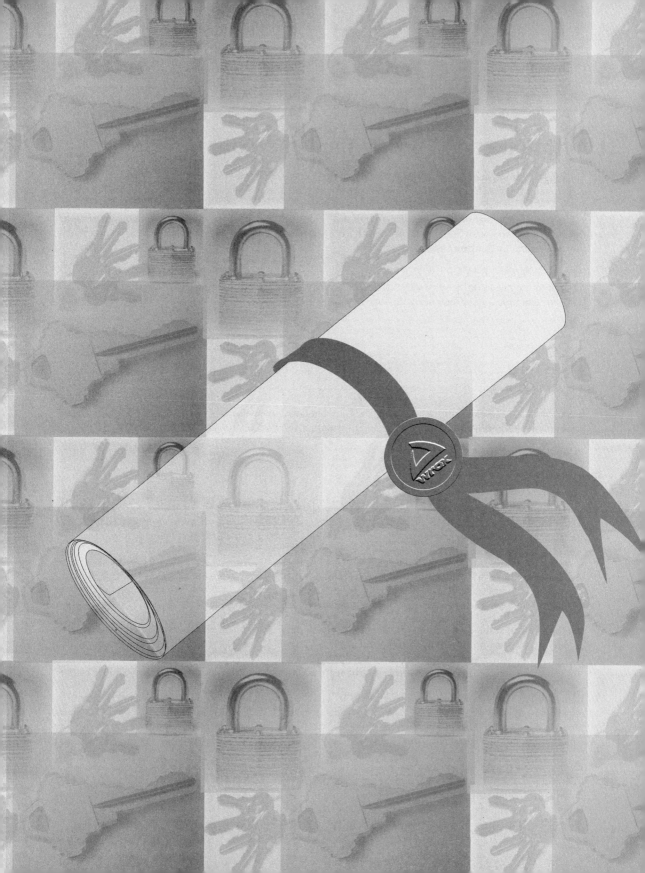

Additional Techniques

Within the body of this book, we've concentrated on the basic cryptographic primitives, like message digests, encryption, and digital signatures, as well as session-key encryption and SSL. There are a number of well-established ways to use these primitives to achieve certain effects, some of which we've illustrated. However, to secure your particular application, you may need more tools than the ones we have already provided. In this appendix we'll quickly talk about some additional protocols and techniques that you may find useful to augment the approaches we've already described – some of these techniques (like timestamping and nonces) we've already encountered in passing.

The topics we'll be looking at here are:

- ❑ Secure e-mail
- ❑ Timestamping
- ❑ Secure logging
- ❑ Using a nonce

As we mentioned at the start of the book it's important to use proven algorithms and protocols whenever possible. Many of them have been rigorously tested and validated. When you create your own protocol, you risk creating new problems that an expert would have caught. That's not to say that using existing protocols guarantees success, but it will give you a considerable head start.

If you're looking for something special, say, a protocol for digital cash, then the first place to start is the existing literature and a good overview of a number of protocols and algorithms can be found in *Applied Cryptography: Protocols, Algorithms, and Source Code in C, 2nd Edition* by Bruce Schneier, John Wiley & Sons; ISBN: 0-471117-09-9.

Secure E-Mail

E-mail is almost always sent in the clear over the Internet. If you wish your communications to be private, you need to find some way to protect your e-mail. There are two common forms of secure e-mail in use today: **S/MIME** (**Secure/Multipurpose Internet Mail Extensions**) and **PGP** (**Pretty Good Privacy**). Neither is well supported in Java, but libraries can be purchased that add the appropriate capability.

Secure e-mail typically provides two services:

❑ Encryption

❑ Authentication

If encryption is used, then the message can only be read by its intended recipient. Authentication allows the recipient to be certain that the message truly came from the person who signed it. Session-key encryption is used to encrypt the messages, and digital signatures are applied to supply authentication. The particular algorithms are dependent on what form of secure e-mail used.

There are a number of possible uses for secure e-mail. Let's say you have reports that are generated weekly that need to be sent to key employees. It would be nice to secure those reports so that only those employees could read them. Also, by signing the reports with the sender's private key, no one could forge the reports. An additional use of secure e-mail is issuing authenticated commands. Network Solutions, for instance, allows its customers who set up domain names to require PGP authentication on any requests for changes.

S/MIME

Secure/Multipurpose Internet Mail Extensions (S/MIME) is a format for secure e-mail put forward by RSA Security Inc., and implemented in three of the most popular e-mail clients:

❑ Netscape Communicator

❑ Microsoft Outlook

❑ Microsoft Outlook Express

The S/MIME protocol is defined in RFC 2633 (which can be found at www.ietf.org/rfc/rfc2633). S/MIME is currently at version 3.0, but most implementations only support version 2. The differences are fairly minor, however. In the S/MIME format for encrypting and digitally signing e-mails:

❑ Keys are delivered in X.509 certificates

❑ Signatures are most commonly performed using RSA

❑ Encryption is done with a session-key, usually TripleDES, with the key encrypted using RSA

At the time of the writing, there were no free S/MIME libraries for Java that could be used commercially, and, in the table below, a few of the companies selling such libraries are identified. Other companies will no doubt begin offering S/MIME libraries, including RSA Security Inc. These libraries are however, likely to be expensive

Provider	URL	Notes
DSTC	security.dstc.edu.au/projects/java/misc/s-mime.html	Free for non-commercial use
IAIK	jcewww.iaik.tu-graz.ac.at/Smime/Smime.htm	
ISNetworks	www.isnetworks.com/smime/	30-day trial available
Phaos	www.phaos.com/e_security/prod_smime.html	

Using S/MIME is not difficult if you have the appropriate classes, but there is no standard way in Java to create and send such a message. Instead, you'll have to use provider-specific APIs.

Alternatives to S/MIME

Due to its expense, you may find it unfeasible to use S/MIME in your applications. Some alternative options are:

❑ Writing your own S/MIME implementation – This is unlikely to be much more feasible than purchasing an implementation due to the amount of work involved in writing an S/MIME implementation.

❑ Creating your own e-mail protocol – You could perform your own session-key encryption and/or digital signatures and attach the files to your e-mail messages. These would likely not be as secure as S/MIME, but it may be appropriate for certain applications.

❑ Avoiding encrypted e-mails – You could send notifications in plaintext e-mail, and then provide that actual information itself on a web server secured with SSL. It would be advisable to use some sort of authentication, such as SSL client authentication, in order to ensure that an eavesdropper could not access the server's information.

❑ Using PGP – We're about to discuss PGP and using it as an option over S/MIME. The situation under PGP isn't really any better. It's still difficult to find libraries for a reasonable price, but there is a project in the works to provide PGP support in Java, run by Cryptix (see below).

PGP

PGP ("Pretty Good Privacy") was written by Phil Zimmermann in 1991, and was the first widely used e-mail encryption protocol. It is quite similar to S/MIME, but uses a different form of certificates.

Rather than use the hierarchical trust model of X.509, PGP uses **peer-based trust**, where each user decides which certificates he or she will trust. This works well in a community of technical experts, but falls short in an enterprise where individual users do not understand cryptography or PKI.

That being said, PGP can be quite useful for the same things as S/MIME from within Java. As long as the certificates you will be using are established beforehand, the two are practically equivalent (the latest specification for PGP – known as **OpenPGP** – is available at www.ietf.org/rfc/rfc2440.txt).

Unfortunately, Java's support for PGP is only marginally better than its support for S/MIME. There is only one project that we are currently aware of that is implementing the latest version of PGP (OpenPGP) in Java: the Cryptix OpenPGP project, at http://www.cryptix.org/products/openpgp/index.html. Cryptix has an implementation of an older version of PGP (v 2.x) that is complete, but it is not compatible with current versions of PGP or with OpenPGP. Cryptix's OpenPGP was not complete at the time this book was written.

Solutions

OK, so Java support is lacking in encrypted e-mail. What can be done? Hopefully the expiration of the RSA patent will spur the development of implementations. Perhaps Sun will even add S/MIME to JavaMail, which would be particularly welcome. Perhaps some enterprising developer reading this book will decide to work on Cryptix's OpenPGP implementation or even contribute an S/MIME library. If you need secure e-mail support in Java right now, though, you're probably going to have to go with a proprietary solution. However, as we mentioned in our section on S/MIME, there are alternatives to using secure mail, such as sending short messages that tell a user to visit a secure web page.

Timestamping

Timestamping is an extremely simple concept with a great number of sophisticated uses. Essentially a timestamp provides proof that some information existed at a specific point in time. One must begin by establishing a machine that has a source of time that everyone involved will agree upon. This will be known as the **Time Stamp Authority** (**TSA**). Perhaps it synchronizes with an official time source, such as the one run by the International Bureau of Weights and Measures, or through GPS transmissions. It isn't even truly required that it be synched to anything, but all parties involved in the system using the service must agree that that the Time Stamp Authority is authoritative for time. Thus, if there is a disagreement about what time it is, the authority is correct. Sometimes this authority is called a **timeserver**.

The TSA provides a timestamping service. It accepts arbitrary data from a client, then computes a message digest of that data along with the current time, and signs that resulting message digest. This signature is then returned to the client. Anyone can authenticate the signature with the TSA's public key, provided they know the original information that was submitted to the time stamp authority. The timeserver may also log timestamp requests, but that is optional. Typically clients send in a hash to be timestamped, so that they don't have to send in the entire document that they want timestamped.

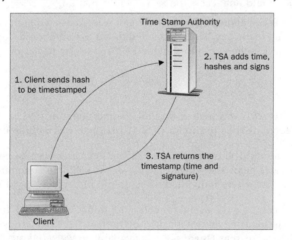

Now, provided that one trusts the TSA, one can be assured that timestamped data *must* have existed at the time it was stamped. One simply has to hash the data, and then hash it again with the time it was signed, and validate the signature against that. If it matches, the timestamp is valid, and if not, it was forged.

By timestamping a hash of the data, rather than the data itself, the TSA is not allowed to see the original data. This allows the client to feel safe in requesting a timestamp on sensitive data, as it is not computationally feasible to reconstruct data given only the hash.

Timestamping Issues

As we indicated above, how much a timestamp can be trusted depends directly on how much one can trust the Timestamp Authority. Where do they get their time? Is the time source stable, tamperproof, and likely to be around for enough time to support the system being used? For instance is it a regular PC relying on the internal clock, or is it specialized hardware synchronizing with the National Institute of Standards and Technology (NIST)? Even if you trust the source of the time itself, how much do you trust the security of the private key being used for timestamping? If the private key is compromised, then all timestamps created by it are compromised as well.

Different applications will have different requirements for the reliability of the Timestamp Authority. If you're deploying an e-commerce application and want to log when purchases are made, you have very different timestamp requirements from a legal firm wishing to establish an intellectual property database.

Uses for Timestamping

There are quite a number of uses for a timestamping service. The most obvious is a form of digital notary, where signed contracts are submitted to a timestamping service in order to prove that the contract was signed at a particular time. Another use for a TSA is in protecting intellectual property (IP). IP can be submitted to the TSA, thus proving that it existed at a particular point in time. If a lawsuit arose regarding the property, it could be proven who had a copy of it earliest, based on timestamps. A TSA can also be used to create expiring tokens. By using the TSA, a server can know when a token was created, and that it was not forged.

Timestamping in Java

There's no standard way to timestamp in Java. You can do it in a number of different ways, provided that the time, the digital signature, and the original data or a hash of it can be transmitted and stored. A method of timestamping needs to be established, including the algorithm used for the digital signature on the timestamp.

To illustrate these concepts we're going to write a simple example of a timestamp service and validator. Our timestamper will accept an arbitrary hash in SHA-1 format, which it will then hash with the current time. It will then return that original hash, along with the time and a digital signature on the second hash.

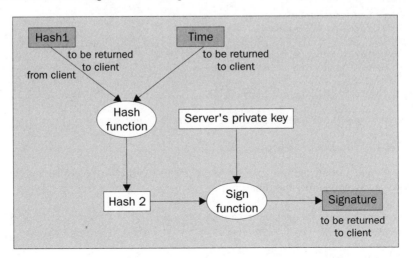

The time will be a 64-bit `long`, representing the number of seconds since January 1, 1970. (the value we get when we call `System.currentTimeMillis()` in Java). We'll hash it as a sequence of 8 bytes, in **big-endian** format.

We'll use a 1024-bit RSA key to sign, giving us a 128-byte signature. Since we're using SHA-1, our hash will be 20 bytes long.

Our timestamp, then, will look like this:

Since we know how long the hash, the time, and the signature are (20 bytes, 8 bytes, and 128 bytes respectively), we can just use a single `byte` array (of 156 bytes) to transport the data.

Timestamp Server

We'll begin by writing the timestamper itself. Our timestamper (`Timestamper.java`) will read in a file and output the timestamp, as in the illustration above. We will use a keystore to read in the private key. Once again we've broken the code up with comments to aid readability – the code available from www.wrox.com is fully commented.

```
import java.security.*;
import java.io.*;

public class Timestamper {
```

We'll store the keystore in a file called `timestamper.ks`. We'll store that filename as a constant. We also need a member variable to store an instance of our message digest and to hold our private key:

```
private static final String KEYSTORE_FILENAME = "timestamper.ks";
private MessageDigest mHasher;
private PrivateKey mPrivateKey;
```

Our constructor takes a private key and fetches an instance of our message digest:

```
public Timestamper(PrivateKey privateKey) {
  mPrivateKey = privateKey;
  try {
    mHasher = MessageDigest.getInstance("SHA-1");
  } catch (NoSuchAlgorithmException nsae) {

    // This should never happen, as the JDK comes with SHA-1

    throw new RuntimeException("SHA-1 Unavailable");
  }
}
```

We'll have only one public method: `timestamp()`. This method will read from an input stream and return a `byte` array containing the timestamp:

```
public byte[] timestamp(InputStream input)
  throws SignatureException, IOException {
```

We're going to use a `byte` array output stream to store the resulting timestamp. We know our timestamps are 156 bytes long, so we'll initialize our output stream with that value:

```
ByteArrayOutputStream output = new ByteArrayOutputStream(156);
```

The first thing we need to do is hash the input in its entirety and write that hash to our output:

```
mHasher.reset();
int i;
while ((i = input.read())!= -1) {
  mHasher.update((byte)i);
}
byte[] hash1 = mHasher.digest();
output.write(hash1);
```

Next we need to get the time and write that, as bytes, to our output:

```
long time = System.currentTimeMillis();
byte[] timeBytes = longToBytes(time);
output.write(timeBytes);
```

We'll produce a second hash from the first hash and the time:

```
mHasher.update(hash1);
mHasher.update(timeBytes);
byte[] hash2 = mHasher.digest();
```

Now we'll sign that hash. We're using RSA signatures, which are included in JDK 1.3. If we can't get an RSA signature object, we fail with an exception.

```
Signature signer = null;
try {
  signer = Signature.getInstance("SHA1withRSA");
  signer.initSign(mPrivateKey);
} catch (NoSuchAlgorithmException nsae) {

  // Probably don't have RSA signatures installed

  nsae.printStackTrace();
  System.err.println("Check that an RSA provider is installed.");
  throw new RuntimeException("No suitable provider");
} catch (InvalidKeyException ike) {
  throw new SignatureException("InvalidKey");
}
signer.update(hash2);
byte[] signatureBytes = signer.sign();
```

We've got our signature, so we can write it to the output and return the `byte` array from the output stream.

```
output.write(signatureBytes);
byte[] outputBytes = output.toByteArray();
return outputBytes;
}
```

Now we'll write a main() method for executing the timestamper. We'll take three arguments:

- ❏ The file to be timestamped
- ❏ The password for the keystore
- ❏ The file to place the timestamp in

We'll start by checking those arguments and displaying usage information if they aren't included:

```
public static void main(String[] args) throws Exception {
  if (args.length != 3) {
    System.err.println
      ("Usage: java Timestamper sourcefilename password destinationFilename");
    System.exit(1);
  }
```

We start by opening up our keystore with the password provided:

```
String defaultType = KeyStore.getDefaultType();
KeyStore keystore = KeyStore.getInstance(defaultType);
char[] password = args[1].toCharArray();
FileInputStream keystoreStream = new
  FileInputStream(KEYSTORE_FILENAME);
keystore.load(keystoreStream, password);
keystoreStream.close();
```

Now we need to fetch the private key stored in that keystore. The default key is stored under the alias mykey, so we'll fetch that out using the password the user entered:

```
PrivateKey privateKey =
  (PrivateKey)keystore.getKey("mykey", password);
```

We have our private key, so we can construct a new timestamper:

```
Timestamper timestamper = new Timestamper(privateKey);
```

The timestamper processes data from an input stream, so we'll pass in a file input stream for the file we want to timestamp. We'll get the timestamp as a byte array.

```
FileInputStream input = new FileInputStream(args[0]);
byte[] timestampBytes = timestamper.timestamp(input);
input.close();
```

We'll simply write that byte array out to the file the user specified and we're done:

```
FileOutputStream fos = new FileOutputStream(args[2]);
fos.write(timestampBytes);
fos.close();
}
```

Lastly, we need a utility method for converting a `long` to a `byte` array. This is fairly simple; we just shift and mask the 8 bytes stored in a long and place them in a new array:

```
private byte[] longToBytes (long longToConvert) {

  byte[] output = new byte[8];
  output[0] = (byte)(longToConvert >>> 56);
  output[1] = (byte)(longToConvert >>> 48);
  output[2] = (byte)(longToConvert >>> 40);
  output[3] = (byte)(longToConvert >>> 32);
  output[4] = (byte)(longToConvert >>> 24);
  output[5] = (byte)(longToConvert >>> 16);
  output[6] = (byte)(longToConvert >>> 8);
  output[7] = (byte)longToConvert;
  return output;
  }
}
```

Timestamp Client

The client is quite simple as well. We'll accept a timestamp, an input file, and a certificate, and will check the timestamp against the data by computing the hash and comparing the signature. Since the timestamp includes the date, we'll print that out.

```
import java.security.*;
import java.security.cert.*;
import java.io.*;
import java.util.Date;
import java.util.Arrays;

public class TimestampClient {
```

We have a constant that holds the filename of the timestamper's certificate:

```
private static final String CERTIFICATE_FILENAME = "timestamper.cer";
```

We have three member variables: the timestamper's public key, a message digest, and a signature object for verifying the timestamp.

```
private PublicKey mPublicKey;
private MessageDigest mHasher;
private Signature mSigner;
```

Our constructor takes the public key of the timestamper. We'll use that to verify the signature on the timestamp:

```
public TimestampClient (PublicKey publicKey) {
  mPublicKey = publicKey;
  try {
    mHasher = MessageDigest.getInstance("SHA-1");
    mSigner = Signature.getInstance("SHA1withRSA");
  } catch (NoSuchAlgorithmException nsae) {
    throw new RuntimeException("Missing algorithm: " + nsae);
  }
}
```

We have one public method: checkTimestamp(). It takes a byte array containing the timestamp and an input stream of the data that was timestamped:

```
public boolean checkTimestamp(byte[] timestamp, InputStream input)
  throws SignatureException, IOException {
```

We start by hashing the input:

```
mHasher.reset();
int i;
while ((i = input.read())!= -1) {
  mHasher.update((byte)i);
}
byte[] hashFromFile = mHasher.digest();
```

Now we need to pull the original hash out of the timestamp and check that they match. If not, we know the data has changed and we can return false.

```
byte[] hash1 = new byte[20];
System.arraycopy(timestamp,0,hash1,0,20);
if (!Arrays.equals(hashFromFile, hash1)) {
  return false;
}
```

Because the hashes match, we know this is the correct data. We'll display the time it was timestamped, which we can pull from the timestamp byte array:

```
byte[] timeBytes = new byte[8];
System.arraycopy(timestamp,20,timeBytes,0,8);
```

We need to convert that byte array into a long, which we'll do with an internal convenience method, bytesToLong(). Then we can use the long to construct a date object. Then we will display that date.

```
long time = bytesToLong(timeBytes);
Date date = new Date(time);
System.out.println("This data was timestamped on: "+date);
```

Now we want to check the signature. We start by hashing the first hash with the time, as that is what was done to create the original signature:

```
mHasher.update (hash1);
mHasher.update(timeBytes);
byte[] hash2 = mHasher.digest();
```

Now we'll check the signature itself and return the result.

```
try {
  mSigner.initVerify(mPublicKey);
} catch (InvalidKeyException ike) {
  throw new SignatureException("Invalid public key");
}
mSigner.update(hash2);
```

```
    byte[] signatureBytes = new byte[128];
    System.arraycopy(timestamp,28,signatureBytes,0,128);

    boolean result = mSigner.verify(signatureBytes);

    return result;
}
```

Our main() method will check the timestamp on a file. The user will pass in two arguments:

❏ The file that was timestamped

❏ The file containing the timestamp

```
public static void main(String[] args)
    throws Exception {

    if (args.length != 2) {
        System.err.println
            ("Usage: java TimestampClient sourceFilename timestampFilename");
        System.exit(1);
    }
```

We start by loading the timestamp bytes from the timestamp file and loading the public key from the certificate file:

```
FileInputStream fis = new FileInputStream(args[1]);
ByteArrayOutputStream baos = new ByteArrayOutputStream();
int i;
while ((i = fis.read()) != -1) {
    baos.write(i);
}
byte[] timestampBytes = baos.toByteArray();
baos.close();
fis.close();

fis = new FileInputStream(CERTIFICATE_FILENAME);
CertificateFactory certFactory =
    CertificateFactory.getInstance("X.509");
java.security.cert.Certificate cert =
    certFactory.generateCertificate(fis);
fis.close();
PublicKey publicKey = cert.getPublicKey();
```

Now we'll create a timestamp client with the timestamper's public key and ask it to check the timestamp on the file the user passed in:

```
TimestampClient client = new TimestampClient(publicKey);

FileInputStream input = new FileInputStream(args[0]);
boolean validTimestamp =
    client.checkTimestamp(timestampBytes, input);
input.close();
System.out.println("Timestamp valid: "+validTimestamp);
}
```

Lastly, we have our convenience method for converting a byte array into a long.

```
    private long bytesToLong(byte[] bytes) {
      long result = 0;
      int tempInt;
      for (int i=0;i<8;i++) {
        result = result << 8;
        tempInt = bytes[i];
        if (tempInt < 0) {
          tempInt = tempInt + 256;
        }
        result = result + tempInt;
      }
      return result;
    }
  }
```

Running the Example

In order to run the example, you'll need to have RSA signature support in your JDK. If you're using 1.3, it's already available to you. If you're using 1.2, you can add support with a JCE listed in Chapter 3.

In order to run the example, you need to create a keystore that will hold the server's private key, and a corresponding certificate that will hold the public key. Create the keystore with the following command:

```
C:>\keytool -genkey -keyalg RSA -keystore timestamper.ks
```

You will need to select a password for the keystore. Use the same password to protect the key as well. Since there's only one key in the keystore, there's no need to protect it separately.

To export the certificate, enter:

```
C:>\keytool -export -keystore timestamper.ks -file timestamper.cer
```

This should give the feedback:

```
Enter keystore password:
```

On entering the appropriate password you should get the message:

```
Certificate stored in file <timestamper.cer>
```

Now you can timestamp a file. You'll need to create that file, or use an existing one. For this example, create a file called test.txt and then timestamp it with:

```
C:>\java Timestamper test.txt password timestampOnTest.bin
```

Where *password* is the password you used to create the keystore. The timestamper will place the binary timestamp in the file timestampOnTest.bin. To verify it, run the TimestampClient:

```
C:>\java TimestampClient test.txt timestampOnTest.bin
```

You should see output similar to the following:

```
This data was timestamped on: Fri Mar 30 13:40:31 GMT +01:00 2001
Timestamp valid: true
```

We can modify the original data, and the timestamp will no longer be valid. Change something in the file `test.txt`, and run the client again. You should see the following output:

```
Timestamp valid: false
```

Secure Logging

In a system where security is important, access must be logged. Intelligent attackers will attempt to cover their tracks by deleting or modifying logs if they manage to gain access to a system. Therefore it is important to establish a secure log that is more difficult to modify than a simple text file stored on a machine that could be compromised.

There are a number of different ways to implement logging, depending on your requirements. Two possible requirements are:

❑   No messages get lost after they are logged

❑   No messages can be forged after the fact

If you require that no messages are lost, you may wish to use a separate machine that is hardened against attack and does nothing but log requests. Create a database that allows data to be added and read, but not modified and use it to store the information. The security of your logging then depends on the security on that database. You couldn't be sure that all of the logs in the database were accurate, but you would know that none of the messages that you sent had been modified or deleted. By encrypting the connection to the database and using client-authentication, you could know that logged messages were good up to the point at which a compromise occurred.

If it is necessary that messages cannot be forged after the fact, you could timestamp each log entry (or batches of them for efficiency). This could be combined with the previous methodology if required, or used in place of it, which would eliminate the requirement of a separate logging machine. This does run the risk of an attacker being able to cover his tracks by deleting log entries, but at least you can be sure that no entries could be inserted into the log before the current time.

Using a Nonce

We've discussed using a **nonce** briefly in chapters 6 and 8. A nonce is a temporary piece of data that is generated on the fly for a specific, short-term purpose, usually as a piece of information that must be signed to prove identity. It's used to prevent replay attacks (one in which someone records an authentication exchange and plays it back to the server, attempting to be authenticated).

Let's take a look at an example to understand the use of a nonce more fully. Assume there is a server and a client is attempting to authenticate to it. The server generates some random data, appends it to the current time, and sends it to the client. The client then signs it with its private key, and returns the signature to the server. Assuming the server has the public key, it can validate the signature and know that the client actually possesses the appropriate private key. Using the nonce means that the next time someone comes in to authenticate, the server will generate a new nonce that must be signed again. The client cannot have eavesdropped on the previous authentication and simply resubmit that signed data, as the signature won't be valid on the new nonce.

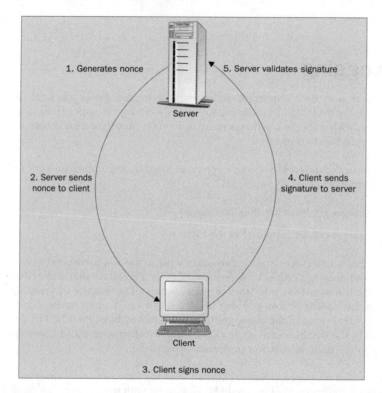

Using a nonce is a very common technique for establishing identity. It's used in SSL for authentication, but it could be used on its own in other situations if SSL is too heavyweight. HTTP Digest Authentication uses this approach, and we used it in Chapter 6 when writing a simple digital signature authentication server.

Summary

In this appendix we've attempted to briefly broaden your exposure to security approaches by looking at options for securing e-mail communications such as using S/MIME, PGP, or even getting recipients to download communications from a secure web server.

Additionally we've fleshed out the other more generally applicable techniques of timestamping, secure logging, and using nonces.

MySQL Database and JDBC Driver

In order to run some of the code in this book, you'll need a database. You can use just about any database that has JDBC drivers, including but not limited to: Oracle, Postgres, and SQL Server. If you don't have a database handy, you can use MySQL, which is a freely available open source database. You can download it from http://www.mysql.com. In this appendix, we're going to give instructions for installing and configuring MySQL on Windows.

Installation

Start by downloading the latest stable version of MySQL for Windows from the MySQL site (currently version 3.23). Once you've downloaded it, unzip it and run `Setup.exe`. Choose the typical installation and allow the installer to do its work.

Starting up MySQL

If you've installed using the MySQL defaults, MySQL will be in the directory `c:\mysql`. Navigate into the `bin` subdirectory, `c:\mysql\bin`. Run the program `winmysqladmin.exe`, which will briefly display a window with some information about MySQL, and then before you can actually do anything it will minimize itself into an icon in the taskbar:

The green light indicates that the server is running. If you click on the icon and select Show me from the menu that pops up, you will get the admin tool:

When you need to stop MySQL, you can do so by right-clicking on the traffic icon in the top-left corner and selecting WinNT | Stop the Service. Don't do this right now though, as we need to create the user and tables we'll be using for the examples.

You can access the database directly by executing mysql.exe, which will bring up a command-line prompt allowing you to enter SQL commands. Here's what you should see if you run mysql.exe:

```
Welcome to the MySQL monitor.  Commands end with ; or \g.
Your MySQL connection id is 2 to server version: 3.23.36

Type 'help;' or '\h' for help. Type '\c' to clear the buffer

mysql>
```

Entering exit will allow you to close down the SQL window, but don't do this yet as we'll be using it shortly to configure the databse.

Configuring MySQL for the Examples

Now we're going to configure MySQL for the examples. We need to create a database, create some tables in that database, and create a user with a password to access the database.

Start by calling up the command-line tool for MySQL, mysql.exe. We're going to start by creating the database, projava, by entering the following command in the mysql window:

```
CREATE DATABASE projava;
```

In that database we want to create two tables: account and credit_card, which we'll do by executing the following commands in mysql:

```
USE projava;

CREATE TABLE account (
   account_id INT8 PRIMARY KEY,
   customer_name VARCHAR( 40 ),
   balance FLOAT,
   cert_serial_number VARCHAR( 255 )
);

CREATE TABLE credit_card (
   account_id INT8 PRIMARY KEY,
   session_key VARCHAR( 255 ),
   cc_number VARCHAR( 100 )
);
```

Next, we want to create a user, projava, with a password of sasquatch who can access the database:

```
GRANT ALL PRIVILEGES ON * TO projava@localhost IDENTIFIED BY 'sasquatch';
```

Now your database is configured. You need to shut it down and bring it back up to have it see the changes to the user table.

Accessing MySQL from Java

We will be accessing MySQL from Java using JDBC, which are Java's built-in APIs for database access. They are all part of the java.sql package in the core JDK. In order to actually use JDBC, however, you need to have a JDBC driver for the database you will be using. You can download a JDBC driver for MySQL from http://mmmysql.sourceforge.net/ (although there is one provided with the code download).

These JDBC drivers are written entirely in Java, so you do not need to download a version specific to Windows. At the time of this writing, the most current production MySQL driver was version 2.0.4. Download that binary driver, or a more recent version if you prefer, and we will use it to connect to our database.

Once you've downloaded the driver, you may need to change the name of the file so that Java will recognize it as a JAR file. We're going to call it mysql.jar.

Now we're going to write a short test (JDBCTest) to determine whether or not we can access the database from Java. We'll just execute a simple SQL select statement. If an exception gets thrown, we'll display the exception.

```java
import java.sql.*;

public class JDBCTest {

    private static final String DRIVER_NAME="org.gjt.mm.mysql.Driver";
    private static final String DB_URL="jdbc:mysql://localhost/projava";

    private static final String QUERY="SELECT * FROM credit_card";

    public static void main(String[] args) throws Exception {
        Class.forName(DRIVER_NAME);
        Connection conn = DriverManager.getConnection(DB_URL);
        Statement stmt = conn.createStatement();
        ResultSet rslt = stmt.executeQuery(QUERY);
        rslt.next();
        rslt.close();
        stmt.close();
        conn.close();
        System.out.println("Success! Connected to database.");
    }
}
```

Place the JDBC driver on your classpath, and execute the above class with:

```
C:\> java JDBCTest
```

You should see the message:

```
Success! Connected to database.
```

Troubleshooting

If you get an exception, there are a number of possibilities:

❑ The JDBC driver is not on the classpath – Make sure that the driver file you downloaded is in your classpath and that the filename ends in .jar. You may also want to try opening it in WinZip and make sure that it downloaded correctly.

❑ Your database is not running – Make sure you ran the program winmysqladmin.exe before executing the Java application.

❑ Your user and tables do not exist – Run the commands listed earlier in this appendix that detail creating the user and tables for the application.

Once the test application succeeds, your installation of MySQL is ready to be used.

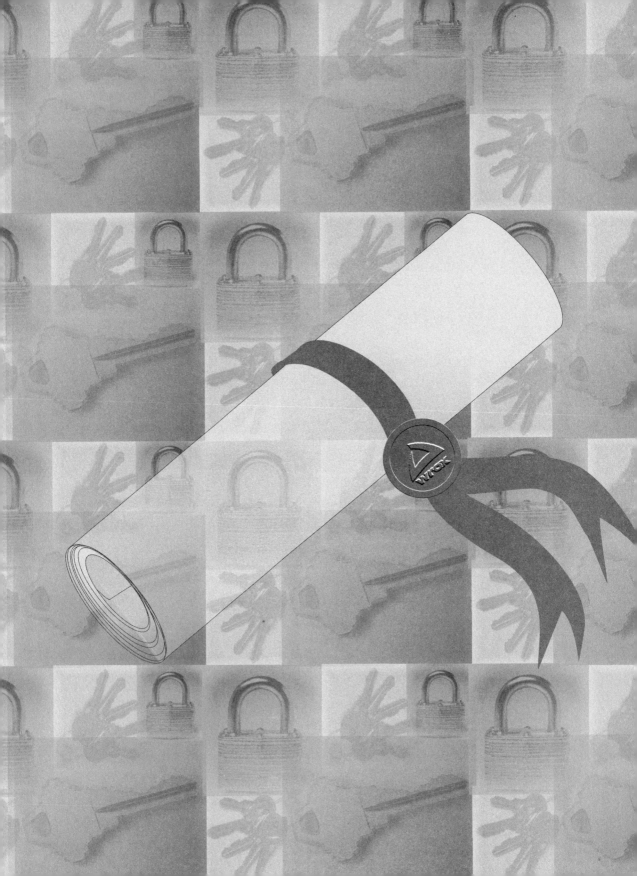

BASE64 Code

As mentioned in Chapter 4, there is a BASE64 encoder and decoder in the sun.misc package, but, since its location could change in future release of Java, we are providing the following classes as a replacement.

BASE64Decoder

```java
package com.isnetworks.base64;

/**
 * Utility class to do Base64 decoding, as defined by RFC 2045,
 * section 6.8 (http://www.ietf.org/rfc/rfc2045.txt)
 * Uses the same class and function names as Sun's implementation from
 * sun.misc
 */

public class BASE64Decoder {

    /**
     * Bit mask for one byte worth of bits in Base64 encoding.
     * Equivalent to binary value 11111111b.
     */

    private static final int EIGHT_BIT_MASK = 0xFF;

    /**
     * Decode an input String using Base64
     * @param data The String to be decoded
     * @return The appropriate byte array
     */

    public byte[] decodeBuffer( String data ) {
```

```
    // Create a wrapper around the input to screen out non-Base64 characters

    StringWrapper wrapper = new StringWrapper( data );

    // A Base64 byte array is 75% the size of its String representation

    int byteArrayLength = wrapper.getUsefulLength() * 3 / 4;

    byte result[] = new byte[ byteArrayLength ];

    int byteTriplet = 0;
    int byteIndex = 0;

    // Continue until we have less than 4 full characters left to
    // decode in the input.

    while ( byteIndex + 2 < byteArrayLength ) {

      // Package a set of four characters into a byte triplet
      // Each character contributes 6 bits of useful information

      byteTriplet = mapCharToInt( wrapper.getNextUsefulChar() );
      byteTriplet <<= 6;
      byteTriplet |= mapCharToInt( wrapper.getNextUsefulChar() );
      byteTriplet <<= 6;
      byteTriplet |= mapCharToInt( wrapper.getNextUsefulChar() );
      byteTriplet <<= 6;
      byteTriplet |= mapCharToInt( wrapper.getNextUsefulChar() );

      // Grab a normal byte (eight bits) out of the byte triplet
      // and put it in the byte array

      result[ byteIndex + 2 ] = (byte)( byteTriplet & EIGHT_BIT_MASK );
      byteTriplet >>= 8;
      result[ byteIndex + 1 ] = (byte)( byteTriplet & EIGHT_BIT_MASK );
      byteTriplet >>= 8;
      result[ byteIndex ] = (byte)( byteTriplet & EIGHT_BIT_MASK );
      byteIndex += 3;
    }

    // Check if we have one byte left to decode

    if ( byteIndex == byteArrayLength - 1 ) {

      // Take out the last two characters from the String

      byteTriplet = mapCharToInt( wrapper.getNextUsefulChar() );
      byteTriplet <<= 6;
      byteTriplet |= mapCharToInt( wrapper.getNextUsefulChar() );

      // Remove the padded zeros

      byteTriplet >>= 4;
      result[ byteIndex ] = (byte)( byteTriplet & EIGHT_BIT_MASK );
    }

    // Check if we have two bytes left to decode

    if ( byteIndex == byteArrayLength - 2 ) {
      // Take out the last three characters from the String
```

```
      byteTriplet = mapCharToInt( wrapper.getNextUsefulChar() );
      byteTriplet <<= 6;
      byteTriplet |= mapCharToInt( wrapper.getNextUsefulChar() );
      byteTriplet <<= 6;
      byteTriplet |= mapCharToInt( wrapper.getNextUsefulChar() );

      // Remove the padded zeros

      byteTriplet >>= 2;
      result[ byteIndex + 1 ] = (byte)( byteTriplet & EIGHT_BIT_MASK );
      byteTriplet >>= 8;
      result[ byteIndex ] = (byte)( byteTriplet & EIGHT_BIT_MASK );
    }

  return result;
}

/**
  * Convert a Base64 character to its 6 bit value as defined by the
  * mapping.
  * @param c Base64 character to decode
  * @return int representation of 6 bit value
  */
private int mapCharToInt( char c ) {
  if ( c >= 'A' && c <= 'Z' ) {
    return c - 'A';
  }

  if ( c >= 'a' && c <= 'z' ) {
    return ( c - 'a' ) + BASE64Encoder.LOWER_CASE_A_VALUE;
  }

  if ( c >= '0' && c <= '9' ) {
    return ( c - '0' ) + BASE64Encoder.ZERO_VALUE;
  }

  if ( c == '+' ) {
    return BASE64Encoder.PLUS_VALUE;
  }

  if ( c == '/' ) {
    return BASE64Encoder.SLASH_VALUE;
  }

  throw new IllegalArgumentException( c + " is not a valid Base64
                                              character." );
}

/**
  * Simple class to wrap around the String input to ignore all of the
  * non-Base64 characters in the input.  Note that although '=' is
  * a valid character, it does not contribute to the total number
  * of output bytes, and is therefore ignored
  */
private class StringWrapper {

  /**
    * The input String to be decoded
    */
```

```java
    private String mString;

    /**
     * Current position in the String
     */

    private int mIndex = 0;

    /**
     * Total number of Base64 characters in the input
     */

    private int mUsefulLength;

    /**
     * @param c Character to be examined
     * @return Whether or not the character is a Base64 character
     */

    private boolean isUsefulChar( char c ) {
        return ( c >= 'A' && c <= 'Z' ) ||
               ( c >= 'a' && c <= 'z' ) ||
               ( c >= '0' && c <= '9' ) ||
               ( c == '+' ) ||
               ( c == '/' );
    }

    /**
     * Create the wrapper and determine the number of Base64 characters in
     * the input
     * @param s Input String to be decoded
     */

    public StringWrapper( String s ) {
        mString = s;
        mUsefulLength = 0;
        int length = mString.length();
        for( int i = 0; i < length; i++ ) {
            if( isUsefulChar( mString.charAt( i ) ) ){
                mUsefulLength++;
            }
        }
    }

    /**
     * @return Total number of Base64 characters in the input.  Does
     * not include '='
     */

    public int getUsefulLength() {
        return mUsefulLength;
    }

    /**
     * Traverse the String until hitting the next Base64 character.
     * Assumes that there is still another valid Base64 character
     * left in the String.
     */

    public char getNextUsefulChar() {
        char result = '_';  // Start with a non-Base64 character
        while ( !isUsefulChar( result ) ) {
            result = mString.charAt( mIndex++ );
        }

        return result;
    }
}
}
```

BASE64Encoder

```
package com.isnetworks.base64;

import java.util.*;

/**
 * Utility class to do Base64 encoding, as defined by RFC 2045,
 * section 6.8 (http://www.ietf.org/rfc/rfc2045.txt)
 * Uses the same class and function names as Sun's implementation from
 * sun.misc
 */

public class BASE64Encoder {

    /**
     * Byte value that maps to 'a' in Base64 encoding
     */

    final static int LOWER_CASE_A_VALUE = 26;

    /**
     * Byte value that maps to '0' in Base64 encoding
     */

    final static int ZERO_VALUE = 52;

    /**
     * Byte value that maps to '+' in Base64 encoding
     */

    final static int PLUS_VALUE = 62;

    /**
     * Byte value that maps to '/' in Base64 encoding
     */

    final static int SLASH_VALUE = 63;

    /**
     * Bit mask for one character worth of bits in Base64 encoding.
     * Equivalent to binary value 111111b.
     */

    private final static int SIX_BIT_MASK = 63;

    /**
     * Convert a byte to an integer.  Needed because in Java bytes
     * are signed, and for Base64 purposes they are not.  If not done
     * this way, when converted to an int, 0xFF will become -127
     * @param b Byte value to be converted
     * @return Value as an integer, as if byte was unsigned
     */
```

```
private int convertUnsignedByteToInt( byte b ) {
  if ( b >= 0 ) {
    return (int)b;
  }

  return 256 + b;
}

/**
 * Encode an array of bytes using Base64
 * @param data[] The bytes to be encoded
 * @return A valid Base64 representation of the input
 */

public String encode( byte data[] ) {

  // Base64 encoding yields a String that is 33% longer than the byte
  // array

  int charCount = ( ( data.length * 4 ) / 3 ) + 4;

  // New lines will also be needed for every 76 charactesr, so allocate a
  // StringBuffer that is long enough to hold the full result without
  // having to expand later

  StringBuffer result = new StringBuffer( ( charCount * 77 ) / 76 );

  int byteArrayLength = data.length;
  int byteArrayIndex = 0;
  int byteTriplet = 0;
  while ( byteArrayIndex < byteArrayLength - 2 ) {

    // Build the 24 bit byte triplet from the input data

    byteTriplet = convertUnsignedByteToInt( data[ byteArrayIndex++ ] );

    // Each input byte contributes 8 bits to the triplet

    byteTriplet <<= 8;
    byteTriplet |= convertUnsignedByteToInt( data[ byteArrayIndex++ ] );
    byteTriplet <<= 8;
    byteTriplet |= convertUnsignedByteToInt( data[ byteArrayIndex++ ] );

    // Look at the lowest order six bits and remember them
    byte b4 = (byte)( SIX_BIT_MASK & byteTriplet );

    // Move the byte triplet to get the next 6 bit value

    byteTriplet >>= 6;
    byte b3 = (byte)( SIX_BIT_MASK & byteTriplet );
    byteTriplet >>= 6;
    byte b2 = (byte)( SIX_BIT_MASK & byteTriplet );
    byteTriplet >>= 6;
    byte b1 = (byte)( SIX_BIT_MASK & byteTriplet );

    // Add the Base64 encoded character to the result String
```

```
    result.append( mapByteToChar( b1 ) );
    result.append( mapByteToChar( b2 ) );
    result.append( mapByteToChar( b3 ) );
    result.append( mapByteToChar( b4 ) );

    // There are 57 bytes for every 76 characters, so wrap the line when
    // needed

    if ( byteArrayIndex % 57 == 0 ) {
      result.append( "\n" );
    }
  }

  // Check if we have one byte left over

  if ( byteArrayIndex == byteArrayLength - 1 ) {

    // Convert our one byte to an int

    byteTriplet = convertUnsignedByteToInt( data[ byteArrayIndex++ ] );

    // Right pad the second 6 bit value with zeros

    byteTriplet <<= 4;

    byte b2 = (byte)( SIX_BIT_MASK & byteTriplet );
    byteTriplet >>= 6;
    byte b1 = (byte)( SIX_BIT_MASK & byteTriplet );

    result.append( mapByteToChar( b1 ) );
    result.append( mapByteToChar( b2 ) );

    // Add "==" to the output to make it a multiple of 4 Base64 characters

    result.append( "==" );
  }

  // Check if we have two byte left over

  if ( byteArrayIndex == byteArrayLength - 2 ) {

    // Convert our two bytes to an int

    byteTriplet = convertUnsignedByteToInt( data[ byteArrayIndex++ ] );
    byteTriplet <<= 8;
    byteTriplet |= convertUnsignedByteToInt( data[ byteArrayIndex++ ] );

    // Right pad the third 6 bit value with zeros

    byteTriplet <<= 2;

    byte b3 = (byte)( SIX_BIT_MASK & byteTriplet );
    byteTriplet >>= 6;
    byte b2 = (byte)( SIX_BIT_MASK & byteTriplet );
    byteTriplet >>= 6;
    byte b1 = (byte)( SIX_BIT_MASK & byteTriplet );
```

```
      result.append( mapByteToChar( b1 ) );
      result.append( mapByteToChar( b2 ) );
      result.append( mapByteToChar( b3 ) );

      // Add "==" to the output to make it a multiple of 4 Base64 characters

      result.append( "=" );
    }

    return result.toString();
  }

  /**
   * Convert a byte between 0 and 63 to its Base64 character equivalent
   * @param b Byte value to be converted
   * @return Base64 char value
   */

  private char mapByteToChar( byte b ) {
    if ( b < LOWER_CASE_A_VALUE ) {
      return (char)( 'A' + b );
    }

    if ( b < ZERO_VALUE ) {
      return (char)( 'a' + ( b - LOWER_CASE_A_VALUE ) );
    }

    if ( b < PLUS_VALUE ) {
      return (char)( '0' + ( b - ZERO_VALUE ) );
    }

    if ( b == PLUS_VALUE ) {
      return '+';
    }

    if ( b == SLASH_VALUE ) {
      return '/';
    }

    throw new IllegalArgumentException( "Byte " + new Integer( b ) + " is
                                        not a valid Base64 value" );
  }

  /**
   * Simple test method to make sure everything works correctly
   * Creates 100 randomly sized arrays of random bytes, encodes them,
   * decodes them, and checks to make sure the result matches the input
   */

  public static void main( String args[] ) throws Exception {

//    sun.misc.BASE64Encoder encoder = new sun.misc.BASE64Encoder();

    BASE64Encoder encoder = new BASE64Encoder();
```

```
//    sun.misc.BASE64Decoder decoder = new sun.misc.BASE64Decoder();

    BASE64Decoder decoder = new BASE64Decoder();

    for( int j = 0; j < 100; j++ ) {
      byte test[] = new byte[ (int)( 100000 * Math.random() ) ];
      for( int i = 0; i < test.length; i++ ) {
        test[ i ] = (byte)( 256 * Math.random() );
      }

      String string = encoder.encode( test );
      byte result[] = decoder.decodeBuffer( string );

      if ( !Arrays.equals( test, result ) || test.length != result.length )
      {
        System.out.println( "ARRAYS DO NOT MATCH!" );
      }
    }
  }
}
```

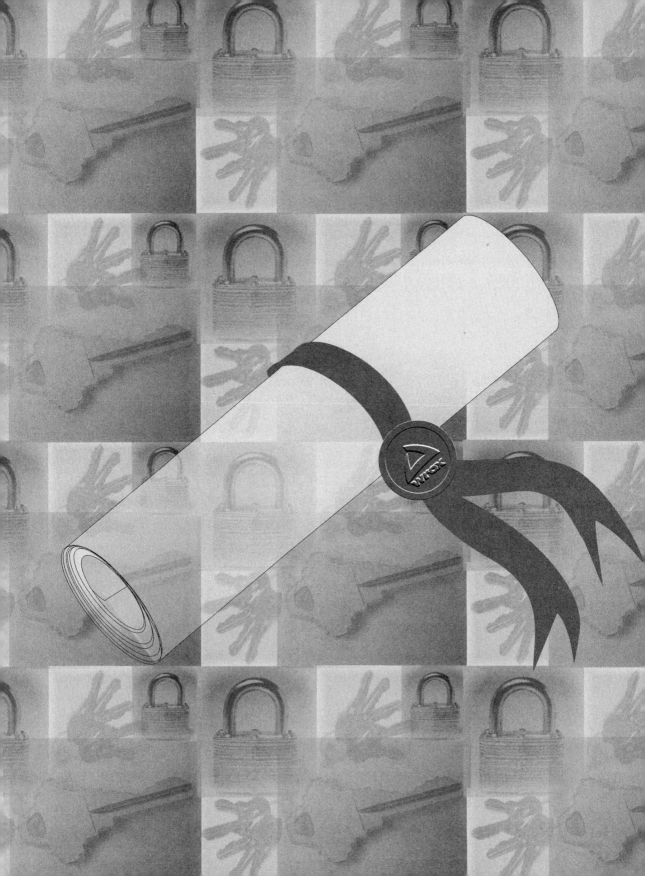

EncryptedObject

As mentioned in Chapter 4 in JDK1.2 extensions are prevented from using the class loader to create objects that are neither standard objects, nor extensions. The class presented below (EncryptedObject) is functionally equivalent to SealedObject, but can be used with custom classes.

```java
import java.io.*;
import java.security.*;
import javax.crypto.*;
import javax.crypto.spec.*;

/**
 *  EncryptedObject
 *
 *  This class is a reimplementation of javax.crypto.SealedObject.
 *
 *  It exists to enable sealing custom objects that are not
 *  located in the trusted classes directory (lib/ext).
 *
 */

public class EncryptedObject implements Serializable
{

/**
     *  Byte array for the encrypted version of the
     *  serialized object
     */

    private byte[] mEncryptedObject;
```

```java
/**
 *  Byte array for the encoded parameters to
 *  the algorithm being used for encryption
 */

private byte[] mEncodedParameters;

/**
 *  The algorithm being used for encryption
 */

private String mEncryptionAlgorithm;

/**
 *  The name of the parameter algorithm
 */

private String mParameterAlgorithm;

/**
 *  Constructs an EncryptedObject from a serializable
 *  object with a given cipher.
 */

public EncryptedObject (Serializable object, Cipher cipher)
                            throws IOException, IllegalBlockSizeException
{
  ByteArrayOutputStream baos = new ByteArrayOutputStream();
  ObjectOutputStream oos = new ObjectOutputStream(baos);
  oos.writeObject(object);
  oos.flush();
  try
  {
    mEncryptedObject = cipher.doFinal(baos.toByteArray());
  } catch (BadPaddingException bpe) {
          throw new IllegalBlockSizeException(bpe.toString());
  }

  mEncryptionAlgorithm = cipher.getAlgorithm();
  AlgorithmParameters parameters = cipher.getParameters();

  if (parameters != null)
  {
    mEncodedParameters = parameters.getEncoded();
    mParameterAlgorithm = parameters.getAlgorithm();
  }
  oos.close();
}

/**
 *  Returns the algorithm used to encrypt the object
 */

public final String getAlgorithm()
{
  return mEncryptionAlgorithm;
}

/**
 *  Returns the object decrypted with the given cipher
 */
```

```
public final Object getObject(Cipher cipher)
                              throws IOException, ClassNotFoundException,
                              IllegalBlockSizeException, BadPaddingException
{
  ByteArrayInputStream bais =
    new ByteArrayInputStream(cipher.doFinal(mEncryptedObject));
  ObjectInputStream ois = new ObjectInputStream(bais);
  return ois.readObject();
}

/**
 *  Returns the object decrypted with the given key
 */

public final Object getObject(Key key)
                              throws IOException, ClassNotFoundException,
                              NoSuchAlgorithmException, InvalidKeyException
{
  AlgorithmParameters parameters = null;
  Cipher cipher;
  Object object;

  if (mEncodedParameters != null)
  {
    parameters = AlgorithmParameters.getInstance(mParameterAlgorithm);
    parameters.init(mEncodedParameters);
  }
  try
  {
    cipher = Cipher.getInstance(mEncryptionAlgorithm);
    cipher.init(Cipher.DECRYPT_MODE, key, parameters);
    object = getObject(cipher);
    } catch (NoSuchPaddingException nspe) {
            throw new NoSuchAlgorithmException(nspe.toString());
    } catch (InvalidAlgorithmParameterException iape) {
            throw new IOException(iape.toString());
    } catch (BadPaddingException bpe) {
            throw new IOException(bpe.toString());
    } catch (IllegalBlockSizeException ibe) {
            throw new IOException(ibe.toString());
    }
  return object;
}

/**
 *  Returns the object decrypted with the given
 *  key, using the provider requested
 */

public final Object getObject(Key key, String provider)
                              throws IOException, ClassNotFoundException,
                              NoSuchAlgorithmException, NoSuchProviderException,
                              InvalidKeyException
{
  AlgorithmParameters parameters = null;
  Cipher cipher;
  Object object;
```

```
        if (mEncodedParameters != null)
        {
          parameters = AlgorithmParameters.getInstance(mParameterAlgorithm, provider);
          parameters.init(mEncodedParameters);
        }
        try
        {
          cipher = Cipher.getInstance(mEncryptionAlgorithm, provider);
          cipher.init(Cipher.DECRYPT_MODE, key, parameters);
          object = getObject(cipher);
        } catch (NoSuchPaddingException nspe) {
                throw new NoSuchAlgorithmException(nspe.toString());
        } catch (InvalidAlgorithmParameterException iape) {
                throw new IOException(iape.toString());
        } catch (BadPaddingException bpe) {
                throw new IOException(bpe.toString());
        } catch (IllegalBlockSizeException ibe) {
                throw new IOException(ibe.toString());
        }
        return object;
    }
}
```

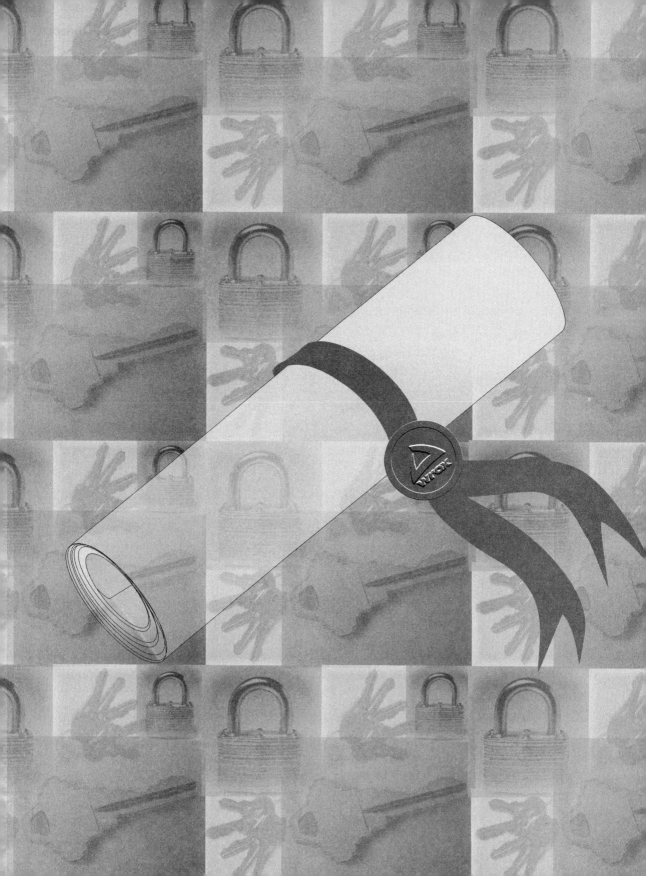

Index

A Guide to the Index

The index is arranged hierarchically, in alphabetical order, with symbols preceding the letter A. Most second-level entries and many third-level entries also occur as first-level entries. This is to ensure that users will find the information they require however they choose to search for it.

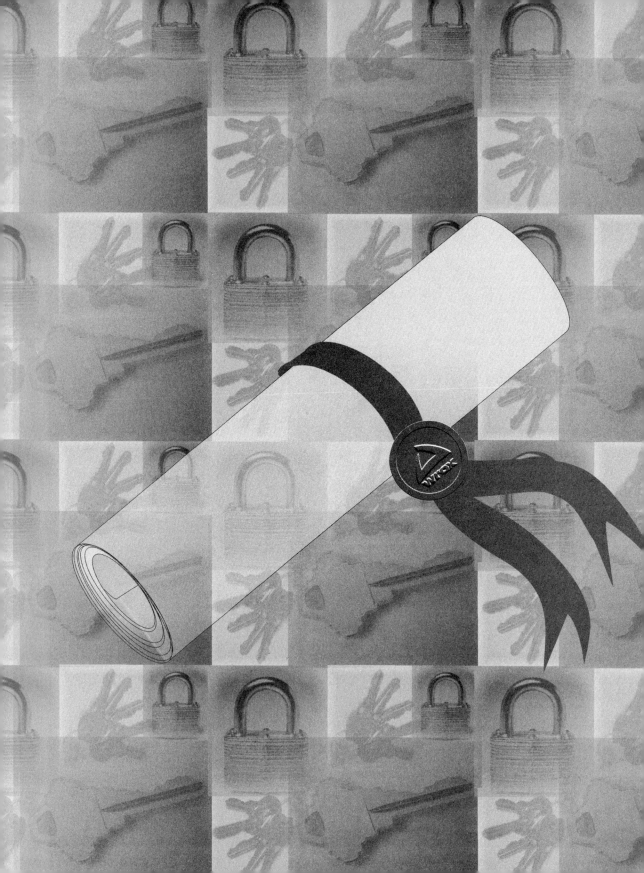

p2p.wrox.com
The programmer's resource centre

A unique free service from Wrox Press
with the aim of helping programmers to help each other

Wrox Press aims to provide timely and practical information to today's programmer. P2P is a list server offering a host of targeted mailing lists where you can share knowledge with your fellow programmers and find solutions to your problems. Whatever the level of your programming knowledge, and whatever technology you use, P2P can provide you with the information you need.

ASP — Support for beginners and professionals, including a resource page with hundreds of links, and a popular ASP+ mailing list.

DATABASES — For database programmers, offering support on SQL Server, mySQL, and Oracle.

MOBILE — Software development for the mobile market is growing rapidly. We provide lists for the several current standards, including WAP, WindowsCE, and Symbian.

JAVA — A complete set of Java lists, covering beginners, professionals, and server-side programmers (including JSP, servlets and EJBs)

.NET — Microsoft's new OS platform, covering topics such as ASP+, C#, and general .Net discussion.

VISUAL BASIC — Covers all aspects of VB programming, from programming Office macros to creating components for the .Net platform.

WEB DESIGN — As web page requirements become more complex, programmer sare taking a more important role in creating web sites. For these programmers, we offer lists covering technologies such as Flash, Coldfusion, and JavaScript.

XML — Covering all aspects of XML, including XSLT and schemas.

OPEN SOURCE — Many Open Source topics covered including PHP, Apache, Perl, Linux, Python and more.

FOREIGN LANGUAGE — Several lists dedicated to Spanish and German speaking programmers, categories include .Net, Java, XML, PHP and XML.

How To Subscribe

Simply visit the P2P site, at **http://p2p.wrox.com/**

Select the 'FAQ' option on the side menu bar for more information about the subscription process and our service.